MW00790906

The Castration of Oedipus

To Jody with congratulations and very best wishes for the brilliant academic career which lies ahead.

[illegible]

June 13th, 1997

The Castration of Oedipus

Feminism, Psychoanalysis, and the Will to Power

J. C. Smith and Carla Ferstman

WITH AN INTRODUCTION BY *Ann Scales*

New York University Press

NEW YORK AND LONDON

Copyright © 1996 by New York University

All rights reserved

Manufactured in the United States of America

Library of Congress Cataloging-in-Publication Data
Smith J. C. (Joseph Carman), 1930-
The castration of Oedipus : feminism, psychoanalysis, and the will to power / J. C. Smith and Carla Ferstman ; with an introduction by Ann Scales.
p. cm.
Contents: Thinking the unthinkable—The sexuality of politics—Knowledge and the languaging body—The dialectics—The dialectics of fantasy—The dialectics of signification—The dialectics of desire—Ariadne and Dionysus—Medusa depetrified—Oedipus.
ISBN 0-8147-8018-0 (cloth : acid free).—ISBN 0-8147-8019-9 (pbk. : acid free)
1. Psychoanalysis and feminism. 2. Feminist theory. 3. Postmodernism. I. Ferstman, Carla, 1968- . II. Title.
BF175.4.F45S65 1996
150.19'5—dc20 95-41726
CIP

New York University Press books are printed on acid-free paper, and their binding materials are chosen for strength and durability.

10 9 8 7 6 5 4 3 2 1

I sing the body electric
The armies of those I love engulf me and I engirth them,
They will not let me off till I go with them, respond to them,
And discorrupt them, and charge them full with the charge of
the soul.
Was it doubted that those who corrupt their own bodies
conceal themselves?
And if those who defile the living are as bad as they who
defile the dead?
And if the body does not do fully as much as the soul?
And if the body were not the soul, what is the soul?

—Walt Whitman,
Leaves of Grass

Contents

Abbreviations

Freud

SE	*The Standard Edition of the Complete Works of Sigmund Freud,* ed. James Strachey. 24 vols. (London: Hogarth Press, 1966).

Derrida

Ap	*Aporias* (Stanford: Stanford University Press, 1993).
Df	"Difference," in *Margins of Philosophy* (Chicago: University of Chicago Press, 1982).
DS	"The Double Session," in *Dissemination* (Chicago: University of Chicago Press, 1981).
EM	"The Ends of Man," in *Margins of Philosophy* (Chicago: University of Chicago Press, 1982).
EO	*The Ear of the Other* (Lincoln: University of Nebraska Press, 1985).
Glas	*Glas,* trans. John P. Leavey Jr. and Richard Rand (Lincoln: University of Nebraska Press, 1986).
PC	*The Post Card* (Chicago: University of Chicago Press, 1987).
Pit	"The Pit and the Pyramid," in *Margins of Philosophy* (Chicago: University of Chicago Press, 1982).
Pos	*Positions* (Chicago: University of Chicago Press, 1978).
PP	"Plato's Pharmacy," in *Dissemination* (Chicago: University of Chicago Press, 1981).

Sp *Spurs: Nietzsche's Styles* (Chicago: University of Chicago Press, 1979).

Goux

OP *Oedipus, Philosopher* (Stanford: Stanford University Press, 1993).

P "The Phallus: Masculine Identity and the 'Exchange of Women,' " in *Difference* 4 (spring 1992), "The Phallus Issue."

Lacan

E *Êcrits: A Selection*, trans. A. Sheridan (New York: W. W. Norton, 1977).

F *The Four Fundamental Concepts of Psycho-Analysis* (New York: W. W. Norton, 1981).

FS *Feminine Sexuality*, ed. Juliet Mitchell and Jacqueline Rose (New York: W. W. Norton, 1982).

OS "Of Structure as an Inmixing of an Otherness Prerequisite to Any Subject Whatsoever," in *The Languages of and the Criticisms of the Sciences of Man*, ed. Richard Macksey and Eugene Donato (Baltimore: Johns Hopkins University Press, 1970).

S I "Freud's Papers on Technique, 1953-1954," in *The Seminar of Jacques Lacan, Book I* (New York: W. W. Norton, 1991).

S II "The Ego in Freud's Theory 1954-1955," in *The Seminar of Jacques Lacan, Book II* (New York: W. W. Norton, 1988).

S III "The Psychoses, 1955-1956," in *The Seminar of Jacques Lacan, Book III* (New York: W. W. Norton, 1993).

S VII "The Ethics of Psychoanalysis, 1959-1960," in *The Seminar of Jacques Lacan, Book VII* (New York: W. W. Norton, 1992).

Tel *Television* (New York: W. W. Norton, 1990).

Laplanche

L&D	*Life and Death in Psychoanalysis* (Baltimore: Johns Hopkins University Press, 1976).

Laplanche and Pontalis

FO	"Fantasy and the Origin of Sexuality," in *Formations of Fantasy*, ed. Victor Burgin, James Donald, and Cora Kaplan (London: Methuen, 1986).
LP	*The Language of Psycho-Analysis* (New York: W. W. Norton, 1973).

Nietzsche

In most cases, Nietzsche's works are cited in the text by section numbers. Where Nietzsche did not use section numbers, the reference will be to a page.

BGE	*Beyond Good and Evil*, trans. R. J. Hollingdale (London: Penguin Books, 1973).
BT	*The Birth of Tragedy*, trans. Walter Kaufmann, in *Basic Writings of Nietzsche* (New York: Modern Library, 1968).
D	*Daybreak*, trans. R. J. Hollingdale (Cambridge: Cambridge University Press, 1982).
EH	*Ecce Homo*, trans. R. J. Hollingdale (London: Penguin Books, 1979).
GM	*On the Genealogy of Morals*, trans. Walter Kaufmann, in *Basic Writings of Nietzsche* (New York: Modern Library, 1968).
GS	*The Gay Science*, trans. Walter Kaufmann (New York: Vintage Books, 1974).
HH	*Human, All Too Human*, trans. R. J. Hollingdale (Cambridge: Cambridge University Press, 1986).
Pt N	*The Portable Nietzsche*, trans. Walter Kaufmann (London: Penguin Books, 1982).
T	*Twilight of the Idols*, in *The Portable Nietzsche*, trans. Walter Kaufmann (London: Penguin Books, 1982).

TL	*On Truth and Lies in an Extra-Moral Sense,* a fragment published posthumously, in *The Portable Nietzsche,* trans. Walter Kaufmann (London: Penguin Books, 1982).
UD	*On the Uses and Disadvantages of History for Life,* in *Untimely Meditations,* trans. R. J. Hollingdale (Cambridge: Cambridge University Press, 1983).
UM	*Untimely Meditations,* trans. R. J. Hollingdale (Cambridge: Cambridge University Press, 1983).
WP	*The Will to Power,* trans. Walter Kaufmann and R. J. Hollingdale (New York: Vintage Books, 1968).
Z	*Thus Spoke Zarathustra,* trans. R. J. Hollingdale (London: Penguin Books, 1969).

Introduction

These authors have a lot of nerve. They have swum into the treacherous waters among the already rocky shores of psychoanalysis, postmodernism, and feminism, but not only that. They have written a book that claims to be *doing* each of those enterprises simultaneously rather than redescribing or reinterpreting them. Even more outrageously, they claim to be pushing psychoanalysis, postmodernism, and feminism to those perspectives' logical conclusions.

At no point do the authors attempt to define the three disciplines. They start, rather, with certain notions that are fundamental to each. They believe, fundamental to feminism, that women are oppressed, in every conceivable, cruel way. Something must be done about it if women are to be minimally protected or maximally "liberated," or, indeed, if the history of this species is to be other than stories of misery upon misery. They believe, fundamental to postmodernism, that in this postquantum-mechanical, post-Nietzchean, literally postmodern world, there is no "objective" reality. We cannot separate what we believe we "know" from how we know it. Everything that we "know," all that we are, is a function of language. They believe, fundamental to psychoanalysis, that there is a developmental process of "genderization," which process is not rational but driven by primal needs. Further, the genders constructed are not symmetrically related: for our "languaging biped species," the process requires that the genders be differently understood, and even hierarchically ordered.

One could challenge the authors' simplification of these presuppositions (which of course I have simplified much further for the purposes of this introduction) or ask why these suppositions are not necessary to their respective disciplines or how subschools of each discipline actively deny the respective suppositions. The power of this book, however, requires the reader to suspend those objections temporarily, in order to ask: *What if* the disciplines as characterized were combined? *What if* each discipline were taken to its logical limits? *What if* the disciplines had to meet each other—what would be the result?

In order to get that far, these authors claim that each of those disciplines (or sets of disciplines) can afford to sacrifice some of its most cherished tenets. They work in that "sacrifice" concept right off the top, and it ain't that easy to swallow.

Feminism must give up its belief in the ideal of equality and in other prediscursive concepts such as nature and justice. Postmodernism has to give up its preoccupation with endless indeterminacy and allow itself to be used in the service of political ends and psychical transformation. Postmodernism must allow that there are morally compelling cases (such as the historical torture of women) and that, at least in those cases, postmodernism can be method rather than entirety. Psychoanalysis, having in its Lacanian form begun the purge of biological necessity, must now realize the contingency of its patriarchal conclusions. Allowing the inversion particularly of its Oedipal hypothesis (regarding the psychically violent separation of the [male] infant from the mother), it must recognize the primacy of the female, at least on the level of psychic reality.

Why would anyone want, even for the sake of argument, to make such sacrifices? In public discourses, battles seem to be won by fortifying rather than blurring the lines among points of view. In the academy, awards come from being aligned with a point of view and by picking away at competitors. It pays to be a loyal soldier in a particular army (some more than others), or at least to be a consistent, predictable resister of other ways of thinking. There is also reward in ownership. I could argue that many of the insights both of postmodernism and contemporary psychoanalysis are at best redundant of, and at worst ripped off from, radical feminism. I am sure that students of postmodernism and psychoanalysis could make parallel, oppositional arguments. The incentives to compartmentalize, to claim, to be uncontaminated, to assert truths are not trivial. One's economic, political, and existential security can depend on it. These authors ask a lot of us.

As I am a radical feminist activist/lawyer/law teacher, my appreciation of this book must flow from what it can do for feminism. There's an obstacle right there, insofar as the authors place, and require readers to accept, at least some value in psychoanalytic theory. The other perspectives serve to whip psychoanalysis into shape, to render it useful today. (That is, postmodern method can clarify Freud's essentialist mistakes, and feminism can negate the prescriptive aspects of the Oedipal passage.) Thus, the primary concern of these authors is with the "why" of male dominance. As they note, there has always been an ambivalent relationship between feminism and psychoanalysis. Feminism is expert in the "what" of male dominance. Sometimes we cannot help but confront the why, usually out of compassion for our brothers. Though psychoanalysis can offer such explanations, those explanations seem always to import the sexually bimorphic terms of the Oedipal passage: phallic possession or lack, seduction, and castration. Of these terms, feminism is deeply and rightly suspicious, not only because of the Freudians' demonstrated misogyny but also because of the depressing stasis and morbidity implicit in the theories and the threat that any alliance with psychoanalysis will put us forever in the pit of "cultural feminism."

And that is a dark, deep pit. These authors state that contemporary feminisms tend toward the liberal ideal of equality, or otherwise toward essentialism, "advocating some form of the female supremacy over the male rooted in the biological differences between the sexes, or . . . some kind of mysticism about the female body."[1] I guarantee that this is a gross oversimplification of feminist *theory*. But it is an accurate description of how feminism has been *treated*. Feminist work, for all its insight and nuance, has been bludgeoned into the categories, roughly, of liberal and cultural feminism. Anything that is not liberal feminism (which the important work is not) gets called "cultural feminism," or less politely "Femi-Nazism," or even that most feared of all evils, "male-bashing." Why redomesticate that dog?

Five years ago, in a telephone conversation with J. C. Smith, I was describing how my early published work had been criticized for resorting to psychoanalytic theory and questioning whether feminism ought not to just abandon that approach. In the midst of my complaints and hardlining, J. C. interrupted to say (and those who know him can hear this exactly in their minds), *"But Ann, how else can you understand this crazy world and the crazy men who run it?"* How indeed? Why should feminists accept the risks of entertaining psychoanalysis yet again? The short answer to that came again from J. C. Smith, during a faculty lunch seminar in January of 1993, while I was visiting at the University of British Columbia. In a fifty-minute span, Professor Smith shared the skeletal structure of this book, focusing on the relevance of Nietzsche to a postmodern, psychoanalytic feminism. One of our colleagues earnestly asked, But doesn't this whole theory undermine the goal of equality? J. C.'s short response: *"Equality is a male game."*

Those five words refocused my thinking and, I believe, encapsulate the greatest contribution of this book to feminist thought. Radical lawyers of all stripes have known for a long time that the discourse of equality was not "real," and surely not neutral. Our greatest theorists, particularly Catharine MacKinnon, have demonstrated how "equality" is manipulated to patriarchal ends. As shifting sands these are, MacKinnon long since predicted the path of almost every grain.

The authors of this book focus on the idea that women have settled, and that some feminist theories allow women to settle, for mere "patriarchal civility." This idea had its best feminist articulation in Andrea Dworkin's classic (absolutely fundamental reading) Right-Wing Women. J. C. Smith and Carla Ferstman complement Dworkin's approach by pursuing that settlement to its psychical origins and by showing how the settlement is mandated by a blind (yea, Oedipal) commitment to the ideal of equality.

The authors do not advocate an abandonment of equality discourse but a more strategic relationship to it. Those of us in the field have known that for some time and have proceeded accordingly. But these authors, in their central metaphor, give us a different way to understand why we must deploy the concept of equality with caution.

When Oedipus "answered" the riddle of the Sphinx, he made man the measure of all things. In the view of these authors, Oedipus symbolizes not only a wrong-headed and incomplete problem of childhood development but stands also for the ridiculous (though understandable) human desire for there to be answers to life's riddles. That is the basic impulse of modernity and its greatest political achievement—liberalism.

Contemporary liberalism has swept Nietzsche's lessons under a procedural rug. Thus, within liberalism, though there may not be a "right" answer among competing points of view, those points of view are presumed rational, and the world is right so long as the rational conversation among points of view continues. "Mistakes" (such as torture and genocide) will be disclosed in the fullness of time. We can fix those "errors." It is all right. Everything is really going quite smoothly.

As radical feminism has long since demonstrated, this is the central metaphysic of patriarchy, as well as its insurance policy. Modernity and liberalism guarantee that real problems cannot even be fully realized, much less fixed. Equality is the centerpiece of this regime. Equality—conceived in rational, even mathematical, terms—provides the moral imprimatur for fixing nothing. In the United States, the weight of this imprimatur is evident in the public hysteria over the "injustice" of affirmative action (and that doctrine's dramatic demise in constitutional law). There was once a complex question: What to do about centuries of oppression? Now there is an easy answer: whatever we do, it can't be by means of acknowledging centuries of oppression.

Thus, "equality" as an abstract end is an Oedipal "solved riddle." That of course misses the point of riddles and produces a "blindspot" (that metaphor again) about how patriarchal metaphysics is generated, sustained, and deployed with such seamless success. True believers in the ideal of equality cannot see how they are doomed to be sharecroppers on Apollo's farm. As the authors put it: "My faith in the system as one which will protect my interests, ensure my voice and give me justice — O Almighty Justice!, is a system which at its very roots seeks to keep me down. Give me laws, give me rights entrenched in constitutions — let them proclaim that I as woman am a person, for this I did not know."[2]

This book is *really* scary (to unreformed liberals and their beneficiaries) because it not only exposes the fallacies of equality at a psychological level, it also proposes the supremacy of the female as an alternative. Is this anything other than the "cultural feminism" trap? These authors go to lengths to explain how their postmodern, psychoanalytic feminism is not simply the replacement of Oppressor A with Oppressor B. First, they advocate the recognition of "female supremacy" as distinguishable from "female superiority." The latter implies male inferiority, which is not their claim. The difference is crucial to their call for male sacrifice: the male's gift does not flow from his vilification. Rather, it is the joyful counterpart to his liberation from the neurotic, debilitating illusion of control. His sacrifice to HER is matched by the gift to him of his own animality.

All of this takes place in the realm of "psychic reality." For a feminism driven by something other than the equality game or by biological/psychological essentialism, we must locate our efforts, to use the Lacanian terms central to this book, "in the registries of the Imaginary and the Symbolic." It is only then that feminism will be realized for what it is: a path toward social and psychical transformation rather than a "phallic 'seizure of power.' "[3] Properly understood, these authors' alternative narrative of matriarchal consciousness "is not an opposition within patriarchy but its grand antithesis."[4]

Really? We really need to know and that depends on the strength of the book's central thesis. "There can be no self without a discourse, no discourse without a master signifier, no master signifier without a grand metaphor, no grand metaphor without a primal fantasy, no primal fantasy except through the body of the female."[5] The thesis rests on the middle chapters, the neo-Lacanian arguments about the connections between childhood anxieties, language, and repression. These chapters will strike some feminists as a load of French vomit. (In fairness to the authors, however, though they use lots of the lingo of postmodernism, their arguments helped to demystify at least the Lacanian branch of that study for me. I'm sure some will object that the demystification could occur only because the authors' arguments are not really postmodernist—I'm not equipped to judge.) But these middle chapters are necessary to thwart biological determinism, to get to the matrix of language, and therefore to the contingency of maleness as the "privileged signifier."

I would have neither the knowledge nor the inclination to make such an argument in such terms. That is why I need this book. With a carefully constructed argument, it further informs what we already knew about both the contingency of patriarchy and the uselessness of its metaphysics. I want to say that this book advances a discussion that had become depressing in its compartmentalization and predictable traps. The authors, however, would be the first to retort that the notion of "advancing" is one of our species' strangest symptoms.

In any case, this book is a great chew, and also fun. I'm sure the authors recognize the compliment. They have willingly exposed their own vulnerabilities and accepted the risks and, in their confession to the high crime of "grand theory,"[6] implicitly allowed that their mission may be undermined by its own terms. They understand the pitfalls and the rather endearing misguidedness in the "will to theory." At the end of the day, their own creation may be subject to Nietzsche's bottom line: "I hope that at this artificial inflation of a small species into the absolute measure of things one is still permitted to laugh?"[7]

Having said that, there are parts of the arguments in this book that are not fun and are indeed deeply troubling. (Every reader can no doubt make her own different list.) For example, fundamental to this work is a claim to the urgency and frustration of male mammalian sexuality. Catharine MacKinnon has called this the "hard-wiring" defense of male aggression;[8] it has been a mightily convenient explanation for many atrocities. This book of course posits the hard wiring very differently and raises the question of whether that business that won't go away could ever be a link in a liberatory chain. Again, these authors have a lot of nerve.

Much of the controversial material in this book arises from the (by now) self-evident theoretical proposition that what we call "knowledge" is produced by contrast between and among presumed opposites, in an endless spiraling "economy." The authors go much further (or much backward, from a postmodernist point of view). They argue that sexuality/genderization is the *basic* contrast and that all knowledge is dependent on sexuality, which is in turn based on their central notion that humans must have some fantasy/understanding of "the generative power of nature."

That leads them to two other, more extravagant claims. First, that a domination/submission dialectic has been?/will always be? necessary to the human psyche. Second, that there is a *jouissance* in masochism (at least for the male). They could not have hit more controversial chords.

I will not attempt to summarize the connections among these ideas, which are the substance of this book. The authors go on to make detailed distinctions between pathological (bad) masochism and perverse (good) masochism. Their conclusions about sacrifice and castration depend on those distinctions. As of publication time, I have not determined whether my uneasiness is substantive or a reaction to the language of domination/submission, master/slave dialectic, *jouissance* of masochism, and all the other terms that have received recent popularity through a Frenchified abstraction of real traumas.

I have provisionally chosen, perhaps incorrectly, to understand these connections and distinctions in a larger psychical context. I think of them in terms of the pain of individuation—the struggle involved in having a self when the self is an entirely vulnerable, and inevitably temporary, construct. Though I am not otherwise given to grand theory, I recognize this struggle in much human endeavor, whether as a psychoanalytic explanation (per the Oedipal passage or the alternative to it proposed in this book), as a theological necessity (as in most "Eastern" religions), or as a metaphysical mistake (or the mistake that is metaphysics), which has had massively stupid and horrid consequences (the exposure of which was Nietzsche's great contribution).

These reservations notwithstanding, this book makes many specific, not necessarily grand-theory-dependent contributions, four of which have settled forever in my brain. First is the psychoanalytic deconstruction of equality, described above, which I believe adds a new dimension to what we already understand and practice.

Second is the reinvigoration of Nietzsche in terms useful to the feminist millennium. Only Luce Irigaray, among widely read authors, has been able to give Nietzsche back to feminist social theory with any success. The effort of these authors, in my view, is even better. That may not matter to many readers. I suspect, however, that there are feminists besides me who have had a heretofore embarrassed attraction to (and inspiration from) Nietzsche's work, in spite of its misogynist moments, which these authors try to explain and in any case go beyond.

Third is the extraordinary exploration in this book of the connections among religion, law, and pornography. Several activists/scholars have long suspected that religion and pornography were mirror images; they knew, if only intuitively, that de Sade and Saint Paul are each other's evil twin, as these authors state unequivocally. The authors' construct has its genesis in the work of Mary Daly, Andrea Dworkin, Catharine MacKinnon, and Jane Caputi—among others. But here we have something new. Even for those of us who are suspicious of linear constructs, the logos-law-penis axis described in this book is critical grist for our mill; it may even be a genuine breakthrough.

Fourth, the insights that J. C. Smith and Carla Ferstman provide about poor old Oedipus himself have both social and personal therapeutic value. Many of us know an Oedipal figure: a person who has surrendered the possibilities of life to the patriarchal institutions that make claim to certainty, the institutions that promise everything but at the literal end of the day deliver nothing. Those are really the terms of the bargain for lots of women. But many of us (particularly, perhaps, those of my generation who have attended the elderly) also know such a man: a former prince in Apollo's court who finds himself, at his animal end, literally and/or figuratively blind and crawling about in institutional excrement.

This business of finding or denying joy, of embracing or resisting resistance to certainty, is of consequence for everybody. Those topics are the real focus for J. C. Smith and Carla Ferstman. In that context, there are some specific conclusions of this book that ring true for me. The costs of the once presumably necessary "Oedipal separation" have been astronomical for all organisms and for the earth herself. Our species must come to terms with its animality if we are to realize Nietzsche's "YES" to life. That minimally requires alternative forms of male heterosexuality, which means that men must relinquish the power that is in fact their misery. Some sacrifice (in the authors' term, "castration") is inevitable: the question is how and by whom and with what results. No one who has glimpsed this alternative psychic reality (in the authors' parlance, no one who has seen HER) would want to turn back to the miserable stories of history and personal demise.

I am in the privileged position of knowing both J. C. Smith and Carla Ferstman. They live in that alternative psychic reality and transform the people around them who—by whatever twists of fate—are lucky enough to be open to them. (It is not irrelevant that one of these authors—the guy, as it turns out—has shared an inspiring relationship with an astonishing woman for the last forty years.) I therefore cannot separate this book from my experience of the authors. I can only urge the readers to allow these possibilities into their own lives.

This book pushed every button on my personal and political pads. There is a raging argument in my head with the authors and with myself. These people are obviously learned and obviously mad. They are clearly strange and strangely clear. They must be on to something.

Ann Scales
Albuquerque, New Mexico
January 1995

ONE

Thinking the Unthinkable

Psychoanalysis, Postmodernism, and Feminism

Contemporary critical social theory points to three perspectives: the psychoanalytic, the postmodern, and the feminist. Though each has its own independent core, incorporating aspects from one or more of the other perspectives can be beneficial and has the result of strengthening or clarifying the respective theoretical structure. There is substantial literature combining any two of these three perspectives. Each alliance turns out to be a case of one perspective co-opting some aspect of the others while at the same time rejecting one or more of the basic presuppositions upon which the perspective rests. Thus, we have postmodern feminism, postmodern psychoanalysis, and psychoanalytic feminism. There is not, as yet, however, a full integration of these three points of view. Jane Flax wrote a book entitled *Thinking Fragments,* in which she exposed the fundamental contradictions of the three perspectives and came to the conclusion that a unified theory was not possible. She concluded that "no neat integration, new synthesis, or *Aufhebung*" of these three perspectives is either possible or desirable.[1] While a total convergence of these three perspectives may not be possible, or for that matter even desirable, they may be so integrated that it will be neither possible nor desirable to separate their discourses or methodologies.

We disagree with Flax in that we think a synthesis *is* possible. Whether or not it would be desirable is an open question. For there to be any unification, each perspective must sacrifice some of its basic tenets or presuppositions. Psychoanalysis and feminism must give up or reverse valued or cherished, and fairly fundamental, components. Postmodernism, when pitted against these two discourses, must allow itself to reach its natural conclusions and avoid the desire to sidetrack or to get caught in the detail along the way. The desirability of a psychoanalytic-postmodern-feminism will depend upon the nature of these sacrifices. One of the primary objectives of this book is to explore how there would be a unified theory within which each position could maintain its integrity, while simultaneously exploring the desirability of making the necessary modifications. This text was not designed as a defense of any one or all of these three different perspectives. We assume these discourses as givens. Our intent is to create a treatise that makes the necessary modifications to each perspective in order to bring them together into an integrated whole.

Our objective is to demonstrate the natural results that flow from such an integration, rather than to persuade the reader of the viability of the unification. Theorists committed to psychoanalysis, postmodernism, and feminism must, in scrutinizing the premises of this endeavor, either find flaws in the method of unification and develop it differently or they must continue to think in terms of fragments. Since people generally prefer to rid their worldviews of contradictions, this may place the reader in somewhat of a dilemma. What is important, however, is that in struggling with these issues we enrich our understanding and are willing at least to think about and tolerate views that, in terms of the predominant psychic reality, may at first glance appear to be distasteful or unacceptable. We would not go so far as to say that this is the only form the unification can take. We think, however, that it is the best way to combine them while maintaining their essential elements.

Psychoanalytic theory, postmodernism, and feminism are all radical and critical approaches to theory. When they are combined, the degree of radicalness is compounded. There are unstated limits and boundaries that restrict what we can say and discuss about human sexuality. We generally function within these conceptual boundaries, but by taking a more radical hypothesis we can locate and critically examine these confines and possibly roll them back a little. Despite decades of "intermittent but intense dialogue," we do not fully know whether or not male and female sexual natures are essentially different or how far women's sexuality has been muted by repression, nor do we fully understand the complex relationship between sexuality and aggression.[2] Carol Vance, in posing such questions, points out that discussion of human sexuality is permeated with emotional ambiguity, intrapsychic anxiety, and fears of dissolution, self-annihilation, and dependency. "Having been told that pleasure threatens civilization, we wonder: what if there is no end to desire?"[3] One cannot help but ask why, after two thousand years of the ideology of equality, do we still have gender discrimination, and why after several decades of universal suffrage, do we still have only token female representation in the structures and hierarchies of power? Why, after substantial legislative reform and a new age of fundamental rights, is violence against women still pervasive?

We will argue that the transformation in discourse has failed to alter the reality of live practice because the practice itself is neurotic rather than merely mistaken. One cannot alter misogyny by appealing to reason any more than one can cure neurotics of their neuroses by pointing out and explaining how unreasonable their behavior is. The employment of the concept of neurosis as a metaphor for male misogyny is, we will argue, valid. Misogyny can be viewed as a neurosis of the male collective psyche and therefore as a collective neurosis.[4] Neurotic behavior of individuals is altered, defused, or transcended by the psychoanalytic process of uncovering the source of the neurosis and bringing it into conscious awareness. A collective neurosis such as misogyny can only be defused or transcended by an analogous process. An examination of the interrelationships between psychoanalysis, postmodernism, and radical feminism will reveal how the deconstructive process parallels that which takes place between the analyst and the analysand.[5]

We do not purport to provide answers for any of the questions set out above as we write this book from a hypothetical perspective based upon presuppositions that for the purpose of our writing, we take for granted. The book does suggest answers to some of these questions, answers that are conditional upon the validity of the presuppositions that we assert underlie psychoanalysis, postmodernism, and feminism. These are presuppositions that the reader may or may not accept. In looking at some of the above questions from the perspective of a unified psychoanalytic postmodern feminism, the reader ought to be able to gain new insights about the nature and complexity of these issues, and hopefully it will be helpful for readers in formulating their own responses to some of these critical issues. By maintaining this study at the hypothetical level we hope to isolate our examination of the nature and structure of human sexuality and its relationship to social order from some of the emotional baggage that we as authors, and you as readers, will inevitably bring to these themes.

This book is written in the style of grand theory. There is no reason why postmodern scholarship cannot be comprehensive or sweeping, so long as one keeps in mind that it is just a story not *the* story. As such, this kind of scholarship should be compared to theater. It is a play, a story, a myth, a discourse, a stage, as are also all other comprehensive or sweeping theories. When one writes, stages, or acts a play, one ought not to have to keep reminding the audience that it is a play. When the play is in progress, the author, director, and actors try to make it as convincing as possible for the sake of the play or the theatrical event. We hope that the reader will approach this book in the spirit of theater.

The Dialectics of Authors and Their Texts

Jacques Lacan, the most profound of all of the disciples of Freud, said of Freud, "the father of psychoanalysis, what did he do but hand it over to the women, and also perhaps to the master-fools? As far as the women are concerned, we should reserve judgment; they are beings who remain rich in promise, at least to the extent that they haven't yet lived up to them. As for the master-fools, that's another story altogether" (S VII, 182). If women have not fully lived up to the challenge of Freud's legacy, which, according to Lacan, Freud bequeathed them in the form of psychoanalytic theory, it may well be because they have not, as yet, fully integrated feminism and psychoanalysis. If there are master fools, certainly the postmodernist fits this description as the trickster and the subversive. The master fool of all time is Friedrich Nietzsche. Nietzsche wrote the most outrageous, profound, unreasonable, irrational things, and if that is not the role of the master fool, then what is? The postmodernists—those who embrace the legacy of Nietzsche—are master fools. So it well may be that the feminists and postmodernists are, in the final analysis, the true heirs and beneficiaries of the Freudian Pandora's box we call psychoanalysis. In any case, we, the authors of this text, have written as woman and master fool.

The psychoanalytic tradition founded in the work of Lacan is postmodern in that it is poststructuralist and consistent with deconstruction, while the school of psychoanalysis grounded in the work of Melanie Klein, for example, presupposes a modernist theory of cognition. The postmodernist is the person who explores the limits of knowledge at the boundaries of language. Lacan would certainly fit this definition. Just as there are postmodern and modernist psychoanalytic perspectives, there are postmodern and modernist feminisms. Modernist feminisms tend to be essentialist, advocating some form of supremacy of the female over the male rooted in the biological differences between the sexes, or they revert to some kind of mysticism about the female body. Or, further, they tend to submit to an ethereal truth of equality, of sameness. There are psychoanalytic feminisms and feminists who consider Freud and Lacan rather as enemies than allies. There is, however, a special convergence in critical social theory between psychoanalysis, postmodernism, and feminism.

Much of contemporary critical social theory in the English-speaking world consists of commentaries on French texts, such as those of Lacan, Derrida, Foucault, Cixous, Irigaray, and Kristeva, who in turn are reacting to German texts such as those of Hegel, Marx, Nietzsche, Freud, and Heidegger. The problem with reading many of these texts is that it is often difficult to understand them unless you already have a good grasp of what they say, and it is difficult to get that without first having read the texts. One technique is to read some of the excellent commentaries, interpretations, commentaries on the commentaries, and interpretations of the interpretations. This book uses the texts themselves to construct a narrative or exposition of the authors. This is precisely what Lacan does with the texts of Freud and invites us to do so with his own text. In this way we are not just talking in the abstract about psychoanalysis, or postmodernism, or feminism, but are doing it.

Throughout this book we make extensive use of the texts of Nietzsche, Freud, and Lacan. Lacan, in particular, suggested to those who attended his famous seminars that any attempt on their part to restate his position would lead to a misunderstanding. "I'm not surprised that something of a misunderstanding remains to be dispelled, even in people who think they're following me," he writes. "[I]f I were to try to make myself very easily understood, so that you were completely certain that you followed, then according to my premises concerning interhuman discourse the misunderstanding would be irremediable" (S III, 164).

This book, therefore, can not only be contrasted with the books that attempt to explain for the reader what Nietzsche, Freud, and Lacan wrote and taught, but also with some of the excellent commentaries on psychoanalytic or postmodern feminist social theory. This book attempts to forge a synthesis by making the necessary changes in each perspective that is required in order to create a convergence with the other two, rather than discussing what changes would have to be made and whether or not they are desirable. Whether or not the changes made in each perspective in order to achieve a convergence are to be welcomed is left as an open question for the reader to contemplate and consider.

This book should not be taken as constituting an argument for the creation of a synthesis of psychoanalysis, postmodernism, and feminism. Our purpose in writing the book is to create a text that manifests such a synthesis. Our argument is that if you take as presuppositions the basic tenets and methodologies of psychoanalysis, postmodernism, and feminism and bring them together by deleting those elements that are inconsistent with what is fundamental to each of the others, then the theory should look very much like what we set out in this volume. This is our goal, and this is the standard by which we invite the reader to judge the book.

This book limits itself to an analysis of heterosexual relationships. As such, it ignores the fundamental reality of lesbians and homosexuals. This was not an effort to negate, but merely an effort not to distort and to leave for another day. We wish the text to stand as completely independent as possible from our own private views, many of which, of course, will be reflected in the text. We have attempted not to allow our own views to distort or modify the synthesis. That is to say that we have attempted to let the synthesis take its own form and speak for itself, even though our views may not accord with it. We have also tried not to use the synthesis to press our own views. In fact, being two authors, female and male, we ourselves do not hold the same views consistently. This fact has not been a problem in coauthoring the book because we have tried to let the text itself govern its own development. That is, we have sought to bring about the closest possible union of the views and the fundamental and essential texts of Freud, Lacan, and Nietzsche, the three sets of texts that are most closely interrelated and most fundamental to psychoanalytic social theory and postmodernism. We believe that this approach will allow readers to confront issues and raise questions that they might not otherwise have considered in reading commentaries on or the texts of Nietzsche, Freud, or Lacan in isolation from each other and from the feminist perspective. In particular, we wish the reader to explore more deeply the implications of psychoanalysis and postmodernism for feminism, particularly when they are used in consort.

The unifying theme of this book is the political. We are interested not only in what a synthesis of psychoanalysis, postmodernism, and feminism would be like, but also in what kind of politics such a synthesis would lead to. Again, our interest in writing this book is not to promote this kind of politics but to develop and outline it. Consequently, the arguments in the book are not arguments in favor of the adoption of the analysis but arguments for the analysis taking this particular form as against other possible forms. This difference may appear subtle, and we may have crossed over the line at times for which we apologize and ask the reader's indulgence. It is for this reason that we have not developed counterarguments against this kind of politics.

We have diligently attempted to exemplify postmodern methodology in the writing of the book. We invite the reader to contemplate the relationship between sexuality and politics, gender and power. We will seduce the reader to suspend the belief in an objective external reality and absolute truth and to take as well a feminist perspective. In this way we hope to lead the reader to explore the place where the public and the private converge; where subjectivity and objectivity meet; where sexuality and politics intersect; where gender, sexuality, and power come together; and where the inner world of psychic reality and the external world of material reality fuse.

The methodology of postmodernism and psychoanalysis is much the same, and in a way each presupposes the other.[6] One can only fully appreciate Freud when one has read Nietzsche, and one can only grasp the significance of Nietzsche after reading Freud.[7] It is no accident that the deconstructionist movement is deeply rooted in the writings of both Freud and Nietzsche.[8] Deconstruction entails close analysis, and close analysis requires deconstruction.[9] Deconstruction and psychoanalysis are parallel processes such that when we envisage postmodern psychoanalytic theory or psychoanalytic postmodernism, they amount to much the same thing. The concepts of each can be explained in terms of the nomenclature of the other.

The relationship of radical feminism to each is different than the relationship of poststructuralism and deconstruction to psychoanalytic theory. Radical feminism is presupposed by neither; nevertheless, the actual practice of either ought to have led to the same set of presuppositions that underlie radical feminism. The discourse of radical feminism came into being independently of the discourse and perspective of psychoanalytic theory, poststructuralism, and deconstruction. Nietzsche, Freud, Lacan, and Derrida are males who failed to take their methodology to the limits of its potential, to the deconstruction and delegitimization of male domination. Consequently, their work remains incomplete. Radical feminism, therefore, is the methodology, discourse, and perspective that permits the analysis of the texts of psychoanalysis and the deconstruction of the texts of poststructuralism. When the methodologies are intertwined in this manner, the boundaries between them begin to disintegrate.

The Sacrifice

Psychoanalysis must sacrifice the privileged position of the phallus, while at the same time maintaining the underlying theoretical structure that led to the placing of the phallus in a privileged position. To do this, we must show that Freud was right about the methodology of psychoanalysis but made a wrong turn at some point in its application. While Freud was clearly not a feminist, and many feminists have been and are highly critical of Freud, others have forged an alliance between feminism and psychoanalytic theory. The fundamental contribution of psychoanalytic theory to feminist social theory lies in its capacity and potential for explaining the origins of sexuality, sexual difference, gender difference, male domination, rape, perversion, pathology, the structure of the family, and group or collective behavior. The paradox of feminism and psychoanalysis is, however, that the explanations are in terms of phallic possession or lack, seduction, and castration, all of which seem to privilege the Oedipal structure. This gives the male the dominant position as the possessor of the phallus and legitimizes male domination. The relationship between traditional psychoanalytic theory and feminism, while important for each, remains ambivalent at best.

From this unified perspective we have concluded and argue that a feminism rooted in the ideology of equality (as contrasted with the practical politics of equality) is inconsistent with psychoanalysis. Therefore, in order to mesh feminist theory with psychoanalysis, feminism must sacrifice liberal notions of equality. Psychoanalysis requires a feminism based on sexuality, and the psychoanalytic perspective of sexuality presupposes difference, castration, and lack—not equality. Equality is not sexy. There is no libidinal force behind equality. A feminism that chooses to concentrate on distribution of power rather than upon the nature and structure of human sexuality must reject Freud, and a feminism that is willing to consider the sexual dimension must confront Freud. At the same time, a psychoanalysis that is consistent with feminism must treat the privileged position of the male as a neurotic and pathological symptom arising from repression. Psychoanalysis and feminism can only be fully integrated within a theory that embraces a dialectic of difference that may well be inconsistent with gender equality. Feminism may well have to choose between liberalism and psychoanalysis. It can align itself with one or the other, but not with both.

For both Freud and Lacan sexual difference is necessarily asymmetrical, and, furthermore, no symmetrical relation between men and women is possible. Sexual identity is culturally constructed through fantasy structures that are made to cohere with biology.[10] The problem that feminism has with Lacan is that there appears to be no way out of this impasse. Postmodernism must take the giant leap into the domain of sexuality and gender and test the bounds of the liberal conceptions of sexual and gender symmetry. The result is a precarious positioning on the edge of discourse, a frightening discourse of binary oppositions and gender hierarchies.

What is at issue is how the explanations are to unfold. Whether the relationship between feminism and psychoanalysis is to be that of a close integration such that it will be difficult to measure where one ends and the other begins or whether it is to remain inharmonious will depend upon whether or not a different form of sexuality, gender structure, and psychic reality can be said to coexist as an oppositional alternative to the Oedipal analysis, while at the same time maintaining the essential theoretical structure of psychoanalytic theory. If psychoanalytic theory could be extended in this manner, then the process of individuation would be seen as a dialectical process between two forms of psychic sexuality and reality, each of which could furnish a set of gender structures having a reverse asymmetry. Each would provide a female and male sexual and gender structure.

Feminism requires that the category of "woman" be taken as a presupposition. Psychoanalysis, on the other hand, assumes that the category of "woman" can only be defined in terms of the lack of the phallus. Traditional psychoanalytic theory has serious defects that center around its assumptions and presuppositions about women. Freud was haunted by women, obsessed with women, and in the end failed to understand them.[11] In traditional psychoanalytic theory man claims the position of subject, observer, and woman is designated the other—that which is to be observed. There have been and continue to be a substantial number of female psychoanalytic theorists who have focused their gaze in the same direction as the male,[12] that is, on the female, in attempting to correct the many misrepresentations, projections, errors, and mistakes that the male as observer of the female has made.

There is, however, a fallacy in this configuration of males observing females and describing the nature of femininity, and females saying, "No, women are not really like that—the male is mistaken." The fallacy is that there is a subject making the observations of something that is other than itself, when in reality what is happening is that the males are projecting a fantasy structure of their own sexual psychic reality onto the female. The conclusions that Freud reached about women and their sexuality are about women as they exist within the fantasy structures of male psychic reality. If we wish to gain an understanding of women as a construct of the fantasy structure of male collective psychic reality, we must start by looking inside the psyche of the male since that is where the concept of femininity originates—as a male defense mechanism to protect the male ego against the seduction of the female as (M)other. Women psychoanalysts and feminist theorists have been reluctant to take on the task of describing what is inside the male psyche as this would create the same dangers of projection in reverse. What psychoanalytic theory lacks and desperately needs is an equivalent group of male theorists who would concentrate on analyzing the structure of male sexuality and psychic reality, such as the many important female psychoanalysts and feminist theorists have done in regard to female sexuality and the female psyche. There is an extensive body of literature about female sexuality and femininity. There is no corresponding body of psychoanalytic literature about male sexuality and masculinity. Freud asked, "What does woman want?" rather than asking "What is wrong with the man?" or "Why is the man a problem for women?" The need is to understand the man who is the projector of the fantasy structure "woman," which women adopt as the mask of femininity in order to participate within the framework of male desire. What is required to bring about a synthesis between psychoanalytic theory and feminism is a dialectical, postmodern psychoanalysis.

The writings of Jacques Lacan are and will continue to be a core theme in the dialogue between feminism and psychoanalysis because they furnish feminism with a version of psychoanalytic theory that begins the purge of biological essentialism—toward a postmodern psychoanalysis. The intercourse of the two will be contentious and difficult in that Lacan's writings themselves are formidable, opaque, complicated, and problematic, generating many interpretations of his thought, as well as interpretations of the interpretations. Just as Freud was not a feminist, neither was Lacan. As stated by Jane Gallop, "There never was an alliance between the person Lacan [the body of Lacan's writing] and feminism. What there has been is an alliance some feminists have made with Lacanian thought."[13] A postmodern Lacanian psychoanalysis would push the boundaries of sexual difference and recognize the binary positions of hierarchy and power. It would acknowledge the final purge of biological essentialism—and would understand the male and female points of reference to be mere positions in the signifying chain, positions susceptible to bifurcation.

The Dialectic

Freud's dialectical method is manifest in his celebrated dualisms between ego and id, sex and ego, Eros and Thanatos, along with the pleasure principle and the primacy of masochism. Whether or not Freud's substantive theories are valid,[14] psychoanalytic theory must take as its presuppositions the oppositional poles of the sexual and ego drive, material and psychic reality; the ego and the self; conscious and unconscious; repression and neurosis; the primacy of sexuality; and the structure of unconscious fantasy, which plays out in terms of the phallus, seduction, and castration, if it is to remain true to the legacy of Freud. When it comes to gender, however, the distinctions between masculinity and femininity, male and female, male sexuality and female sexuality, father and mother, are based on the possession of the phallus, and the corresponding lack. This is not a dialectical distinction and is, therefore, inconsistent with the dialectical methodology that Freud uses wherever possible. To surrender the privileged position of the phallus in psychoanalytic theory in exchange for a dialectic would be a major modification of traditional psychoanalytic theory. Yet feminism demands the castration of Oedipus. The question that must be asked is whether the sacrifice of the privileged position of the phallus is desirable from the perspective of psychoanalytic social theory? Can the theoretical body survive the operation?

From the position of a Freudian psychoanalysis that accepts the duality of Eros and Thanatos, we find ourselves as languaging biped primates, caught in a dialectics in which we can embrace our animality or reject it; embrace our sexuality or reject it; embrace our bodies or reject them; embrace the short ephemeral dance of life or reject it; submit ourselves to life or rebel against it. These are not necessarily choices over which we have control. They are choices contingent upon the structure of our particular neurosis. If male domination is a neurosis, the dialectical dynamics are derived from the play of this factor in our fantasy structures by which we relate ourselves to the other/nature/nonhuman. We get meaning from the metaphorical similarities and differences we draw with the other. An explanation of the self is essential to the creation of the self. An explanation is incomplete without an account of origin—a critical factor in the fantasy structures of the self. The difference between a biological essentialism and the fantasy structures by which we formulate our visions of the self constitutes the difference between the modern and the postmodern.

A psychoanalytic feminism that advocates a dialectical pole in opposition to male domination must be postmodern. It cannot seek its justification in terms of a transcendent order of things—nature, justice, truth, reality, goodness, fixed ideal, nor any other form of foundationalism. It must be a feminism beyond good and evil that depends upon no legal enforcement, bill of rights, rule of law, legislative scheme, human rights commissions, police protection, ideological orthodoxy, or founding mothers. Other forms of feminism (modernist) will require these. The postmodern feminists may well use these but not as foundations, only as strategies in the game.

It must be a feminism that is beyond both hope and despair and must avoid any utopian vision. It will be a feminism of survival, a desperate form of politics, a subversive feminism. The surrender of purpose, hope, and utopia will allow for a feminism of play, irony, and duplicity; a feminism that embraces contingency, indeterminacy, ambiguity, and ambivalence. It must be a seductive feminism that can reverse illusion and fantasy by embracing their oppositional structures. Such a feminism would embrace the postmodern vision rather than merely using it as a tool of deconstruction. Patriarchy presupposes modernism, that is to say, an objective reality independent of the observer. A feminism that turns patriarchy upside down and proclaims a matriarchy that is simply a reversal of patriarchy cannot be postmodern. While the lesbian alternative must always be there as a legitimate and reasonable choice for women, a postmodern feminism must be able to provide a heterosexual alternative to male domination. Patriarchy requires women to embrace female submission and is rooted in the eroticization of male domination. A psychoanalytic postmodern feminism must use fantasy against fantasy, eroticization of power against the eroticization of power, and neurosis against neurosis. It would turn a psychic reality rooted in Eros or life against a psychic reality grounded in Thanatos or death. Since all gender structures are the result of the neuroses produced by the conflict between the sexual and the ego drives, a psychoanalytic feminism must be one that points toward a healing of the psyche.

The politics of revolution have not helped the cause of women all that much. The politics of the left have tended to exploit the talents and energy of the women of the left as much as have politics of the right exploited the women who have identified with the right. The politics of postmodernism are particularly appropriate for a truly radical feminism, which focuses on the empowerment of women rather than on an equality with a male standard. Within the politics of postmodernism success or failure is not in issue. It is the process that is important, whatever the chances of success may be. It is a politics of those who are serious at play rather than serious people who play at politics. It is a politics of subversion that transcends. It is a politics that seeks to destabilize ideologies and institutions so that change can take place from within rather than being imposed from the peaks.

To the degree that Freudian psychoanalytic theory is grounded upon biological foundations, it will be foundationally inconsistent with postmodernism. Later, however, Freud abandoned biological essentialism and developed themes that were foreshadowed by Nietzsche. It is this aspect of Freudian theory that permits a postmodern psychoanalysis. Nietzsche's focus was on culture and society while Freud concentrated on the individual psyche. Nietzsche, in one sense, was a precursor of psychoanalytic social theory. His genealogical method and approach to history are the analog of the psychoanalytic process. His "will to ignorance" (WP, 609) and "active forgetfulness" (GM, II, 1, 3) are structurally similar to Freud's ideas about repression. His view of truth as illusion (TL, 46–47) is a counterpart to Freud's ideas about psychic reality (SE, XIII 159–61; SE, XVII, 244–45, 248–51).[15] Nietzsche referred frequently to the unconscious (GS, 9; HH, II, 37; D, II, 119, 129; WP, 74, 289, 676).[16] His strategy of intersubstituting opposites and reversing perspectives demonstrated two terms of an oppositional pair to be mere accomplices of each other (BGE, 2, 34, 47, 200–201; T, 486),[17] a method akin to the analytic process of using the analysand's narrative to uncover what has been repressed (SE,

XVI, 385; XIX, 50 n, 235–39). Nietzsche's view of consciousness as a disease (GS, 354) corresponds to Freud's view of the neurosis of normality (SE, XXIII, 219, 220, 235, 238, 239, 250). His view of truth as error and the truth in the lie (EH, 34, 126–27; WP, 5, 261, 278–79, 493–95, 572, 616, 853, 1011; GM, III, 19; GS, 347; D, 117) is presupposed by deconstructionism,[18] as is his denial of an ultimate reality (BGE, 4; GS, 54, 57, 58; WP, 12, 13, 80, 461, 567, 580, 583–86, 616).[19] The postmodern perspectival construction of reality comes directly from Nietzsche (D, 119; Z, 62; GS, 92; HH, 208),[20] and Nietzsche's perspective of history as interpretation (UM, 72–7, 95–7; UD, 3, 7; GS, 344) and his genealogical approach to origins (D, 44, 49, 446; GM, pref. 4–7; GM, II, 6, 12; HH, 3, 16, 274) underlie the deconstructive histories of sexuality, mental illness, and Foucault's penal system.[21]

A fruitful interchange between feminism and psychoanalysis and between feminism and postmodernism is now in progress.[22] One aspect of that discussion is essentialism, the view that at least some aspect of what it means to be human or what we call *human nature* is natural or, in other words, biologically determined and consequently cannot be changed.[23] The ideological discourses of the legitimization of male domination are necessarily and inevitably essentialist. Consequently, postmodernism, which necessarily and inevitably denies the possibility of absolute or objective knowledge, furnishes a powerful counterargument to the legitimacy of patriarchy. Freud made a serious error when he concluded that the psychic reality of the Oedipal passage reflected material reality. This assumption underlies Freud's classification of non-Oedipal psychic reality as perverse. Consequently, Freud constituted the Oedipal theory as not only descriptive but as also prescriptive. Freud's view of material reality was tainted with modernity. Postmodernism can help clarify the nature and structure of material reality, and feminism can negate the prescriptive aspect of Oedipal theory.

SHE Who Must Be Obeyed

There is one central, predominant figure who appears throughout this book. She is a particular type of woman, difficult to describe. According to Freud, she doesn't even exist and cannot exist. Yet he met her once, although he was unaware of it at the time. When analyzing one of his own dreams, he referred to Rider Haggard's novel *SHE*, which he called "A *strange* book, but full of hidden meaning . . . the eternal feminine," and he alludes to "thoughts which . . . went too deep to become conscious . . . that had been stirred up by the mention of Rider Haggard's *She*" (SE, V, 453–54).[24] In the novel, the Eternal Feminine, the all-powerful female figure who couldn't be killed, was called by those under her authority "She Who Must Be Obeyed." How does one describe what cannot exist? In Freud's terms, she would be the woman who does not suffer from a lack. Women do not have penises, and for Freud the absence of a penis is a lack. We are not referring to the Freudian phallic woman or phallic mother, as she is the woman who lacks a penis but thinks or acts just as if she had one. Such a woman would still suffer from a lack. The figure we wish to think and write about would not have a penis but would not be defined as having or suffering from a lack. Such a woman would be unthinkable for Freud. If the woman is so defined, and psychoanalysis remains committed to an asymmetrical view of gender, then the woman would possess something that the male did not have. The male would then be the one defined in terms of a lack, and for Freudian psychoanalysis this would be to think the unthinkable.

Interestingly enough, she does exist for Carl Jung, and her existence for Jung was one of the factors that inevitably led to his break with Freud. The recognition of her existence, however, ensures that Jungian analytical psychology presupposes a gender symmetry of a kind, which Jung deals with in terms of the anima, the animus, and androgyny. This, however, makes Jungian analytical psychology essentialist. Jung assumes that certain characteristics, which both sexes possess, are more fundamentally connected to one sex than to the other. It is in terms of these essentialist connections that the anima and the animus are defined.[25] However, this woman, for the Jungian, is monstrous and must be killed by the Hero. SHE is the all-consuming mother from whom everyone, male or female, must escape. Jung, therefore, tells us that if we meet the monster, we must destroy her. For Jung, SHE exists but is incomplete in a different way in that she lacks a masculine side. SHE is monstrous because she is all-female and therefore lacks balance.

We reject the essentialist position that there are any characteristics whatsoever that are biologically determined. It is our position that the self is formulated within discourse, that is to say, structured through discourse. When, therefore, we write about this woman, who doesn't exist for Freud but does exist for Jung, who counsels us to murder her, we are writing about a certain kind of discourse rather than a certain kind of woman. This woman does not exist for Lacan because the kind of discourse that could produce this kind of subjectivity cannot exist. The reason it cannot exist is that, so far as Lacan is concerned, all discourse must be structured by the privileged signifier. The privileged signifier is the phallus, and the kind of discourse necessary to produce this kind of woman cannot have the phallus as the privileged signifier.

Language, for Lacan, presupposes the category of the Subject. The Other comes out of language itself, as the Subject must remain, by its very nature and structure, outside language, as a presupposition of language. Males, because they have the phallus, are selves generated out of the Subject, while females, lacking the phallus, are selves generated out of the Other. The woman with whom we are concerned is impossible for Lacan because, given that discourse is structured by the privileged signifier, she cannot exist as a self generated out of the Subject. She is the woman who is a self as a manifestation of the Subject rather than a self as a manifestation of the Other. If we assume the possibility of her existence, this woman who is a self as a manifestation of the Subject, then she would have the Gaze and the Voice. We can, therefore, refer to the woman who is a self as a manifestation of the Subject as SHE WHO MUST BE OBEYED, or SHE for short. Given the asymmetrical nature of gender, which is a fundamental presupposition of psychoanalysis, if the woman can have the Gaze and the Voice, the male can correspondingly be the object of the Gaze, described and defined by the Voice. This male would be castrated because he would lack, within the terms of the discourse, whatever it was that the woman possessed that defined her self as a manifestation of the Subject. Since SHE cannot exist within the confines of traditional psychoanalysis, we must approach her through the castrated male. We must view Oedipus as castrated. This, of course, is what he does to himself when he puts out his own eyes and flees his position of power and wealth. Hence, we title this book *The Castration of Oedipus.*

This produces a problem for feminism, one that lies at the heart of the ambivalent relationship between feminism and psychoanalytic theory. There is no such thing, as yet, as a psychoanalytic feminism, and possibly there never will be. Feminism is committed to both the empowerment of women and to gender equality. Psychoanalytic theory is committed to gender asymmetry. How, then, can these two presuppositions converge?

They could converge only in terms of some kind of theory of female supremacy, which for both feminism and psychoanalysis is unthinkable. Even if we were to think about the unthinkable, it would have to be based on the one assumption that the postmodern perspective requires—that gender structure is not biologically determined. On that one presupposition, all three perspectives do accord.

A consistent and integrated merging of psychoanalysis, postmodernism, and feminism will only be possible and desirable if there are alternative forms of heterosexual male sexuality. These alternative forms, if they exist, must be perverse if they are to point to a way out of the Lacanian impasse because the sexuality must be a denial of, and a revolt against, the Law of the Father and it must manifest itself in the form of a different kind of masculinity. At the same time, it must provide a category of "woman" that is not defined in terms of lack or castration.

One could well ask why a book should be either written or read about the unthinkable, or about the discourse of SHE, if SHE does not exist? The issue to be examined is whether a discourse exists out of which a woman could structure a subjectivity, a self as SHE. Are there women as such who are not phallic males, that is to say, females who have structured their subjectivity, their self, out of a phallic discourse? This question challenges Lacan in a very fundamental way. The point of this book is to challenge psychoanalysis, postmodernism, and feminism at a very fundamental level, at the level of their presuppositions.

For this reason the book starts from the presupposition as a hypothetical that there is a discourse within which a woman can structure a self as SHE. The single preface to this entire work, therefore, are two simple words, WHAT IF? This book originated in a seminar that one of the authors has taught for a number of years on psychoanalysis, postmodernism, and feminism and in which the other author was at one time enrolled as a student. The seminar used a number of videos and films, the purpose of which was to evoke SHE in the psyche of the students. The students would then confront HER in their own psyche and would thereafter do some preliminary self-analysis as to their conscious and unconscious reactions to HER. The seminars have generally been made up of an equal number of females and males. Each student was asked to keep a personal journal of his or her reactions to the readings, the videos and films, and the discussions. Some of the students were hostile to HER and wanted to kill HER. They then understood at a "gut level" the Jungian theory of individuation of the self as the Hero who must battle the monstrous female mother, SHE. Others, particularly some of the females, wanted to negate HER with argument and discourse. They wanted no part of HER, that is, they wanted no part of HER in themselves. SHE triggered masochistic fantasies in the psyche of some males, and they wanted to worship HER and sacrifice their phalluses to HER. A few found HER so scary that they withdrew from the confrontation.

The purpose of the seminar was to encourage the student to use these reactions to engage the important theoretical issues of feminist legal theory. Almost every student who went through the exercise felt it to be of a great benefit for approaching feminist issues. They thereafter would see these issues in a new way. They were now engaged in these issues on a personal level with a broader view of their difficulty and complexity. What the students liked about the approach of the seminar was precisely that they were engaged in the theoretical issues and material on this very personal level. Each person came out of the seminar with a different perspective. The students were led to approach the seminar as a text to be interpreted. The interpretation included what they brought to it themselves as much as the text itself.

This book is written from the same perspective. It is written the way it is in order to produce a reaction in the psyche of the readers, which the reader is encouraged to examine. Whatever the reader takes away from the reading of this text, it ought to include what they bring to it. The exercise of self-analysis is important for the reading of this book. Otherwise the reader will miss its point altogether. If this book is treated as a book like any other, as an argument for a particular position, then whoever the reader is, whether Freudian, Jungian, Lacanian, and whatever kind of feminist—liberal, Marxist, essentialist, or civil libertarian—he or she will be offended. The authors will be seen to be reverse discriminators, man-haters, or gender fascists. If the reader finds it difficult to separate the authors from the text, or to read the text as a hypothetical, then this itself ought to be revealing about the reader's own psyche. The very fact that the authors feel it necessary to approach this topic in such a defensive and guarded way is also revealing.

As authors, however, we must take at least one position or perspective as fundamental, and on that we may be challenged. This position is that of postmodernism. Our method and underlying cognitive presuppositions are those that are generally referred to as postmodern or poststructuralist.

Interpreting Texts

There are certain texts in which a point is reached where no further knowledge, insights, and perceptions are to be gained, irrespective of the experience that the interpreter brings. There are other texts, however, that are so complex and rich that there appears to be no end to what can be drawn from them. Such texts generally are disturbing and challenging on their face, and the more we study them, the more disturbing and challenging they become. They remain a central focus of analysis and interpretation long after the death of their authors. There is more contained in these texts than is evident on the surface, and an interaction takes place between the experience the reader brings and the text itself. Consequently, they are subject or susceptible to interpretations that would not necessarily have been present in the minds of their authors. Such are the texts of Nietzsche, Freud, and Lacan. In the past few decades there has been a material resurgence of interest in the writings of Nietzsche and Freud, and the works of Lacan will absorb social theorists for decades to come. So long as we continue to study Lacan, we will need to keep reading Freud and Nietzsche.

We have playfully embraced the irony of writing a feminist book using texts that have been considered misogynous and inaccurate in their depictions of women and femininity. We have attempted to stage a confrontation between feminism and these texts and to produce a convergence. Whether or not we are successful is not a major concern to us. What we hope the reader will learn from the exercise is that feminism has only begun to confront human sexuality. There is much more to be learned. Legal theory, court actions, human rights codes, affirmative action, and progressive legislation are all important, but they will not, in and of themselves, change the praxis of the relationships that shape the destinies of women and men. In the final analysis, what happens in the bedroom may be of more importance to the ending of male domination of the female than what happens in courts or legislatures.

How can one write a feminist book and base it on the texts of Nietzsche, Freud and Lacan? There is a way, which is suggested by Derrida, and we have adopted his methodology in writing this book on psychoanalytic, postmodern feminism. Derrida, in dealing with the problem of the Nazi's interpretation and use of the texts of Nietzsche and whether or not Nietzsche failed in some way in not foreseeing the possibility of their use and interpretation in that manner, tells us that "the effects or structure of a text are not reducible to its 'truth,'—to the intended meaning of its presumed author, or even its supposedly unique and identifiable signatory" (EO, 29). He then questions "how reactive degeneration could exploit the same language, the same words, the same utterances, the same rallying cries as the active forces to which it stands opposed," adding that "neither this phenomenon nor this peculiar ruse eluded Nietzsche." A similar question can be proposed by feminists regarding the writings of Nietzsche, Freud, and Lacan: how can their patriarchal, male, and phallic-centered texts be used as an active force against patriarchy and male domination? Derrida explains:

> The question that poses itself for us might take this form: Must there not be some powerful utterance-producing machine that programs the movements of the two opposing forces at once, and which couples, conjugates, or marries them in a given set, as life (does) death? . . . Neither of the two antagonistic forces can break with this powerful programming machine: it is their *destination;* they draw their points of origin and their resources from it; in it, they exchange utterances that are allowed to pass through the machine and into each other, carried along by family resemblances, however incompatible they may sometimes appear. . . . The "programming machine" that interests me here does not call only for decipherment but also for transformation—that is, a practical rewriting according to a theory. . . . [I]f one does more than extract short sequences . . . then one will clearly see that what passes elsewhere for the "same" utterance says exactly the opposite and corresponds instead to the inverse, the reactive inversion of the very thing it mimes. (EO, 29–30)

In Derrida's discussion of *Ecce Homo* and *On the Future of Our Educational Institutions,* he refers to Nietzsche's contrasting pairs of Christ and Dionysus and Nietzsche's biographical parental reference in *Ecce Homo* to his mother—the living feminine or life—and his father—the dead man or death. The contrasts that these two pairings represent also run through the writings of Freud and Lacan, inviting us to explore the oppositional reading and interpretation of their texts. What we have attempted in this book is to use the patriarchal, male-oriented, phallic-focused texts of Nietzsche, Freud, and Lacan and "reconstitute the entire syntax of the system" around the primary signifier in place of the privileged. The texts of Freud and Lacan are incomplete and open in the same way as those of Nietzsche and invite the reader to engage the text in this fashion. We have, therefore, throughout this book, attempted to approach the texts of Freud and Lacan with the same degree of respect, admiration, and challenge as Derrida would have us approach the texts of Nietzsche.

The texts of Freud and Lacan, like those of Nietzsche, deal with Eros and Thanatos. As well, they deal with the sexual drive and the ego drive, the Subject and the Other, the mind and the body, pleasure and pain, the conscious and the unconscious, the self and the other, birth and death, female and male, and femininity and masculinity. These dialectics, dualisms, and oppositional pairs are very much interrelated. The powerful programming machine that Derrida postulates can equally function between these oppositional and antagonistic forces, conjugating and marrying them in a similar fashion.

TWO

The Sexuality of Politics

The Oedipal Passage

Clearly, there can be no full integration of feminist theory and psychoanalysis as long as psychoanalysis continues to maintain that the Oedipal passage is a necessary representation of unconscious life and that a successful Oedipal passage of an individual, whether male or female, is the measure of effective individuation. So long as psychoanalytic theory treats a successful Oedipal passage as the norm against which perversion is to be measured, the relationship between feminism and psychoanalysis must remain equivocal and paradoxical. If, on the other hand, the Oedipal passage is considered to be only a possible materialization and not necessarily the best, and if non-Oedipal sexualities and gender positions are also possible that lead to healthier forms of individuation and social life, then Oedipal sexuality will not retain its position as a norm. Equally, the relationship between postmodernism and psychoanalysis will remain problematic if the Oedipal passage is an essential representation, manifestation, and materialization of unconscious life.

The Oedipal passage alone seems to dominate our psychic reality. Very few would seriously argue that the Oedipal analysis is not a valid description of the process of genderization. The gender positions that are its end product seem to reconfirm the analysis. Even so, many of Freud's views as they relate to the primal scene, fantasies of seduction, penis envy, and femininity as castration have always been, and still remain, highly controversial, even within Freudian circles. All of these themes have one factor in common. They deal with origins: the origin of the child, the origin of the self, the origin of the ego, the origin or emergence of sexuality, the origin of sexual differences, the origin and development of gender differences, the origin of femininity and masculinity, the origin of neuroses, and the origin of desire (LP, 332). The disputes within the Freudian community are not so much about origin, seduction, and castration as they are about how these topics are to be interpreted and played out in the explanations of the origin of human psychic development.

The resolution of the Oedipus complex and its relationship to the structure of sex and gender turns on the problem of castration. The phallic lack defines castration and determines the nature of sexuality and gender. The phallus is the privileged point of reference that determines dominance and submission. The girl must submit to the status of being castrated, and the boy to the fear of castration, in order to allow the emergence of desire.[1] According to Lacan, "What analytic experience shows is that, in any case, it is castration that governs desire, whether in the normal or the abnormal" (E, 323). The boy treads on the path to desire by exchanging the father for the mother as the object of his ego ideal. For the girl, the passage is more difficult. Freud permits the girl three choices: a withdrawal from sexuality altogether, femininity, or masculinity (the masculinity complex). For the girl, there is no ideal exit from the Oedipus complex in that not only does the Oedipus complex "neuroticize" the girl, it pathologizes female sexuality. The political implications of phallic sexuality are clear. They ensure male domination over the female and reproduce from generation to generation the structure of the patriarchal family, the "feminization" of women and their sexual exploitation.

The concept of the phallus is critical in psychoanalytic theory. It has three parts: the generative power of nature, the law of desire, and the sexual organs of reproduction. The concept of the phallus is traditionally identified with the male penis. It is clear, however, that the phallus is much more than the penis in psychoanalytic discourse. The penis is an organ of the male body and as such is a material reality. The phallus belongs to the world of psychic reality. Its meaning entails that which is endowed or given to the possessor of the penis within the framework of psychic reality. Correspondingly, the mammary glands and uteri of women are material realities, while at the level of psychic reality the breasts and womb take on significance and meaning that have no counterpart in the world of biological material reality. Attributing the generative powers of nature to the breasts and womb would constitute a dialectical alternative to the phallus, or, in other words, a primary signifier repressed and denied by the privileged signifier. At the level of psychic reality castration means not having the phallus. Traditional Freudian theory assumes that the female is castrated by nature because she lacks a penis. Females, however, are castrated within the framework of Oedipal sexuality not because they lack the penis but because in male patriphallic psychic reality the generative powers of nature are not identified with females' reproductive organs.

If the generative power of nature is to be identified with any reproductive organs it ought to be those of the female, as the female in mammalian species has a much greater role to play in reproduction than does the male. The male carries 50 percent of the genetic code, whereas the female not only furnishes the other 50 percent, but her body is host to the fetus, gives it birth, and nourishes it. The attachment of the generative power of nature to the male penis constitutes a castration of the female by depriving her of the generative power of nature. The female is not castrated by her nature but by male patriphallic psychic reality imposed upon her through the Oedipal passage.[2] The generative power of nature lies either with the female, in which case it attaches to the womb and the breasts, or it lies in the male, attaching to the penis. If the male has the phallus and gives it to the female (recognizes that the generative powers of nature lie with her) then he castrates himself as a voluntary sacrifice. All of this shapes desire or is shaped by desire within the realm of psychic reality. If we are to conceive of a matriphallus, it is the phallus of the male that is given to and consequently owned and controlled by the (M)other. Since the male remains attached to it, when he gives it to her, he is giving her dominion over himself and embracing submission.

In the pre-Oedipal stage, the child recognizes the mother as having the generative power of nature—the source of her power, authority, and preeminence—as she learns that her origin is her mother. The authority of the mother is natural in that it requires no justification other than being a mother, giving birth, and nurturing. Its relationship to sex is general and not specifically genital. It is the generative power of nature that the female loses through castration in the Oedipal passage. If this is correct, then the initial stage of infant male sexuality is non-Oedipal matriarchal sexuality, in which the child wishes to give his little phallus to the mother. This is transformed into Oedipal patriphallic sexuality as the male child adopts the gender structure and sexuality of male patriphallic psychic reality, by which he is led to believe that eventually he will own one all for himself.

The paternal phallus is a conceptual structure that links the male mind with the penis. It is the possession of the phallus that makes a male a father. The concept of the father and the concept of the paternal phallus are inextricably linked. A father, as correctly defined by Freud, is a man who owns or possesses a woman, that is to say, who exercises authority over women or a woman.[3] Thus, the paternal phallus is the source of the law. Lacan states that "The phallus is the privileged signifier of that mark in which the role of the logos is joined with the advent of desire" (E, 287). The will of the father is the law, and the proclamation of the will is a production of the mind. The archetypal paternal phallus is a dialectical structure between the poles of the logos and the penis and reflects the structure of male mind/body dualism. Oedipal patriphallic psychic reality uses religion, law, and pornography to castrate the female. The Law of the Father is the midpoint between penis and logos.

Oedipus and the Monster

The woman is castrated. She suffers a lack. The Oedipal passage as the paradigm of normal individuation for the female condemns her always to be a self generated from the Other. Her subjectivity will always be that of the Other, and not as a manifestation of the Subject. SHE, whose self is a manifestation of the Subject, is not castrated. SHE suffers no lack. Was SHE originally in the discourse and then castrated so SHE is now only she, or was SHE never there at all? For Freud, the latter was true. For Jung, SHE was there, but, as SHE was not to be found in Sophocles' texts *(Oedipus the King, Oedipus Colonus)*, SHE was not a significant figure. He took his material from the Hero myths in which SHE, portrayed as the female monster, was always slain by the Hero in mortal combat. However, Jean-Joseph Goux in his book *Oedipus, Philosopher* tells us that SHE was there, and he subjects the text of the two plays to "rigorous and thoroughgoing analysis with the tools of anthropology, comparative mythology, and narratology" to establish HER presence (OP, 1). SHE is the Sphinx, the threatening female monster, part woman, part animal, who confronted Oedipus. Instead of engaging the monster in mortal combat as is the task of the Hero, Oedipus engaged HER in an intellectual contest and, while winning the contest, Oedipus failed to kill HER, and SHE killed HERSELF instead. By failing to kill HER, the sin of incest with his own mother became inevitable. For Goux, the central theme of the Oedipal myth is not patricide, which is only a side issue, but matricide failed. Freud, therefore, according to Goux, missed an essential element. Goux writes in his introduction that "it is within a specific historical institution of subjectivity, within the framework of a particular symbolic mechanism (of which the Oedipus myth is the most powerful manifestation), that something like the 'Oedipus complex' has been able to command attention and elicit description." He explains that the Hero who is to become king must first kill "the female dragon, the female serpent, the female monstrosity, in bloody combat" and thus liberate the bride by "murdering a dangerous, dark feminine force" (OP, 2).

It was not our SHE who Oedipus met on the road and failed to kill. The SHE he met exists in a mythic discourse that is structured by the privileged signifier. Consequently, SHE exists as monster. The SHE of the monomyths is defined in terms of a phallic discourse. No female can structure a self as a manifestation of the Lacanian Subject from such a discourse. This SHE must be beheaded so that SHE is no longer SHE but only a dead she, or a castrated she, without Gaze or Voice. The presence of the SHE as Subject rather than monstrous Other would have to come out of the structure of a very different kind of discourse, a discourse that would challenge the privilege of the phallus as the exclusive master signifier.

According to Goux's interpretation of the discourse of the Oedipal mythic structure, "Oedipus is the dramatic type who exemplifies a new posture that philosophy takes on," which Goux calls "anthropocentering" (OP, 119) in that man becomes the measure of all things. In so doing Oedipus takes over the realm of Apollo, and for doing this Apollo curses and punishes Oedipus. The realm of the gods is in the unconscious, so that Freud could not recognize the relationship between the conscious and the unconscious without discovering, at the same time, the Oedipus complex. "The Sphinx . . . is a mixture of animality and humanity. By solving the riddle with the answer 'man' Oedipus suppresses that mixture, dissolves the monstrosity. He makes man—who is now self-conscious—the answer that can be used against any obscurity" (OP, 164). Oedipus, the new rational man of Greek science and philosophy, made the Sphinx go away by pronouncing the word "man." But where did the Sphinx go? She killed herself but is now merely moved into the underworld of the unconscious. Lacan tells us that the unconscious is structured like a language. But is the discourse of the unconscious structured by the privileged signifier? If not, then in what realm is the Sphinx, banished by the pronouncement of the word "man"?

Goux tells us that Oedipus, by killing his father and causing his mother's death, became the new rational agent of the discourse of reason, the discourse of science, mathematics, and Western law. Without father and mother he is the citizen of the universal state. Oedipus therefore marks the shift from mythos to logos, but the logos is a part of the phallus. The discourse of gender equality, which is central to so much of feminist discourse, is a product of a discourse structured by the privileged signifier. Goux writes that "The move to overthrow idealism and take possession of the Earth completes philosophy's Oedipean destiny. Foreseen by Descartes to a limited extent, accomplished by Marx and by Nietzsche, the movement whereby human reason, having become instrumental, takes possession of 'Nature/Matter/Earth' is a movement that unfolds, organizes, and amplifies what mythic language evoked with horror, in archaic personalized and sexualized terms, as possession of one's own mother" (OP, 175). It is, therefore, in the configurations of the Oedipal myth as they bring together themes of patricide and matricide, mythic monsters and the discourse of rationality, that we should commence our search for "SHE WHO MUST BE OBEYED." It is in the unconscious, the text between the lines, the truth of the lie of the narrative, that we must search for the text from which SHE shall emerge—if the text is there at all.

Reality

Psychoanalytic theory is concerned with three realities: "material reality," "psychical reality," and "the reality of unconscious wishes and their 'truest shape': fantasy" (FO, 8).[4] Material reality is what goes on in the external world. Psychical or psychic reality is the inner world of the individual that is projected onto the external world, based on the premise that "what appears to us as immediate reality consists of carefully processed images."[5] Fantasy comes out of an imaginal framework rooted in perception. It is the inner reality of the individual projected onto the external world. Most people assume that their psychic reality is in fact material reality. Psychic reality lies between material reality and the reality of unconscious fantasy and is structurally related to both. There is, of course, no sharp division between these three realities. Material reality, which impinges on our consciousness, merges with the reality of unconscious fantasy to shape our psychic reality, which is our own vision of ourselves and the world.

Human sexuality is the dominant focus of psychoanalytic theory. The masculine and the feminine are the primary metaphors of human thought; and the two sets of reproductive organs are the grand metonymical links that we forge with the generative or creative powers of nature. "Sex, sexuality, and gender form a knot" in that while we can think of sex in biological terms and gender in psychological terms, the psychoanalytic perspective of "sexuality" "seems to have nothing to say about sex and gender" even though sexuality is "inextricably bound up with both biological sex and sociological gender."[6] The distinction between sex, sexuality, and gender spans the three kinds of reality: material, psychic, and unconscious. If we relate the three levels of reality to this knot, biological sex would seem to have more to do with material reality and sexuality would have more to do with psychic reality and the reality of unconscious fantasy while gender would seem to have a place in all three.

Material Reality and Sexuality

Human sexuality is the focal point of psychoanalytic theory. Perceived biological sexual differences are the bases of gender discrimination and, therefore, will continue to be a pivotal concern of feminism. By deconstructing human discourse, we find what lies between the lines and underneath the text: namely, sex. Accordingly, human sexuality must be the central unifying subject of the triad of psychoanalysis, feminism, and postmodernism.

Let us metaphorically assume, for a moment, that "nature" was sentient and the evolutionary process was purposeful. Let us further assume that bimorphic sexuality, by which the genetic code is split each time reproduction takes place, is the most efficient mechanism of evolutionary change and that the most effective method of ensuring reproduction is by hormonally inducing unpleasure through sexual tension, which impels the animal to seek release in the form of sexual pleasure through copulation. One could hormonally induce the unpleasure to the degree that the animal would vacillate between eating and copulating when faced with the possibility of a choice between satisfying hunger or the sexual drive. If one increased the amount of hormones in the "design" of the species, the animal would always choose sexual pleasure. If, however, the satisfaction of the drive for sexual release meant doing battle with a larger male in order to achieve access to the female, the animal would choose to satisfy hunger since the unpleasure of conflict would outweigh the unpleasure of sexual tension. If the unpleasure of sexual tension were increased to the degree that it outweighed even the unpleasure of mortal combat, then the animal would be driven to attack the potential rival, no matter what the cost in terms of pain.

In the female of the species, one would want to enhance the ability of the female to select her mate. One would therefore "build in" either a lesser amount of unpleasure or a greater tolerance for sexual deprivation. At the same time, one might want to increase the degree of pleasure so that it was greater than that of the male in order to encourage the female to permit penetration, but without the desperation of being driven by desire. This is very similar to the existing state of mammalian sexuality, whereby the struggle for access serves two powerful evolutionary processes, the propagation of the strongest genetic codes through the survival of the fittest and the facilitation of the female's selection of her mate ensured by the extreme unpleasure of sexual tension in the male.

Imagine further that this species causes the evolution of language and consciousness such that it becomes aware of its biological "bondage" to the reproductive process and knowledgeable of its own impending and inevitable death. Suppose further that in the evolutionary process the species breeds out estrus and is subject to constant and ever recurring sexual unpleasure, and suppose that the erotic unpleasure is visually stimulated through the mere sight of parts of the anatomy of the female rather than through smell, such that it is thus even more difficult for the male to escape the unpleasure. At the same time, the female not only has a greater capacity for tolerating sexual abstinence but is not erotically stimulated by the visual, over which there is little control, but rather by arousal based on a tactile mechanism. Humans are mammals, and human sexuality is fundamentally mammalian. Why should we expect human sexuality to be any different than that described above?[7]

While biological sex does not determine phallic possession, and hence traditional gender roles, there are, nevertheless, relationships between the material reality of biological sex and the psychic reality of phallus possession, castration, and gender structure. These relationships are evident in the fact that humans have bred out estrus and are consequently almost continually subject to sexual arousal; that the human male, at the same time, has the hormonal stimulation of most mammalian species, which forces it to struggle and compete for sexual access; that the erotic triggering mechanism is visual rather than based on smell; that the human male is subject to a constant, reoccurring cycle of sexual arousal, and consequential unpleasure, and is therefore dependent on the female for release from the unpleasure of unrequited sexual tension. At the same time the human male has conscious awareness of all of this and of his own impending and inevitable death as well. Moreover, given that most human psychic processes go on at the unconscious level and that humans have the capacity to repress into the unconscious those aspects of material reality that they find painful, and replace them with illusions in the form of psychic reality, we can understand why gender structures are the way they are—even though they are not as determined as the foregoing suggests.

Psychic Reality and Sexuality

Patriarchy is the massive delusionary conceptual system that denies the psychological burden of animality.[8] The reliance of the human male on the female for release from the intense unpleasure of unrequited sexual desire and the power of the female to give or deny pleasure or relief, together with memories of the loving and all-fulfilling mother, combine to create a relationship of power and dependency. It is the primeval dominant/subservient relationship between the sexes of most species of mammals. The image of herds of female animals dominated by a single large male who fights off all rivals is a fantasy of males immersed in patriarchal mythic systems. One can equally conceive of the same arrangement in terms of the males biologically committed to never ending bouts of conflict, unpleasure, and pleasure such that it is the male who is the enslaved. If we adopt the metaphor of master/slave to the woman/man sexual relationship, Nietzsche's genealogical approach to morality can be applied to the legal discourse of authority, obligation, and duty. Duty or obligation is the central core of the normative systems of morality, law, and religion.

Nietzsche developed a "naturalistic" explanation for the phenomena of normative discourse.[9] Patriarchy is a normative system that embraces religion, morality, and law. Nietzsche's genealogical method of analysis, which he applied to Christian morality, is equally applicable to patriarchy. Nietzsche understood the function of normative discourse to be a weapon of the powerless against the powerful that serves to delegitimize the exercise of the will to power of those who possess it. Just as the capacity to withhold economic benefits is a form of power upon which the entire capitalist system rests,[10] so the capability to deny sexual satisfaction is a very compelling form of power. The biological and hormonally induced need of the human male for constant, recurring sexual satisfaction and the capacity of the female to give or deny creates the analog of a master/slave relationship in terms of this power. The metaphor of "a slave of passion" is not without foundation. The morality of patriarchy robs the female of the will to power and turns a capacity to deny sexual satisfaction into a duty to provide it. The Law of the Father provides that *"thy desire shall be to thy husband, and he shall rule over thee."*[11] The text between the lines reads *"your husband has the right to enjoy your body, and this right will be exercised without limit, without being stopped from impulse, until he is satiated."*[12]

The primary form of the species has meaning in and of itself—the being that reproduces. The survival of the species, that is the perpetuation of the genetic code, is the only consistent pattern to be found in life forms. The being that reproduces requires no legitimization, no definition, no word. Women and mothers are primary and therefore are "real." Masculinity is secondary and requires legitimization, definition, conceptualization. "[M]others are 'real,' fathers are only conceptual."[13] The Great Mother simply is. The heavenly father has to proclaim his existence—"I AM THAT I AM."[14] Man-father-husband had to create himself by proclaiming himself. Man-father-husband-God-king is a conceptualization driven by desire. Man is therefore the product of the WORD. "In the beginning was the Word, and the Word was with God, and the Word was God."[15] Patriarchy, which is standard morality, law, religion, culture, and history, turns the "slavery" of the sexual dependency of the human male into the slavery of male authority whereby the woman exists for the enjoyment of the man.

The Reality of Unconscious Fantasy and Sexuality

Freud, in his analysis of fantasy, introduces the concept of primal or original fantasy, which he termed *Urphantasien* (LP, 331). According to Laplanche and Pontalis, "The original fantasies constitute this store of unconscious fantasies of all neurotics, and probably of all human beings" (FO, 17). They state:

> The original fantasy is first and foremost fantasy—it lies beyond the history of the subject but nevertheless in history—a kind of language and a symbolic sequence, but loaded with elements of imagination; a structure, but activated by

contingent elements. As such it is characterized by certain traits which make it difficult to assimilate to a purely transcendental scheme, even if it provides the possibility of experience (FO, 18).

Original fantasies contain three themes: "Fantasies of origins: the primal scene pictures the origin of the individual; fantasies of seduction, the origin and upsurge of sexuality; fantasies of castration, the origin of the differences between the sexes" (FO, 19). "Like myths they [the original fantasies] claim to provide a representation of, and a solution to, the major enigmas which confront the child" (FO, 19). For the child, fantasy is the setting for desire (FO, 26). These early fantasies have the structure of the original fantasy wherein the child seeks an answer to her or his origin, awakening eroticism and sexual difference. Within the setting of fantasy, the child experiences the seductive role of the mother as she washes, dresses, and caresses the child (FO, 26). Desire is "engendered" by difference. Difference exists in terms of masculinity and femininity. Masculinity and femininity are determined by avowal or disavowal of the phallus. Avowal or disavowal of the phallus is fantasized and symbolized in terms of castrating and being castrated.

Since the original fantasy is a universal fundamental structure of unconscious fantasy, it will be reflected in the structure of foundational myths, which are the fantasies of the collective psyche. These foundational myths also may take two different forms, depending upon whether the generative power of nature is attributed to the mother/female or the father/male. The foundational mythic systems of the West, such as the Judeo, Christian, and Islamic religions and the Greek myths, constitute collective fantasies that reflect the structure of the original fantasy—creation, seduction, castration. "In the beginning God created the heaven and the earth."[16] "And God said let us make man in our image, after our likeness; and let them have dominion over the fish of the sea, and over the fowl of the air, and over the cattle, and over all the earth, and over every creeping thing that creepeth upon the earth."[17] "The mother is no parent of that which is called her child, but only nurse of the new-planted seed that grows. The parent is he who mounts. A stranger she preserves a stranger's seed."[18] The logos, pure mind and spirit, is opposed to the flesh and animal body that seduces the mind through the pull of desire. The higher law denounces and disparages sexual pleasure as it contaminates and defiles pure mind and brings the spirit down to the level of the body.

When the generative power of nature is attributed to the mother/

female, the structure of the original fantasy spanning creation-seduction-castration will take a different form. The archetypes and the collective mythic narratives will be female-oriented rather than male in the foundational mythic structure of the collective. The generative powers of nature are identified with women through the Great Goddess who gives birth to all life. Entry into desire is through castration. The difference, however, is that it is the male who embraces castration by presenting his phallus to the female rather than entering desire by affirming the phallus in himself and in dominion over her—and thus, by definition, castrating the female. Matriarchal or non-Oedipal sexuality and patriarchal or Oedipal sexuality are not the same as male and female sexuality or feminine and masculine sexuality. Each kind is archetypal and prescribes gender roles. The archetypal structure of non-Oedipal sexuality is that of the Goddess and the Consort, Dionysus, or that of Parvati and Shiva. The gender structure is that of powerful females and males who are willing to sacrifice themselves for the ongoing process of life or Eros. The archetypal structure of Oedipal sexuality is that of God-King-Paterfamilias, who exercises authority over the inferior female who exists to serve the Father.

Oedipal patriphallic sexuality is pathological but not perverse. It is pathological because it pathologizes female sexuality and forces women to adopt femininity.[19] Furthermore, it is antilife and consequently death-oriented. It is not perverse because it defines the law. Non-Oedipal matriphallic sexuality is perverse because it subverts the Oedipal law that underlies the structure of the social order. It is symbolically incestuous because it seduces the male into surrendering the boundaries of the ego-oriented self in order to merge with the (M)other. "[T]he seduction of the mother's look challenges the social and familial order, indeed, we could say, perverts it."[20]

The Reality of Herstory and Sexuality

Postmodernism is essential for a psychoanalytic feminism that advocates and seeks the elimination of the submission of the female to the male. Let us approach this issue from the perspective of questions such as "Does the phallus exist?"; "Does the logos exist?"; "Does the Goddess really exist?" Questions of this form do not make sense in the context of postmodernism nor do they make sense in terms of Lacan's distinction between the Imaginary, the Symbolic, and the Real. Nothing can be said to exist in the Real because existence can only be given meaning in terms of the Imaginary and the Symbolic. There is no question but that the Goddess is a part of the Imaginary and the Symbolic and will always be so, so long as God, the logos (in whatever form it may take, whether scientific or religious), the father, and the phallus are a part of the Imaginary and the Symbolic. The postmodern feminist doesn't believe or disbelieve in the Goddess but plays within the discourse of the Goddess. If, as Shakespeare proclaimed, all the world is a stage, then there is no point in asking the question of what lies outside the play.

If one argues with the existence of the Goddess then one has to enter the arena of the modern, and in that arena the male controls the discourse. Therefore, God and the logos can exist, but the Goddess cannot. Women and feminism are on a much more level playing field within the postmodern perspective than they are within the discourse of modernism with its existing external and paternal world, objective reality, and truth. Look as one will, one will not find a Goddess there.

"Was there actually an age of matriarchal consciousness in the distant past?" would seem to be a lucid, direct question to a historian. For the postmodernist, history is always present in that it is only an interpretation of artifacts and texts of the past. History is just his story—a construction that entails selection, which entails exclusion, which always leaves open the possibility of another interpretation.[21] It is collective male psychic reality that purports to be objectively known material reality. The idea of what *really happened,* for the postmodernist, is meaningless. All we have and can ever have are interpretations. There is no final, comprehensive, true, or absolute interpretation because all interpretation selects and excludes. Lacan speaks of "this present synthesis of the past which we call history" (S I, 36). He tells us that "History is not the past. History is the past in so far as it is historicised in the present" (S I, 13). "[W]hen all is said and done, it is less a matter of remembering than of rewriting history" (S I, 14). Every construction of history will contain something that the observer-interpreter will bring to the texts and artifacts that will affect the process of selection and exclusion. The observer cannot be separated from what is observed. If truth can never be absolute, then neither can history. In one sense, therefore, the past is always present within a framework of forgetting and remembering, and what we forget is more telling than what we remember, whether it is the massacre of women as witches or the destruction of aboriginal peoples as savages.

The question "Was there actually an age of matriarchal consciousness in the distant past?" is problematic for psychoanalytic social theory as well as for the postmodernist. What we term "history" is our collective psychic reality, which is formed from the convergence of our collective material reality and our collective reality of unconscious fantasy, which, in turn contains our collective unconscious wishes, manifested in the form of our myths. When we examine our mythic structures, which span history, religion, art, and law, and the artifacts of the earliest centers of culture, there can be little question but that matriarchal consciousness formed a part of the collective unconscious and psychic realities of humankind. From the perspective of psychoanalysis, the very virulence of the misogyny in some early cultures, the extreme forms that patriarchy took in a number of ancient societies, and the eventual universality of patriarchy are all compelling evidence of the repression of matrisexual psychic reality, which identifies the generative power of nature with the mother. The question of whether or not there actually was an age of matriarchal consciousness in the distant past is problematic for psychoanalytic theory because it assumes that there is only a material reality and that it is capable of being discovered and known objectively. From the perspective of psychoanalysis, this is simply not the case.

The question of whether or not there was an actual age of matriarchal consciousness is also problematic for feminists because it has been males who have written the histories and interpreted the artifacts. It is a complicated one for feminists because the very question is asked in the context of a view of history and an interpretation of artifacts and texts that is male and phallocentric.

Nietzsche's genealogical method and his theory of discovering "truth" through oppositional substitution, Derrida's methodology of deconstruction, Freud's method of analysis as interpreted by Lacan—all furnish us with a response to the question of whether or not there was ever an age of matriarchal consciousness. Since there has been and is an age of patriarchal consciousness, there must be an age of matriarchal consciousness. Patriarchy is one facet of a paired opposition: Maleness-patriarchy requires femaleness-matriarchy. Jehovah could not exist without the Goddess existing. It is only in opposition to the Goddess that God became meaningful. It is only in opposition to the mother that the father became meaningful. The age of matriarchal consciousness is the *truth* in the lie of patriarchy. It is the *reality* in the illusion of the grand mythic systems we call history, culture, and religion.

The age of matriarchal consciousness was not discovered, conceived, or constructed upon the basis of archaeological discoveries of artifacts that could be interpreted in terms of goddess worship. It was constructed by two males—Bachofen and Frazer[22]—and the texts were interpreted or reinterpreted in terms of it. The archaeological effort took place by "digging" underneath the narratives of patriarchy. The narratives of patriarchy presumed and required their opposing counternarratives. Later, a vast number of artifacts were discovered that could be interpreted in terms of this narrative discourse. It should not be surprising that artifacts that invite an interpretation in terms of a matriarchal narrative were found predating the artifacts of an age of male sky gods, kings, and paterfamilias.

The denial of an age of matriarchal consciousness on the grounds that there never was a period in human history when male domination did not exist is an interpretation driven by desire. Matriarchal consciousness was and still remains the repressed and excluded counternarrative of patriarchal consciousness. The Old Testament is permeated with the struggle between the Goddess and Jehovah. God is the binary opposite to the Goddess. Paternal authority is similarly the opposite to maternal primacy; Eve to the Amazon; Christ to Pan or Dionysus; the horned consort of the Goddess to Satan; the crucifixion to the sacrifice of the sacred king to fertilize the earth; the cross to the serpent of the Goddess; the phallus to the womb; fornication to reproduction; the religious preoccupation with death to life; and the superiority of male over female to male sexual and emotional dependency on the female. The narratives of the Hero are stories of struggle against that which is feared—the Medusa, the Amazon, the Siren—in other words, SHE, the powerful female who is a self as a manifestation of the Subject. The glories of war and the progress of civilization are the opposition to the ever haunting thought that all that seems to matter in nature is the propagation of the genetic code. According to Camille Paglia, although women were at the center of early symbolism, "not a shred of evidence supports the existence of matriarchy anywhere in the world at any time,"[23] in the sense of a peaceful society ruled by women that was overthrown by warring men. While it well could be the case that matriarchal consciousness did not entail the political rule of women over men, it is difficult to imagine an age of matriarchal consciousness in which women were dominated by men as they are in patriarchy. The construction of the past is a part of the process of becoming. History, culture, and religion are a part of the narrative discourses within which we construct our sense of our selves. To deconstruct them entails the deconstruction of gender, and the deconstruction of gender requires the deconstruction of history, culture, and religion—and the construction of herstory.

The Dionysian Passage

Both Nietzsche and Derrida interpret narratives with a rigorous awareness both of what the author is blind to or excludes and what the reader brings to her or his interpretation, both consciously and unconsciously. All narratives, whether life stories, fiction, myth, or grand theories, are woven out of or are created in response to other narratives. Behind every grand story lies a counter grand story. The analyst elicits a narrative from the analysand and deconstructs the story in terms of the substitution of opposites, to discover the contents of the narrative repressed in the unconscious. The analyst, in aiding and encouraging the analysand to bring the counternarrative into consciousness, enables the analysand to defuse and transcend the preanalysis narrative. Since the personal life narratives of both analyst and analysand are constructed in terms of shared grand narratives and mythic structures, material from within the unconscious of both the analyst and the analysand is exchanged and interwoven. In the process of introducing the repressed into consciousness, neurosis becomes tolerable even though it may not be fully cured. When the analysand is able to immerse her- or himself in the excluded and repressed counternarrative, the original narrative is transformed or deenergized.

Postmodernism, poststructuralism, and deconstructionism demonstrate that Freudian psychoanalytic theory is incomplete in that its analytical structure is only half formulated. The "trinity" reveals the dialectic of the text, narrative, and discourse—the veiled cover and that which lies between and underneath. The counternarrative of psychoanalytic theory, which is to be found in between and underneath its own text-narrative-discourse, reveals an underlying oppositional parallel to Oedipal-centered and phallic-oriented theory. To reveal this is not merely to make corrections to mistaken ideas or to add neglected detail. Rather, it is to develop the other side of a dialectical psychic process.

There is another Greek myth that, in a number of ways, represents the pinnacle of the classical Greek dramatic tradition. This is Euripides' *The Bacchae,* with its central character Dionysus. When Dionysus is placed in dialectical opposition to Oedipus Rex or Pentheus, the King of Thebes, we have the framework of a dialectical structure of male psychic reality, the reality of male unconscious fantasy, and male sexuality. "*The Bacchae,*" according to Segal, "is strikingly modern not only because it invites reading contemporary concerns into the fifth century b.c. or fifth-century concerns into the twentieth but because Euripides was confronting a crisis of belief and of language, indeed a crisis of all symbolic expression, that *mutatis mutandi* resembles our own."[24] The dialectical tensions between Dionysus and his cousin, the King of Thebes, mirror the dialectical dynamics of our own phallic individual and collective psyches: the ego versus the id, the Self versus the Other, irrationalism versus rationalism, law and social order versus social chaos and transgression, Eros versus Thanatos, Pan versus Christ, the maternal phallus versus the paternal phallus, matriphallic sexuality versus patriphallic sexuality, Nietzsche versus Plato and Kant, truth versus myth, and modernity versus postmodernity. Pentheus rejects Dionysus' embrace of matriarchy. The adherence to patriarchal value brings about the Logos-King-Father's eventual retribution at the hands of his mother. In a ritualized act of violent dismemberment, mother castrates the law of the son and the father.

To transform ourselves we must transform the self by way of the "talking cure." Language and discourse are products of the collective psyche. They are the madness-pathologies-neuroses of the collective psyche that are reproduced within the psyche of the individual. Traditional psychoanalysis was developed to treat individual neuroses. The madness that we all share is a collective neurosis within the collective psyche. Postmodernism and radical feminism need to be integrated with psychoanalysis in order for the individual to transcend collective neuroses (generally considered as states of normality), as contrasted with the neuroses that arise from individual lived experience. The eventual purpose of the exploration of this triadic relationship is to develop a theory for the treatment of collective neuroses at both the individual and social levels. It will provide an etiology of patriarchy for feminism and suggest a possible "cure" for misogyny. It will also furnish postmodernism with a theory of the collective psyche and a method for transforming discourses. It will turn psychoanalytic theory from an ego psychology to a psychology of the collective that will embrace culture and history. Further, it will shift the traditional focus of psychoanalysis from the mythic structures of the Oedipal to those of the Dionysian. Analysis rooted in the Oedipal mythic structure concentrated on the father. Psychoanalytic theory, since Freud, has focused attention on the mother and the pre-Oedipal period of the development of the psyche. With this has come an alternative mythic structure that more and more is replacing the central focus on the Oedipal. The shift from Oedipus to Dionysus marks a significant trend in psychoanalytic social theory. Norman O. Brown, in a recent essay, states:

> What does it mean to take one's stand under the Dionysian, rather than the Freudian (or the Marxist) flag? It means to discard the pseudo-scientific posture of clinical detachment or political rationality, and recognize madness as the universal human condition, not the distinctive stigma of a separate class distinguished as insane. It means that madness is not an individual but a social phenomenon in which we all participate collectively: we are all in one and the same boat or body. It means also that madness is inherent in life and in order to live with it we must learn to love it. That is the point of honoring it with the name of a god. . . .
>
> "Dionysus, the god of madness, is also death" (Heraclitus). Ever since I read Freud's *Beyond the Pleasure Principle* I have pursued the idea that Life against Death, Eros and Thanatos, were the ultimate terms in which to think about human behavior, or "the psychoanalytical meaning of history." At the same time it was clear to me even in *Life Against Death* that at that deep level which can only be expressed in myth or metaphor, Freud's "instinct theory" needed to be remythologized in terms of Dionysus, that is to say in terms of instinctual dialectics rather than instinctual dualism.[25]

Brown concludes his essay with the words "We participate with each other, connected as well as separated by a sea of death; living each other's death, and dying each other's life."[26] It is, of course, in the analysis of Dionysian consciousness that the work of Nietzsche and Freud may be made to converge most closely.

Beyond the gender crisis lies the animality crisis, and beyond the Oedipal passage lies the Demeter-Dionysian passage that leads to trans-Oedipal psychic reality whereby the generative power of nature is again recognized to lie with the female-mother. In trans-Oedipal psychic reality, the female takes off the mask of femininity and no longer plays the masquerade. The male disavows the illusionary paternal phallus by presenting it by way of sacrifice to the female. Pathological patriphallic sexuality is replaced by perverse matriphallic sexuality. Gender structures are transformed and gender roles become blended. For the male, this entails exchanging Oedipal insanity for Dionysian madness. For the female, the trans-Oedipal state entails shedding the mask of femininity.[27] It involves the empowering embrace of the Great Goddess, the Medusa, the Kali. It is the embrace of the deep pain associated with the acknowledgment of patriarchal suffering and a healing through the affirmation of the labyrinthine chaos of the female body. It is a return to the origins and a descent toward the ominous matrix of sexuality.

There are two grand metaphors for the self. The one is the self as mind trapped within and confined by the body.[28] This is the essential view of the self in all religious discourse and is implicit in all human culture. This metaphor is the foundation of the belief in the human soul or spirit. It differentiates man from nature because only mankind has a soul. It differentiates men from women because mind is identified with maleness and femaleness with the body. Another metaphor of the self is man as the conscious animal, the biped primate with the extra thick cortex. This metaphor entered our consciousness and discourse through Darwin, Nietzsche, and Freud. This metaphorical view is both implicit and expressed in the discourse of both psychoanalytic social theory and postmodernism. Nietzsche subtitles his last work, *Ecce Homo,* "How One Becomes What One Is?" What is the appropriate metaphor for humans, the spirit, soul, mind, logos, the slightly-less-than-the-angels, or the biped primate that evolved through evolutionary chance, with a brain of such complexity that it produced the mental phenomena that we call mind or psyche? The challenge of knowing and becoming what one is, according to Nietzsche, is the heaviest demand that can be placed on mankind, and it is the challenge that he throws out to his readers.[29] To know who and what we are we must know in what way we are similar to other animals and in what way we are different. The metaphor of man as mind, however, denies our animality. If the biped primate, sharing mammalian sexuality and mortality, is the most appropriate metaphor for humanity, then accepting our animality is the heavy burden that Nietzsche and Freud challenge us to bear. Patriarchy is "an interpretation of the body and a *misunderstanding of the body*" (GS, pref. 2).

In *Ecce Homo* Nietzsche clearly identifies himself with Dionysus. We will never know whether or not this was the pinnacle of his genius or the beginning of his madness. According to suggestions that Derrida makes in his analysis in *Spurs* of Nietzsche's views on women, it might well be the former.[30] In any case, man cannot become the *Übermensch* without accepting his animality and his sexual dependency. He must accept his membership in the species of the great apes if he is to become something beyond what he is. To transcend the crisis of awareness of death and bondage to the reproductive cycle of mammalian life, we must deconstruct the lies that constitute gender. For the male, this is what it means to *become* Dionysus.[31] To become Dionysus the male must enter into an analytic process by immersing himself as he confronts the texts of radical feminism in the discourse of the (M)other. By so doing, material passes to and from the unconscious in a process that is the analog of transference and countertransference. According to Shoshana Felman, "Lacan is thus a metaphor—or a symptom—of psychoanalysis itself, insofar as psychoanalysis is reenacting a constant revolution in the most basic human questions:—What does it mean to be human?—What does it mean to think? and consequently,—What does it mean to be contemporary?"[32] These questions cannot be answered outside of the discourse of radical feminism. Postmodernism is about what we do and how we live when we realize where these questions take us. It is thinking beyond fragments in a process of becoming.

Freud, Lacan, and Derrida take us to the edge of the *Nietzschean abyss.* They do not take us across the ravine. Thus spoke Zarathustra:

> Man is a rope, tied between animal and overman—a rope over an abyss. A dangerous going-across, a dangerous wayfaring, a dangerous looking-back, a dangerous shuddering and staying still.
>
> What is great in man is that he is a bridge and not a goal; what can be loved in man is that he is a going-across and a down-going for they are those who are going across.
>
> I love the great despisers, for they are the great venerators and arrows of longing for the other bank.
>
> I love those who do not first seek beyond the stars for reasons to go down and to be sacrifices: but who sacrifice themselves to the earth. (Z, I, 4)

How does the man cross over? By going under. How does the man go under? By going into the unconscious. How does the man go into the unconscious? By bringing that which is under consciousness into consciousness. How is that done? By the man recreating himself through a process of becoming. How does the man recreate himself through a process of becoming? By the affirmation of that which has been denied; by the elevation of that which has been repressed; by proclaiming the lie of the truth and the truth in the lie; by substituting opposites and reversing perspectives; by negating the grand myths of history and culture; by replacing that which is privileged with that which is primary and denied by privilege. It should now be clear why psychoanalysis and postmodernism—Nietzsche, Freud, Derrida, and Lacan—will leave the man at the edge of the abyss. They alone cannot link the animal with that which lies beyond the human in the process of becoming.

A consistent and integrated merging of psychoanalysis, postmodernism, and feminism will only be possible and desirable if there are alternative forms of heterosexual male sexuality. These alternative forms, if they exist, must be perverse if they are to point to a way out of the Lacanian impasse because the sexuality must be a denial of, and a revolt against, the Law of the Father, and it must manifest itself in the form of a different kind of masculinity. At the same time, it must provide a category of "woman" that is not defined in terms of lack or castration. These alternative forms of sexuality must provide alternative forms of gender structure for both the female and the male if a meaningful convergence of psychoanalysis, postmodernism, and feminism is possible.

> Zarathustra is a dancer—: how he, who has the harshest, the most fearful insight into reality, who has thought the "most abysmal thought," nonetheless finds in it no objection to existence . . . the eternal Yes to all things . . . "Into every abyss I still bear the blessing of my affirmation" . . . But that is the concept of Dionysos once more. (EH, 108)—Have I been understood?—Dionysos against the Crucified. . . . (EH, 134)

THREE

Knowledge and the Languaging Body

Psychoanalytic theory, postmodernism, and feminism have one important feature in common. They each call into question the very nature of knowledge and inevitably lead us to question how we know what we think we know. Each requires us at some point to use "the instrument of analysis to analyze the instrument of analysis";[1] to conceptualize the process of conceptualization, to take cognizance of the process of cognition, to explain the process of explanation, to observe the process of observation, to become conscious of what is consciousness, to examine the reality of reality and the differentiations of difference, and to articulate within language the question "what is language?"

Psychoanalysis and psychoanalytic social theory are the latter-day and contemporary culminations of a paradigmatic shift in worldview, a cognitive methodology that commenced with the pre-Socratics. It is the evolution of the cognitive process by which Thales postulated that everything is made of water and has led us back from nature, that which is to be known, to the knowing of the knower. Its methodologies may appear idiosyncratic when compared to the techniques of the traditional sciences, but they are unorthodox because of the cognitive difficulties that are entailed in the process of "knowing" the processes of cognition. Science examines nature whereas psychoanalysis examines the examiner of nature, and, in the process, not only does her or his body become an object of knowledge, but the psyche itself, the human mind, becomes an object in relationship to a piece of the mind that still stands apart as the subject doing the observation. This process is consummated in the exploration of language.

Psychoanalysis and postmodernism are about seeing the individual "seeing itself seeing itself" (F, 80). When we push back knowledge in this manner, we eventually end up at its very limits: the dialectics of difference, the arbitrariness of conceptualization, the subjectivity of experience, the relativity of reality, the ambiguity of certainty, the contingency of meaning, the restrictions of perception, the constraints of the neural organization of the brain, the deficiencies of language, and the boundaries of consciousness.

The limits of cognition are biological, neurological, psychological, and linguistic. If we had additional biological sensory systems to interact with the external world or if our existing sensory systems would record or identify a broader or finer set of external environmental changes or phenomena, such as our vision "perceiving" all frequencies of the electromagnetic spectrum rather than just the narrow band of light, we would live in a radically different "reality." If the neurological structure of the brain was expanded in size and complexity, we would conceptualize and experience a different universe. If all of the id became ego, or if all aspects of the processes of the psyche became conscious, we would be a different kind of creature conceptualizing a very different kind of world.

Knowing is a perceptual event taking place within a perceptual system. There is no alternative to nor way to escape from the cognitive processes by which we perceive and conceptualize the objects of knowledge. The observer is a biological system made up of a number of subsystems and is inextricably linked to the observed. Any act of observation is an event within a system that changes the state of the system. The perceptual system is a representation of a nonperceptual system, and the perceptual system is represented by a conceptual system involving language. The limits of language restrict the conceptual system, which in turn places limits on perception.

Knowledge, consciousness, and intelligence present us with a number of interesting anomalies. We don't know what intelligence is because we have no satisfactory theory of intelligence or of the mind or consciousness.[2] We do not even have theories that are, as yet, not proven, needing merely more evidence to resolve the theoretical issues that remain in dispute. Rather, we have no true theories at all. All that we have are models, and models are not theories.[3] A true theory must explain the nature and origin of a phenomenon whereas a model has little or no explanatory power. A great deal of research has been done on the brain and neural nets,[4] but the brain is not the mind. Thanks to the intellectual tradition of psychoanalysis, we know something about the psyche, but psychoanalysis has no theory of consciousness or of intelligence.

An adequate theory of the mind would require an understanding of the relationship between the psyche and the brain. We know that there is a relationship between the two, but we don't know what that relationship is. We don't even have a clear idea of what a true theory of the mind, of consciousness, or of intelligence should look like. We have no explanation for even the simplest of sensory experiences. We know yellow when we see it, the physics of light, and how the eye works as a biological sensory system. We don't have any explanation whatsoever, however, for how the processes of the retina—the optic nerve and the brain—produce within an individual the experience of yellowness. Biology and physics alone cannot explain the phenomena of "seeing" yellow. No one, as yet, has transcended mind/body dualism by providing a satisfactory unified explanation that unites the biological discourses with those of psychoanalysis and cognitive psychology nor has anyone bridged the phenomenological gap between the two.

Cognitive science is a collection of separate fields of study, still fully divided between physical and mental sciences. We have no "satisfactory explanation of how we know what we know, stated in terms of the physics and chemistry, the anatomy and physiology, of the biological system,"[5] nor do we have a satisfactory explanation of how we know what we know or think we know stated in terms of the philosophy of the mind, psychology, cognitive science, or psychoanalysis. We do know, however, that if we start from the extreme of theoretical physics on the one side and of psychoanalysis on other, and we push the boundaries of knowing as far as we can, we will end up at the same place. The issues of "knowledge" and "knowing" will dissolve into questions about language. Whatever the area of knowledge, if we ask the question "How do we know what we know?" we reach and cannot transcend the limits of the cognitive processes. Objective reality and ultimate truth are linguistic artifacts we use when we decide we do not wish to pursue the question of how we know what we know. Werner Heisenberg, concluded that "I do not know what the words *fundamental reality* mean . . . our thinking hangs in the language."[6] In answer to the question *Would you go so far as to say that . . . language has actually set a limit to our domain of understanding in quantum mechanics?*, Heisenberg responded by saying, "Words as *position* and *velocity* and *temperature* lose their meaning when we get down to the smallest particles."[7] Conceptual structures such as Stephen Hawking's "point of singularity," the expanding or contracting universe, or the big bang are simply ineffective metaphors. They are fundamentally meaningless given that time and space are internal to the universe, whatever state it is in before, during, and after the big bang. There is no external time-space reference point for attributing size to such terms as "point" or "expansion." Twentieth-century physics, which conflates time, space, energy, and matter, provides no meaning for "nothingness." We are, therefore, left hanging in language.

The root of the problem of language is that "our language is formed from our continuous exchange with the outer world," and "we are a part of that world."[8] Stephen Hawking declares, "Even if there is only one possible unified theory, it is just a set of rules and equations,"[9] which, of course, are particular parts of the sublanguages of science. Lacan, at the opposite end of the cognitive spectrum, asserts that the unconscious is structured like a language (F, 20). Even philosophy in this century has reverted from metaphysics and ontology to epistemology and the study of language.

Cognition is a dialectical process. Knowledge entails differentiation, and differentiation entails selection. Selection entails exclusion. Exclusion entails omission, and omission entails fallacy. Fallacy leads to a new selection that entails a new exclusion. No discourse can, therefore, be absolute, privileged, objective, or true. Yet we have practices and rules that allow us to ascertain truth and falsity within discourses and evaluate some discourses as better than others. The relativity of reality stems from our total inability to make reference to something transcendent or independent of experience. The concept of reality can only be valid within particular discourses or narratives where people share a certain number of presuppositions. Relativity, however, assumes that experience can be validated. Subjectivity assumes that it cannot. Language is a product of the collective, and people are born into it. Sensory experience is private to each individual. The conceptualization that is entailed by perception means that subjective sensory experience is conceptualized according to collective structures and syntax and chains of signification. Thus, consciousness entails language, and language entails representation. Representation, in turn, is one of the essential correlates of language (F, 80).

Language was not "out there" for humans to discover. It is the product of a complex evolutionary process involving the development of the organs of vocalization and the structure of the brain, both of which evolved as a part of a complex system producing consciousness. Consciousness is not a product of language, and language is not a product of the human brain and the vocalization system. They developed together. Humans are therefore languaging hominoids and the only languaging primates. Language is the outer shell of the sphere of cognition, beyond which we cannot pass, and consciousness, perception, and conceptualization all take place within it. Language determines our humanity. "In short, we are what we are because of speech and syntax."[10]

In the early days of psychoanalysis, Freud, and even Jung, attempted to root the study of the psyche in biology, which in turn would culminate in theoretical physics. Theoretical physicists, however, in reaching the limits of cognition, find that the external world cannot be separated from the internal mental one. According to Roger S. Jones, "Quantum mechanics, then, may just possibly imply an essential role for consciousness in the scheme of things, but it is basically a passive consciousness not an active or creative one. Behind all is the assumption that consciousness along with matter is a random, accidental occurrence in the universe without rhyme or reason."[11] Jones further states that

> The four foundation concepts of physics—space, time, matter, and number— . . . are intimately related to consciousness and are guaranteed of no objective, external status by physics, I prefer to call them metaphors . . . as an act of consciousness that borders on the very creation of things. Thus I emphasize that they are creations of the mind. I see space, time, matter, and number as possibly the deepest expressions of the present stage of our consciousness.[12]

Herbert states that "One of the best-kept secrets of science is that physicists have lost their grip on reality."[13] He concludes that "Science's biggest mystery is the nature of consciousness. It is not that we possess bad or imperfect theories of human awareness; we simply have no such theories at all."[14] In shifting psychoanalytic theory from Freud's metaphorical physical model to language, Lacan establishes the foundations for a very different kind of relationship between physics and psychoanalysis than was envisaged by either Freud or Jung, and provides a place for psychoanalysis as a fundamental and important part of cognitive science. Physics, philosophy, cognitive science, and psychoanalysis converge at the point of "the omnipresence of human discourse . . ." (E, 56). "The big question for the human sciences now is—what is language?" (S II, 119–20).

The Perceptual-Consciousness System

Language and consciousness presuppose each other in that each is a necessary but insufficient condition for the other. Animals with complex communication systems, such as those possessed by ants, bees, whales, or dolphins, do not have language.[15] It is the possession of language that accounts for the gulf between humans and other species. Humanity is inseparable from languaging capability. Conversely, "the thorny question of the origins of language . . . is inseparable from the origin of man."[16] Only humans can have psyches because only humans have language. The analysis of the psyche is an analysis of language, and the analysis of mental processes such as repression, dreaming, and fantasizing is also an analysis of language: "Whether it sees itself as an instrument of healing, of training, or of exploration in depth, psychoanalysis has only a single medium: the patient's speech"(E, 40). Julia Kristeva, in exploring the complex relations between psychoanalysis and language, describes psychoanalysis as "inseparable from the linguistic universe." She emphasizes that, "psychoanalysis sees the patient's speech as its object." "The psychoanalyst has no other means within his reach, no other reality with which to explore the conscious or unconscious functioning of the subject, than speech and its laws and structures."[17]

The structure of language entails a syntactical distinction between subject and object and a related conceptual distinction between self and Other, which presuppose consciousness. As stated by Lacan, "Only a subject can understand a meaning; conversely, every phenomenon of meaning implies a subject" (E, 9). A languaging animal that was not conscious or a conscious animal that did not have language is difficult to even conceive of. Most, if not all, animals have perceptual systems of one form or another, and most mammals evidence the presence of emotional states such as anger or fear. Almost all animals display instinctual behavior; and all animals have brains and communicate in a variety of ways. Animal communication is not structured like a language but like a code where the "sign" bears a fixed relationship to what it signifies. Miller explains:

> Lacan says that language is not a code. A code is computed by the fixed codification of signs to the reality they signify. In a *language,* on the contrary, the various signs—the signifiers—take on their value from their relation to one another. That is the meaning of symbolic order. The symbolic order is effectively a self-contained dimension and is not grounded on correspondence, but on circularity. That is, a

sign is defined through other signs. And when Lacan proposes a definition of the signifier, it is a circular definition he gives: a signifier represents a subject for another signifier. That is not a true definition because in the definition itself, you have the word to define.[18]

According to the above distinction, primates such as the mountain gorilla Koko, who are able to learn extensive word patterns and language functions and how to communicate in nonverbal ways such as signing, would be learning "speech" as a code since language must be learned as an integrated whole to enable the languaging process to function.[19]

Freud was the first to comprehend the dynamics of the unconscious and to search for its governing principles. He argued:

It is essential to abandon the overvaluation of the property of being conscious before it becomes possible to form any correct view of the origin of what is mental. . . . [T]he unconsciousness must be assumed to be the general basis of psychical life. The unconscious is the larger sphere, which includes the smaller sphere of the conscious. Everything conscious has an unconscious preliminary stage; whereas what is unconscious may remain at that stage and nevertheless claim to be regarded as having the full value of a psychical process. The unconscious is the true psychical reality; *in its innermost nature it is as much unknown to us as the reality of the external world, and it is as incompletely presented by the data of consciousness as is the external world by the communications of our sense organs.* (SE, V, 612–13)

Much of the mental processes of speech goes on outside of consciousness. When we read the sign "USED FOOD EQUIPMENT FOR SALE," it is completely open as to whether it should be interpreted as equipment for used food or used *food equipment.* Our mental processes calculate how often *used* modifies *food* and how often it modifies *equipment.* We generally reach the appropriate interpretations without consciously thinking about them.[20] As Lacan tells us, "The question that the nature of the unconscious puts before us is, in a few words, that something always *thinks.* Freud told us that the unconscious is above all thoughts, and that which thinks is barred from consciousness" (OS, 188–89). "It [the unconscious] is a thinking with words, with thoughts that escape your vigilance, your state of watchfulness" (OS, 189).

While Freud discovered a great deal about the structure of that part of the unconscious that was the source of individual neuroses, he failed to provide us with an adequate model for understanding collective behavior, neuroses, and defense mechanisms. Jung provided a model of the collective unconscious in terms of archetypes with some explanatory power. It was the revelation by Lacan, however, that "the unconscious is structured like a language" (F, 20; S III, 166–67) that finally furnished psychoanalytic theory with an adequate and powerful hypothesis, which firmly positions it within cognitive science. Lacan proclaims that "what the psychoanalytic experience discovers in the unconscious is the whole structure of language" (F, 20). Lacan further states that "it is this linguistic structure that gives its status to the unconscious. It is this structure . . . that assures us that there is, beneath the term unconscious, something definable, accessible and objectifiable" (E, 147). "Properly speaking," Lacan tells us, the statement that the unconscious is structured like a language "is a redundancy because 'structured' and 'as a language' for me mean exactly the same thing" (OS, 188). "The unconscious," according to Lacan, "is the sum of the effects of speech on a subject, at the level at which the subject constitutes himself out of the effects of the signifier" (F, 126). Once we recognize that "it is clear that our physics is simply a mental fabrication whose instrument is the mathematical symbol" (E, 74), we will be gradually driven to the conclusion that we cannot break out of the sphere of language that encompasses us. "There is no unconscious except for the speaking being"; "It speaks, does the unconscious, so that it depends on language, about which we know so little . . ." (Tel, 5). Lacan maintains that "it is this linguistic structure that gives its status to the unconscious. It is this structure, in any case, that assures us that there is, beneath the term unconscious, something definable, accessible and objectifiable" (F, 21). "The unconscious is the sum of the effects of speech on a subject, at the level at which the subject constitutes himself out of the effects of the signifier" (F, 126).

Just as the genetic code is passed on from generation to generation through its embodiment or representations in the individuals who make up the species *Homo sapiens*, so language is also passed on from generation to generation through its embodiment or representation in the psyches of these same individuals. While children may be consciously taught specific words, they learn language at an unconscious level. They simply begin to speak as they assimilate language. Their unconscious, which constitutes the major portion of their psyches, is built up in the process of learning language. Lacan explains that "The unconscious is that part of the concrete discourse, insofar as it is trans-individual, that is not at the disposal of the subject in re-establishing the continuity of his conscious discourse" (E, 49). Thus, it may be said that, "the unconscious of the subject is the discourse of the other" (E, 55). "From the Freudian point of view man is the subject captured and tortured by language" (S III, 243). Given that, for Lacan, the unconscious is structured like a language, then it is neither primordial and instinctual nor elementary (E, 170).

The body furnishes the grand metaphors for all meaning. Meaning begins and ends with the body, whereas the self begins with a recognition of the body. Desire begins in the body, whereas difference is rooted in the body. The body is the gateway to seduction, and the body entails our limitations and castrations. "It is to this," states Lacan, "that Freud came to give his approval, his official stamp, when he made the image of the world, whose fallacious archetypes, return once and for all there where they belong, that is in our body" (S VII, 93). Lacan further declares that "Symbols in fact envelop the life of man in a network so total that they join together, before he comes into the world, those who are going to engender him 'by flesh and blood'; so total that they bring to his birth, along with the gifts of the stars, if not with the gifts of the fairies, the shape of his destiny; so total that they give the words that will make him faithful or renegade, the law of the acts that will follow him right to the very place where he is not yet and even beyond his death" (E, 68). According to Kristeva, "Now, when Freud spoke of language, he didn't just mean the discursive system in which the subject makes and unmakes himself. For psychoanalytic psychopathology, the body itself speaks. Remember that Freud founded psychoanalysis starting with hysterical symptoms which he saw as 'talking bodies.' The corporal symptom is overdetermined by a complex symbolic network, and by a language whose syntactic laws must be discerned in order to resolve the symptom."[21]

Pattern and structure are embodied in the material. Thus, the structure of the genetic code that constitutes humans as a mammalian species is embodied within the individuals who constitute it at any particular time. If the bodies disappeared so would the code. Language is also embodied in the material of the brain in ways that we do not understand. If the bodies containing those brains disappear, then so will language. We are born into language. Humans act as though they created language as some kind of invention like the wheel, or discovered it like fire, but in fact, it is language that makes us human. Humans are shaped by two complex adaptive systems, the genetic code and language, and it is through the latter that we do something that we call knowing, which permits us to comprehend the former.

By explaining the structure of mind in terms of language theory and by clarifying the relationship between mind and body in terms of the function of language, Lacan offers the world "a new theory of cognition."[22] The fundamental difference between plant and animal life is that plants have no internal representation of an outside environment. "Indeed, so that a living being doesn't perish every time it turns round, it must possess some adequate reflection of the external world" (S II, 107).

Every animal has a perceptual system that creates an inner representation of the external world. These perceptual systems meet whatever requirements the individual animal species has. A frog's eye doesn't need to formulate pictures for the frog but must merely record the movement of insects. Thus, the frog's eye has evolved to give an inner representation to its brain of the spatial location and movement of the insect.[23] "[I]n the end, the living organism can only receive, record, what it is constructed to receive—more precisely, that its functions are far more constructed in order not to receive than to receive. It doesn't see, it doesn't hear, what isn't useful to its biological subsistence" (S II, 322). Animals' perceptual systems not only give them an internal representation of the external world but also a representation of their bodies. This would include those parts that fall within the vision of their eyes; of external surfaces through their senses of touch, heat, and cold; and to some extent their internal state, through the sensation of pain, hunger, and sexual or erotic sensations, which are centered in parts of the reproductive organs. Animals' perceptual systems are instinctual rather than conceptual. The animal therefore functions with an instinctive perceptual system that spans the external and the internal, converging at points that mark the inside from the outside. This perceptual system permits the organism to modify its behavior and to learn to distinguish between beneficial and harmful forms of behavior, which enhances the reproductive potential of the species as well as ensuring the preservation of the individual creature.

The human brain has achieved the capacity to create a system of symbols to represent the perceptual system. Within the perceptual system, there are no sharp borders between the external world of the environment, the internal world of the creature, or the surface where they converge. The animal learns to make distinctions between the external and the internal required for reproduction and survival. Within the human, there is an additional complication in that there is no clear boundary between the perceptual system and the symbolic system. Perception takes place before language and the unconscious, at the level of contact with the external world. Once the symbolic system of language is in place, however, the perceptual world is no longer direct—it is filtered through the symbolic system. The two systems merge into a conceptual-perceptual representation of the external world, the internal state of the human body, and the surfaces where they converge. The human has to learn the meaning of external and internal and must develop a sense of self. Each infant must learn to gradually formulate the divisions between self and Other, and self and mother. "The perceptual system is a kind of sensitive layer, sensitive in the sense of photo-sensitive" (S II, 140). Perception is itself represented by a symbolic system that allows the storing as memory, and the communication of information concerning the monitoring of the states of the perceptual system. The perceptual and symbolic systems combine in a "perception-consciousness system" (S II, 110, 140–41).

Consciousness functions like a metarepresentational system. "This is the original adventure through which man, for the first time, has the experience of seeing himself, of reflecting on himself and conceiving of himself as other than he is—an essential dimension of the human, which entirely structures his fantasy life" (S I, 79). Consciousness thus creates a fundamental schism within the human in that one's own body becomes an object for the self. According to Lacan, "It is very odd to say, there's a truly strange incoherence in saying—man has a body. . . . It is very strange to be localized in a body, and this strangeness can't be minimized. . . . It is completely useless to make great declarations about returning to the unity of the human being, to the soul as the body's form. . . . The division is here to stay" (S II, 72–73). Consciousness is not a pinnacle of evolutionary progress. "This perspective leads to an anthropomorphism which is so deluded that one has to start by shedding the scales from one's eyes, so as to realize what kind of illusion one has fallen prey to" (S II, 48). Lacan refers to modern man's understanding that he is the pinnacle of a progressive evolutionary process as an incoherent and idiotic form of scientific atheism (S II, 48). Rather, "consciousness is linked to something entirely contingent, just as contingent as the surface of a lake in an uninhabited world—the existence of our eyes or of our ears" (S II, 48). "He [Freud] cannot find the slightest tendency towards progress in any of the concrete and historical manifestations of human functions, and this really has a value for the person who invented our method. All forms of life are as surprising, as miraculous, there is no tendency towards superior forms" (S II, 326).

Instincts and Drives

According to Freud, "Psychoanalysis early became aware that all mental occurrences must be regarded as built on the basis of an interplay of the forces of the elementary instincts" (SE, XVIII, 255). Freud proposed a distinction between two groups of elementary or basic drives, the ego and the sexual drives. In the original German text, Freud uses the term *Instinckt* when referring to instincts in animals and *Trieb* when referring to the drive. Unfortunately, for the sake of clarity, the English standard edition of his works misleadingly uses the English word *instinct* to translate both the German words *Instinckt* and *Trieb* (F, 49, 161–63). Instincts are hereditary behavior patterns peculiar to animals. "If now we apply ourselves to considering mental life from a biological point of view," Freud states, a drive would appear to us "as a concept on the frontier between the mental and the somatic, as the psychical representative of the stimuli originating from within the organism and reaching the mind, as a measure of the demand made upon the mind for work in consequence of the connection with the body" (SE, XIV, 121–22). Freud acknowledged that animals have a wide variety of instincts or engage in a broad spectrum of instinctual behavior. Nevertheless, animal instincts seem to fall into two broad categories: reproductive instincts, which relate to the preservation of the species as such, and self-preservation instincts, which are associated with the safety and security of the individual members of the species. In animals, the self-preservation instincts are secondary to the reproductive instincts. The better the individual members of a species can survive, the better are the species' chances to reproduce and endure.

In the animal world, the welfare of the species will always have an evolutionary priority over the safety or well-being of the individual members that constitute it. Females frequently will risk death to protect their young, as will males of the species, and often the sexual instincts of male animals will lead them to aggressive and violent behavior in the struggle for access to the females. In animals, instincts do not come into conflict precisely because there is no evolutionary contradiction between the two kinds of instincts and because animals lack self-consciousness, so there is no risk of a contradiction between the interest of the individual and the interest of the species. Freud states:

I am in fact of the opinion that the antithesis of conscious and unconscious is not applicable to instincts. An instinct can never become an object of consciousness—

> only the idea that represents the instinct can. Even in the unconscious, moreover, an instinct cannot be represented otherwise than by an idea. If the instinct did not attach itself to an idea or manifest itself as an affective state, we could know nothing about it. When we nevertheless speak of an unconscious instinctual impulse or of a repressed instinctual impulse, the looseness of phraseology is a harmless one. We can only mean an instinctual impulse the ideational representative of which is unconscious, for nothing else comes into consideration. (SE, XIV, 177)

"Within human sexuality," Laplanche informs us, "the instinct, a vital force, loses its quality and its identity in the drive, its metaphorico-metonymical 'derivative' " (L&D, 125).

Reproductive and self-preservation instincts are universal among mammals. They manifest themselves in the form of certain nonconceptual mental phenomena, such as sexual tensions and pleasure, and emotions such as fear and aggression. In the human species, the sexual and self-preservation instincts have become drives that are conceptually structured representations of aspects of those instincts. Drives require language and consciousness. They are the mental representations, conceptualizations, and manifestations of our consciousness of the feelings, compulsions, pleasures, and unpleasures of instinctual experience. Animals cannot have drives, and humans, living as they do within language and consciousness, cannot have pure instincts. When Freud explores the question of the degree to which any human behavior might be instinctual, he uses the phrase "something analogous to instinct in animals" (SE, XIV, 195; SE, XVII, 120). Nowhere does Freud find in the animal kingdom a counterpart to or an analogy with drives since other forms of animal life do not have the kind of mental existence that is a necessary condition for instincts to be transformed into drives.

The transformation in the evolutionary development of the human from the sexual and self-preservation instincts to the sexual and ego drives is an integral part of the development of language and consciousness. The transformation, however, results in a dialectical tension that does not exist at the stage of animal instinct. The sexual drive constitutes a threat to the ego and is thus in conflict with the ego drive. The conflict arises because the instincts for the preservation of the species are more powerful than those that serve to protect its individual members. As a result, the ego drive will always be weaker than the sexual drive and continually vulnerable to being overpowered. If this were not the case, it is unlikely that altruism, love for children, or desire for the preservation of the human species would be sufficient to preserve the human race. The world population problem is not due to a love for children but to the precarious positioning of the ego drive in relation to the sexual drive. The ego experiences the imperatives of the reproductive instincts, which ensure the survival of the species, as a threat and a challenge to its own aims, integrity, and unity. The ego is sexually driven to constantly compromise itself. "In the course of things it happens again and again that individual instincts or parts of instincts turn out to be incompatible in their aims or demands with the remaining ones, which are able to combine into the inclusive unity of the ego" (SE, XVIII, 11). The essence of the ego is individuation. It recognizes and prizes the individuality and independence of the body from the rest of the world and seeks mastery or control over it.

Consequently, Freud suggests that one can conceptualize the relationship between the two drives in two equally well-justified ways: "On the one view, the individual is the principal thing, sexuality is one of its activities and sexual satisfaction one of its needs; while on the other view the individual is a temporary and transient appendage to the quasi-immortal germ-plasm, which is entrusted to him by the process of generation" (SE, XVI, 125). While individuals may be able to defend themselves against some unpleasurable external stimuli through action, they are defenseless against those stimuli that originate in instinct. According to Freud,

> The power of the id expresses the true purpose of the individual organism's life. This consists in the satisfaction of its innate needs. No such purpose as that of keeping itself alive or of protecting itself from dangers by means of anxiety can be attributed to the id. That is the task of the ego, whose business it also is to discover the most favorable and least perilous method of obtaining satisfaction, taking the external world into account. . . . The forces which we assume to exist behind the tension caused by the needs of the id are called *instincts.* They represent the somatic demands upon the mind. . . . (SE, XXIII, 148)

> We have been able to trace them [neuroses] back to the basic situation in which the sexual instincts have come into a dispute with the self-preservative instincts, or, to put it in biological . . . terms, a situation in which one aspect of the ego, as an independent individual organism, comes into conflict with its other aspect, as a member of a succession of generations. A dissension of this kind may perhaps only occur in human beings, and on that account neurosis may, generally speaking, constitute their prerogative over the animals. The excessive development of their libido and—what is perhaps made possible precisely by that—their development

of a richly articulated mental life seem to have created the determinants for the occurrence of such a conflict. (SE, XVI, 414)

Two of Freud's most important discoveries, however, are that "the life of our sexual instincts cannot be wholly tamed, and that mental processes are in themselves unconscious and only reach the ego and come under its control through incomplete and untrustworthy perceptions—these two discoveries amount to a statement that *the ego is not master in its own house*" (SE, XVII, 143). According to Freud, "science has so little to tell us about the origin of sexuality that we can liken the problem to a darkness into which not so much as a ray of a hypothesis has penetrated" (SE, VIII, 57). Freud further asserts, "For in humans it may happen that the demands of the sexual instincts, whose reach of course extends far beyond the individual, seem to the ego to constitute a danger which threatens its self-preservation or its esteem. The ego then assumes the defensive, denies the sexual instincts the satisfaction they desire and forces them into those by-paths of substitutive satisfaction which become manifest as nervous symptoms" (SE, XVII, 138).

Freud assures us that "psycho-analysis has never forgotten that there are instinctual forces which are not sexual." Nevertheless, "a sharp distinction between the sexual instincts and the ego-instincts" is fundamental to psychoanalysis, and all neurosis "is due to a conflict between the ego and sexuality" (SE, XVI, 351). Moreover, "The neuroses are the expression of conflicts between the ego and such of the sexual impulses as seem to the ego incompatible with its integrity or with its ethical standards. Since these impulses are not *ego-syntonic*, the ego has *repressed* them" (SE, XVIII, 246). "The theory of repression is the corner-stone on which the whole structure of psycho-analysis rests" (SE, XIV, 16), and "the essence of repression lies simply in turning something away, and keeping it at a distance, from the conscious" (SE, XIV, 147). The repressed sexual drive then assails the ego and returns in the form of a neurotic symptom. "The neuroses are the expression of conflicts between the ego and such of the sexual impulses as seem to the ego incompatible with its integrity" (SE, XVIII, 246). Moreover, "The assumption that there are unconscious mental processes, the recognition of the theory of resistance and repression, the appreciation of the importance of sexuality and of the Oedipus complex—these constitute the principal subject-matter of psycho-analysis and the foundations of its theory" (SE, XVIII, 247). Sexuality is the repressed par excellence (L&D, 39).

Using the same pattern, the common reproductive behavior of herd animals, for example, can be described in two different ways. If we project the description from the perspective of the individual male members of the species, we would describe the situation in which the strongest, most aggressive male, defeats all rivals to become the leader of the herd. The herd belongs to him as the dominant male and he controls the females of the herd and drives away the young males as they reach reproductive maturity. If one were to describe the same reproductive patterns from the perspective of the primacy of the species, one would envision a group of female animals that, when in estrus, trigger an uncontrollable sexual frenzy in the males that forces them to struggle and battle for access to the females, thus ensuring the transmittal of the superior genetic code to future progeny. The males could thus be conceived as trapped and enslaved by their sexuality, inextricably bound to the reproductive process. It is interesting to note that any species-oriented description gives primacy to the female role, whereas individual-oriented descriptions give preeminence to the role of the male.

Both descriptions are, however, human projections onto nature. What is interesting, nevertheless, is that descriptions from the individual perspective are predominant in human descriptions of the animal world. This tells us more about the predominance of the ego drive in the psyche of the human than it does about the reality of animal reproductive behavior. If the reproductive instincts were weaker than the instincts of self-preservation in a particular species, then the species would, in all likelihood, eventually become extinct. This is equally true for the human species. Ego-oriented descriptions of animal behavior, therefore, reflect the repression that is produced by the conflict between the sexual and ego drives. In the reproductive behavior of the honey bee, on the other hand, it would be difficult to privilege the role of the male, and, consequently, a species-oriented projection is the only plausibility. When an individualistic perspective is applied, we take by way of analogy the negative image of the queen bee and apply it to nonsubmissive women.

The interrelationship of the sexual instinct-drive and the self-preservation instinct-drive is, in the evolution of the human species, extremely complex. With the breeding out of estrus, resulting in a state of constant sexual receptivity, and the shift from an olfactory to a visual arousal mechanism in the male, humans became probably one of the most sexually driven animals on the face of the earth. On the other hand, with the evolution of consciousness and the development of the ego, the self-preservation instinct is transformed into a powerful drive for the preservation of the ego, which is identified with the bodily image in what Lacan refers to as the "imago." There is a consensus among many experts that human sexuality was the primary factor in the evolution of consciousness and language.[24] Thus, the word is inextricably linked to the genitals. And if human sexuality is similar to most forms of animal sexuality, where the male is sexually driven to seek access, then we should find that the word will be inextricably linked to the penis. According to Lacan, "The reality of the unconscious is sexual reality" (F, 150, 152) because "sexual division, in so far as it reigns over most living beings, is that which ensures the survival of a species" (F, 150). He goes on to say,

> Existence, thanks to sexual division, rests upon copulation, accentuated in two poles that time-honored tradition has tried to characterize as the male pole and the female pole. This is because the mainspring of reproduction is to be found there. Around this fundamental reality, there have always been grouped, harmonized, other characteristics, more or less bound up with the finality of reproduction. I can do no more than point out here, what, in the biological register, is associated with sexual differentiation, in the form of secondary sexual characteristics and functions. We know today how, in society, a whole distribution of functions in a play of alternation is grounded on this terrain. . . . (F, 150).
>
> [I]t is through sexual reality that the signifier came into the world—that man learned to think. (F, 151)

The recognition of the dialectics between body and mind; the interests of the individual in, and the biological determinants for, the preservation of the species; and the demands of libido and ego—all of which form the underlying structure of the mental life of the human—was Freud's great discovery. According to Freud,

> We finally arrive at the connections we are in search of, if we take as our starting-point the opposition we have so often asserted between the ego and the libido. As we know, the generation of anxiety is the ego's reaction to danger and the signal for taking flight. If so, it seems plausible to suppose that in neurotic anxiety the ego is making a similar attempt at flight from the demand by its libido, that it is treating this internal danger as though it were an external one. This would therefore fulfill our expectation that where anxiety is shown there is something one is afraid of. But the analogy could be carried further. Just as the attempt at flight from an external danger is replaced by standing firm and the adoption of expedient measures of defense, so too the generation of neurotic anxiety gives place to the formation of symptoms, which results in the anxiety being bound. (SE, XVI, 405)

Freud was, of course, very cognizant of the complexity of sexuality and the many forms it could take, sometimes in defense of the ego rather than as a threat to it. "The pathogenic conflict is thus one between the ego-instincts and the sexual instincts." Even when it would appear that two sexual trends are antagonistic to each other, the conflict still remains one between the ego and sexuality since "one is always, as we might say, 'ego-syntonic' while the other provokes the ego's defense. It therefore still remains a conflict between the ego and sexuality" (SE, XVI, 351).

Lacan states, "It is clear, in effect, that genital libido operates as a suppression, indeed a blind suppression, of the individual in favor of the species, and that its sublimating effects in the Oedipal crisis lie at the origin of the whole process of cultural subordination of man" (E, 24). "The theory of instincts," he states further, "cannot but take into account a fundamental bipartition between the final ends of the preservation of the individual and those of the continuity of the species" (S I, 120). Individuals merely carry the genetic code of the collective. Species remain while individuals are born and die. "If the individual which develops is quite distinct from the fundamental living substance which the germ-plasm constitutes, and which does not perish, if the individual is parasitic, what function does it have in the propagation of Life? None. From the point of view of the species, individuals are, if one can put it that way, already dead. An individual is worth nothing alongside the immortal substance hidden deep inside it, which is the only thing to be perpetuated and which authentically and substantially represents such life as there is" (S I, 121). Consciousness creates a dichotomy of interest between the ongoing survival of the species, for which the individual is irrelevant, and the survival of the individual, who has, at best, a very limited interest in the perpetuation of the species.

Lacan's Theory of Language

Lacan does not confuse thought, consciousness, or the unconscious with language. He says that "I have never said that the unconscious was an assemblage of words, but that the unconscious is precisely structured" (OS, 187). Thought is not the same as language or the unconscious, though the three are intimately related. What Lacan does say is that "the unconscious is structured like a language" (F, 20); that "what the psychoanalytic experience discovers in the unconscious is the whole structure of language" (E, 147); and that "there is no unconscious except for the speaking being" (Tel, 5). Lacan implicitly assumed that both thought and consciousness are equally structured like a language. If it is the case that consciousness, the unconscious, and thought are structured like a language, then whatever we believe reality to be at any particular time will also be structured like a language (E, 106). "It is the world of words that creates the world of things" (E, 65). The distinctions that we make between subject and object, the observer and the observed, the self and the Other, equally reflect the structure of language. It is only within the framework of language that we become and are, and will remain, human. "Man speaks, then, but it is because the symbol has made him man" (E, 65).

Lacanian language theory is premised on the Swiss linguist Ferdinand de Saussure's arbitrariness of the sign.[25] The relationship between the sign, its sound, and its meaning is purely arbitrary. "To pinpoint the emergence of linguistic science we may say that . . . it is contained in the constitutive moments of an algorithm that is its foundation. This algorithm is the following:

$$\frac{S}{s}$$

which is read as: the signifier over the signified, 'over' corresponding to the bar separating the two stages" (E, 149). The relationship between the signifier and the signified is not one to one. There is no necessary relationship between the signifier and that which it signifies. Meaning, therefore, is a matter of convention.

The signifier is a sign that doesn't refer to any object but refers to another sign in such away as to designate the absence of the first sign. The one signifier gets its meaning in opposition to the other: "I spoke about day and night. Day and night are in no way something that can be defined by experience. All experience is able to indicate is a series of modulations and transformations, even a pulsation, an alternation, of light and dark, with all its transitions. Language begins at the opposition—day and night. And once the day is there as a signifier, it lends itself to all the vicissitudes of an arrangement whereby it will come to signify things of great diversity" (S III, 167–68). Moreover, "[I]t isn't what appears in the foreground that is important," Lacan writes, "What's important is the opposition between two sorts of links that are themselves internal to the signifier. . . . This binding of opposites is essential to the functioning of language" (S III, 225). Lacan conceives of language as a simultaneous system of chains of signifiers that are structured in terms of groups of opposition (S III, 54).

Lacan firmly declares and insists that we will never understand the nature of language and how it functions so long as we cling to the illusion that "the signifier answers to the function of representing the signified, or better, that the signifier has to answer for its existence in the name of any signification whatever" (E, 150). "The trap, the hole one must not fall into, is the belief that the signified are objects, things" (S III, 32). He adds, "Now, in no way can we consider that the fundamental endpoint is to point to a thing. There is an absolute non-equivalence between discourse and pointing. Whatever you take the ultimate element of discourse to be reduced to, you will never be able to replace it with your index finger" (S III, 137–38). Further, "The signified is not the things in their raw state, already there, given in an order open to meaning. Meaning is human discourse insofar as it always refers to another meaning" (S III, 119). The word *tree,* for example, does not get its meaning by standing for an external object. Rather its meaning is derived from a set of related signifiers such as life, plants, plants that in contrast are not trees, leaves, branches, trunks, roots and so on. There are other uses of the word *tree.* It is used, for example to refer to a kind of diagram that has stems and branches. These signifiers belong to what Lacan calls a "chain of signification" or a "chain of signifiers."

Meaning lies within the framework of sets of signifiers, which are fundamentally structured, woven, chained, meshed by language. "In fact, what characterizes language is the system of signifiers as such" (E, 153–54). "[I]t is in the chain of the signifier that the meaning 'insists' but that none of its elements 'consists' in the signification of which it is at the moment capable. We are forced, then, to accept the notion of an incessant sliding of the signified under the signifier." Every chain of signification has attached to it "a whole articulation of relevant contexts," suspended, as it were (E, 153–54). A meaning will always refer to another meaning (S III, 33). Words, therefore, cannot have meaning in isolation.

In addition to the arbitrary nature of the sign in relationship to meaning, there is a second fundamental property of language that Lacan integrates into language theory: the capacity that language has to use a finite number of symbols to create an infinite amount of discourse. A finite set of symbols, which constitute a language, can be combined and recombined in an infinite number of ways to symbolically represent a universe that unfolds for the knower in an infinite number of combinations. This stems from the ability of language to constitute a unified system. "[T]here is no language *(langue)* in existence for which there is any question of its inability to cover the whole field of the signified, it being an effect of its existence as a language *(langue)* that it necessarily answers all needs" (E, 150). We are born into language, and for children to learn it, they must grasp it as a unified whole (S III, 228). It is for this reason that it is difficult for us to grasp how language emerged in the early stages of the development of our species. We can imagine what it might have been like before language and after language but not what it was like between these two points (S II, 5). Lacan explains further that the symbolic universe constitutes a totality and that "everything which is human has to be ordained within a universe constituted by the symbolic function" (S II, 29–30). It is the dialectical structure of language, which is reflected in the oppositional structure of the signifiers, that gives language this property of completeness such that it constitutes a totality (S II, 30). However small the number of symbols that humans had in the early stages of language, that number would form the totality for that universe. The symbolic order takes on its universal character right from the start, such that once the symbolic function is in place it will imply the totality of everything that is human at that time and place (S II, 30, 287). "[I]t's the whole of reality that is covered by the entire network of language" (S III, 32).

This capacity is derived from the two primary language functions of metaphor and metonymy. Any conjunction between two signifiers can constitute a metaphor, provided there is a disparity of the images such that there is a poetic spark that can conjoin that which is different (E, 165). "The creative spark of the metaphor does not spring from the presentation of two images, that is, of two signifiers equally actualized. It flashes between two signifiers one of which has taken the place of the other in the signifying chain. . . . *One word for another:* that is the formula for the metaphor" (E, 157). Thus, "language is at its most effective when it manages to say something by saying something else" (S III, 224) or to signify *something quite other* than what it says" (E, 155). Metonymy, considered the opposite of metaphor, involves the substitution for something that has to be named, the name of its container, or its part, or the name of something that is connected to it (E, 156; S III, 220–21).

The Primary and the Privileged

Language presents us with chains of signification within which there are oppositional signifiers. The opposition between signifiers and chains of signification will be such that one is generally taken to be primary and its opposite given the status of the secondary, or one is selected as privileged over the other. The very idea of privileging assumes a contrast. A privileged signifier assumes a primary signifier. The preference, advantage, or dominance given to that which is privileged is a denial of the primacy of the primary. A term that is the standard within the framework of material reality becomes the adjusted term within psychical reality.[26] The privileging of fantasy over material reality that is entailed in repression reverses the relationship between the standard and the adjusted forms of the signifiers. A primary chain of signification within the framework of the articulation of material reality will lie under and be opposed to a privileged chain of signification within the framework of fantasy.

The relative primacy of terms are measured according to derivation as well as in terms of their hierarchical positioning in chains of signification. The concept of law is therefore primary in terms of the concept of a cause of action. The latter presupposes the former. Many terms that appear in pairs cannot be measured in terms of primacy and derivation. For example, neither up/down, black/white, near/far, or night/day can be classified as primary or secondary. Both terms are secondary with respect to concepts of position, color, or time, the meaning of which they presuppose.

Whereas some pairs of terms will not be classified as primary with respect to derivation, one term or pole of the dichotomy may still be privileged. For example, in much discourse, good is privileged over evil, day over night, up over down, and white over black. The privileged position of the term is always subject to reversal within a different discourse. The privileged position comes from a fantasy structure rather than from material reality.

A privileged term in a terminological dichotomy may or may not reverse a primary relationship based on presupposition or derivation. The two terms may be equally derivative, or the primary term may also be given a phantasmic privilege. Repression is at work, however, when a signifier becomes privileged, when it presupposes the existence or meaning of a primary signifier but the primary signifier is given an adjusted form and the privileged signifier is expressed in the form of the standard or the complete. While one cannot say in terms of time which comes first—the chicken or the egg—in terms of biology the bird is primary in that the egg is a step in the process of its reproduction, but neither egg nor chicken is privileged in terms of fantasy.

In repression, the privileged pole, which will be taken as the standard case, will have a property that the unmarked term will lack, the lack being the basis of its categorization as nonstandard. The property, however, will be phantasmic and not real. The primary signifier will thus be the adjusted term and the secondary signifier the privileged. For example, *Male* is a privileged signifier insofar as it is taken as the standard with the female as the marked nonstandard through the addition of the adjuster *fe* to the standard *male* or the adjuster *ess* added to the standard *god.* Similarly, the use of the male form of the pronoun (he) for the general that includes male and female reflects the phantasmic privileging of the male over the female. Yet the measure of life is the capacity for reproduction, and in reproduction the female is primary: males come out of female bodies. In material reality males are born of females. Males may own or possess females in psychic reality, but in material reality all mammalian life is protofemale. The fetus will always be born female, whether or not the y chromosome is present, unless the hormonal baths are triggered in the early stages of the development of the fetus.[27]

In psychic reality's phantasmic privileging of the male, the primary processes of life are made secondary by marking the metaphorically derived secondary meaning as the standard case and the primary as the marked, adjusted case. The coming into being of a person through birth is primary when contrasted to the making of tools and the things that we make with tools. The made presupposes a maker. Yet, in language, the secondary or derivative is privileged and the primary is marked as an adjusted term, as in *production* and *reproduction*, or *creation* and *procreation.* Why is this the case? The relationship between primary and privileged is derived from, or is the manifestation of, the mind/body dualism. The body is primary because it is a necessary condition for the ego. The ego, however, is the focal point in consciousness of the mind or psyche. It controls the body in the sense that it can move it, or not, as it decides, or even destroy it, as in suicide. But in doing so, the ego falls with the body.

Signifiers, whether primary/secondary or privileged/discriminated against, get their meaning within chains of signification. To the degree that the principal signifiers are primary or secondary, privileged or marked as adjusted or nonstandard, the chains of signification of which they form a part will be primary or secondary, privileged or devalued. Neurotic symptoms will therefore be marked by the repression of the chains of signification that conceptualize material reality and the privileging of the chains of signification in which the phantasmic is conceptualized. "[T]he major function of language is not to find final answers, communicate, or provide information, but to project narcissism, protect egos, mask *jouissance,* negotiate desire."[28] It is for this reason that the primary poles of the dialectical oppositionary signifiers, as measured in terms of material reality, are reversed in psychic reality by the privileging of the secondary signifier over its primary opposite.

The Imaginary, the Symbolic, and the Real

While Freud drew a distinction between material and psychic reality and the reality of unconscious fantasy, Lacan postulates a different set of categories, the Imaginary, the Symbolic, and the Real. These are not parallels to Freud's realities, but cut across all three. "One of the main springs, one of the keys of the doctrine which I expound here," Lacan writes, "is the distinction between the Real, the Imaginary and the Symbolic. . . . This notion of objects is in fact sustained by the straightforward confusion of these three terms" (S II, 250). Freud's material reality is not the same as Lacan's category of the Real. Rather, it is constituted by Lacan's categories of the Imaginary and the Symbolic. According to Lacan, "the living organism can only receive, record, what it is constructed to receive—more precisely, that its functions are far more constructed in order not to receive. It doesn't see, it doesn't hear, what isn't useful to its biological subsistence" (S II, 322). Material reality is of the order of the phantasmic, according to Lacan: "There is, according to analytic discourse, an animal which finds himself speaking, and for whom it follows that, by inhabiting the signifier, he is its subject. From then on, everything is played out for him on the level of fantasy" (FS, 159). Moreover, "To be a psychoanalyst is simply to open your eyes to the evident fact that nothing malfunctions more than human reality" (S III, 82).

Lacan's Imaginary is grounded in the perceptual system, within which image plays a major part. Vision is, for Lacan, the primary center of the perceptual system for it is through vision that the image comes into being. The perceptual, however, is not independent of the conceptual or the cognitive. Sensed perception is shaped and structured within the Symbolic:

> While the image equally plays a capital role in our own domain, this role is completely taken up and caught up within, remolded and reanimated by, the symbolic order. The image is always more or less integrated into this order, which, I remind you, is defined in man by its property of organized structure.
>
> Finally, we can understand the red car within the symbolic order, namely in the way one understands the color red in a game of cards, that is, as opposed to black, as being a part of an already organized language.
>
> There you have the three registers distinguished from one another, and also distinguished from one another are the three planes on which our so-called understanding of the elementary phenomenon can be undertaken. (S III, 10)

The first image that the human forms is that of the body of its mother. From this body and its identification with its own reflection, the infant gains an image of its own body as both self and Other. The primacy of the body in the Imaginary furnishes the foundational image for the register of the Symbolic. In the mirror stage, the infant identifies the body with the ego wherein the subject assumes an image: "there is a specific relation here between man and his own body that is manifested in a series of social practices—from rites involving tattooing, incision, and circumcision in primitive societies to what, in advanced societies, might be called the Procrustean arbitrariness of fashion, a relatively recent cultural innovation, in that it denies respect for the natural forms of the human body" (E, 11). The images of bodily mutilation, torture, punishment, binding and restriction, and in particular the image of castration, demonstrate the primacy of the bodily image in the Imaginary.

The Imaginary and the Symbolic are seamlessly related. "The first symbols, natural symbols, stem from a certain number of prevailing images—the image of the human body, the image of a certain number of obvious objects like the sun, the moon, and some others. And that is what gives human language its weight, its resources, and its emotional vibration. Is this imaginary homogeneous with the symbolic?" (S II, 306). The body itself is the primary image of symbolic relationships of power, domination, and authority, as is evidenced in the concept of the body of the king as embodiment of state, church as body of Christ, corporate bodies, the body politic, and such metaphorical references as the arm of the law, the head of state, the lifeblood of the nation, and, of course, the phallus. As Lacan concludes, "The language embodied in a human language is made up of, and there's no doubt about this, choice images which all have a specific relation with the living existence of the human being, with quite a narrow sector of its biological reality, with the image of the fellow being. This imaginary experience furnishes ballast for every concrete language, and by the same token for every verbal exchange, with this something which makes it a human language—in the most down to earth and most ordinary sense of the word human, in the English sense of 'human' " (S II, 319).

The Real is not knowledge in that it is not the Imaginary and the Symbolic, and what is imaginary and symbolic cannot be the Real. The Real is, therefore, "a hole in discourse" (Tel, xxiii-iv). The Real is not external reality since external reality is in the registers of the Imaginary and the Symbolic. "When discourse runs up against something, falters, and can go no further, encountering a 'there is no' [*il n'y a pas*]—and that by its own logic—that's the Real" (Tel, xxiii-iv). Similarly, "[T]he world is merely the fantasy through which thought sustains itself—'reality' no doubt, but to be understood as a grimace of the real" (Tel, 6). When it comes to the Real, language fails, "Yet it's through this very impossibility that the truth holds onto the real" (Tel, 3). The Real is neither matter nor substance nor void nor nothing. It is neither God, Tao, nirvana, or logos. It cannot be anything for which man has ever found a name since it falls outside of the range of perception or conception. The distinction between externality and internality makes no sense at the level of the Real, as the Real is without fissure (S II, 97). "There is no absence in the real. There is only absence if you suggest that there may be a presence there when there isn't one" (S II, 313).

Lacan warns us to "avoid the illusion that language is modeled on a simple and direct apprehension of the Real" (S III, 117–18). Man approaches the Real (including the real of his own body) through "the play of symbols" (S II, 300). The symbols, however, do not come from the Real (S II, 238). The relationship between the Real and the play of symbols is explained in the following way: "Everything is tied to the symbolic order, since there are men in the world and they speak. And what is transmitted and tends to get constituted is an immense message into which the entire real is little by little retransplanted, recreated, remade. The symbolization of the real tends to be equivalent to the universe, and the subjects are only relays, supports in it. What we get up to in all this is to make a break on the level of one of these couplings" (S II, 322). The Real is neither the big bang nor what was there just before the big bang nor Stephen Hawking's point of singularity nor the electromagnetic time-space continuum nor the grand unified theory nor any other kind of scientific conception. "The exact sciences are, of course, very closely tied to the function of the Real" (S II, 297), but whatever scientific progress we make, it will not be a direct discovery of the Real—the Real will be behind or beyond it. "The little symbolic game in which Newton's system and that of Einstein is summed up has in the end very little to do with the Real. The science which reduces the real to several little letters, to a little bundle of formulae, will probably seem, with the hindsight of later epochs, like an amazing epic, and will also dwindle down, like an epic, to a rather short circuit" (S II, 299). There is the Real, and there is our representation of it, the Imaginary and the Symbolic. There is no deep connection between the two in that the Imaginary and the Symbolic can never escape the human body (S VII, 92). The Cartesian universe is a fantasy in that the Cartesian subject may not be assumed, and therefore there is no immovable point on which Descartes can stand. "It's like Archimedes—you give him his little point outside of the world, and he can move it. But this little point outside the world doesn't exist" (S II, 68).

While language can rearrange itself to symbolize any universe, language itself is not necessarily a unified system. It is made up of many different sets of discourses:

> You know only too well the everlasting disputes there are on every theme and on every subject, with greater or lesser ambiguity depending on the zones of interhuman action, and with the manifest discordance between the different symbolic systems which prescribe action, the religious, juridical, scientific, political systems. There is neither superposition, nor conjunction of these references—between them there are gaps, faults, rents. That is why we cannot conceive of human discourse as being unitary. Every emission of speech is always, up to a certain point, under an inner necessity to err. So we are led, it would appear, to a historical Pyrronism which suspends the truth-value of everything which the human voice can emit, suspends it in the expectation of a future totalisation. (S I, 264)

The interrelationship of Freud's three categories of material reality, psychic reality, and the reality of unconscious fantasy intermesh with Lacan's three categories of the Imaginary, the Symbolic, and the Real.

Each category of the one is divisible into the three categories of the other.
The following diagram suggests how we might usefully correlate these two sets of cognitive triads.

	The Imaginary	The Symbolic	The Real
Material Reality			
Psychic Reality			
Reality of Unconscious Fantasy			

It is within the framework of the dialectic between the primary that reflects material reality and the privileged that reflects the reality of unconscious fantasy that we divide truth from error in the realm of psychic reality. "We have seen that deception, as such, can only be sustained as a function of the truth, and not only of the truth, but of a movement of the truth—that error is the usual manifestation of the truth itself—so that the paths of truth are in essence the paths of error" (S I, 263–64).

FOUR

The Dialectics

Dialectics and the Fold

In his essay *The Double Session* (DS), Derrida develops a textual dialectic located within the text rather than in material reality. Derridean textual dialectics is different than Hegelian dialectics, which polarizes thesis and contradiction as antithesis. It meets at a point Derrida refers to as the fold. The text has two parts, the published, visible, and readable text and the unpublished, unspoken, and hidden text, which lies between the lines and beneath the surface. He states, "This double session will itself have been picked up on a corner, in the middle or the suspense of the two parts of a text, of which only one is visible, readable for having at least been published" (DS, 177). Interpreted in this way, the texts of Nietzsche, Freud, and Lacan consist of two parts—the published text and that which is hidden. Whatever *truth* is to be found will be located at the fold: "The place of interest, then, this corner between literature and truth, will form a certain angle. It will be a figure of folding back, of the angle ensured by a fold" (DS, 177). Only by making visible and publishing the Other, can we see the truth that lies at the fold.

In seeking the "fold where the text confronts the truth," there are, of course, certain inevitable risks. Derrida explains that "Because of a certain fold . . . these texts, and their commerce, definitively escape any exhaustive treatment. We can nevertheless begin to mark out, in a few rough strokes, a certain number of motifs. These strokes might be seen to form a sort of frame, the enclosure or borders of a history that would precisely be that of a certain play between literature and truth" (DS, 183). This text, therefore, constitutes only "a few rough strokes" and "a certain motif." It is "*a dialogue or a dialectic.* At least it should be" (DS, 184).

The dialectics of discourse, while they have no synthesis, do meet at a point of truth where the polarity disappears, where each side becomes a mimesis of the other as one passes through the folds of the hymen. As explained by Derrida,

> What announces itself here is an internal division within *mimesis*, a self-duplication of repetition itself, *ad infinitum*, since this movement feeds its own proliferation. Perhaps, then, there is always more than one kind of *mimesis*; and perhaps it is in the strange mirror that reflects but also displaces and distorts one *mimesis* into the other, as though it were itself destined to mime or mask *itself*, that history—the history of literature—is lodged, along with the whole of its interpretation. Everything would then be played out in the paradoxes of the supplementary double: the paradoxes of something that, added to the simple and the single, replaces and mimes them, both like, and unlike, unlike because it is—in that it is—like, the same as and different from what it duplicates. (DS, 191)

The strange mirror images of domination and submission reflect back and forth, each time displacing and distorting the image it replaces.

The mythic texts of human existence are destined to mime or mask themselves, playing out, back and forth, the paradoxes of the supplementary double, each part alike and unlike, each duplicating the other. The "matrix-form of substance" and the mathematical mapping of reality, and the "oppositions between matter and form" (DS, 191) are alternative images of physical existence that contrast, merge, and reverberate with the image of the self as body, or of the self as mind or soul. The *truth* emerges at the fold, as it is here that it becomes obvious that it is fantasy that supports gender hierarchy and that there is no escape from nor alternative to the discourse of primal fantasy. Cognition takes place within the realm of fantasy, within the registers of the Imaginary and the Symbolic, which are not, and can never be, the register of the Real.

Derrida's inspiration for the concept of the fold comes from a passage in Mallarmé's *Mimique* that he quotes at the beginning *The Double Session*. It reads: "This—'The scene illustrates but the idea, not any actual action, in a hymen (out of which flows Dream), tainted with vice yet sacred, between desire and fulfillment, perpetration and remembrance: here anticipating, there recalling, in the future, in the past, under the false appearance of a present. That is how the Mime operates, whose act is confined to perpetual allusion without breaking the ice or the mirror: he thus sets up a medium, a pure medium, of fiction' " (DS, 175). Derrida explains this passage in the following way:

> "Hymen" (a word, indeed the only word, that reminds us that what is in question is a "supreme spasm") is first of all a sign of fusion, the consummation of a marriage, the identification of two beings, the confusion between two. *Between* the two, there is no longer difference but identity. Within this fusion, there is no longer any distance between desire (the awaiting of a full presence designed to fulfill it, to carry it out) and the fulfillment of presence, between distance and non-distance; there is no longer any difference between desire and satisfaction. It is not only the difference (between desire and fulfillment) that is abolished, but also between difference and nondifference. Nonpresence, the gaping void of desire, and presence, the fullness of enjoyment, amount to the same. . . . But it does not follow that what remains is thus the fullness of the signified, the imitated, or the thing itself, simply present in person. It is the difference between the two terms that is no longer functional. The confusion or consummation of this hymen eliminates the spatial heterogeneity of the two poles in the "supreme spasm," . . . By the same token, it eliminates the exteriority or anteriority, the independence, of the initiated, the signified, or the thing. Fulfillment is summed up within desire; desire is (ahead of) fulfillment, which, still mimed, remains desire, *"without breaking the mirror."* (DS, 209–10)

The dialectics that we analyze meet, but there is no synthesis, no resolution, merely a passing back and forth and an accommodation. They fold into each other in mirrored reversals, in mimesis.

When males and females pass through the hymen, the self is transformed in a "supreme spasm," "fulfillment is summed up within desire," and the mirror remains intact. "What does the hymen that illustrates the suspension of differends remain, other than Dream?" Derrida asks (DS, 210). The Dream is our psychic reality, and our psychic reality is a dream. "Dream, being at once perception, remembrance, and anticipation (desire), each within the others, is really none of these. It declares the 'fiction,' the 'medium, the pure medium, of fiction' . . . a fiction that is not imaginary, mimicry without imitation, without verisimilitude, without truth or falsity, a miming of appearance without concealed reality. . . . There remains only traces, announcements and souvenirs, foreplays and after effects . . . which no present will have preceded or followed" (DS, 210–11). When the hero stares through the membrane of the hymen, he sees the Sphinx, the Medusa, the female monster. When the hero breaks through the hymen he is castrated and the consort emerges on the other side. When the female passes through the hymen the daughter bride becomes the Goddess. She becomes SHE. The fold is the point where Subject and Other converge, without synthesizing. It is the chasm between two mountain ranges:

To repeat: the hymen . . . is an operation that *both* sows confusion *between* opposites *and* stands *between* the opposites "at once." What counts here is the *between,* the in-between-ness of the hymen. The hymen "takes place" in the "inter—" in the space between desire and fulfillment, between penetration and its recollection. But this medium of the *entre* has nothing to do with a center. . . . The hymen enters into the antre. . . . Cave, natural grotto, deep dark cavern. . . . The *interval* of the *entre,* the in-between of the hymen: one might be tempted to visualize these as the hollow or bed of a valley . . . without which there would be no mountains, like the sacred vale between the two flanks of the Parnassus, the dwelling place of the Muses . . . the space between two palisades." (DS, 212)

All knowledge commences with grand metaphors that metaphorically join one or the other sex, either the female or the male, with the generative power of nature. Knowledge is essentially structured on an erotic foundation whereby sexual reproduction is equated with the generative power of nature. Knowledge itself, however, is illusory and mythic and can privilege either the male or the female. Subject/Other, human/nature, mind/body, and male/female are the foundations on which all knowledge is built. They are all dialectics of discourse, and all are dialectically related. They all meet at a fold where the textual distinctions merge. The human is a part of nature, and nature is a construct of the human. The mind conceives the body, and the body furnishes the mirror image for the mind to attach to. It is at the point of the fold that the *truth* emerges, that the mind/body separation is not real. Its dialectics function within, and not external to, language. Intense feelings of pain can be experienced as pleasure, whereas what one experiences as pleasures in a particular fantasy structure would be considered pain if the Imaginary and Symbolic content were absent. The dialectics of pleasure and pain are textual and not material. The ego identifies itself with the body, but is separate from it.

The function of the master signifier is to establish the metaphorical and metonymical relationships between the human and nature. In this relationship, human is Subject and nature is Other. The sexual bifurcation implicit in knowledge also dichotomizes the human in terms of Subject and object. The foundations are laid for all knowledge in this set of bifurcations. There is nothing inherent in language or in the structure of knowledge that determines which dialectical pole will be privileged at any given time or place. Even when one pole is privileged, any individual can move counter to mainstream culture and redefine their "self" in terms of an oppositional master signifier.

We perceive through the conceptual structure of language, and whether we perceive polarities or unities depends as much on the conceptual structure through which we perceive material reality as it does on what is perceived. When in space, up and down are a matter of choice. On earth, we privilege down according to the force of gravity. The actual direction changes according to whether we are in the northern hemisphere or the southern hemisphere. The dialectics of discourse are therefore different than the dialectics of material reality and meet at the fold. For Derrida, the dialectics of discourse are a dialogue that the mind carries on with itself (DS, 184), a dialogue "divided into two halves only through the fiction of a crease" (DS, 227).

The Subject and the Other

The problem "that touches the most sensitive point of the nature of language" is, according to Lacan, the "question of the subject" since the Subject "cannot simply be identified with the speaker or the personal pronoun in a sentence" (OS, 188). Language entails speech, and speech entails the Subject. The Subject is a function of, or is produced by, speech and is therefore a category within the function of language. It always stands behind the ego, the body, the self, and even the mind. We can think (as the Subject) about our ego, our mind or psyche, but we can't conceive of *our Subject* since it is still the Subject doing the thinking. It is the Subject who speaks when one says "I can't make up my mind." It, according to Lacan, "makes himself an object by displaying himself before the mirror" (E, 42). He defines the mirror stage of the child "*as an identification,* in the full sense that analysis gives to the term: namely, the transformation that takes place in the Subject when he assumes an image" (E, 2) that permits the child to say "I" and "me." Kristeva explains that "as a signifying system in which the speaking subject *makes* and *unmakes* himself, language is at the center of psychological and more particularly psychoanalytic studies."[1] According to Lacan, "It [psychoanalysis] is governed by a particular aim, which is historically defined by the elaboration of the notion of the Subject. It poses this notion in a new way, by leading the subject back to his signifying dependence" (F, 77).

Lacan defines the Subject as "what, in the development of objectification, is outside of the object" (S I, 194). What is not Subject is Other, and what is Other is not the Subject. "[L]anguage is constituted by a set of signifiers. . . . The definition of this collection of signifiers is that they constitute what I call the Other" (OS, 193). He tells us that "All that is language is lent from this otherness and this is why the subject is always a fading thing that runs under the chain of signifiers. For the definition of a signifier is that it represents a subject . . . for another signifier" (OS, 194). According to Jacques-Alain Miller, "The subject is nothing more than the effect of the combination of the signifiers."[2] Lacan asserts that "language and its structure exist prior to the moment at which each subject at a certain point in his mental development makes his entry into it" (E, 148), and "If the subject is what I say it is, namely the subject determined by language and speech, it follows that the subject, *in initio* begins in the locus of the Other, in so far as it is there that the first signifier emerges" (F, 198). The Other is that which is not Subject, and "the unconscious is the discourse of the *Other* (F, 13). "The unconscious is the sum of the effects of speech on a subject, at the level at which the subject constitutes himself out of the effects of the signifier" (F, 126).

The interrelationship of Subject and signifier is complex. Miller explains that each is anterior to the other at one and the same time: "We must hold together the definitions which make the subject *the effect of the signifier* and *the signifier the representative of the subject.*" He calls it "a circular non-reciprocal relation."[3] Lacan similarly states that "The subject is born in so far as the signifier emerges in the field of the Other. But by this very fact, this subject—which was previously nothing if not a subject coming into being—solidifies into signifier" (F, 199). A signifier from which a Subject emerges is a master signifier. While Descartes concluded that he thought because he doubted, Lacan concludes that "by virtue of thinking, I am" (F, 35).

The Subject is that which is not *other,* but Lacan points out that "We must distinguish two *others* . . . an other with a capital, and an other with a small o. . . . In the function of speech we are concerned with the Other" (S II, 236).

> [W]hen the Other with a big O speaks it is not purely and simply the reality in front of you, namely the individual holding forth. The Other is beyond that reality. (S III, 52)

> In true speech the Other is that before which you make yourself recognized. But you can make yourself recognized by it only because it is recognized first. It has to be recognized for you to be able to make yourself recognized. This supplementary

dimension—the reciprocity—is necessary for there to be any value in this speech of which I've given you some typical examples—You are my master or You are my woman. (S III, 51)

The Subject is thus realized "in his signifying dependence in the locus of the Other" (F, 206).

When the Subject begins to speak, it is about itself (E, 70): "It is therefore always in the relation between the subject's ego (moi) and the 'I' (je) of his discourse that you must understand the meaning of the discourse if you are to achieve the de-alienation of the subject. But you cannot possibly achieve this if you cling to the idea that the ego of the subject is identical with the presence that is speaking to you" (E, 90). "The ego . . . is only one element in the objectal relations of the subject" (S I, 194), which also include the self, the mind or psyche and the body, or any combination of these objectal forms of dialectical identification with the Other, which emerge from the discourse of the Subject (E, 2). Lacan states that "I say—*the Other is, therefore, the locus in which is constituted the I who is speaking with him who hears*. . . . there is always an Other beyond all concrete dialogue, all interpsychological play" (S III, 273). Moreover, "The Other is the locus in which is situated the chain of the signifier that governs whatever may be made present of the subject—it is the field of that living being in which the subject has to appear. And I said that it has on the side of this living being, called to subjectivity, that the drive is essentially manifested" (F, 203).

The constitution of the Subject from the structure of the unconscious is "in its essence, through and through, sexual" (F, 203). The Subject requires a doubling. "The question of the two is for us the question of the subject, and here we reach a fact of psychoanalytical experience in as much as the two does not complete the one to make two but must repeat the one to permit the one to exist . . . and only one repetition is necessary to constitute the status of the subject" (OS, 191). The self emerges from the Subject-Other as a sexual and gendered self according to the way it is structured, the one in relationship to the Other, by the master signifier. All knowledge has a sexual foundation,[4] and self-knowledge is consequently gendered. The master signifier links the self with that which is not self and Subject with Other and other (Lacan's big *O* and little *o*).

Pinker tells us that "Chomsky's claim that from a Martian's-eye-view all humans speak a single language is based on the discovery that the same symbol-manipulating machinery, without exception, underlies the world's languages. Linguists have long known that the basic design features of language are found everywhere."[5] Lacan writes, "Before strictly human relations are established, certain relations have already been determined. They are taken from whatever nature may offer as supports, supports that are arranged in themes of opposition. Nature proves—I must use the word—signifiers, and these signifiers organize human relations in a creative way, providing them with structures and shaping them" (F, 20). Before there can be any formulation of a subject who thinks, the structures that permit persons to recognize themselves as subjects must already be in place: "Only a subject can understand a meaning; conversely, every phenomenon of meaning implies a subject" (E, 9).

The Subject, as a category presupposed by language, has the Gaze and the Voice. It is a presupposition of language, while the self, which is formulated in and through language, is a manifestation of the Subject. This subject (Lacan's little *s* as contrasted with the capital *S*) is the self as the manifestation of the Subject. There is a self, however, that is a manifestation of the Other. It has neither Gaze nor Voice and is therefore an object self that suffers a lack as defined by the master signifier. The subjectivity of otherness is essential for the subjectivity of the self as a manifestation of the Subject. Biological sex does not determine gender hierarchy. The combination of the animal instincts, which have a biological foundation, and the drives, which are their conceptualization in language, makes gender hierarchy inevitable for the languaging primate. It is only when passing through the fold, breaking through the hymen to the other side of the textual dialectic, that one can recognize the point where Subject and Object converge.

The Subject/Other dialectic is the first of a related set of dualisms that underlie knowledge. These dualisms lead Lacan to conclude that "Life goes down the river, from time to time touching a bank, staying for a while here and there, without understanding anything of what happens. The idea of the unifying unity of the human condition has always had on me the effect of a scandalous lie" (OS, 190). He further states: "In simple terms, this only means that in a universe of discourse nothing contains everything, and here you find again the gap that constitutes the subject. The subject is the introduction of a loss in reality, yet nothing can introduce that since by status reality is as full as possible. . . . When the subject takes the place of the lack, a loss is introduced in the word, and this is the definition of the subject" (OS, 193).

Mind/Body Dualism

Human cognition demands the capacity to distinguish and differentiate and the ability to categorize in terms of binary oppositions. The fundamental structure of language is binary, as is the configuration of cognition. Language entails the speaker-thinker-Subject and all else. Cognition is that which is drawn between the Subject manifesting itself as "self," and Other; or the knower and the known. The complexity arises when we conceive of our bodies as objects because our minds inhabit them and own them. This is implicit in such statements as "I have the right to do what I want with my own body." When we know the knower, the knower is unavoidably objectified. We may thus speak of our ego, our psyche, and our soul. The Subject must always be assumed and separated from whatever we identify and treat as an object. Since the body is an essential part of the self, the owner of the body is correspondingly less than the self:

> Whereas it is certain that, if there is for us a fundamental given even before the register of the unhappy consciousness has emerged at all, it's precisely the distinction between our consciousness and our body. This distinction makes our body into something fictitious, from which our consciousness is entirely incapable of detaching itself, but on the basis of which it conceives itself—these are not perhaps the most adequate terms—as distinct. The distinction between consciousness and body is set up in this abrupt interchange of roles which takes place in the experience of the mirror when the other is involved. (S I, 147)
>
> A person's own body, and above all its surface, is a place from which both external and internal perceptions may spring. It is *seen* like any other object, but to the *touch* it yields two kinds of sensations, one of which may be equivalent to an internal perception, thus a person's own body attains a special position as an object among other objects in the world of perception. (SE, IX, 25)

It is the capacity to develop language that enables humans to cognitively judge that they have a mind, psyche, or soul. Knowledge, being a representational system, requires a separation between the observer and that which is observed. Since one's own body is an object of observation, mind/body dualism is implicit in consciousness. One can only know what the subject is by objectifying it. This entails a second meta- or superknower to observe the self. A direct examination of the self by the self is impossible because that which one wishes to examine always moves back one step in the process and is therefore beyond direct examination.

Language is not a human creation, but rather human beings are products of language. As stated by Steven Pinker, "Language is not a cultural artifact that we learn the way we learn to tell time or how the federal government works. Instead, it is a distinct piece of the biological makeup of our brains. Language is a complex specialized skill, which develops in the child spontaneously, without conscious effort or formal instruction, is deployed without awareness of its underlying logic, is qualitatively the same in every individual, and is distinct from more general abilities to process information or behave intelligently."[6] Most of the syntactical and semantic processes related to language take place at the unconscious level. The perceptual-conceptual system does not in and of itself require consciousness. The first step in the development of this system is the recognition of the body as a unity distinct from the external world. "The ego is first and foremost a bodily ego; it is not merely a surface entity, but is itself the projection of a surface" (SE, IX, 26). This process takes place in what Lacan terms the mirror stage. "We have only to understand the mirror stage *as an identification,* in the full sense that analysis gives to the term: namely, the transformation that takes place in the subject when he assumes an image" (E, 2). The notion that we are bodies, and not merely sensory perceptions, pleasures, and pains, develops in us as the mediation of an image that we see as external but nevertheless as a reflection of ourselves. "Man's ideal unity, which is never attained as such and escapes him at every moment, is evoked at every moment in this perception" (S II, 166).

The body inflicts sensations on the ego. The primacy of the body lies in the inability of the ego to control it and of the body to impose on the ego various perceptual states of pleasure, unpleasure, and pain, irrespective of what the ego may desire. The ego is privileged in that it is the sentient place of conceptualization and, in turn, has some control over the body. There is, therefore, a great deal of tension within the perceptual-consciousness system, which is merely a manifestation of mind/body dualism. Master signifiers will be primary or privileged, according to how they relate to mind and body. A master signifier is primary if the signified, over which it slides at a particular time, is representational of the body and is privileged if it rides on a signified that is a manifestation of the ego.

The Ego and the Self

The Subject is always distinct from what it says or thinks (S I, 194). "[T]he sender is always a receiver at the same time, that one hears the sound of one's own words" (S III, 24). The ego, conversely, "acquires the status of a mirage, as the residue, it is only one element in the objectal relations of the subject" (S I, 194). The transparency of thought to itself would indicate that "the subject is somewhere, at a privileged point where he is able to have an endoscopy of what is going on inside himself" (S III, 35).

The occupier-owner of the body is the ego, "a notion so upsetting as to warrant the expression Copernican revolution" (S II, 3). Lacan poses the question, "To what inner necessity does the assertion that somewhere there must be an autonomous ego answer?" He states that "This conviction extends beyond the individual naiveté of the subject who believes in himself, who believes that he is himself—a common enough madness, which isn't a complete madness, because it belongs to the order of beliefs" (S II, 11–12). Moreover, "A madman is precisely someone who adheres to the imaginary, purely and simply" (S II, 243). "That the subject ends up believing in the ego is in itself madness" (S II, 247) because it "more or less implicitly perpetuates the substantialism implicit in the religious conception of the soul, as a substance which at the very least is endowed with the properties of immortality" (S II, 7). It answers the inner necessity of denying our animality—being a part of it, bound by it: nothing more than a mammal born—subject to sexual arousal, frenzy, copulation, reproducing, and then dying.

The ego is an "imaginary function" (S II, 36, 193, 243) that is indispensable in the process of constructing the self. It is not an a priori category but a discovery yielded by experience. "[W]e can no longer do our thinking without this register of the ego which we have acquired over the course of history" (S II, 7). Since the ego is an imaginary function, though essential to experience, we must conclude with Lacan that "The fundamental, central structure of our experience really belongs to the imaginary order" (S II, 36–37) and that the reality of the self is not to be found in the ego (S II, 43). "The core of our being does not coincide with the ego. That is the point of the analytic experience" (S II, 44). To the extent that the ego is imaginary, we not only put our very existence into doubt and create for ourselves the problem of *being*, but our very sanity becomes problematic in that the subject believing in the ego is in itself a form of madness (S II, 247). "The ego is structured exactly like a symptom," it is "par excellence, the mental illness of a man" (S I, 16). "*Man is the character who is always asking if he exists,* and he's quite right, and there's only one thing wrong, which is his answering yes. In relation to all the others, the privilege his ego has is that it's the only one which he can be sure exists when he questions himself—and Lord knows he does question himself. Essentially there he is, all alone. And it is because speech is received from this ego that the subject enters into the sweet illusion that this ego is in a unique position" (S II, 268). The ego, which excludes the unconscious, is an object (S II, 50) of a Subject that includes the unconscious (S II, 43, 59; S I, 193–94). When the imaginary function of the ego comes into play, one can see the ego as a reflection of "the point of view of the other" (S II, 112). According to Lacan, "The notion of the ego today draws its self-evidential character from a certain prestige given to consciousness in so far as it is a unique, individual, irreducible experience. The intuition of the ego retains, in so far as it is centered on the experience of consciousness, a captivating character, which one must rid oneself of in order to accede to our conception of the subject. . . . In the unconscious, excluded from the system of the ego, the subject speaks" (S II, 58).

If the ego is a privileged object of the Subject, an "I" that is different from the "me" of the ego, then the question arises as to who is the Subject, and to tackle that question "is to tackle the very roots of language" (S II, 134) because "this subject who speaks is beyond the ego" (S II, 175). The ego, though "a mirage," is "a sum of identifications" (S II, 209): "Freud states in a thousand, two thousand different places in his writings, namely that ego is the sum of the identifications of the subject, with all that implies as to its radical contingency. If you allow me to give an image of it, the ego is like the superimposition of various coats borrowed from what I would call the bric-a-brac of its props department" (S II, 155).

The psyche, as a system that can symbolically represent the sensory perceptual system and can also represent itself, does not exist as such at birth but evolves within the infant as she or he assimilates language. "We are bound to suppose," states Freud, "that a unity comparable to the ego cannot exist in the individual from the start; the ego has to be developed" (SE XIV, 76–7). Moreover, "The ego is the center point of consciousness in that it is the 'me' which communicates with the subject" (S III, 14).

The Primary and the Privileged

The physical human body is primary because it is a necessary condition for language. Language, conversely, is not a necessary condition for the human body. The ego, self, or psyche have no physical existence but are products of the languaging body, and thus secondary. Since they constitute thinking and consciousness, and the body does not, they are in a privileged position as they reduce the very conceptualization of the body. That there is no such thing as a mental substance either by way of spirit or matter is a fundamental presupposition of psychoanalytic theory and, as well, of postmodernism. Mind/body dualism is therefore a dialectic between the primary and the privileged.

In the discourse of material reality, humans are part of nature, whereas in the fantasy structure of psychic reality humanity is the ultimate creation of God, the pinnacle of evolutionary progress, and the master of and owner of the natural environment. Similarly, life is primary since only a living thing can die. Death presupposes life, but life does not necessarily presuppose death. In phantasmic psychic reality, the prevention of death is privileged over life in view of how we value children and the resources we are willing to spend on their welfare, compared to what we spend on war and weaponry. The sexual drive is primary and the ego drive privileged. Because of the privileged position of the ego, the sexual drive can be repressed. However, the primacy of the sexual drive is always maintained as it can return from the unconscious in the form of neurosis. Whatever defenses the ego may use against the sexual drive the sexual drive will overwhelm with libidinal energy, turning them into symptoms, neuroses, perversions, or pathologies.

The privileged status of mind often creates the illusion that the mind exists independently of the body and that the body is a mere vessel of the mind. The delusions that the magical immortal processes of the soul can by pure mind alter the physical are manifestations of the privileged position of the mind.[7] When the body thinks, it thinks it is thinking independently of the body: "Before strictly human relations are established, certain relations have already been determined. They are taken from whatever nature may offer as supports, supports that are arranged in themes of opposition. Nature provides—I must use the term signifier, and these signifiers organize human relations in a creative way providing them with structures and shaping them" (F, 20). Since the languaging body distinguishes between the mental and the physical, body and mind, Subject and Other, knowledge will be bifurcated along the lines of the primary and the privileged. The master signifiers that relate to each aspect will be primary or privileged, accordingly.

Psychoanalytic methodologies lead us to the conclusion that the spirit, the soul, the self, and the ego have no existence apart from the functioning body. A computer loaded with the most sophisticated and powerful software, if turned off and left to decay and rust, is nothing more than a machine. The software, however, continues to function in other machines. Equally, the human is born into language and dies out of it, and at the end of the cycle there is nothing left but a decaying body that can no longer language. So long as the species of humans continues to exist, language lives on in other bodies. The term *God* or the adjective *Divine* have no place in the scientific worldview other than being a particular kind of discourse or metaphor we use when we reach the limits of cognition.

A classical example of the relationship between the primary and the privileged concerns science and religion. The privileged position of religion is reflected in the assumption that religion does not deny science but declares as false whatever science proclaims that is in conflict with religion. Science on the other hand merely treats religion as a psychological phenomenon to be studied and described. Science can afford to ignore religion precisely because it is primary, while religion cannot ignore science but must claim a privileged position in defining it. Primacy and privilege are aspects of the discourse as they relate to the physical and the mental.

Jacques-Alain Miller, in elucidating Lacan's epistemology, points out that, within the Lacanian theory of language, there is an implicit and fundamental distinction to be made between knowledge and science (EE, 27).[8] Knowledge, Miller states, assumes a unity between the Subject and the object in that "the classical theory of knowledge assumes a co-naturality of subject and object, a pre-established harmony between the subject who knows and the object known" (EE, 27). Science, conversely, "constructs its object" (EE, 28). Knowledge "is fundamentally illusory and mythical" in that all theories of knowledge have sexual connotations. "[K]nowledge, in so far as it is distinguished from science, sings indefinitely the imaginary wedding of the male and the female principles, whether in the form of Aristotle's distinction between form and matter, or the ancient Chinese distinction between *yin* and *yang*" (EE, 28). Lacan's statement that woman does not exist is described according to Miller as a fundamental thesis for epistemology. In knowledge, woman is identified as object and so does not exist as subject. Knowledge therefore represents "a way of taming the woman" (EE, 28). Given the function of the phallus as the privileged signifier and knowledge as the constitution of the male Subject and the female object, it would appear that Lacanian psychoanalytic theory locks patriarchy into the very structure of knowledge that leaves us, so far as feminism is concerned, in a position similar to the one we are in with biological essentialism. There is no way for us to go outside of language and knowledge and still be sentient beings.[9] The recognition of the role of the phallus as the privileged signifier in opposition to the womb as primary signifier allows us to recognize the *rapport sexuel* of knowledge, and a genderization of subject and object that can shift dialectically between a female or male subject. Why should we assume that because the phallus, as privileged signifier, has structured the Imaginary and Symbolic for the last five thousand years, that it has always done so? It is much more likely that language and knowledge as "the illusory and mythical wedding of the sexes" evolved around the structure of a primary signifier, which was eventually repressed by the secondary oppositional signifier.

Science, by which Miller meant the mathematical physics that was born in the seventeenth century, "assumes on the contrary that there is no co-naturality between subject and object, that there is no anesthesia of the opposite sex, that there is no natural sexual tropism" (EE, 28–29). Miller tells us that "Lacan's proposition that there is no sexual rapport (or ratio) may be considered as a sort of secret condition for the emergence of the discourse of science. In a certain way, the men who developed the discourse of science in the seventeenth century must have posed the proposition that there is no sexual rapport. . . . One could say in this sense, that the scientific approach assumes a desexualization of the view of the world, and to use a philosophical expression, a desexualization of being in the world" (EE, 29). According to Miller's interpretation of Lacan, the discourse of mathematical physics escapes the sexuality of knowledge (hence is non-phallic) "because this discourse constitutes itself only from the moment of the extinction of signification, from the construction of systematic networks of elements which are in themselves without signification but which are coherent among themselves" (EE, 30). A scientific object "is a pure creation of mathematical discourse" (EE, 31). "What is called an object is a pure creation of mathematical discourse. . . . The fate of science is tied to formalization, not to measurement" (EE, 31). It "assumes the disjunction of the symbolic and the imaginary, of the signifier and the image" (EE, 32).

The difference between the discourse of knowledge and that of mathematical physics is that in the former the phallus is always present and in the latter it is not because science entails "the extermination of all imaginary symbolism":

[H]eavens, the creation, the earth sung the glory of God and the grandeur of His plan. It is precisely the discourse of science, since the emergence of mathematical physics, that makes the world become silent. Lacan sums up this proposition, which I believe is unquestionable, by saying that science assumes that there exists in the world the signifier which means nothing—and for nobody. That the signifier can be found in the world, a signifier which is organized and which responds to laws, but which is not linked with a subject who would express himself through it—this is an entirely modern and scientific idea. The signifier may exist independently of a subject who expresses himself through it s mediation. This is a signifier separated from its signification; a signifier without intention. The mathematization of physics answers to this requirement. (EE, 34)

God "is silent and hidden and he calculates." God ceases to speak, but doesn't disappear entirely, which is why "science is not . . . as atheist as is generally believed" (EE, 35).

Science, according to Miller, assumes God in two forms. "In the first place, it assumes God as Descartes recognized him, as the guarantor of truth, that is to say, as an element which does not deceive" (EE, 35). This is because "science is always linked with the idea that there is already knowledge . . . in the real: an articulated network of signifiers which function in the real independently of the knowledge that we may have of it" (EE, 35). The second way science assumes God is "as supposed subject of knowing" (EE, 36). This Cartesian subject of science, who has emptied himself of representations and the imaginary, is "an entirely desubstantialised subject for whom all natural adherences have been undone" (EE, 38). Moreover, "[T]his subject of science which emerges with Descartes is, at the same time that it emerges, rejected by the discourse of science" (EE, 39). It paradoxically presents itself as a discourse void of subject and at the same time as the discourse of the supposed impersonal subject of knowing, that the academics purport to represent.

The Dialectics of Sexuality

No clear distinction can be drawn in psychoanalysis between biology and culture or, consequently, between sexuality and gender or biological sex and sexuality. This is so because we cannot delineate between Freud's material reality or biology and psychic reality, the realm of culture, sexuality, and gender. All of this becomes clear when we contrast Lacan's distinction between the Imaginary, the Symbolic, and the Real with Freud's material reality, psychic reality, and the reality of unconscious fantasy. Material reality can only be known in terms of the Imaginary and the Symbolic. It is a part of knowledge and is not, therefore, the same as Lacan's the Real. Similarly, psychoanalysis does not sit above the dialectic as a grand arbitrator but is itself equally structured by the same dialectic. We, as languaging primates, can never escape the registries of the Imaginary and the Symbolic. Traditional psychoanalysis failed to carry through its dialectic to the point that it recognized the existence of the primary signifier. It failed to recognize that the privileged signifier has no meaning in and of itself but only as a negation of and reaction to the primary signifier.

Traditional biology as it relates to mammalian reproduction is structured by the privileged signifier and is consequently phallic. The *Oxford English Dictionary* defines the clitoris as "A homologue of the male penis, present, as a rudimentary organ, in the females of many of the higher vertebrate."[10] When Freud discusses the female vaginal orgasm, he speaks within this domain. The existence or nonexistence of the vaginal orgasm is a question for biology to decide in terms of the physiology of the female via female experience. Yet Freud relied on neither of these sources for his postulations.

Freud considered female sexuality a mystery, which after thirty years he still failed to understand. A mystery consists of that which we do not know and cannot find out. Why is the shared experience of over 50 percent of the world's population mysterious? Why is it that we can know male sexuality and not know that of the female? Clearly, female sexuality cannot be *known* in terms of a signifier that defines it in terms of lack, and privileges the penis. Any chain of signification that is structured by the phallus could not possibly conform to female experience and, in the absence of an alternative master signifier, will always remain a mystery to males. Any discourse in which the male is the observer and the female the object of observation, in which the male has the sole Voice and the Gaze, will never provide an adequate explanation or description of female sexuality or answer the question, "What does the woman want?" The recognition of the dialectical function of the master signifiers is essential for a psychoanalysis that is able to come to grips with the issues of biological sex, sexuality, and gender.

96

One of the most detailed psychoanalytic studies of female sexuality is Dr. Mary Jane Sherfey's book *The Nature and Evolution of Female Sexuality*.[11] She brings to her study an exploration of such diverse fields as physiology, anatomy, comparative embryology, endocrinology, gynecology, paleontology, evolutionary biology, population genetics, primatology, theology, anthropology, psychiatry, and, of course, psychoanalysis. While bringing diversity to her analysis, Sherfey nevertheless focuses on the biological aspects of human sexuality. She asserts that "One of the biological theories of the nineteenth century most thoroughly integrated into medicine and psychiatry has been the theory of the innate, embryonic bisexuality of all vertebrates" (N, 30). On this premise, human skills, attitudes, abilities, emotions, and actions are divided into those that are inherently male and those inherently female. The clitoris was considered to be a diminutive or undeveloped penis, and the male orgasm the standard measure of sexual experience. This certainly confirms Lacan's positioning of the phallus and maintains the consistency of phallic supremacy within these various disciplines.

Freud's recognition of essential masculine and feminine characteristics, his conception of female sexuality in terms of phallic castration, and his postulation of the vaginal orgasm, all reflect the fact that Freud constructed his theory of female sexuality on the biological premises of embryonic bisexuality and male primacy. Sherfey asserts that contemporary psychoanalytic theory ultimately reflects this dated "truism" (N, 30–34). "Thus it is," she states, "that psychoanalytic theory has led us through a series of perfectly logical steps to a position which is, in essence, anachronistic: a scientific restatement of the Eve-out-of Adam myth." She concludes that, on the evidence, "The early embryo is not undifferentiated: 'it' is a female. In the beginning, we were all created females; and if this were not so, we would not be here at all" (N, 38). Genetic sex is established at fertilization, but the influence of the sex genes is not brought to bear until the fifth to sixth weeks of fetal life. Female development is autonomous in that "no ovarian inductor substance or estrogens are elaborated because none are needed. Female differentiation results from the innate, genetically determined female morphology of all mammalian embryos" (N, 39). The male embryo, on the other hand, is required to undergo a differentiating transformation of the sexual anatomy brought about by a hormonal bath of androgen, which masculinizes the original female genital tract (N, 40). "The primacy of the embryonic female morphology forces us to reverse long held concepts on the nature of sexual differentiation. Embryologically speaking, it is correct to say that the penis is an exaggerated clitoris, the scrotum is derived from the labia majora, the original libido is feminine, etc." (N, 46). She further suggests that "it is unfortunately true, I believe, that had the traditional view been substantiated by embryology—and all embryos were innately males from which the females derived—a large number of people would have loudly leaped to the conclusion that such was unassailable proof of the innately masculine nature of the sexual drive, clear evidence for the scientific affirmation of the Eve-out-of-Adam myth, and 'objective' confirmation of masculine superiority argued from the logic of creation" (N, 46). She draws this probability to our attention in order to emphasize that an argument for innate female superiority cannot, and ought not, be made on the basis of the primacy of embryonic female morphology. The distinction between primary and secondary reflects the distinction between modern and postmodern epistemology. In our view, the concept of a privileged signifier assumes that it receives a priority over another signifier when there is no justification for the preference in terms of either material reality or in relationship to the Real. The supremacy of privilege is therefore based on illusion.

According to Freud's "clitoral-vaginal transfer theory," early female orgasms are centered in the clitoris, and with maturity, they invariably shift to the vagina. Sherfey states:

> Thus the original Freudian transfer theory has now become almost a statement of female psychosexual development as an evolutionary ideal toward which most women must still strive. Only a few superior women have the highly evolved or trained cortex necessary to produce the vaginal orgasm. Therefore vaginal orgastic competency becomes a function of the higher centers and the intellect. Again we are led by clear logic to the very uncomfortable position stating that the majority of women remain biologically inferior, retarded in their psychosexual evolution compared to men, not sufficiently evolved emotionally and intellectually to achieve the vaginal orgasm. (N, 35)

The question of the existence or nonexistence of the vaginal orgasm is, according to Sherfey, a biological problem that must be answered by biology (N, 28). She argues that a study of the anatomy and physiology of the female vagina will conclusively show that the vaginal orgasm is a physiological impossibility because *"no part of the vagina itself produces the orgasmic contractions"* (N, 93). To her, the evidence seems overwhelming that *"it is a physical impossibility to separate the clitoral from the vaginal orgasm as demanded by psychoanalytic theory"* (N, 85). "With maturation, the erotogenic zone of the lower third of the vagina does not supplant the clitoral zone; *it must be assimilated with the entire clitoral-labial complex into a single functional structure"* (N, 116).

Sherfey tells us that the reason the transfer theory was never fully denied or strongly opposed by women psychoanalysts was that "people *want* the vaginal orgasm to exist" (N, 28). The notion of a vaginal orgasm is closely interrelated with the idea that at a biological level the sexual function of the female is to satisfy the sexual desires of the male, which in turn leads to the reproduction of the species. Only the male penis, or a phallic substitute, can produce a vaginal orgasm for the female. The vaginal orgasm thus biologically determines the sexuality of the female in terms of reproduction and the sexual satisfaction of the male. She is thus the passive sexual object rather than the active sexual subject. The vaginal orgasm is, therefore, an essential part of patriphallic psychic reality.

The implications of the primacy of the clitoral orgasm for women's sexuality are frightening for the patriphallic male. Physiologically, there can be no limit to the number and frequency of clitoral orgasms. As Sherfey points out, "Multiple orgasms in women are well explained by the physiodynamics of the sexual cycle" (N, 105). From the scientific data, she concludes that "the more orgasms a woman has, the stronger they become; the more orgasms she has, the more she can have. To all intents and purposes, *the human female is sexually insatiable in the presence of the highest degrees of sexual satiation* (N, 112). The clitoral orgasm need not require the male penis. In fact, as Masters and Johnson point out, most males have difficulty maintaining an erection long enough to produce a single orgasm, let alone multiple orgasms; therefore, very few males can give the female full sexual satisfaction. Male inadequacy is the implication of the clitoral orgasm. A further implication is the nonessential nature of the male for female sexual satisfaction. Given that female sexuality commences between mother and daughter, lesbian sexuality can be a superior alternative to heterosexuality as long as the male continues to view the point of the relationship as the fulfilling of his desire. Given the reality of the multiple clitoral orgasm, the only satisfactory heterosexual relationship, so far as the female is concerned, is that in which the male embraces as his desire the fulfillment of the female's desire. This is a total reversal of patriphallic heterosexual psychical reality. Sherfey concludes that the "ruthless subjugation of female sexuality, which, of course, necessarily subjugated her entire emotional and intellectual life" and the concurrent family and kinship social order was "essential to man's becoming—and remaining—man" (N, 137–38).

The converse of patriphallic heterosexuality would be matriphallic heterosexuality. By "matriphallic" we do not suggest that the female has a phallus or possesses the equivalent of the male phallus. Matriphallic heterosexuality is where the male places his phallus at the service of the female. He gives it to her and by doing so gives himself, as he is attached to it. He embraces the fulfillment of her desire as the object of his desire. He is prepared to compete with any form of lesbian sexuality. She becomes the subject, and he the object, of her desire. In making the sacrificial gift of his phallus, the Gaze is passed over to her. Rather than observing her nudity as his right, he becomes the voyeur. According to Lacan, "We can apprehend this privilege of the gaze in the function of desire, by pouring ourselves, as it were, along the veins through which the domain of vision has been integrated into the field of desire" (F, 85).

The foundational point of all knowledge is the Subject. The Subject must be in place for knowledge to exist, and the Subject cannot exist without knowledge. Knowing entails a constant reformulation of the Subject as it takes place, and the activity of knowing (imagining and symbolizing the Other) takes place in relationship to the Subject. The Other is that which is not Subject. The Subject is that which is not Other. There is no knowledge of the Other that is not dependent on knowledge of the Subject. The differences between the female and male body, the inevitable significance of the potential for reproduction in the face of death, the necessity of the gaze of the Other for the image of the self, the interdependency of sexuality—all function to produce a duality of selves split on the interrelationship of gendered psychic reality in dialectical response to the duality of bimorphic mammalian biological sex. This will not change in the foreseeable future, if ever. The languaging body condemns humans to the dialectics of master signifiers, to two sides that meet in the fold, which mimic each other in the function of signification. The denial of difference within the discourses structured by the privileged signifier leaves our patriphallic psychic reality unchallenged. The primary signifier functions to preserve the separation and integrity of material reality and to use material reality to challenge the illusions of psychic reality.

The Dialectics of the Eros Drive and the Thanatos Drive

Freud introduced a second dualism: the Eros or life drive and Thanatos or death drive. He was led to this dualism by his attempts to reconcile masochism with the pleasure principle. The pleasure principle dictates that the ego seeks pleasure and the release from unpleasure. It is modified by the reality principle, which explains how the individual will postpone or deny momentary pleasure in the face of reality for the sake of future pleasure. While sadism is consistent with the pleasure principle, masochism is not. The phenomenon of the self turning aggression inward led Freud to the discovery of the death drive. Freud writes that "Our speculations have suggested that Eros operates from the beginning of life, and appears as a *life-instinct* in opposition to the *death-instinct*" (SE, XVIII, 62, n. 1). He explains:

> This aggressive instinct is the derivative and the main representative of the death instinct which we have found alongside of Eros and which shares world-dominion with it. And now, I think, the meaning of the evolution of civilization is no longer obscure to us. It must present the struggle between Eros and Death, between the instinct of life and the instinct of destruction, as it works itself out in the human species. This struggle is what all life essentially consists of, and the evolution of civilization may therefore be simply described as the struggle for life of the human species. And it is this battle of the giants that our nurse-maids try to appease with their lullaby about Heaven. (SE, XXI, 122)

The relationship between the sexual-ego drives and the Eros-Thanatos drives has been the topic of much discussion in academic literature. It is as if there are two different conceptual frameworks at work in Freud, whereby he seems to use one dialectic for some purposes and another for a different form of analysis, despite his wish for one comprehensive dialectic.[12] He writes, "The upshot of our inquiry so far has been the drawing of a sharp distinction between the 'ego-instincts' and the sexual instincts, and the view that the former exercise pressure towards death and the latter towards a prolongation of life. But this conclusion is bound to be unsatisfactory in many respects even to ourselves" (SE, XVIII, 44).

Freud has no difficulty in relating the sex and Eros drives. He states that "With the hypothesis of narcissistic libido, and the extension of the concept of libido to the individual cells, the sexual instinct was transformed for us into Eros, which seeks to force together and hold together the portions of living substance" (SE, XVIII, 61 n. 1). According to Laplanche, "[I]t is sexuality which represents the model of every drive and probably constitutes the only drive in the strict sense of the term" (L&D, 8). He goes on to say that "Something is always opposed to sexuality, even if that opposite term is defined differently in various stages of Freud's thought; it may be another kind of drive—what Freud terms self-preservative drives or ego drives—or it may be the ego, as a structure, itself; in the last analysis, it will be the death drive" (L&D, 26). In attempting to equate the ego drive with the Thanatos or death drive, the problem arises that the former is the conceptualization of the instincts that lead toward self-preservation, which seems to be the opposite of a drive toward death. Lacan explains Freud's dilemma:

> Now, in man the function of the ego possesses distinct characteristics. That's the great discovery of analysis—at the level of the generic relation, bound up with the life of the species, man already functions differently. In man, there's already a crack, a profound perturbation of the regulation of life. That's the importance of the notion introduced by Freud of the death instinct. Not that the death instinct is such an enlightening notion in itself. What has to be comprehended is that he was forced to introduce it so as to remind us of a salient fact of his experience, just when it was beginning to get lost . . . what Freud's experience amounted to. He wanted to save some kind of dualism at all costs, just when this dualism was crumbling in his hands, and when the ego, the libido, etc., all of that was tending to produce a kind of vast whole, returning us to a philosophy of nature. (S II, 37)

At first, Freud gave the death drive a biological foundation that almost went as far as to conceptualize the bodily process of aging. Much of Freud's work, however, particularly that of the latter part of his life, rejected the biologicalism of his earlier writings. Lacan, who rejects all aspects of biology as a foundation for psychoanalysis, purges the death drive of all biologicalisms.

The Lacanian version of the life/death dialectic commences with an analysis of the relationship between speech and death. "[T]here is a conjunction in the human world between the speech which dominates the destiny of man and death," Lacan writes (S II, 206). It is speech and symbols that move humans from the instinctual world to the world of drives. Lacan locates the Eros and Thanatos drives at the level of the Imaginary, the Symbolic, and the Real. Just as animals don't have sex but copulate or "rut," animals perish but do not die as death lies in the register of the Symbolic (Ap, 35). As Heidegger wrote, "Mortals are they who can experience death as death. Animals cannot do this. But animals cannot speak either. The essential relation between death and language flashes up before us but remains still unthought."[13] Concerning the concept of death, Derrida writes "Fundamentally, one knows perhaps neither the meaning nor the referent of this word. It is well known that if there is one word that remains absolutely unassignable or unassigning with respect to its concept and to its thingness, it is the word 'death.' Less than for any other noun, save 'God'—and for good reason, since their association here is not fortuitous" (Ap, 22).

Lacan calls the death instinct the mask of the symbolic order (S II, 326). To the degree that humans partake in the death instinct, they remain in part outside life and engage in the register of life from the register of death (S II, 90). "[T]his life we're captive of, this essentially alienated life, existing, this life in the other, is as such joined to death, it always returns to death" (S II, 233). According to Lacan, "The nature of the symbol remains to be clarified. We have come close to its essence by locating its genesis at the same point as that of the death instinct. We are expressing one and the same thing. We are moving towards a point of convergence—what does the signifier essentially signify in its signifying role? What is the original and initiatory function, in human life, of the existence of the symbol qua pure signifier? This question takes us back to our study of the psychoses" (S III, 215). The ego comes into being in the Imaginary and the Symbolic order in tension with the sexual drive. "The symbolic order is simultaneously non-being and insisting to be, that is what Freud has in mind when he talks about the death instinct as being what is most fundamental—a symbolic order in travail, in the process of coming, insisting on being realized" (S II, 326).

Culture lies within the register of the Symbolic and as such reflects the same relationship between death and the Symbolic. Derrida explains:

> [C]ulture itself, culture in general, is essentially, before anything, even a priori, the culture of death. Consequently, then, it is a *history of death*. . . . The very concept of culture may seem to be synonymous with the culture of death, as if the expression "culture of death" were ultimately a pleonasm or a tautology. . . . The difference between nature and culture, indeed between biological life and culture, and, more precisely, between the animal and the human is the relation *to* death, as one most often thinks according to the same philosophical *doxa*. The relation to death *as such*. The true border would be there. (Ap, 43–44)

If death and perishing distinguish the animal from the human, so do birth and reproduction. The concept of life is as much within the register of the Symbolic as is the concept of death. Eros and Thanatos cannot, therefore, be distinguished in terms of death belonging to the register of the Symbolic. Rather, the distinction must be located in the way that reproduction and perishing are manifested in the registers of the Imaginary and the Symbolic.

Just as the ego reacts to the sexual in terms of affirmation and acceptance, or denial and negation, the ego confronts the animality of the body in similar terms. The oppositional relationship between the sexual drive and the ego drive is manifested in the form of the fundamental symptoms and neuroses that can be reduced to the acceptance or denial of our animality.

According to Freud, "Negation is a substitute, at a higher level, for repression" (SE, XIV, 186). "Thus the content of a repressed image or idea can make its way into consciousness, on condition that it is *negated*" (SE, XIX, 235). Negation entails judgment and thus, "The polarity of judgment appears to correspond to the opposition of the two groups of instincts which we have supposed to exist" (SE, XIX, 237). "Affirmation—as a substitute for uniting—belongs to Eros; negation—the successor to expulsion—belongs to the instinct of destruction" (SE, XIX, 237). In negating Eros, the Ego embraces its antithesis—Thanatos. Behind affirmation is unification, but behind negation is a denial that is more than a mere wish to destroy, it is an instinct of destruction, a drive to destroy (S I, 295–96).

The relationship between being born and perishing is not the same as the dialectical relationship of Eros and Thanatos. At the moment of birth, one is immediately vulnerable to death. Perishing is inevitable—it is only a question of how and when. Animality embraces mortality. To affirm animality is to embrace death as well as life. It is to say "yes" to life. The affirmation of Eros is the embrace of animality—our bodies, our sexuality, our mortality. "I grant you that I haven't yet completely lifted the veil—I'll leave that for next time. In order for procreation to have its full sense there must also be, in both sexes, an apprehension, a relation with the experience of death, which gives the term *to procreate* its full sense. Moreover, paternity and death are two signifiers that Freud links in relation to obsessionals" (S III, 293). The negation of animality is a denial of the body by a glorification of the mind; sexuality by privileging production over reproduction and culture over nature; and mortality by the myths of the survival of the mind after the dissolution of the body.

The affirmation or denial of animality is not a rational judgment. Since the polarity of judgments corresponds to the polarity of drives, both the judgments of affirmation or denial are neurotic reactions or manifestations of symptom formations. This is consistent with Lacan's statement that "The function of desire must remain in a fundamental relation with death" (S VII, 351). "Who, more fearlessly than this clinician [Freud], so firmly tied to mundane suffering, has questioned life as to its meaning, and not to say that it has none, which is a convenient way of washing one's hands of the whole business, but to say that it has only one meaning, that in which desire is borne by death?" (E, 276–77).

In this sense, the Eros and Thanatos drives could be better classified as complexes. As stated by Lacan, "Psychosis is no longer interpreted on the basis of the complex economy of the dynamics of the drives but on the basis of procedure used by the ego to escape from various requirements, to defend itself against the drives. The ego again becomes not only the center but the cause of the disorder" (S III, 105). The Thanatos complex is the post-Oedipal state of the psyche. As we are sexually genderized in the Oedipal passage we pass into the Thanatos complex. Patriarchy and male domination, male phallic possession and female lack are all manifestations of the Thanatos complex. The Eros complex reverses the dynamics of heterosexual sexuality and must entail, therefore, female dominance (but not necessarily domination); the primacy of the Womb over the privilege of the Phallus, and male sacrifice in place of female lack. If feminism is not a politics of Eros, then it will inevitably fall within the politics of Thanatos and will never lead to the liberation of women.

The problem of reconciling the two Freudian dialectics stems from linking aggression and masochism with the Thanatos or death drive. Though Freud came to the recognition of the death drive through the discovery of masochism as a primary symptom, it does not follow that aggression should necessarily be linked with the Thanatos drive. It may be the case that aggression can function in both the Eros complex or drive, and the Thanatos complex or drive, depending on the source of the aggression. Primary masochism can function in the service of either Eros or Thanatos. When primary masochism is the product of aggression by the id against the ego, seeking to dissolve the boundaries of the ego in order to unify mind and body, then the aggression is in the service of Eros. When primary masochism is a manifestation of the dialectics between the sexual drive and the ego drive, seeking an integration of the sexual drive with the ego, then it serves Eros since unification is the end product of the Eros drive. If the self-aggression of primary masochism seeks the destruction of the ego rather than unification, then it is functioning in the service of Thanatos.

The Dialectics of Domination and Submission

Lacan's view of the relationship between the self and the Other and the nature of desire, owes as much to Alexandre Kojève's interpretation of Hegel as it does to Freud. Lacan produced a synthesis of Freud and Hegel with respect to the development of the ego and self-consciousness. He frequently appeals to Hegel in the development of his views regarding the formation of the self and specifically to the fundamental Hegelian tenet that "man's desire is the desire of the other" (S I, 146). Lacan argues that the child first develops its sense of a unified self at the age of six to eighteen months from seeing its image in the mirror. The reflecting glass is replaced by the kind and degree of recognition that the Other imparts. The Other thus defines the nature and structure of the self. Identity emerges from an intersubjective, dialectical process of recognition.

Kojève, the brilliant Hegelian scholar, presented a series of lectures between 1933 to 1939 on Hegel's *Phenomenology of Spirit* that had a profound influence on post-World War II French social theory. Kojève's famous *Introduction to the Reading of Hegel* has been a source of inspiration not only to psychoanalysis but also to feminism and postmodernism.[14] Kojève has profoundly influenced French social theory, and most of the important theorists of the sixties attended Kojève's seminars on Hegel during the thirties. The Hegelian perspective has also been a very important one for many feminists such as Catharine MacKinnon and Jessica Benjamin.[15] According to Kojève, "Hegelian Dialectics is not a *method* of research or of philosophical exposition, but the adequate description of the *structure* of Being, and the realization and appearance of Being as well" (RH, 259). The applicability of the creation of self-consciousness through obtaining the recognition of others seems a particularly appropriate paradigm from which to study male domination.

"Man becomes conscious of himself at the moment when—for the 'first' time—he says 'I'. To understand man by understanding his 'origin' is . . . to understand the origin of the I revealed by speech" (RH, 3). The object first shows itself through perception. Contemplation reveals the object through an act of knowing. The individual is only brought back into himself through a desire for the contemplated object. "Desire of a being is what constitutes that being as I and reveals it as such by moving it to say 'I.' . . . It is in and by—or better still, as—'his' Desire that man is formed and is revealed—to himself and to others—as an I, as the I that is essentially different from, and radically opposed to, the non-I. The (human). I is the I of a Desire or of Desire" (RH, 3–4). The self-conscious human being, therefore, implies and presupposes desire.

Action negates or satisfies desire by the assimilation, consumption, or transformation of the desired object, and thus the satisfaction of desire entails the negation of the objects of desire. Desire is a necessary condition for self-consciousness, though not a sufficient condition (RH, 4). If the desire is for the consumption of a natural object such as food, then the subject will be a natural subject, "an animal I," and as such can never attain Self-Consciousness (RH, 5). "For there to be Self-Consciousness, Desire must therefore be directed toward a non-natural object, toward something that goes beyond the given reality. Furthermore, according to Kojève:

> The only thing that goes beyond the given reality is Desire itself. For Desire taken as Desire—i.e., before its satisfaction—is but a revealed nothingness, an unreal emptiness. Desire, being the revelation of an emptiness, the presence of the absence of a reality, is something essentially different from the desired thing, something other than a thing, than a static and given real being that stays eternally identical to itself. Therefore, Desire directed toward another Desire, taken as Desire, will create, by the negating and assimilating action that satisfies it, an I essentially different from the animal "I." This I, which "feeds" on Desires, will itself be Desire in its very being, created in and by the satisfaction of its Desire. (RH, 5)

Since human desire must be directed toward another human desire, there must be a multiplicity of desire in order for self-consciousness to be born. "Man can appear on earth only within a herd" (RH, 6). Social reality consists therefore, of a set of desires mutually desiring one another as desires rather than as objects: "in the relationship between man and woman, for example, Desire is human only if the one desires, not the body, but the Desire of the other; if he wants 'to possess' or 'to assimilate' the Desire taken as Desire—that is to say, if he wants to be 'desired' or 'loved,' or, rather 'recognized' in his human value, in his reality as a human individual" (RH, 6).

Our existence as self-conscious beings "is, finally, a function of the desire for 'recognition.' . . . Therefore, the human being can be formed only if at least two of these desires confront one another" (RH, 7). The first confrontation between two human desires is not on the hunt, at the marketplace of commerce, or on the battlefield. It is in the process of mating and reproduction. Before man confronts man, he first confronts woman. The Hegelian-Kojèvian dialectics of desires from which the self-conscious being emerges, is between mother and child, between woman and man. If, as is postulated by Freud, that desire is rooted in human sexuality and libido energized by sexual difference, then a theory of the emergence of the self and of the dialectics of intersubjectivity must be closely interrelated with a theory of the structure of human sexuality and gender.

Lacan emphasizes that "at every turn, I take my bearings from the master-slave dialectic, and I re-explain it. . . . Hegel gives account of the interhuman bond. He has to account not only for society, but for history. He cannot neglect any of its aspects" (S I, 222–23). "[M]an's desire finds its meaning in the desire of the other, not so much because the other holds the key to the object desired, as because the first object of desire is to be recognized by the other" (E, 58). Lacan merges Hegel with Freud in his theory of the development of the self. He explains:

> Before Darwin, however, Hegel had provided the ultimate theory of the proper function of aggressivity in human ontology, seeming to prophecy the iron law of our time. From the conflict of Master and Slave, he deduced the entire subjective and objective progress of our history, revealing in these crises the syntheses to be found in the highest forms of the status of the person in the West, from the Stoic to the Christian, and even to the future citizen of the Universal State. . . . The satisfaction of human desire is possible only when mediated by the desire and labour of the other. (E, 26)

> We live in a society in which slavery isn't recognized. It's nevertheless clear to any sociologist or philosopher that it has in no way been abolished. This has even become the object of some fairly well-known claims. It's also clear that while bondage hasn't been abolished, one might say it has been generalized. The relationship of those known as the exploiters, in relation to the economy as a whole, is no less a relationship of bondage than that of the average man. Thus the master-slave duality is generalized within each participant in our society. (S III, 132)

"The most naked rivalry between men and women is eternal," Lacan asserts, "and its style is laid down in conjugal relations. . . . Feminine rebellion didn't start yesterday. From master to slave and rival, there is only one dialectical step—the relations of the master to the slave are essentially reversible, and the master sees very quickly his dependency in relation to his slave become established" (S II, 263). Moreover, "Man's desire finds its meaning in the desire of the other, not so much because the other holds the key to the object desired, as because the first object of desire is to be recognized by the other" (E, 58). The Other, for man, is woman. The *jouissances* of domination and submission reflect the correlative tensions between "the narcissistic structure in the coming-into-being of the subject," and aggression (E, 22). Thus the development of the human subject as a gendered being and sexuality are intertwined. Gender, like sexuality, entails domination and submission. Mitchell, in her comment on Lacan's theory of sexuality, explains:

> For all psychoanalysts the development of the human subject, its unconscious and its sexuality go hand-in-hand, they are causitively intertwined. A psychoanalyst could not subscribe to a currently popular sociological distinction in which a person is born with their biological gender to which society—general environment, parents, education, the media—adds a socially defined sex, masculine or feminine. Psychoanalysis cannot make such a distinction: a person is formed through their sexuality, it could not be "added" to him or her. The ways in which psychosexuality and the unconscious are closely bound together are complex, but most obviously, the unconscious contains wishes that cannot be satisfied and hence have been repressed. Predominant among such wishes are the tabooed incestuous desires of childhood. (FS, 2)

Lacan states: "A law is imposed upon the slave, that he should satisfy the desire and the pleasure [*jouissance*] of the other" (S I, 223). The *jouissance* of submission emanates from the satisfaction received from fulfilling the Other's desire to be recognized (S II, 236).

It is within the dialectics of the *jouissances* of control and submission that self-consciousness emerges from the intersubjectivity of the self and the Other. The primary mirror for the emerging self of the child is the mother. In the state of narcissistic bliss and omnipotence before the child distinguishes between self and mother and becomes aware of limitations, the child knows neither control nor submission. Following the narcissistic wound when the child begins to be cognizant of its separateness from the mother and its helplessness, the child is in a state of submission to her and seeks recognition in the eyes of the mother. The child seeks to become the object of the mother's desire.

It is the desire for the Mother that constitutes the child, an I. The child consumes the mother as she or he feeds at her breast, and absorbs her love, attention, and admiration. The breast is the first object of the infant's desire, and the recognition of the eternality of the breast as an object, which commences the process of the emergence of the self. The desire that is presupposed by the being of man is the desire for the mother. Oedipal desire is the child's desire for recognition from the mother, and her willingness to give it. That is, it is the child's desire for the desire of the mother, and not the body of the mother as an object, that constitutes Oedipal desire. The human being is forged out of the relationship between domination and submission, which is confronted first between the mother and child, second as the child witnesses the dynamics of control and submission between the mother and the father, and third in the struggle between the sexes. In other words, humans experience domination and submission long before men risk their lives in the struggle for mastery over other men, which lies at the center of Hegelian dialectics.

Men know themselves as men because of the recognition they receive in the eyes of women, and women seek recognition by being the object of male desire. Gender is the fundamental historical dialectic. The Hegelian master/slave dialectic is secondary, and builds upon the existing foundation in terms of the sexually based dynamics of control and submission. The dialectics of desire for recognition and desire for domination and submission are the same. Sexual satisfaction and recognition of the self are so intertwined that they cannot be entirely separated. It is because of this interrelationship, in part, that the sexual drive is often such a threat to the ego drive.

If it is the case that "Man achieves his true autonomy, his authentic freedom, only after passing through Slavery" (RH, 27), then, applying the Hegelian-Kojèvian analysis to the "war of the sexes," women will only achieve their true autonomy and authentic freedom by passing through submission. "The Master can never detach himself from the World in which he lives. . . . Only the Slave can transform the World that forms him and fixes him in slavery and create a World that he has formed in which he will be free" (RH, 29). Only women can transform and transcend their status as submissive to male authority. "Therefore, it is indeed the originally dependent, serving and slavish Consciousness that in the end realizes and reveals the ideal of autonomous Self-Consciousness and is thus its 'truth' " (RH, 30). It is the person in submission who has an intuition of human reality (RH, 48). Master and slave, domination and submission, are the two sides of the self that meet at the fold. The portal between is a two-way door, and domination and submission fold in on each other at the crease.

We must rid ourselves of the notion that there are separate female and male perspectives of the Subject. The Subject is a category presupposed by language. The self, however, as it includes the body, is gendered. The concept of the gendered self relies on the oppositional relationship of the two signifiers. The dominant-subservient relationship of the master signifiers plays out sexually in terms of the *jouissances* of domination and submission. Each self, according to the structure of the particular master signifier, will achieve its status in terms of dominance and submission. According to Lacan, "The intersubjective relation which subtends perverse desire is only sustained by the annihilation either of the desire of the other, or of the desire of the subject. It can only be grasped at the limit, in its inversions. . . . This means . . . that in the one as in the other, this relation dissolves the being of the subject. The other subject is reduced to being only the instrument of the first, who thus remains the only subject as such, but the latter is reduced to being only an idol offered to the desire of the other" (S I, 222).

The dialectics of domination and submission are based on difference. The most significant difference between selves is that found in the body. Neither femaleness nor maleness determines which is dominant and which is subservient. This can only be determined by their chains of signification. In the same way, domination and submission between males is structured in terms of difference. Racial differences are obvious and therefore form the most significant foundations for domination and submission between males. The desire to accumulate wealth furnishes an imaginary and symbolic foundation for domination through the exercise of economic power. If the fantasy is shattered and the illegitimate privilege is denied, then one is faced with a reversal of domination and submission. As a result, the primary chains of signification permit the formation of the self in terms of female domination and male submission because the female is identified with the primary in the set of dialectics. So long as mind/body dualism, and all the related dialectics, have a sexual manifestation within knowledge, the dialectics of domination and submission will be the framework within which the self is formulated. The dialectics of domination and submission parallel the dialectics of subjectivity as selves as manifestation-of-the-Subject and selves as manifestation-of-the-Other. The self as subject will be dominant and the self as other will be submissive. Humans, whether female or male, can pass through the fold from one to the other. At the point of passage, as they break through the hymen, they will catch a glimpse of the *truth* of gender.

FIVE

The Dialectics of Fantasy

Reality

Distinctions between appearance and reality are inevitable when one concentrates on the biological limits of knowledge and on the subjectivity of sensed experience. Each person presupposes or assumes his or her own existence as the knower, as a given, and the external world as other and object. At the same time, reality is a human construct that is relative to a particular discourse or set of discourses. There is no transcendental appeal to an objective measure outside of or beyond the limits of human perception, mental life, and language. Nevertheless, as one encounters the external world within the framework of language, one is compelled to recognize that the perceptions, conceptions, and discourses that constitute knowledge (Lacan's registers of the Imaginary and the Symbolic) are at best metaphorical representations of that which is not knowledge (the Real). As such, one can evaluate and compare a given interpretation as being better than another. In this sense, appearance can be measured against material reality.

When one examines the myriad of languaging functions, it quickly becomes clear that while observing, describing, explaining, and theorizing have to do with discovering or establishing reality, other functions are concerned with establishing appearance, often at the expense of reality. Such languaging functions would include desiring, rationalizing, justifying, legitimizing, hallucinating, and lying. The denial of reality through such languaging functions is effective only when appearance is accepted as reality. Effectiveness is dependent on the blurring or eradication of the distinction between appearance and reality. In psychic reality, appearance is taken as reality.

The fundamental presupposition of our educational, legal, and political systems is that the reality-establishing functions of languaging predominate and that the appearance functions are idiosyncratic—the exception rather than the rule. The fundamental presupposition of psychoanalysis is just the opposite. As stated by R. H. Hook, "Freud showed that it is, in fact, the other way around: by nature man has an undiscriminating preference for whatever offers immediate gratification and it is only harsh reality that forces him to be rational. He attempts mentally to construct the world as he desires it and it is only when the world does not work that he is obliged to start again, only this time taking frustrating reality into account."[1]

Freud drew a fundamental distinction between what he termed "primary process thinking" and "secondary process thinking."[2] Primary process thinking establishes appearance. While the structure of primary process thinking is neurotic and pathological, it underlies the "so-called normal activities of the mind" such as dreams, fantasies, myths, and rituals in which "time and space have an altered significance, and if represented at all, are dealt with in a manner altogether different from that of secondary process."[3] Secondary process thinking is concerned with the establishment of reality, and therefore logic and rationality are dominant. The centrality of this distinction is attested to by Maurice Bénassy and René Diatkine who state that "Freud's revolutionary contribution to psychology was not so much his demonstrating the existence of an unconscious . . . as his proposition that there are two fundamentally different kinds of mental processes, which he termed primary and secondary respectively. . . . That is to say, unconscious tendencies of the organism are governed by original laws that are different from the laws governing secondary processes, preconscious or conscious. These laws function according to the unpleasure-pleasure principle."[4]

Key to primary thinking is the illusion that our predominant thought is secondary thinking. The maintenance of the illusion that humans are primarily rational, logical, truth-seeking, sentient beings is a fundamental aspect of primary thinking. The central concept in primary thinking is that of fantasy or phantasy,[5] or the delusion that we are different than we *really* are, that the world is different than it *really* is. According to Freud, psychic reality, the appearance of which is taken to be reality, is structured as fantasy, in which case the structure of "normalcy" is neurotic, psychotic, and pathological. How, then can we still distinguish between "normalcy" and "madness"? The sane are those whose psyches function within the structure of collective fantasies, and those who are adjudged to be mad are persons whose governing fantasy structures are idiosyncratic. Thus, as Foucault tells us, from the Middle Ages onward, a man was considered to be mad if his speech could not be said to form part of the common discourse of men.[6]

Why would Freud designate the kind of thinking that produces illusion as *primary* and the kind of thinking through which we formulate our conceptions of material reality as *secondary?* The mental processes of repression and neurosis, which produce dreams, fantasy, myth, and illusion, are more powerful than those mental processes that seek a material reality. Repression and neurosis are primary because they predominate. The conceptual world within which we live is governed by psychic rather than material reality. The psychic is therefore privileged over the material. Primary thinking is *primary* because of its privileged position in the signifying chain of neurotic psychic reality. Secondary thinking, on the other hand, reflects the Imaginary and the Symbolic registers which attempt a closer approximation to the Real and produce the chains of signification that are primary in light of our knowledge of material reality with regard to fantasy.

Patriarchy is both an explanation and a justification of male domination. According to Humberto Maturana, two things happen when a particular discourse is accepted as explanation:

> (a) What we do is to propose a reformulation of a particular situation of our praxis of living, and,
>
> (b) our reformulation of our praxis of living is accepted by the listener as a reformulation of his or her praxis of living.[7]

The patriarchal praxis of living is substantially detached from *reality.* Feminists would have little difficulty in applying the terms "neurotic," "psychotic," and "pathological" to the patriarchal praxis. While many would be deeply troubled by much of traditional psychoanalytic theory, few feminists would dispute the distinction between material and psychic reality while viewing male domination and the ideology of patriarchy as psychic reality. Nor should an analysis of "normalcy," which is almost universally patriarchal, give rise to any serious intellectual predicaments for the feminist. An analysis of human knowledge in terms of fantasy ought therefore to be an ideal focal point for the discourses of psychoanalysis, postmodernism, and feminism. Patriarchy, as a product of primary thinking, is privileged in the registers of the Imaginary and the Symbolic. Consequently, feminism is a product of secondary thinking. Feminism must therefore establish its foundations in the registers of the Imaginary and the Symbolic. Moreover, these foundations must be established in terms of a metaphorical relation to the Real in the constructions and conceptualizations that we classify as material reality, in contrast to fantasy. The distinction between material reality and fantasy does not leave feminism in an essentialist position so long as it is recognized that the distinction is within registers of the Imaginary and the Symbolic—in terms of a contrast between primary and privileged signifiers and chains of signification. The distinction between a primary and privileged signification must be measured in terms of a relationship with the Real.

Bénassy and Diatkine argue that "Fantasy is built up by the organism in its constant relationship with the environment. It is learned, built up of inherited physical structures, individual acquisitions. It is constructed of memories of perceptions and memories of fantasies" to which language gives structure and a social dimension.[8] Thus, "fantasy is a human way of fitting organism to environment."[9] Reality, as Lagache reminds us, "is ambiguous; its opposition to fantasy is not radical," and "the same ambiguity is found in the reality principle—which is basic both to objective knowledge and to the well-known misrepresentations of defense mechanisms."[10] "The history of science," he states, "itself shows how deeply the most archaic fantasies have permeated the search for truth: the scientific outlook is the result of a slow process of elimination of fantasy."[11] He goes on to say that "reality is not only a fantasy about the other, but is also largely the fantasy of the other. The sense of reality is inculcated as a maxim of morality: we often explain to someone that he is taking his desires, hence his fantasies, to be reality. In every field, up to and including scientific research, objectivity is taken as a moral value and a moral rule. There would be a gain in clarity if we spoke, not of real or external objects, but of independent objects, that is to say, of entities independent of fantasy."[12] He concludes that "The triad, fantasy, reality, and truth, is taken to be the basis of human existence, of science, and of psychoanalysis. Reason is not entirely absent from the fantasy system, or reason would find nothing to lay hold of."[13]

Fantasy

Fantasy has been a central concern of psychoanalysis from its inception (FO, 5). Early in the development of psychoanalytic theory, Freud was perplexed as he more and more came to recognize "the low valuation of reality" and "the neglect of the distinction between it and phantasy" (SE, VI, 368). He later states that "The phantasies possess psychical as contrasted with *material* reality, and we gradually learn to understand that *in the world of the neuroses it is psychic reality which is the decisive kind*" (SE, XVI, 368). Jean Laplanche and Jean-Bertrand Pontalis go so far as to assert that "An explanation of the stability, efficacy and relatively coherent nature of the subject's phantasy life is precisely the goal to which Freud's efforts and the efforts of psycho-analytic thought as a whole, are directed" (LP, 314). and that "In point of fact, psycho-analysis endows the phantasy world from the very start with the coherence, organization and efficacy which as clearly implied, for example, by the term 'psychical reality' " (LP, 332). Hanna Segal suggests that "[T]hinking is a modification of unconscious fantasy . . . brought about by reality testing"[14] and that "The richness, depth, and accuracy of a person's thinking will depend on the quality and malleability of unconscious fantasy life and the capacity to subject it to reality testing."[15] According to Segal, the very origin of thought "lies in this process of testing fantasy against reality; that is, that thought is not only contrasted with fantasy, but based on it and derived from it."[16] She explains that "it would be naive to think that the infant learns reality thinking by discarding his fantasies. On the contrary, the infant approaches reality armed, as it were, with expectations formed by his unconscious fantasy. By testing them in reality, he gradually learns which are applicable and which modes of his own functioning enable him to deal with reality."[17] Just as fantasy and material reality merge in psychic reality, so fantasy and the recollection of actual events merge in memory. In fact, according to Freud, the activities of *phantasy* carry more weight in neurosis than does external reality, since on the phenomenological level there is no intrinsic evidence that could distinguish perception memory and fantasy memory (SE, XVIII, 244).[18]

Fantasy is governed by the pleasure principle. Freud explains:

> In the theory of psycho-analysis we have no hesitation in assuming that the course taken by mental events is automatically regulated by the pleasure principle. We believe, that is to say, that the course of those events is invariably set in motion by

an unpleasurable tension, and that it takes a direction such that its final outcome coincides with a lowering of that tension—that is, with an avoidance of unpleasure or a production of pleasure. In taking that course into account in our consideration of the mental processes which are the subject of our study, we are introducing an "economic" point of view into our work. (SE, XVIII, 7)

In *The Two Principles of Mental Functioning,* Freud states that "With the introduction of the reality principle, one mode of thought-activity was split off; it was kept free from reality-testing and remained subordinated to the pleasure principle alone. This activity is *phantasying*" (SE, XII, 222). "[I]n the activity of phantasy," he states, "human beings continue to enjoy the freedom from external compulsion which they have long since renounced in reality" (SE, XVI, 372). The ideational representations of instincts are reflected in desires and fears, as we wish for pleasurable satisfactions and attempt to avoid unpleasure. "Phantasy has the closest of links with desire," and "desire has its origin and its prototype in the *experience of satisfaction*" (LP, 317). Lagache explains that "We postulate the existence of unconscious fantasies as indications of desires or fears that are not revealed as such; . . . There is, however, an indissoluble link between fantasy and desire: Aristotle's dictum . . . that there is no desire without fantasy, finds its counterpart in the psychoanalytic principle that there is no fantasy without desire—or without fear. Unconscious fantasy corresponds to the direction of the unconscious desire, to its goal and object."[19]

There is a distinction to be made between fantasies that function at the conscious level where the creator does not realize that it is fantasy, and the conscious function of fantasizing, the daydream in which "imagined satisfactions of ambitious, megalomanic, erotic wishes" can flourish free "from the assent of reality" (SE, XVI, 372). In the daydream, there is no requirement to limit the play of the pleasure principle by the reality principle.[20] When fantasy and material reality are merged within psychic reality, the reality principle places inhibitions on the free range of fantasy:

The first example of the pleasure-principle being inhibited in this way is a familiar one which occurs with regularity. We know that the pleasure-principle is proper to a *primary* method of working on the part of the mental apparatus, but that, from the point of view of the self-preservation of the organism among the difficulties of the external world it is from the very outset inefficient and even highly dangerous. Under the influence of the ego's instincts of self- preservation, the pleasure principle is replaced by the *reality-principle*. This latter principle does not abandon the intention of ultimately obtaining pleasure, but it nevertheless demands and carries into effect the postponement of satisfaction, the abandonment of a number of possibilities of gaining satisfaction and the temporary toleration of unpleasure as a step on the long indirect road to pleasure. (SE, XVIII, 10)

Unconscious Fantasy

To understand the function of unconscious fantasy, two important properties must be kept in mind. The first is timelessness. According to Freud, "We have learnt that unconscious mental processes are in themselves 'time-less.' This means in the first place that they are not ordered temporally, that time does not change them in any way and that the idea of time cannot be applied to them" (SE, XVIII, 28). If this is so, then the unconscious is not transformed via time-linear progression from a pre-Oedipal, through the Oedipal, to the post-Oedipal state. Change is in terms of addition. In the unconscious, pre-Oedipal structure and content coexists with the Oedipal and post-Oedipal. The pre-Oedipal unconscious fantasy structures remain powerfully in force and affect consciousness and behavior throughout an individual's life.

The second property is that the unconscious knows no contradiction or negation. Freud wrote that

The nucleus of the *Ucs* consists of instinctual representatives which seek to discharge their cathexis; that is to say, it consists of wishful impulses. These instinctual impulses are co-ordinate with one another, exist side by side without being influenced by one another, and are exempt from mutual contradiction. When two wishful impulses whose aims must appear to us incompatible become simultaneously active, the two impulses do not diminish each other or cancel each other out, but combine to form an intermediate aim, a compromise.

There is in this system no negation, no doubt, no degrees of certainty: all this is only introduced by the work of the censorship between the *Ucs* and the *Pcs.* Negation is a substitute, at a higher level, for repression. In the *Ucs* there are only contents, cathected with greater or lesser strength. (SE, XIV, 186)

Since unconscious fantasies neither negate nor contradict each other, they remain fully and powerfully in force without being weakened or diluted. At the unconscious level, sexual, Eros, ego, self-preservation, and death instincts coexist, converge, diverge, reverse, and conflate, without diminishing their independent force. Even at the level of consciousness, where negation and contradiction are manifest, their force remains powerful and dynamic since they are less likely to be processed in terms of rationality and logic. Much of human contradiction can be traced to the influence of primary instincts as manifested through pre-Oedipal, Oedipal, and post-Oedipal unconscious fantasy structures.[21]

Unconscious fantasy can profoundly affect and shape psychic reality in the forms of desires, wishes, actions, symbols, images, dreams, play, and artistic creation.[22] Fantasy, is a "unique *focal point* where it is possible to observe the process of *transition* between the different psychical systems *in vitro*—to observe the mechanism of repression or of the return of the repressed in action" (LP, 316). The convergence of daydreams, fantasy material that the individual is not conscious of as fantasy, and unconscious fantasy is most striking where the content of the fantasy is sexual. Sexual fantasies such as those induced by pornography, for example, affect male beliefs as to the nature of reality,[23] and sexual psychic reality is saturated with unconscious fantasy. Why this is the case is made clear by Freud when he tells us that "The pleasure-principle long persists . . . as the method of working employed by the sexual instincts, which are hard to 'educate' and, starting from those instincts, or in the ego itself, it often succeeds in overcoming the reality-principle, to the detriment of the organism as a whole (SE, XVIII, 10).

The existence and configuration of unconscious fantasy, of course, can only be established by inference from the structure of conscious fantasy such as daydreams, the content of collective fantasies in the conscious such as myths, and from other forms of psychoanalytical evidence.[24] Susan Isaacs went so far as to assert and defend the proposition that fantasy is "the primary content of unconscious mental processes" and that everything that happens in the unconscious unfolds within the framework of fantasy.[25] According to Lagache, "Psychoanalytical investigation cannot dispense with the concept of unconscious fantasy; . . . every psycho-analytical interpretation and construct involves unconscious fantasy" and "unconscious fantasy is included in the reactivation of memory by desire."[26]

Fantasy is the "human way of fitting organism to environment,"[27] and the process of fantasy construction commences in very early infancy as the psyche develops in relationship to the infant's body and that of the mother.[28] According to Hook, "The earliest phantasies are about bodies and represent instinctual aims towards objects, serving from the beginning as a defense against tension and anxiety."[29] "The mental representative of an instinct," he further states, "is a phantasy, and the operation of an instinct is represented by a phantasy of the satisfaction of that instinct by its appropriate object. The earliest object is the breast or nipple."[30] Freud speaks of "instinctual stimuli" that arise from within the organism itself rather than from the outside (SE, XIV, 118). He refers to them as "needs" that can only be satisfied by "an appropriate (adequate) alteration of the internal source of stimulation" (SE, XIV, 119). Freud further describes an instinct as "a concept on the frontier between the mental and the somatic, as the psychical representative of the stimuli originating from within the organism and reaching the mind, as a measure of the demand made upon the mind in consequence of its connection with the body" (SE, XIV, 121–22).

Freud makes clear that while one may speak of an unconscious or a repressed instinctual impulse, "We can only mean an instinctual impulse the ideational representative of which is unconscious, for nothing else comes into consideration" (SE, XIV, 177). He describes that "One of the vicissitudes an instinctual impulse may undergo is to meet with resistances which seek to make it inoperative. Under certain conditions . . . the impulse then passes into the state of 'repression' " (SE, XIV, 146). The essence of repression, he states, *"lies simply in turning something away, and keeping it at a distance, from the conscious"* (SE, XIV, 147). The first phase of repression is what Freud termed "primal repression," which is constituted by a denial of entry into consciousness of the ideational representation of the instinct. The second phase, "repression proper," constitutes the denial of the mental derivatives of the repressed representation of the instinct. Repression creates substitute formations and symptoms that indicate a return of the repressed material into consciousness in a variety of different forms (SE, XIV, 154). The "damming-up consequent on frustrated satisfaction" results in an unchecked and "uninhibited development in phantasy." "If these derivatives," Freud states, "have become sufficiently far removed from the repressed representative, whether owing to the adoption of distortions or by reason of the number of intermediate links inserted, they have free access to consciousness" (SE, XIV, 149). Thus, the "end products of the unconscious fantasy are the conscious fictions of thought and action,"[31] which one is not aware of as fantasy, even though the material of the fantasy is in consciousness.

Repression and defense mechanisms serve to protect the fragile ego from the frustrations of unfulfilled desire and fear. Most, if not all, fantasies take the form of explanation, and explanations are often fantasies or a mixture of fantasy and reality. The explanatory function of fantasy as ego defense is implicit in the role that fantasy plays in comforting the ego. It justifies Freud's conclusion that fantasy is more significant than the memory of an actual historical event for the subsequent course of mental development, and carries more weight in neurosis than does external reality.

Anna Freud clarified the role played by fantasy as an ego defense.[32] Susan Isaacs stresses that the defense mechanisms function in terms of unconscious fantasy.[33] She defines fantasy "as the primary content of unconscious mental processes."[34] Laplanche and Pontalis point out that "phantasy is also the locus of defensive operations" (LP, 318). Segal, while pointing out the widely recognized role of fantasy as a defense mechanism, suggests that, at first glance, the role of fantasy as "a flight from reality and a defense against frustration" seems contradictory to the concept of fantasy as an expression of instinct. She suggests, however, that the contradiction is more apparent than real "since fantasy aims at fulfilling instinctual striving in the absence of reality satisfaction" and that "that function in itself is a defense against reality."[35] Given that (a) "everything that happens in the unconscious happens in terms of phantasy" and "defense mechanisms operate on and modify phantasies,"[36] (b) that fantasy is rooted in instinct; and (c) further that instincts link the mental and the physical (SE, XIV, 123), we can only conclude with Freud that the mental and the biological can never be entirely separated. "Man is not a being different from animals or superior to them; he himself is of animal descent, being more closely related to some species and more distantly to others" (SE, XVII, 141). At the same time we must never lose sight of Lacan's transformation of Freudian psychoanalytic theory into a theory of human cognition. We can trace the roots of unconscious fantasy from the primal drives through their proliferations in the form of substitute formations, which return into consciousness in a variety of derivative forms, such as reversal into the opposite, negation, projection, introjection, condensation (where elements of two or more fantasies combine to form a third), and displacement ("where cathetic energy attaching to one phantasy is transferred to another so that the second stands in place of the first in the distribution of energy cathexes").[37]

Psychic reality consists of the ideational representations that our material bodies will neither permit us to repress or deny, and the fantasy structures that, within the limits of material reality, are possible even if not reasonable. These are integrated into an explanatory mythic structure. It is the inconsistencies between the two that are the bedrock of neuroses, and, as Freud states, *"in the world of the neuroses it is psychic reality which is the decisive kind"* (SE, XVI, 368). The distinction between the "I" and the "not-I" is essential for consciousness and the formation of the ego, fundamental to the concept of the body, a precondition of the concept of reality, and indispensable for language and most of its functions. "The form of fantasy," as Bénassy and Diatkine have argued, "depends upon the level of ego-organization."[38] They define ego as "the system of integrated action of the human organism in its environment, fantasy being an essential element in the system"[39] and give the following explanations of the ego in its relationship to fantasy:

> (a) The ego is an experience, and it is experienced as integrated. Thus we can speak of ego feelings and ego boundaries. . . .
> (b) This ego-experience has psychophysiological, that is physico-chemical correlations. . . . It has no meaning to describe correlations between a concept and physico-chemical events. It has meaning to describe them between an experience and events in the brain. We can speak of an integrated interplay between different nervous functional systems. . . .
> (c) The ego has a history, and its development can be described in terms of successive levels of integration, each one being considered from the phenomenological as well as from the physico-chemical point of view (or language). . . .
> (d) The ego is the field in which conflicts are expressed. Any conflict can be described as the conflict of different patterns of integration, on the phenomenological and/or the physico-chemical level.
> (e) The object relationship can be a description of the ego. It can be considered as the experienced integration of the movement from subject to object and back, or as the physico-chemical integration of the movement from subject to object and back. . . . If we add that pleasure is integrating and unpleasure disintegrating we see how easy it is to consider the ego in the object relationship as experiencing a *dialectical* relationship to the world.[40]

They conclude that, "We see now why it is so easy to connect fantasy to ego as well as to instincts, when we deal with ego and instincts in this way."[41]

Fantasy and Myth

Each ego is constructed within the framework of psychic reality. The psychic reality of each individual is the product of the ego confronting the material reality of the external world and, in the process, constructing fantasy configurations that defend the ego against the pain that is the inevitable product of consciousness. It represses the content that cannot be integrated into the fantasy structures of conscious psychic reality. Much of what goes on in each sentient individual is a part of a collective process. Indeed, the concept of the group or collective psyche or mind is fundamental to psychoanalytic social theory.[42] To the degree that humans make up a single species having a common biological structure, and to the degree that humans share languages, histories, and cultures, they will share psychic realities. To the degree that they share psychic realities, they will share fantasy structures and collective defense mechanisms. The very structure of each ego will contain elements that will furnish a configuration of self or identity in terms of shared factors such as gender, race, nationality, tribe, and family. Each shared identity is formulated within conscious fantasy structures: history, religion, morality, and law.

Myths are the fantasies of the collective. To the degree that people have similar instincts, desires, and fears, they will develop similar fantasy structures, which will serve as collective defense mechanisms. "The work of the myth, like the dream work," Hook states, "is to turn these phantasies into a form acceptable to the ego; like the dream, the manifest content of the myth is made up of elements drawn from the daily life and experience of the people, as well as from material generally regarded as suitable for myth-making."[43] Devereux, in describing the defensive functions of myth, states that "culture in providing myths or beliefs for the cold storage of certain fantasies and insights, keeps them out of 'private circulation' " and "provides a set of standard defenses against, and solutions for 'type conflicts' characteristic of a given cultural milieu."[44]

Like myth, symbols play an important role in psychoanalytic theory, particularly in the analysis of dreams. Hook points out that "These (time and space) are also the mechanisms by means of which symbols are formed and we may expect to find a close relationship between the study of symbolization and symbolic thinking and an understanding of primary process."[45] Symbol, myth, and ritual share the function of "the binding and discharge of psychical energy."[46] Collective fantasies, myths, rituals, and symbols share an underlying fantasy structure. Hook concludes that

> What the psychoanalyst finds when he studies the reports of ethnographers is that the material "rings true" in terms of observations made in the psychoanalysis of individuals. That is to say, on the level of primary process the psychoanalyst's

observations made within the framework of Western society correspond with observations made on material from other cultures widely dispersed in time and space. . . .

The elucidation of the psychoanalytic meaning of cultural products such as myths, depends upon the existence of primitive phantasies and a "psychic apparatus" common to all men—both of which it has been the achievement of psychoanalysis to investigate and clarify. Myths and legends, of which the classical example is *Oedipus Rex,* have furnished psychoanalysis with some of its most fecund material.[47]

The Original Fantasy

Given that the aetiology of fantasy lies in the instincts or drives, and given that Freud identifies what he terms "primal instincts," we would expect that something equivalent to primal fantasies would also be recognized by Freud as fundamental. He introduced the concept of primal fantasy as the *Urphantasien,* the primal or original fantasy. According to Freud, original fantasies ("the observation of sexual intercourse between the parents, of seduction, of castration, and others") constitute the store of unconscious fantasies "of all neurotics, and probably of all human beings" (SE, XIV, 269). In response to Freud's assertion, Laplanche and Pontalis state: "These words alone suggest that it is not solely the empirical fact of frequency, nor even generality, which characterizes them. If 'the same fantasies with the same content are created on every occasion' [SE, XVI, 370], if, beneath the diversity of individual fables we can recover some 'typical' fantasies, it is because the historical life of the subject is not the prime mover, but rather something antecedent, which is capable of operating as an organizer" (FO, 17).

Freud's only explanation for this antecedent feature was that of phylogenesis, which would locate it in some "mythical prehistory of the species" (FO, 17).[48] The foundation of that which is capable of operating as an organizer, they say, must be sought, "in something which transcends both individual experience and what is imagined." "[T]he discovery of the unconscious as a structural field, which can be reconstructed . . . according to certain laws . . . permit the quest for origins to take on a new dimension" (FO, 16). Laplanche and Pontalis are at pains to point out, however, that the phylogenic explanation ought not to be replaced by a structural one. They state that "The original fantasy is first and foremost fantasy—

 it lies beyond the history of the subject but nevertheless in history—a kind of language and a symbolic sequence, but loaded with elements of imagination; a structure, but activated by contingent elements. As such it is characterized by certain traits which make it difficult to assimilate to a purely transcendental scheme, even it provides the possibility of experience" (FO, 18). The structure of the primal or original fantasy in the unconscious must be differentiated from the version of the fantasy as it is manifested in consciousness. Freud found that the conscious manifestation of the primal fantasy or fantasies generally took a specific set of forms. He tells us that "Among the occurrences which recur again and again in the youthful history of neurotics—which are scarcely ever absent—there are a few of particular importance, which also deserve on that account, I think, to be brought into greater prominence than the rest. As specimens of this class I will enumerate these: observation of parental intercourse, seduction by an adult and threat of being castrated. It would be a mistake to suppose that they are never characterized by material reality; on the contrary, this is often established incontestably through inquiries from older members of the patient's family" (SE, XVI, 368–69). Freud calls the scene of parental coitus "the primal scene" (LP, 331).

In place of Freud's phylogenetic explanation, Laplanche and Pontalis explain original or primal fantasies in terms of a "prestructure which is actualized and transmitted by the parental fantasies" (FO, 27). Most children contemplate the sexual relationships of their parents. Young children who actually do witness their parents in intercourse will have that image fixed in their minds, and children who don't will project their later conceptions of intercourse back onto their parents, as a part of their understanding of who and what they are. The primal scene is an evolving fantasy structure which changes with the sexual development of the child. The image of the coming together of opposites, of a penetrating male, and a receptive female permeates Oedipalized relationships. It is an image of a man on top of a woman.

Whether real or fantasized, scenes of parental intercourse, seduction by an adult, and threats of castration are specific content that reflect an underlying structure:

> If we consider the themes which can be recognized in primal phantasies (primal scene, castration, seduction), the striking thing is that they have one trait in common: they are all related to the origins. Like collective myths, they claim to provide a representation of and a "solution" to whatever constitutes a major

enigma for the child. Whatever appears to the subject as a reality of such a type as to require an explanation or "theory" these phantasies dramatise into the primal moment or original point of departure of a history. In the "primal scene," it is the origin of the subject that is represented; in seduction phantasies, it is the origin or emergence of sexuality; in castration phantasies, the origin of the distinction between the sexes. (LP, 332; FO, 19)

The primal fantasy is essential to the development of the ego in that it provides an explanation and therefore a meaning for the "I"-Subject-self. There can be no theory of origins without explanation, and no explanation without meaning. Bénassy and Diatkine write, "As Jones (1958) said of Freud, 'For him a question of meaning usually became at once the question of origin.' This feeling of time, or history, or evolution, whatever you choose to call it, was so strong in Freud that we could say it is the hallmark of his way of thinking."[49] A theory of the self or the "I" must not only contain an explanation of the origin of the individual but must also account for or explain the body and its relationship to the external environment. It must, therefore, explain origin. An explanation of origin must incorporate difference. Difference entails limitation and the recognition of limitation is to suffer a loss. The structure of original fantasies, therefore, is that of origin, difference, and limitation or loss.

Laplanche writes that "To be sure, the necessity of *affirming the primal or originary*, both in the form of the 'individual myth' and in historical or prehistorical myth, may be identified as one of the fundamental, founding orientations of Freud's thought" (L&D, 123). The child's questions: Who am I? What am I? Am I a female or a male? Am I or am I not someone capable of procreating? are its quest for origins and the structure of unconscious fantasy. Lacan explains:

There is nevertheless one thing that evades the symbolic tapestry, it's procreation in its essential root—that one being is born from another. In the symbolic order procreation is covered by the order instituted by this succession between beings. But nothing in the symbolic explains the fact of their individuation, the fact that beings come from beings. The entire symbolism declares that creatures don't engender creatures, that a creature is unthinkable without a fundamental creation. In the symbolic nothing explains creation.

Nor does anything explain why some beings must die for others to be born. There is an essential relationship between sexual reproduction and the appearance of death, the biologists say, and if this is true then it shows that they, too, mull over the same question. The question of what links two beings in the appearance of life only arises for a subject when he or she is in the symbolic, realized as a man or as a woman, but so long as an accident has prevented him or her form acceding to it. This may just as easily occur to anyone by virtue of his or her biographical accidents.

Freud raises these same issues in the background of *Beyond the Pleasure Principle.* Just as life reproduces itself, so it's forced to repeat the same cycle, rejoining the common aim of death. For Freud this reflects his experience. Each neurosis reproduces a particular cycle in the order of the signifier on the basis of the question that man's relationship to the signifier as such raises.

There is, in effect, something radically unassimilable to the signifier. It's quite simply the subject's singular existence. Why is he here? Where has he come from? What is he doing here? Why is he going to disappear? The signifier is incapable of providing him with the answer, for the good reason that it places him beyond death. The signifier already considers him dead, by nature it immortalizes him.

As such, the question of death is another mode of the neurotic creation of the question—its obsessional mode. (S III, 179–80)

Freud noticed that "A child's intellectual interest in the riddles of sex, his desire for sexual knowledge, shows itself accordingly at an unexpectedly early age" (SE, IX, 134). He states that "At about the same time as the sexual life of children reaches its first peak, between the ages of three and five, they also begin to show signs of the activity which may be ascribed to the instinct for knowledge. . . . [T]he first problem with which it deals is the riddle of where babies come from" (SE, VII, 194–95). It is the oldest and most burning question that confronts immature humanity" (SE, IX, 135). The question of where do babies come from is a way of asking "Where do I come from?" The child seeks an explanation of its origin in order to gain a sense of self or identity. "This [the question where babies come from], in a distorted form which can easily be rectified, is the same riddle that was propounded by the Theban Sphinx" (SE, VII, 194–95). In this, "the first, grand problem of life . . . we seem to hear the echoes of this first riddle in innumerable riddles of myth and legend" (SE, IX, 213). The sexual theories of children as symbolic creations in response to the neurotic compulsions of the emerging ego "reply to the same necessities as do myths" (E, 168)—the demand for an explanation of origin as essential for a conceptualization of the ego.

The question of origin for the child cannot be separated from that of its relationship to its mother, even when the content of a primal or original fantasy of a particular child is that of the primal scene. The primal fantasy, therefore, will be rooted in separation and engulfment anxiety, the narcissistic wound as a result of the loss of the state of primal omnipotence and narcissistic bliss, and infant sexuality in relationship to the mother. Every child is born of a mother and sooner or later becomes consciously aware of this fact. According to Freud, it is in relation to the mother who the child first experiences difference; it is the mother who first awakens sexual desire in the infant; and it is in relation to the mother that the child first experiences the desire for, or fear of, castration. The Oedipus complex of the male child reflects a desire for (re)union with the mother, in which the desire to recover the state of narcissistic bliss by (re)uniting the self in the mother converges with the erotic feelings of emerging sexuality. The male child wishes to give himself, with his penis, to the mother, which is to say that the child wishes to become a gift of the phallus to the mother. He shall be the phallus at the disposal of the mother. The price of the gift, however, is the surrender of the self. Laplanche and Pontalis explain that "If we add that Freud constantly insisted on the seductive role of the mother (or of others, when she washes, dresses or caresses her child) [SE, VII, 223], and if we note also that the naturally erogenous zones (oral, anal, uro-genital, skin), are not only those which most attract the mother's attention, but also those which have an obvious exchange value (orifices or skin covering) we can understand how certain chosen parts of the body may not only serve to sustain a local pleasure, but also be a meeting place with maternal desire and fantasy, and thus with one form of original fantasy. . . . By locating the origin of fantasy in the auto-eroticism, we have shown the connection between fantasy and desire" (FO, 26).

Each individual passes through three crises: separation, in which the individual suffers the loss of narcissistic bliss and omnipotence as the psyche of the infant begins to differentiate between itself and the mother (which in turn produces the dialectical conflict of separation and engulfment anxiety); genderization, wherein the self is conceptualized as masculine or feminine; and the animality crisis, wherein the self internalizes or incorporates the limitations of its mind and body. These three crises mark the three stages of individuation: the pre-Oedipal, Oedipal, and post-Oedipal.[50] At every stage of development, the individual will have a theory of its self directed toward birth, sexuality, and death—all of which will reflect the fundamental structure of original fantasy—origin, difference-sexuality, and limitation-castration. Birth is origin; sex is differentiated in terms of gender and death in terms of ultimate castration. Freud conceived of the fear of death as "a development of the fear of castration" (SE, XIX, 58).

The Oedipal passage connotes a shift to a secondary primal fantasy, the Father Fantasy. The father owns the mother and, by owning her, owns her child. Origin is in the name of the father, and the penis becomes the source of life. The return to the mother is forbidden, and the desire to make the gift of the phallus becomes the roots of the fear of castration. The Father Primal Fantasy does not replace the Mother Primal Fantasy. Both coexist in the unconscious, though only the content of the Father Primal Fantasy maintains itself in consciousness.

Though the primal scene may focus on parental intercourse, the primal fantasy, of which the primal scene is a part, does not. It includes the child's view of growing inside the mother and being born. Children ask questions about where they come from. It is their origin that is of primary concern. It is only later that the primal scene is woven into the primal fantasy, which is whatever the child believes its origins to be. The child's primal fantasy, when it includes an image, real or imaginary, of the primal scene, and the child's birth continue to be an ongoing conjunction of opposites, of hierarchies—a father on top and a mother, who is the source of life and nourishment, on bottom.

Original Fantasies of the Collective

The original fantasy of the collective, by which we form our sense of self, will have two forms: primary and privileged. Each will contain a fundamental or master signifier to which all others in the chain of signification will relate. The master signifier will get its meaning from, and give meaning to, the other signifiers in the chain. The primary original fantasy will more closely conform to material reality, and the privileged will more closely conform to the neurotic structure of the symptoms.

The primary and privileged forms of the original fantasy are dialectically related in that they furnish alternative interpretations of the signified. Because the privileged original fantasy and its signifiers are derived from primary fantasy and the privileged original fantasy is privileged as the standard in language, the two forms of original fantasy will reflect the dialectical tensions existing between the sexual and ego drives or the Eros and Thanatos drives. The primary form of original fantasy will reflect primary neuroses, and the privileged will reflect the form of the neurotic symptoms of ego defense such as reversal, negation, and sublimation. The privileged form of the original fantasy will be the norm, and the repressed primary form will be the perverse. Thus, normality is a form of madness when the primary is repressed and the secondary is privileged. It is in this way that we can comprehend Lacan's view that the symptoms are truly structured in language. Original fantasy is the unifying explanation combining and underlying all of the fundamental dialectics or dichotomies of language—contrasts, metaphorical comparisons, and metonymical identities such as male/female, man/nature, body/soul, human/animal, and womb/phallus.

If Lacan is correct in his assertion that the unconscious is structured like a language, then it is very likely that the unconscious is structured ideationally. Conversely, if the instincts are represented in the unconscious ideationally, as is asserted by Freud, then it must follow that the unconscious is structured like a language, and the content of the original fantasies will be ideational representations of separation and engulfment anxieties and fears and the emerging sexual "instincts." According to Hook, "Elementary phantasies are not lost but persist and undergo transformation into complex phantasies which may be taken over by the secondary process and built into such complicated constructions as models or pictures of world order . . . and other culturally important derivatives."[51] As the child develops, the content of original fantasies, as they are manifested in consciousness, will transform as the nature of the fears and desires are modified by the contingencies of living. The underlying structure will still remain: origin-difference or seduction-loss, limitation or castration. The ideational structure of "mother" and "father" will incorporate the ideational structure of the parentally based primal or original fantasies of the collective. These fantasies of the individual will incorporate mythic structures of origin, seduction, and castration.

Languaging also serves an explanatory function that is generally used to give meaning to differentiations and often takes the form of a narrative. The foundational explanation of human cognitive life is the grand story or narrative that explains who and what we are in relation to that which we are not and explains what "that which is not the self" actually is. The structure of such explanations inevitably accounts for origins, differences, and the limitations that being a self entail. The narrative of explanation commences with descriptive differentiations between the processes that we call birth, copulation, and death. Metaphorically, or in fantasy, they are given meaning in terms of origin, seduction, and castration. Fantasy structures are represented in terms of symbols and metaphors that are woven into narratives. A people's view of themselves as a collective is formulated out of the structure of the primal parental fantasies and is saturated with symbols and metaphors drawn from the primal fantasies of the individual. Symbols of mother, father, sister, brother, daughter, son, birth, death, breast, womb, and penis permeate human mythic structures, and themes of creation, seduction, and castration infuse their narratives.

These collective primal or original fantasies are representations of collective instincts, collective projections functioning as collective defense mechanisms. Even in contemporary societies, our grand theories or explanations of the world, the cosmos, and our place within it are the product of "primary process thinking," only somewhat limited by harsh reality. We still conceptualize in terms of mother nature, mother earth, the fatherland, and brotherhood; the Eternal Father is still in His heaven, and we still conquer and tame nature and view ourselves as the pinnacle of a progressive evolutionary process. As Hook states, "The primary units of thinking are phantasies, simple or complex, and the basic operation of the primary process is their manipulation by symbolization, one coming to stand in the place of another in an endless series. This is the basis of Ernest Jones' statement that civilization is the result of an endless process of symbolic substitutions, whilst Melanie Klein saw in symbolization the process by means of which the infant apprehends reality and endows it with value."[52]

The sexual and ego instincts exist "side by side" in the unconscious, without negation or contradiction and without one deleting the instinctual force of the other. They both will be represented as primal fantasies having the unconscious psychic reality structured as origin-seduction-castration, whether as unconscious fantasy or as conscious fantasy not recognized as fantasy. In consciousness, the Eros instinctual fantasy will contradict the ego instinctual fantasy. There will be a dialectical tension, one which is nonexistent at the unconscious level.

In the primal fantasy, the sexual instinct will be shaped by material reality. The ego will differentiate between life and that which is not-life, and the distinction will be based on reproduction. The classification will be given a hierarchical ordering, with life being more highly valued than not-life. A further fundamental distinction will be drawn between the female and male in terms of that which can reproduce and that which cannot, that which is primary in the process of reproduction and that which is secondary. For the reproduction narrative, the female will be given a more prominent position than will the male insofar as she is primary and he secondary. The process by which the male will be sexually aroused and driven to copulate with the female will be explained within the fantasy narrative as a seduction that produces the erotically driven desire to surrender his phallus to the female or to place it at her service. The desire of the male will be to fulfill the desire of the female. At the level of conscious fantasy the life of the individual will be given meaning by flowing alongside or following the path of nature or Eros. Children will be highly valued. Females will sacrifice for children and males for females.

The ego instinct or drive, although having the primal origin-seduction-castration structure of unconscious wish and fantasy, will manifest itself in a very different and contradictory narrative at the level of conscious fantasy. Origin will be explained in terms of male "creation." The sexual dependency of the male on the female will be felt and feared as a threat to the ego.[53] Copulation will be seen as a loss, a giving up of something—a threat to the boundaries of the ego. The female will be viewed as castrated so that she can be objectified and therefore "fucked" without a surrender. The erotic desire for castration will be replaced by a fear of the castrating female in the ego instinctual primal fantasy. The meaning of life will be found in rebelling against and transcending nature.

There is overwhelming symbolic and mythic evidence, as reflected in artifacts and ancient texts from around the world, that for thousands of years a primal fantasy having a common structure of origin-seduction-castration has permeated the collective psyche. This is a collective projection of the unconscious original fantasy. The central figures of the narrative are the Mother Goddess and the Consort Son or Lover who fertilizes her. The symbols are wombs, breasts, and penises—the phallic representations of the reproductive organs. The narratives have a common script. The Consort is seduced into surrendering his phallus as a voluntary sacrifice to the Mother. The seduction entails a castration. The castration is the gift of the phallus to the Mother. One of the most common symbols of the male phallus is the serpent. The serpent is generally in the Goddess's possession; she holds it in her hand, has it wrapped around her waist, or has serpents as hair as in the case of the Medusa. The gift of the phallus was ritualized in terms of the sacrifice of the sacred king—a male animal substitute—or ritual castration. The Lord-Consort to the Mother Goddess was the god of the loss of boundaries of the self, as in Dionysus or Shiva, for in the final analysis the surrender of his phallus to the Mother entails the sacrifice of his ego. These myths in turn are the source of sets of secondary myths that focus on single themes such as seduction or castration.

For the last several thousand years, the primal myth of the collective remained mostly in the unconscious. Consider for a moment the proliferation of museum artifacts: the rock carving goddess of Laussel, circa 22,000–18,000 B.C.; the mammoth ivory goddess of Lespugue, 20,000–18,000 B.C.; the mammoth ivory head of a goddess circa 22,000 B.C., found at Brassempouy, Landes, France; the magnificent goddess of Willendorf, circa 20,000–18,000 B.C.; the clay goddess, 20,000 B.C., found at Dolni, Vestonice, Czechoslovakia; the mammoth ivory goddess figure, circa 16,000–13,000 B.C., found at Mal'ta, Siberia; the powerful Mother Goddess figure seated on a thrown between two lions or leopards, circa 6000–5,800 B.C., found at Catal Huyuk, Anatolia; the many goddess figurines found at Malta; and the serpent-holding Minoan goddesses of Crete—to name but a few. Compare these with the amount of attention they have received in academia, whether the subject area is history, religion, literature, anthropology, archeology, the classics, law, or philosophy. Surely this reflects a collective repression.

The list of goddesses and their son lovers or consorts are many: Inanna and Dumuzi in Sumeria, Ishtar and Tammuz in Babylonia, Isis and Osiris in Egypt, Cybele and Attis in Anatolia, Aphrodite and Adonis in Greece, and Parvati and Shiva in India. Themes of seduction and the ritual of sacrifice-castration are prevalent in the fantasy structures of the ancient past. In modern times, the primal Eros fantasy manifests itself, on the one hand, in terms of a resurging interest in and an attempt to reproduce the rituals of matriarchal paganism and ancient fertility rites and, on the other hand, in terms of male erotic fantasies of domination by powerful females as well as masochistic, ritualistic sexual practices, well served by the pornography industry.

While the Eros primal fantasy is structured by material reality, the ego primal fantasy is in direct contradiction to material reality and serves as a defense mechanism against it, particularly for the male. The ego instinctual primal fantasy is a paradigm example of what Segal describes as fantasy aimed at "fulfilling instinctual striving in the absence of reality satisfaction" and thus functions as a defense against reality.[54] Some of the most common forms that defense mechanisms take are those such as "reversal into the opposite, negation and projection" (LP, 318). Since (a) the sexual and ego instincts are conceptually represented in fantasy in terms of the conceptual oppositional structure of life and death and (b) since the structure of the Eros fantasy is shaped in conformity with material reality—and the ego fantasy is a defense mechanism against material reality—it becomes clear why the primal ego fantasy is a reversal of, in opposition to, and a negation of the primal Eros fantasy.

The paradigm script of the narrative of the primal Eros fantasy is that of the Great Earth Mother Goddess who gives birth to life. She is projected onto the cosmos. Her Lover Son or Consort is seduced into voluntarily sacrificing himself in some form of symbolic castration whereby he is torn apart, dismembered, or ritually sacrificed to fertilize the earth and is again reborn, with the cycle ever repeating itself. The Judeo-Christian-Islamic tradition is the paradigm example of the primal ego fantasy, with Christianity as an almost reverse mirror image of the Eros primal fantasy. The Consort is replaced by the Father who is projected onto the cosmos. The Great Earth Mother Goddess is replaced by the Sky God Heavenly Father. Origin by reproduction is replaced by origin by creation through an action of pure thought—the exercise of the will:

> 1. In the beginning, God created the heaven and the earth.
> 2. And the earth was without form, and void; and darkness was upon the face of the deep, and the spirit of God moved upon the face of the waters.
> 3. And God said, Let there be light: and there was light.[55]

Freud describes the mythic process of creation by an act of will or the speaking of words "the omnipotence of thoughts" (SE, XIV, 75). Whereas metaphorical explanation of origin in terms of birth or the hatching of a cosmic egg is a fantasy representation of material reality, creation by mental projection is a denial of anything we know in material reality.

In the Eros primal fantasy, man is born of woman, whereas in the ego primal fantasy the man is created first and the woman is taken from him:

> 7. And the Lord God formed man of the dust of the ground and breathed into his nostrils the breath of life; and man became a living soul.
> 21. And the Lord God caused a deep sleep to fall upon Adam, and he slept: and he took one of his ribs, and closed up the flesh instead thereof.
> 22. And the rib, which the Lord God had taken from man, made he a woman, and brought her unto the man.
> 23. And Adam said, This is now bone of my bones, and flesh of my flesh: she shall be called Woman, because she was taken out of Man.[56]

And thus we have origin in terms of creation as opposed to reproduction. "The mother is no parent of that which is called her child, but only nurse of the new-planted seed that grows. The parent is he who mounts. A stranger she preserves a stranger's seed."[57]

In the Eros primal myth, the serpent is the symbol of the male phallus, which is given to the Mother as a sacrificial gift. The Mother is always in possession of the serpent, the symbolic representation of the male penis. Thus, the Consort is castrated in that his ego is sacrificed for the sake of ongoing life. The seduction is a positive act. The sacrifice is made sacred, and the sexual is, for the male, an erotically driven gift rather than the sexual satisfaction of the self. In the ego primal fantasy, the serpent is the cursed tempter, the seduction is evil, and the woman is castrated.

> 13. And the Lord God said unto the woman, What is this that thou hast done? And the woman said, The serpent beguiled me, and I did eat.
> 14. And the Lord God said unto the serpent, Because thou hast done this, thou art cursed above all cattle, and above every beast of the field; upon thy belly shalt thou go, and dust shalt thou eat all the days of thy life.
> 15. And I will put enmity between thee and the woman, and between thy seed and her seed; it shall bruise thy head, and thou shalt bruise his heel.
> 16. Unto the woman he said, I will greatly multiply thy sorrow and thy conception; in sorrow thou shalt bring forth children; and thy desire shall be to thy husband, and he shall rule over thee.[58]

Castration befalls the woman rather than the man, and the gift of the male phallus is forbidden. For the male to give the phallus, and for the female to accept it, is the original sin, the epitome of perversion, and the essence of rebellion against the Law of the Father. The sacred dying son is sacrificed to fulfill the will of the Father and is then resurrected. After this sacrifice, no male needs to renew the sacrifice. Pan or Dionysus, the Consort, dies when Christ mounts the cross. The horned Consort becomes the Christian devil, and the symbols of death prevail over life.

The Primary and Privileged Positioning of Jouissance

The *jouissances* of domination and submission manifest the structure of unconscious fantasy, which in turn is reflected in the structure of psychic reality and of the imaginary and the symbolic. Lacan states that

> We are faced with a world of language, which every now and then, gives us the impression that there is something essentially neutralizing, uncertain about it. There isn't one philosopher who hasn't insisted, and rightly so, on the fact that the

very possibility of error is tied to the existence of language. Each subject doesn't simply have to take cognizance of the world, as if it all happened on the level of noetics, he has to find his way about in it. If psychoanalysis means anything, it is that he is already engaged in something which has a relation with language without being identical to it, and that he has to find his way about in it—the universal discourse.

The concrete, universal discourse, which has been unfolding since the beginning of time, is what has truly been said or rather really been said—to fix our ideas, we can get to that point. The subject locates himself as such in relation to that, he is inscribed in it, that is how he is already determined, by a determination belonging to a totally different register from that of the determinations of the real, of the material metabolisms which caused him to come forth into this semblance of existence which his life. His function, in so far as he continues this discourse, is to rediscover his place in it, not simply as orator, but, here and now, as entirely determined by it. (S II, 282–83)

The capacity to procreate and the procreative powers of nature—the metaphorical relationship between the female body and the natural world—are essential to the primal fantasy. Only females reproduce, and it is this that has "given rise to the great fantasy of *natura mater,* the very idea of nature, in relation to which man portrays his original inadequacy to himself" (S I, 149). Very young children soon learn the facts of life—that they are born of mothers. "As to the child, there's not a shadow of doubt—whether male or female, it locates the phallus very early on and, we're told, generously grants it to the mother." (S III, 319). It is not the phallus specifically that the child grants to the mother, it is the generative power of nature—the power of origins—that the child recognizes in the mother, and the child wishes to be the object of the mother's desire. If the child learns that the mother needs something else to complete the generative power, the child wishes to furnish it or be it. It is the process of Oedipal genderization and sexualization that splits the generative power of nature from the mother and identifies it with the father when the penis becomes the phallus. Lacan points out that

Thus, to begin with, we can formulate more correctly the Kleinian fact that the child apprehends from the outset that the mother "contains" the phallus. But it is the dialectic of the demand for love and the test of desire which dictates the order of development.

The demand for love can only suffer from a desire whose signifier is alien to it. If the desire of the mother *is* the phallus, then the child wishes to be the phallus so as to satisfy this desire. Thus the division immanent to desire already makes itself felt in the desire of the Other, since it stops the subject from being satisfied with

> presenting to the Other anything real it might *have* which corresponds to the phallus—what he has being worth no more than what he does not have as far as his demand for love is concerned, which requires that he *be* the phallus. (FS, 83)

The primary fantasy is repressed by the privileged. Hence the dialectics. The primary fantasy is the truth in the lie of the privileged fantasy. It lies underneath and between the lines of the privileged. Whatever form a privileged fantasy may take, there will lie between the lines, and underneath the text, its dialectical opposition in the form of a primary fantasy. It is the privileged rather than the primary master signifier that structures language—hence culture, hence institutions, hence gender. "So the pact of speech goes far beyond the individual relation and its imaginary vicissitudes—there's no need to look very deep into experience to grasp it. But there is a conflict between this symbolic pact and the imaginary relations which proliferate spontaneously within every libidinal relation" (S II, 261).

A psychoanalytic postmodern feminism assumes that the female is primary and the male secondary, that the male has been and presently is privileged and the female repressed. Between the primary and the privileged the dynamics of domination and submission can go either way. The human develops his or her sense of self within the reversible dialectics of domination and suppression, within a dialectics of the primary and the privileged. Both primacy and privilege are determined by language and formulated within the structure of language. Both primary and privileged original fantasies share the same structure of unconscious psychic reality, of origin, difference, and limitation, that play out as the generative power of nature, seduction, and castration. Each fantasy is a chain of signification structured by a master signifier. In order for the privileged signifier to exist within the structure of language, the primary signifier had to come first. The relationship between the primary master signifier and the privileged master signifier is that of oppositional signification:

> [T]he notion of the coming of the day, is something that is properly speaking ungraspable in any reality. The opposition between day and night is a signifying opposition, which goes infinitely beyond all the meanings it may ultimately cover, indeed beyond every kind of meaning. If I took day and night as examples, it's of course because our subject is man and woman. The signifier *man* and the signifier *woman* are something other than a passive attitude and an active attitude, an aggressive attitude and a yielding attitude, something other than forms of behavior. There is undoubtedly a hidden signifier here which, of course, can nowhere be incarnated absolutely, but which is nevertheless the closest to being incarnated in the existence of the word *man* and the word *woman*. (S III, 198)

Aren't we astounded that philosophers didn't emphasize ages ago that human reality is irreducibly structured as signifying?

Day and night, man and woman, peace and war—I could enumerate more oppositions that don't emerge out of the real world but give it its framework, its axes, its structure, that organize it, that bring it about that there is in effect a reality for man, and that he can find his bearings therein. The notion of reality that we bring to bear in analysis presupposes this web, this mesh of signifiers. This isn't new. It's constantly being implied in analytic discourse, but is never isolated as such. This isn't necessarily a drawback, but it is one in, for example, what has been written on the psychoses. (S III, 199)

Freudian Oedipal theory, which privileges the father and the phallus, presupposes the primacy of the mother. "This is the part of Freud's work, of Freudian thought, that is often returned to in all the developments that are currently taking place on pre-oedipal relations, which ultimately consist in saying that the subject always seeks to satisfy the primitive maternal relation" (S III, 84–85). The dialectics between the primary and the privileged determines the pattern of repression that Freud explains in terms of the ego confronting a material reality that it finds to be threatening or painful. This is the primary. The ego defends itself by denying, negating, and repressing it into the unconscious from whence it returns in the form of neuroses. The sexual drive is what is most threatening to the ego insofar as the ego has so little control over it. It is the sexual drive that establishes the primacy of the body for the ego, the primacy of the preservation of the species over self-preservation, the primacy of life over death, and the primacy of the mother. Lacan declares that "I point out to you in advance that this involves the feminine function in its essential symbolic meaning and that we can refind it only at the level of procreation" (S III, 86). The primacy of procreation, and hence of the mother and hence of the female, is evident. "This is what characterizes neurosis; it is both the most obvious thing in the world and the thing one doesn't want to see" (S III, 86). Primacy and privilege lie behind the symptoms of language. Either the primary or the privileged may be dominant. If the privileged is dominant, what is primary is still primary, and the neuroses continue. If the primary is dominant then privilege is lost, and the domination of the female and corresponding submission of the male will be less neurotic and not likely to be pathological.

The process of Oedipal genderization and sexualization produces the denial of Eros in the form of the Thanatos complex. The privileged signifier is master of the chains of signification that are the manifestations in language of the neurotic symptoms that constitute the structure of the privileged primal fantasy. The basic structure of Oedipal genderization and sexualization is misogyny. The *jouissance* of male domination is inevitably misogynous, and the *jouissance* of female submission embraces misogyny in that it entails the assimilation of a self-image centered on lack and corresponding inferiority. The *jouissance* of female domination and male submission are philogynous. The love that a man and a woman have for one another at an individual level relates to the primary and the privileged signifiers in relation to the *jouissance* of domination and submission. Lacan states:

> Let us look at it from the woman's perspective. The love the wife gives her spouse is not directed at the individual, not even an idealized one—that's the danger of what is called life in common, the idealization isn't tenable—but at a being beyond. The love which constitutes the bond of marriage, the love which properly speaking is sacred, flows from the woman towards . . . all men. Similarly, through the woman, it is all women which the fidelity of the husband is directed towards. . . .
>
> [A]ll . . . isn't a quantity, it is a universal function. It is the universal man, the universal woman, the symbol, the embodiment of the partner of the human couple. (S II, 260–61)

Here we are faced again with bifurcations and dialectics. We cannot separate our genderization and sexualization from the other bifurcations and in particular from mind/body dualism. Mind/body dualism seems to inevitably result in Thanatos whereas the unification of mind and body ultimately leads to Eros.

What is this universal man and universal woman, and what is their relationship to the gods? Lacan leaves us with the death of God and the death of Pan (the Goddess never did exist for Lacan), but the phallus still reigns as the privileged signifier. Lacan tells us that "Man survives the death of God, which he assumes, but in doing so, he presents himself before us. The pagan legend tells us that at the moment when the veil of the temple was rent on the Aegean Sea, the message resounded that 'The great Pan is dead' " (S VII, 178). What is dead in the realm of material reality may be very much alive in the realm of psychic reality and the reality of unconscious fantasy. In the realm of the Imaginary, the Symbolic, and the Real, what does the death of God or of Pan entail?

Shortly before he died, Joseph Campbell gave two series of interviews at approximately the same time. One was with the broadcaster and commentator Bill Moyers, and the other was with a Jungian analyst, Fraser Boa. Boa had rented a suite at the Royal Hawaiian Hotel on Waikiki Beach for the filming of his series of interviews, and he and Campbell were chatting and having coffee by the ocean when, Boa related:

Two sparrows landed on the sand near our table. The female squatted, but the male, as if not trusting her demure invitation, stayed his distance, circling round while she chirped and flippantly pecked at the sand. . . . Suddenly, there was a wild flurry of wings. The male sparrow had accepted the invitation, and the female was having none of it. She pushed her tail down hard against the sand and drove him back with a series of fierce attacks. Then she sat down and began innocently preening her feathers. The male, as if paralyzed somewhere between his instinctual urge and his fear of another rejection, continued to circle. They repeated the ritual two or three times till finally he puffed his feathers, darted past her sharp beak, and quickly consummated the relationship. Then they flew away.[59]

Joe threw his arms up into the air and laughed. "There, that's the story! That's the *whole* story." In the final analysis, Campbell tells us there is no meaning to life, only a description of the process of reproduction.

Let us hypothesize that the male bird suddenly is endowed with language. The bird asks itself What am I? Whom am I? Where did I come from? What does it all mean? The languaging, conscious bird seeks an explanation and soon fantasizes "The Story of the Cosmic Egg." After several cycles of being sexually driven to copulate with the female, being rejected, pecked, but finally selected, the bird projects another story onto the cosmos, "The Story of the Big Cock in the Sky."

SIX

The Dialectics of Signification

The Master Signifiers

The master signifiers (the primary and the privileged) link the Imaginary and the Symbolic to the Real. The Imaginary and the Symbolic are in the realm of human cognition, whereas the Real is outside, connected only by metaphor. Consequently, the *representation* is never the same as *what is represented.* The Real cannot be known directly but only metaphorically, and therefore the Real can be represented but the representation is not and can never be the Real. All we can do is improve the metaphors. As Nietzsche stated: "the physical explanation, which is a symbolization of the world by means of sensation and thought, can in itself never account for the origin of sensation and thought; rather physics must construe the world of feeling consistently as lacking feeling and aim—right up to the highest human being. And teleology is only a history of purposes and never physical!" (WP, 562)[1]

The primary and privileged signifiers are dialectically and oppositionally related, and language and cognition are dialectically structured by both. The dialectical opposition is a product of mind/body dualism, the inescapable mental state of a languaging body. This mind/body dichotomy will appear in the form of the conflicting sexual and ego drives. The sexual is the conceptualization in the Imaginary and Symbolic of the reproductive instincts, and the ego drive is the conceptualization of the instinct for self-preservation. The primary signifier establishes the human as a part of nature by confirming the animality of the species. Conversely, the privileged denies that which makes the human a part of the natural as the languaging biped primate and instead projects mind onto the cosmos as the fantasy structure of the logos.

The Imaginary will be in the form of the grand metonymical reference to the human sexual and reproductive organs. The grand metonymical image of the privileged signifier is the penis, which takes the form of the phallic imagery of the pillar, the sword, and the huge inflated penis of Priapus. The central signifier of maleness in the register of the Symbolic is the Father. The master metaphor that relates the Imaginary and the Symbolic to the Real is the logos as disembodied mind. The logos, as the grand projection of the inflated ego, links the male as the possessor of the generative power of nature, with the Real. The female must remain as lacking and secondary in all aspects of human cognition as structured by the privileged signifier.

The grand metonymical image of the primary signifier is that of the female external and internal reproductive and sexual organs as represented by the imagery of the cauldron, the cave, the ocean, the horn of plenty—all womb-like images. The central signifier of femaleness in the register of the Symbolic is the Mother. The master metaphor, which connects the Imaginary and the Symbolic in the human with the Real, is the matrix of chaos out of which life emerges. The womb and the phallus are thus the dialectically related master signifiers of sexually bimorphic human cognition. All cognition begins with a separation of the human from the Other, and the relationship between them. That is the function of the master signifiers.

According to Lacan, "no signification can be sustained other than by reference to another signification." He goes on to say that "by doubling a noun through the mere juxtaposition of two terms whose complementary meaning ought apparently to reinforce each other, a surprise is produced by an unexpected precipitation of an unexpected meaning" (E, 150). He explicates this discussion with his now well-known image of the two doors:

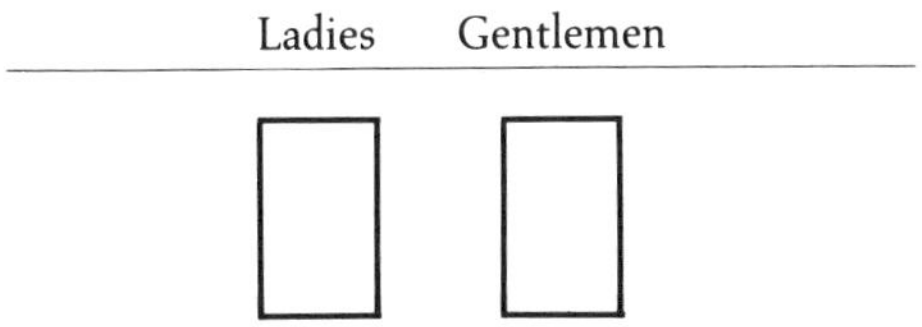

Just as the meaning of signifiers is developed in terms of the juxtaposition of two dialectically complementary terms—female/male, ladies/gentlemen, rights/duties, and so on, the very process of signification itself requires a juxtaposition of two dialectically complementary master signifiers. In this way, the privileged signifier presupposes the primary.

Master Signifiers and Original Fantasies

In Lacan's mirror stage, the individual develops a sense of ego and self, likeness and similarity. With the recognition of the Other comes the inevitable confrontation with sexual difference. By seeing the image of the body in the mirror, the child creates a unity for its own self. The narrative of the emergent self must explain the origins of the self—how the self originates in that which is not the self but existed before the self—and it must account for sexual difference. The child conceptually assimilates its sense of similarity and/or difference in relation to the parental figures. In *Beyond the Pleasure Principle,* Freud discusses a child's play with a bobbin on a string. As the child casts the bobbin away, his mother interprets what he utters as *fort* (away); and when the child pulls it close, he is interpreted as uttering *da* (here) (SE, XVIII, 14). Through play, the child differentiates between self and (M)other; subject and object. Here, as always, one step forward, two steps back.

The self originates in the (M)other, and, consequently, the separation from the (M)other is the beginning of difference and the recognition of limitation. The narcissistic wound is the first experience of loss.[2] Origin is explained in terms of birth and separation from the (M)other. The self will be experienced as separate from but like the (M)other if the body is female and different from the (M)other if the body is male. The next major differentiation the child makes is between that which is human and that which is not human or is other to the human. One of the first differentiations that the child makes within the realm of the Other is the recognition of animals as somewhat similar to humans. Later, the child learns to differentiate between the living or organic and the nonliving or inorganic. The child knows that its teddy bear is animal and somewhat like humans. The child may talk to its teddy bear and give it a name. At the same time, the child knows that the teddy bear is not alive like the family dog. It is life in nature and being alive as a human that establishes a relationship between humans and nature in terms of the register of the Imaginary and the Symbolic.

The narrative of origins, essential to every human being, tribe, and society, is not a simple one to tell or discover. Gender and sexual difference develop within individuals with insatiable libidinal desires, creating dependencies that acknowledge lack. Material reality contains no meaning for the self or for life but is merely descriptive. On the contrary, meaning is formulated through metaphor and metonymy in the context of projection, introjection, repression, denial, neuroses, perversion, and pathology, the symptoms of the defense mechanisms of the ego. The collective explanations of origin that constitute the original fantasies reflect the primal structure of creation, difference, and limitation. These signifiers include the mother figure with her womb and its external opening as well as her breasts and the penile father. The content of the fantasies blend material reality, psychic reality, and the reality of unconscious fantasy.

Psychic reality is based on the premise that "what appears to us as immediate reality consists of carefully processed images."[3] Knowledge is derived from an imaginal framework rooted in perception and the Symbolic. The metaphor for men as minds, within an imaginal network presupposing the polarity and bifurcation of mind/body dualism, leaves bodies as vessels and images of penetration as the metaphorical representation of the female. Sex and death are the basic preoccupations of human conceptual experience. Mother, father, self, male, female, sex, and death are the experiential raw material out of which we forge our mythic systems and worldviews.

Fantasy prevails over material reality in the psychic reality of our world-view because desire demands fulfillment and appeasement, while truth is gratuitous and unnecessary and can be satisfied by mere belief. From the perspective of psychology, *actual* truth or falsity are inconsequential elements so long as we can maintain a belief that something is true. So long as unconscious fantasy can be conceptualized as psychic reality, it doesn't matter that it may not coincide with material reality.

The human sexual and reproductive organs will inevitably play a symbolic organizational function in the narratives of the origin of the cosmos, life, and the human species. The female womb, breasts, and genitalia and the male penis must, therefore, be part of the cognitive structure of primal fantasy at both the unconscious and conscious levels for both the individual and the collective.

Both the primary and the privileged signifiers structurally embody the configuration of the original fantasy, which is constructed of three parts. These parts will correspond to the three parts of the original fantasy: creation as the generative power of nature; the parental position, which contains the generative power of nature, justifying its primary or privileged position in the master signifier; and the reproductive bodily parts, which furnish the image for the generative power. The master signifier therefore spans the registers of the Imaginary, the Symbolic, and the Real.

The master signifiers indicate the structures that govern gender. In patriphallic society where the privileged fantasy shapes societal relationships and institutions, one can "simply by reference to the function of the phallus, indicate the structures that will govern the relations between the sexes" (E, 289). With two fundamental versions of the original fantasy, there are two master signifiers: the primary (the womb) and the privileged (the phallus). Consequently, there are two possible gender structures, the primary is philogynous and the privileged misogynous. The one-to-one relationship is also a one-to-all relationship. Lacan explains:

> Let us look at it from the woman's perspective. The love the wife gives her spouse is not directed at the individual, not even an idealized one—that's the danger of what is called life in common, idealization isn't tenable—but at a being beyond. The love which constitutes the bond of marriage, the love which properly speaking is sacred, flows from the woman towards . . . *all men*. Similarly, through the woman, it is *all women* which the fidelity of the husband is directed towards.
>
> This may seem paradoxical. But . . . *all* isn't a quantity, it is a universal function. It is the universal man, the universal woman, the symbol, the embodiment of the partner of the human couple. (S II, 260–61)

Lacan states that "for the situation to be tenable, the position must be triangular. For the couple to keep the human level, there has to be a god there. Love flows towards the universal man, towards the veiled man, for whom every ideal is only an idolatrous substitute, and this is that famous genital love which makes our Sundays and which we affect to scorn" (S II, 263). And, equally, if a man is to truly love a woman to the point that she is primary and he seeks to be the object of her desire, rather than objectifying her for the benefit of his desire, then there must be, in like manner, a Goddess there. The triangle of the primary signifier is Goddess-Woman-man, and the triangle of the privileged signifier is God-Man-woman.

The essential issue in the dialectical structure of the original fantasy is which sex has possession-ownership-control of both the female and the male sexual and reproductive organs, and which sex surrenders control over its own sexual and reproductive organs either as a voluntary gift to the other or in obedience to the Law, thus embracing castration? While the dynamics of desire dictate that possession-ownership-control belongs to either one or the other, both possibilities reflect the difference that generates desire and the two primal drives that representationally and symbolically structure human cognition. Both primary and privileged sexuality reflect the libidinal dynamics of control and submission.

The Primary Signifier

The master signifier combines within it the structure of the original fantasy—origin-difference-limitation: the Grand Metaphor, the Law of Gender, and the Grand Metonymy. The primal fantasy is one of the earliest myths of ancient Greece in which the ancient goddess Gaia, the personification of Mother Earth, is born out of Chaos at the beginning of time; from her springs all life. There are fairly obvious links of meaning and overlapping chains of signification between *mother, mater, maternal, maternalize, matriarch, matriarchal, maternity, matter, material, materialize,* and *matrix*. The matrix is the grand metaphorical reference of the primary signifier relating mother to nature as that from which life springs. The middle designation of the primary signifier is the Law of the Mother. It dictates that the mother sacrifices for the child, and the male sacrifices for the female. His desire shall be unto her. His desire will be to be the object of her desire. The womb and the passage that connects the outside to the inside is the third part of the primary signifier, which furnishes the Grand Metonymical reference.

In the diachronic development of human language, the metaphorical usage of sexual references permeates human speech. According to Lacan, a radical relationship "exists between the first instrumental relations, the earliest techniques, the principal actions of agriculture, such as that of opening the belly of the earth, or again the principal actions in the making of a vase . . . and something very precise, namely, not so much the sexual act as the female sexual organ" (S VII, 169). Metaphorical manifestations of the female sexual organs are found in reference to openings, vessels, caves, bodies, and life- and natural life-related functions. Lacan goes on to say:

> One takes note of the fact that the use of a term that originally meant "coitus" is extended virtually infinitely, that the use of a term that originally meant "vulva" is capable of generating all kinds of metaphorical uses. And it is in this way that it

> began to be supposed that the vocalization presumed to accompany the sexual act gave men the idea of using the signifier to designate either the organ, and especially the female organ, in a noun form, or the act of coitus in a verb form. . . .
>
> [S]exual symbolism in the ordinary sense of the word may polarize at its point of origin the metaphorical play of the signifier. (S VII, 168–69)

The womb and female breasts clearly have an imaginary, symbolic, metaphorical, and representational relationship to the female reproductive organs that parallels the relationship between the penis and the phallus. The womb is to the uterus and birth canal what the phallus is to the penis. Since the original fantasies are representational structures of Eros and Thanatos, which in turn stem from the oppositional dialectics of the sexual and ego drives, there must be a parallel dialectical relationship between the two original fantasy symbolic representational systems that depict the drive within the psyche at both conscious and unconscious levels. The dialectical relationship between the two fantasy structures is one of contradiction and negation and is representative of a number of dualistic and oppositional structures such as other/self, body/mind, nature/culture, engulfment/separation, and mother/father. Therefore, both the womb and the phallus are master signifiers; one is primary, the other privileged.

In a symbolic narrative chain, it is difference that must be accounted for and difference that permits the shift from the Imaginary to the Symbolic. Difference entails a comparison with something that is primary or foundational. The (M)other is primary within the Imaginary and the Symbolic as well as within material reality. The (M)other is the norm or standard against which difference is measured, either as a different self within the dialectics of other/self or as a different sex in the dialectics of female/male. "[E]ach of the terms must appear as the *differance* of the other, as the other different and deferred in the economy of the same" (Df, 17).

Since the two oppositional and dialectical representations of the primal fantasy (origin-difference-limitation) are negations of each other, the phallus and the womb function very differently in primary and privileged fantasy. In the primal fantasy, the generative power of nature lies with the (M)other, and the womb is the *everything but* the phallus. The phallus is given by the male to the (M)other by way of a sacrifice induced by seduction. The phallus of the primary original fantasy or Eros chain of signification will therefore function contrary to and as a dialectical opposite to the phallus of the privileged original fantasy or Thanatos chain of signification. Freud or, for that matter, Lacan, were never wrong, but their positions were not taken to their logical conclusions. They both depart from the dialectical methodology of psychoanalysis by concentrating on phallic privilege and failing to develop the repressed primary. As a result, they present only one side of the dialectic. The material reality of mammalian bimorphic sexuality will never permit us to completely exclude the reproductive functions of one or the other sex—to diminish it or devalue it, yes, but to eliminate it, never.

In the representational structure of the Eros or sexual drive, the male is seduced into giving possession-ownership-control of the penis to the (M)other, and this is conceptualized as a castration (despite the fact that the penis remains attached to the male). The male genitalia are exceptionally vulnerable to being severed. Castration is therefore a key motif in the register of the Imaginary. The castration-sacrifice of the penis to the (M)other transforms the male into the Consort. We therefore have a chain of signification whereby the phallus is the privileged signifier but is possessed, owned, and controlled by the womb and the breasts. Psychic reality, which is representationally structured by the Eros or sexual fantasy, is "matriphallic" because the (M)other possesses, owns, and controls the penis, which has been presented to her as a gift of sacrifice as the culmination of the seduction.

When the Eros and Thanatos drives are represented as original primary and privileged fantasy in symbolic structures, origin becomes the generative power of nature, and both female and male sexual and reproductive organs must be in the explanatory narrative. The questions of difference, seduction, and castration are determined by who possesses, owns, and controls the two sets of sexual and reproductive organs. They will "belong to" either the male or the female, the mother or the father, in any single original fantasy structure. Though reproduction requires both female and male reproductive organs, desire and difference dictate that only one, either the female or the male, possesses the generative power of nature. The unavoidable result is that the person who doesn't possess the generative power of nature is castrated, his or her reproductive organs controlled by the other.

Possession-ownership-control is determined by the symbolic configuration of the master signifier, which is representational of the original fantasy. In the Eros structure of the primary fantasy, the male is seduced to castrate himself by placing his penis at the disposal of the (M)other. By surrendering in such a way, the male places limits on his ego, and it becomes secondary. It belongs to the (M)other to use as she desires. It is in this way that the female can be said to possess the phallus in matriarchal psychic reality, and the phallus still retains its relationship with the male penis. In mythic structures, the Goddess is served by the Consort. The Consort has the penis, but it is available to the Goddess at her bidding. This is often symbolically represented by the Goddess holding the serpent, the primary symbol of the phallus in the structure of the original primary fantasy. It is also represented in mythic structure by the separation and dismemberement of the male phallus, as in the myth of Isis and Osiris.[4] In writing about the mythic structure of matriphallic sexuality, Esther Harding states that "This involves the sacrifice of his demand, a sacrifice which is not only symbolized by castration, but may indeed appear in reality as the need to renounce for the time being his desire for sexual satisfaction with this woman, whom he yet loves. It is a voluntary castration for the sake of Eros."[5] In the structure of male masochistic fantasy, which reflects matriarchal psychic reality and sexuality, the control by the dominant woman is essential.

The sexual and gender structures of the primary signifier reflect the erotic dynamics of control and submission, control being with the female and submission with the male. In her study of male masochism, *Dominant Women, Submissive Men,* Gini Scott describes how control or fantasy of control of the male penis by the dominant female generates intense sexual arousal in the male, and the postponement or denial of sexual relief to the male is, in and of itself, sexually exciting.[6] Masochism of this kind is *perverse* because it seldom entails standard penetration of the female body by the male. The female possesses and controls the male penis in the male fantasy framework of matriphallic sexuality.

The Privileged Signifier

An understanding of the dialectical relationship between Eros and Thanatos is essential to an understanding of the function of the phallus as the privileged term within the Symbolic order. There would be no representational structure such as a sexual drive if there were not a drive detailing the individuation of the ego. Conversely, there would be no ego drive unless there was something oppositionally related to it. The ego experiences the sexual drive as a loss of control and a surrender of the boundaries of the self. Consequently, a set of defense mechanisms is pivotal to the representational structure of the ego drive. The master signifier is the meeting point of the representational structures of the ego and Eros drives, and it functions as the primary signifier in the primary original fantasy and as the privileged signifier in the Symbolic chain that constitutes the privileged fantasy. As the reality of unconscious fantasy structures the conscious fantasies of the individual and the fantasies and mythic structures of the collective, the content in both the conscious and the unconscious develop dialectically. Neither one has meaning unless placed in dialectical opposition to the other. The representational structure of the ego drive within the Symbolic order arises as a defense against the sexual or Eros drive. Consequently, the fantasy structure of the Eros or sexual drive lies underneath, or between, the lines of the fantasy structure of the ego drive. The defense against the seduction of the (M)other is the Father; the defense against engulfment and the desire to castrate oneself is reflected in the fear of castration.

In the representational structure of the ego drive, reunion or a return to the (M)other is forbidden, as it means a surrender of the ego. The seduction to castrate oneself through presenting the phallic penis as a sacrificial gift to the (M)other is resisted as it presents itself as taboo, the original sin. The Symbolic configuration is the Law of the Father. The male retains the phallus and has possession-ownership-control of the Mother as if by right: over her breasts, womb, and external genitalia. Unlike the male, the reproductive function of the mother requires much of her body, and her reproductive organs cannot be separated from the entirety of her body in the register of the Imaginary. Consequently, the male cannot own the female reproductive organs without owning her entirely. Possession of reproduction requires possession of women. Male control of reproduction entails male control of the female. This is the promulgation of the Law of the Father. The woman is doubly conceptualized as castrated in that she neither possesses, owns, or controls the penis nor possesses, owns, or controls her own body. The castration of the (M)other and the possession of the phallus make the male a Father rather than a Consort. The phallus is either given to the mother or the mother belongs to the phallus—there is no moderation.

There are three parts to the structure of the phallus that function within the fantasy of patriphallic psychic reality, which is representational of the primary ego or death drive. These are the logos, the Law of the Father, and the Law of God—champion of disembodied mind. Each are essential for phallic structure. The phallus must account for the generative power of nature by a symbolic and metaphorical relationship to the male sexual and reproductive organs. In order to carry this generative meaning, the phallus must embody an explanation of origin. To account for difference it must privilege the sexual organ of the male over those of the female, keeping any explanation of origin consistent with the privileged sexual organ. Finally, the phallus must justify the control over the sexual and reproductive organs of the female, whose role in reproduction is relegated to a secondary position. This is done by asserting the Law of the Father, by reinforcing mind/body dualism and, in so doing, privileging the mind.

The Phallus As Logos

The logos explains and accounts for origin. It is the emblem of "Truth," of rationality, of scientific empiricism—and it serves as a promulgation of patriarchal law. Its aim is justification; its method is denial. If one has a penis, one has the logos, and if one has the logos, one has the penis. The possession of logos/penis furnishes the justification for and the legitimacy of the Law of the Father and entitles the phallus to possess, own, or control the breasts, womb, and external genitalia of the Other. The phallus is therefore a paternal conceptual structure that links the male mind (logos) with the penis. The phallus, as the privileged signifier, is the Imaginary and Symbolic representation of the generative power of nature. It is the possession of the phallus that makes a male a father, and it is being a father that gives the man the right to own and possess a woman, that is to say, to exercise authority over women and over woman. Possession of the phallus is only possible for the male by adherence to the logos. The male must submit to lying truths and must erect defences, simulacrums, totems, totalities. The paternal phallus is the source of the law.

The will of the Father is the law, and the proclamation of the will, the law, is a production of the mind. At the same time, the penis is the source of new life and the act of causing a female to conceive is conceptualized as an act of male creation. Penis is therefore inextricably and hopelessly joined to mind. Consequently, the archetypal paternal phallus is a bifurcated structure between the poles of the logos and the penis. As such, it reflects the structure of male mind/body dualism. And it is the law that joins the two poles and maintains the balance between them, and forbids the surrender to seduction.

"The phallus," according to Goux, "is a *masculine* principle of generation, of production. In that sense, *it is the very manifestation of intelligence*" (P, 46). He goes on to say that "What from the very beginning of philosophy associates the father with the idea, the mother with matter, could not be formulated more clearly. The idea that idealism would initially be a *paterialism* (as opposed to materialism) can only be deduced immediately from that assumption and its consequences. Philosophy, once developed, could only be the development of that split" (P, 47).

Pure mind or logos creates the form, the idea, and the ideal. "Matter is only a receptacle and a wet-nurse: it is sterile and receives without giving. The only true principle of generation, including perceptible things, is in the *logos*" (P, 47). "As the male organ of generation, the phallus is therefore essentially *logos* or source of the *logos:* rational power, or intelligible reason. The erect male organ is not perceived by the Greeks primarily as a physical reality, but indeed as the emblem of the *logos* or, as it were, the *logos,* itself made visible" (P, 49).

It is the relationship between the logos and the penis in the structure of the phallus that leads Lacan to link language with the law of the Father. "But when we talk of the Symbolic order . . . there is creation. That is why *in principio erat verbum* is ambiguous. It's not for nothing that in Greek, it was called logos" (S II, 292). The essential link, however, is the structure of original fantasy: language-explanation-origins-differentiations-limitations-original fantasy. The logos, however, is only essential to the original fantasy representation of the ego drive. It is a particular version of origin but not the only one, and certainly not the first. It is origin itself that is fundamental. The logos narrative rises as a defense to and a repression of the sexual and Eros drive. It is a denial of the role of the female in reproduction in material reality, and it is a repression of the submission to the seduction of the castration by sacrifice, or as Goux states:

What the phallic metaphor of the One betrays is what must have occurred for it to be possible, the monopolization of the power of engendering (informing, organizing, directing) by the masculine paternal. And that constituted a new historic step with respect to the conception, even more archaic, of an essentially maternal fecundity, one which is more in conformity with the patent, immediate, and sensible reality of pregnancy and childbirth. The males had to confiscate the maternal power of engendering, a primal gift, in order for the imaginary of the phallic exclusivity that philosophy perpetuates to prevail. As long as the *genitrix* with large womb (herself assimilable to Earth and to Nature) was adored and envoked as the mysterious site of all generation, the existence of the *genitor*, only conjectural, was of little consequence. According to the myths and to philosophy. . . a struggle was nessary in order for *pater*. . . to lower the fecund *genitrix* to the subaltern rank of *mater*—simple matter that only receives, for childbirth, its form and information from the unique masculine.

The philosophical expression of this domination and this exclusivity is clear. In the division between idea and matter, only the idea is fecund. It is the idea that forms and informs a passive receptacle. . . . [T]he sexed resonance of this division remains even in the loftiest speculations. (P, 50–51)

Further on, Goux explains:

The mother, matter, nature, the immediate, the sensible—all of this is on the side of the corruptible, the variable, and the mortal (like the body and the penis itself), while the father, the idea, the spirit, the represented—and also the phallus—are on the side of the invariable and the eternal. From this it is clear that the penis is the natural organ that "belongs" to the mother (joins with her, attaches to her realm) and that it must be abolished in order for this juncture to be destroyed and replaced by the spiritual juncture that phallic simulacrum ensures. It is in this manner that the initiate (the masculine subject) will be able to gain eternal life, absolute renewal.

Disclosing that the process penis/castration/phallus is implicated in this movement is not to propose a reductive (or depreciative) interpretation but rather to elevate the genealogy of an operation to the level of its resistant (and constantly resurgent) mythical expression, which our horizon of thought opens to interpretation. (P, 56)

The Name of the Father

The male claim to the possession of the generative power of nature is rooted in the idea that creation takes place as an expression of an act of the will. Pure disembodied mind is the only Real, and matter is brought into being by a mental act. "In the beginning . . . God said *let there be*. . . ."[7] This is the fantasy of the reality of disembodied mind (or Logos) as the first cause of existence. All religions postulate a disembodied mind as the source and origin of being. It may be differentiated as is the case of the logos, the logical or mathematical structure of the universe, the realm of the Platonic Ideal, or it may be undifferentiated as is the case in Eastern religions such as the Brahman of Hinduism, the nirvana of Buddhism, and the Tao of Taoism. They are the first cause or origin of the material world: mind produces matter.

In the matching dialectics of mind-male and body-female, the male as father is the embodiment of the logos. God is a spirit. The male as father claims to embody the generative power of nature because he embodies the logos as mind. *Concept* lies behind being, and the idea behind the material. *Conception* takes place when the male places life inside the female and she then is said to *conceive*. The idea of the father therefore entails the male as logos or mind inside a physical body. It is a manifestation of the Thanatos drive and serves to separate mind and body in opposition to the Eros drive, which serves to unify. This is well understood by Lacan when he describes the delusion of the father's function in generation as "the begetting of the soul" and "the begetting of the mind" (S III, 213). He explains that "The father belongs to a Reality that is sacred in itself, more spiritual than any other, since ultimately nothing in lived Reality strictly speaking points to his function, his presence, his dominance" (S III, 215). At the same time, he describes the identification of the father with the generative power of nature as a delusion that "can up to a point be described as reasoning madness, in the sense that in certain respects its articulation is logical, though from a secondary point of view that madness should achieve a synthesis of this nature is no less a problem than its very existence" (S III, 217).

In the privileged fantasy, the beginning was pure mind, and pure mind conceived a creation. Man was created by pure mind in its image, or by embodying it. Within each man is a part of the eternal logos. Man requires the body of a woman to procreate, but since he is the embodiment of the generative power of nature as pure mind, he has authority over, possesses, and owns the body of women. As stated by Lacan, "It is in the *name of the father* that we must recognize the support of the Symbolic function which, from the dawn of history, has identified his person with the figure of the law" (E, 67).

"Before the Name-of-the-Father there was no father, there were all sorts of other things . . . but before the term *father* was instituted in a certain register historically there was certainly no father" (S III, 306). There can be no father in the primary original fantasy nor where the primary signifier governs the Symbolic and the Imaginary. If the male gives the phallus to the female as a sacrificial gift, recognizing within her the generative power of nature, then the male is not and cannot be a father. "[T]he father, has his own and that's that, he neither exchanges it nor gives it. There is no circulation . . . The father, as father, has the phallus—full stop" (S III, 319). Either the father embodies the generative power of nature or the mother does. There is no primal fantasy in which they share since the primal fantasy carries the structure of unconscious fantasy, which is creation, difference, and limitation—and not equality. The mother either embodies the generative power of nature, in which case she is *everything but* the phallus, or she is the father's receptacle in which he produces life, in which case she is *nothing but* the womb. In the privileged form of the original fantasy, "It's the signifier *procreation* in its most problematic form, the one that Freud himself evokes in relation to obsessionals, which isn't the form *being a mother* but the form *being a father*" (S III, 292). Lacan elaborates:

> [T]he function of *being a father* is absolutely unthinkable in human experience without the category of the signifier.
>
> What can it mean *to be a father?* You are familiar with the learned discussions, ethnological or other, one immediately enters into to establish whether primitives who say that women conceive when they're placed in such and such a spot possess the scientific notion that women become fertilized once they have duly copulated. These inquiries have nevertheless seemed to some to be perfectly foolish, since it's difficult to conceive of human animals stupid enough to fail to notice that when one wants to have kids one has to copulate. This is not the point. The point is that the sum of these facts—of copulating with a woman, that she then carries something within her womb for a certain period, that this product is finally expelled—will never lead one to constitute the notion of what is *to be a father.* I'm not even speaking about the entire cultural cluster implied in the term *being a father,* I'm simply speaking of what it is *to be a father* in the sense of procreation.
>
> A rebound effect is necessary for the fact that man copulates to receive the sense it Really has, but to which no Imaginary access is possible, that the child is as much his as the mother's. And for this effect of action in return to occur, the elaboration of the notion of *being a father* must have been raised by work that has taken place through an entire cluster of cultural exchanges to the state of major signifier, and this signifier must have its own consistency and status. The subject may well know that copulating is *really* at the origin of procreation, but the function of procreation as a signifier is something else." (S III, 292–93)

The privileged original fantasy structures the phallus, and the phallus gives the structure to gender and Oedipal sexuality. It does so not because of the material facts of human procreation but in spite of the material reality of females' producing children out of their bodies. "The signifier *being a father* is what creates the highway in sexual relations with a woman. If the highway doesn't exist, one finds oneself faced with a number of elementary minor paths, copulation and then the woman's pregnancy" (S III, 293). "I've guided you by the hand long enough for you to perceive that speech, and especially this essential form of speech in which we announce ourselves as a *thou*, is a complex mode that is far from reducible to the intuition of two centers exchanging signals. As the relation of subject to subject is structured in a complex mode by the properties of language, the specific role the signifier plays in it has to be located therein" (S III, 289).

When the ego conceives of itself as separate from and owning a body, then it is eternal and can know no death. If one conceives of oneself as an "I" that includes body and mind, we are faced with creation and destruction. "All I need do is think about myself [*moi*]—I am eternal. From the moment I think about myself [*moi*], no destruction of me [*moi*] is possible. But when I say *I*, not only is destruction possible, but at every instance there is creation" (S II, 292). The ego is fragile because of its vulnerability to narcissistic deflation by interaction with others and with the body. "Think about the *I am* of *I am the one who am*. This is what makes for the problematic nature of the relation to the other" (S III, 288). The ownership of women as a right of phallic possession is the extreme form of male egoistic narcissism. Narcissism is "the central Imaginary relation of interhuman relationships" (S III, 92). The Law of the Father establishes the domination of the father over the female. "By a girl, by a young woman, or even by an aged one, nothing must be done independently, even in her own house. In childhood a female must be subject to her father, in youth to her husband, when her lord is dead to her sons; a woman must never be independent."[8] Since "Every legitimate power always rests, as does any kind of power, on the symbol" (S II, 201), the phallus as the privileged signifier structures human sexuality according to the *jouissances* of male control and female submission. Lacan asks:

> Why does this minimal schema of human experience which Freud gave us in the Oedipus complex retain its irreducible and yet enigmatic value for us? And why privilege the Oedipus complex? Why does Freud always want to find it everywhere, with such insistence? Why do we have here a knot that seems so essential to him that he is unable to abandon it in the slightest particular observation—unless it's because the notion of father, closely related to that of the fear of God, gives him the most palpable element in experience of what I've called the quilting point between the signifier and the signified? (S III, 268)

The logos is not the penis, and, as pure mind, it is in diametrical opposition to the penis as flesh. Every patriphallic man carries within him the ongoing war between Apollo and the figure of Priapus. The Law of the Father keeps the poles linked in opposition, maintaining the female in submission to make her ever available to the penis but separating her and excluding her so that the logos is not polluted by her sexuality.

Jacques Derrida links the logos with the father. "But what is a father?" he asks.

> One would then say that the origin or cause of *logos* is being compared to what we know to be the cause of a living son, his father. One would understand or imagine the birth and development of *logos* from the standpoint of a domain foreign to it, the transmission of life or the generative relation. But the father is not the generator or procreator in any "real" sense prior to or outside all relation to language. In any way, indeed, is the father/son relation distinguishable from a mere cause/effect or generator/engendered relation, if not by the instance of logos? Only a power of speech can have a father. The father is always father to a speaking/living being. In other words, it is precisely *logos* that enables us to perceive and investigate something like paternity. (PP, 80)

The Religion of God

Religion is the supreme denial of our animality. It is premised on the assumption that the mind is Real and permanent (primary) and the body is illusory (secondary) or merely a passing framework within which mind matures. Mind is sublime and the body mundane. Mind is spiritual while the body is animal. Mind draws us up to God—pure Logos, but the body brings us down, pulls with gravitational force toward the baseness of the animal. Mind is of God and the body of the devil. The friction between the two is constant and causes much tension for the possessor of consciousness. Mind, for its sanctity, must deny, transcend, conquer, and control the body. It invents the concept of sin—when one gives in to the body. Saint Paul proclaims that "It is good for a man not to touch a woman. Nevertheless, to avoid fornication, let every man have his own wife and let every woman have her own husband."[9] He states, "I say therefore to the unmarried and widows, it is good for them if they abide even as I. But if they cannot contain, let them marry: for it is better to marry than to burn."[10] The Buddha is said to have told his followers that "Those who are not wise, act like animals, racing toward female forms, like hogs toward mud."[11] According to Freud, "The man is afraid of being weakened by the woman, infected with her femininity and of then showing himself incapable. . . . Psychoanalysis believes that it has discovered a large part of what underlies the narcissistic rejection of women by men, which is so much mixed up with despising them" (SE, XI, 199).

Mind is male, and the male is the Father, who for Lacan "is at the heart of the experience defined as religious" (S VII, 171). The Law of the Father commands that women, lacking the phallus, the generative power of nature, and the voice of logic, must remain silently obedient. Saint Paul commands female obedience when he prescribes: "Let your women keep silence in the Churches: for it is not permitted unto them to speak; but they are commanded to be under obedience, as also saith the laws,"[12] and "Let the woman learn in silence with subjection. But I suffer not a woman to teach, nor to usurp authority over the man, but to be in silence."[13] Similarly, Allah's declaration of His will revealed to the Prophet Mohammed that "The men are made responsible for the women, since God endowed them with certain qualities. . . . If you experience opposition from the woman you shall first talk to them, then desert them in bed, then you may beat them."[14]

Within the religious discourse, the dialectical tensions between Eros and Thanatos, sexuality and ego, are represented as seduction. In the introduction to his book, *Seduction*, Jean Baudrillard writes:

> A fixed destiny weighs on seduction. For religion seduction was a strategy of the devil, whether in the guise of witchcraft or love. It is always the seduction of evil—or of the world. It is the very artifice of the world. Its malediction has been unchanged in ethics and philosophy, and today it is maintained in psychoanalysis and the "liberation of desire.". . .
>
> Seduction . . . belongs to the order of . . . signs and rituals. This is why all the great systems of production and interpretation have not ceased to exclude seduction—to its good fortune—from their conceptual field. For seduction continues to haunt them from without, and from deep within its forsaken state, threatening them with collapse. It awaits the destruction of every godly order, including those of production and desire. Seduction continues to appear to all orthodoxies as malefice and artifice, a black magic for the deviation of all truths, an exaltation of the malicious use of signs, a conspiracy of signs. Every discourse is threatened with this sudden reversibility, absorbed into its own signs without a trace of meaning. This is why all disciplines, which have as an axiom the coherence and finality of their discourse, must try to exorcise it. This is where seduction and femininity are confounded, indeed, confused. Masculinity has always been haunted by this sudden reversibility within the feminine. Seduction and femininity are ineluctable as the reverse side of sex, meaning and power.[15]

In the final paragraphs of the book, in answer to the question, "Production as destiny, or seduction as destiny?" Baudrillard concludes, "Anatomy is not destiny, nor is politics: seduction is destiny."[16]

There are two extreme levels of defense against the seduction, which correspond to the two poles of the phallus within patriphallic psychic reality—logos and penis. At logos, the defense is voluntary castration by the denial of the body leading toward the configuration of religious masochism. By altogether denying the phallus, one can escape the seduction of sacrificing the phallus to the female, thereby allowing the male to simultaneously avoid the *jouissance* of submission while maintaining his control. The religious male would rather castrate himself for the sake of God than for the sake of life, the mother, and the woman. He gives up the erotic but maintains *control.* The sexual drive, however, attacks the ego in terms of ever reoccurring erotic fantasies, which require the application of ever more severe punishments to the disobedient body. The sexual purity of the monastery is assuredly an illusion. As has become clear in the recent exposure of child sexual abuse by "men of God," the sexual drive will get the ego, one way or another.

The phallus functions as a defense mechanism against seduction. The logos denies the body, the Law of the Father denies the seduction to surrender the phallus, and the penis becomes an instrument of aggression, rape being a prime example. When he does it to her, solely for his pleasure and against her will, he protects himself from the desire to present his phallus to her as the object of her desire. The hostile and misogynous nature of phallic aggression is reflected in such common phrases as "fuck you" and "screw you" and in the many other descriptive ways in which males verbalize "doing it to" a woman. Male fantasies of rape, tying up, punishing, or in other ways causing pain to females, or the actual carrying out of the sadistic fantasies into practice, are an erotic manifestation of desire.

The institutionalization of pornographic imagery, ranging from magazine and television commercials and classical paintings to the coarser forms of sexual imagery of the pornography industry, deny women the self, subject, and ego by portraying them as fantasy objects of desire. Typical pornographic imagery socializes women in terms of a psychic reality that denies them that which men claim as embodiment of the logos. Thus, religion and pornography serve the same basic function: defending men against seduction and the desire to surrender the phallus. The portrayal of women as empty, mindless, egoless vessels, open to and awaiting penetration, affirms and reinforces for males their possession of the phallus. Pornographic imagery is, therefore, a powerful defense mechanism for de-eroticizing matriarchal fantasy structures and eroticizing patriphallic fantasy. Religion and pornography function in a dialectical conjunction at the opposite ends of the phallus—religion at the logos end and pornography at the penis end, and the two are mediated by the Law of the Father. Traditional psychoanalytic theory, if limited to the Oedipal side of psychic reality, functions to legitimize what is essentially a powerful and complex set of defense mechanisms and prescribes them as the norm of human individuation.

The writings of the Marquis de Sade have long been recognized as philosophically and psychologically significant, particularly important when read against the frame of Saint Paul. The two write at opposite poles within the framework of Judeo-Christian discourse and are the mirror images of mind/body dualism. Saint Paul, by advocating celibacy and condemning fornication, denies the penis and elevates the spirit or the logos. The writings of de Sade, on the other hand, rebel against the logos. If one examines the purported or real descriptions of the practices of devil worshippers, they conform very closely to descriptions of Sadean scenes, whereas almost every single act of penis aggression celebrated by de Sade can be found to be prohibited by the Old and New Testaments.

Saint Paul aims for the transcendence of the spirit over the flesh, while de Sade's primary objective is the corruption of innocence and purity of the spirit by reveling in sexual pleasures of the flesh and the contamination of virtue. What Saint Paul and de Sade have in common, however, is that their writings reflect patriphallic fantasy structures that function as defenses mechanisms against the powerful, seductive (M)other. Their writings are anti-Eros and ego-centered. By celebrating rape, sodomy, and in every way negating the desire of the Other, de Sade defends the phallus against the seduction of castration. At the same time, he plays the role of the devil to the sanctity of Saint Paul. Religion is the sacred and pornography the profane. Religion is the affirmation of the logos, and pornography the affirmation of the penis as instrument of the ego. Each requires the other. Each defines itself in terms of the negation of the other. At the level of conscious content, they are contradictory. At the level of the unconscious, they are a part of an integrated patriphallic structure. "There is no contradiction in the unconscious; contradictory primary tendencies exist simultaneously."[17]

A parallel will be found in the fantasy structures of ancient Greece, with the Goddess as the monstrous Medusa with writhing snakes in place of hair, whose gaze will turn a man to stone. Greek sculpture and frescoes show an obsession with the theme of heroes killing powerful women—the Amazons.[18] One of the many pornographic plates shown by Eva Keuls in her book about Greek misogyny is particularly reminiscent of de Sade.[19] It portrays a woman being sodomized from behind while she has a penis forced into her mouth from in front. The pornographic images of the Greek pottery reproduced in Keuls's book have the same structural relationship to Platonic and neo-Platonic thought that the verbal images of de Sade have to Christian theology. The prevalence of sodomy and male pedophilia in ancient Greece reflects a defense against the seduction. The desire for castration is so strong that to allow the penis to come close to the body of a woman in the context of a loving relationship is a monumental risk. Sodomy is therefore the opposite of logos in the grand narrative of the Greek worldview in the same way that fornication is the opposite of the Holy Spirit in the patriphallic fantasy structure constituted by Christianity. Behind the grand stories of patriarchy, sharing the structure of mind/body bifurcation and dualism, lies the repressed alternative narrative of matriarchal consciousness, which is not an opposition within patriarchy but its grand antithesis. If ancient Greece had an equivalent to the Marquis de Sade, he would have played the parallel role to Plato that de Sade does to Saint Paul.

Neither celibate castration within aesthetic religious and monastic representational structures nor phallic aggression are adequate defense mechanisms against the seductive force of Eros or the sexual drive. The first is ineffectual, and the second becomes highly destructive if not kept under control. Bipolar alternatives are seldom efficient because they are extremes. The logos, pure mind and spirit, is opposed to the penis, consummate flesh and animal body. The penis seduces the mind through the pull of desire as the aesthetic is haunted by pornographic erotic fantasy. It is often the priest or the clergy that are most likely to have hidden pornography.[20] The higher law denounces and disparages sexual pleasure as it contaminates and defiles pure mind and brings the spirit down to the level of the body, but the body cannot be denied. There is thus an eternal enmity between the logos and the penis in conscious fantasy structures, and the balance is maintained through the law. Sinful flesh and carnal lust are the enemies of the spirit. Each pole of the dialectic entails its contradictory pole, whether God and the devil, religion and pornography, sin and sanctity, the logos and the penis, or the mind and the body. Within the dialectical structure of the phallus in patriphallic psychic reality the oppositional tensions are mediated by the Law of the Father. The law sets limits on sexual aggression and provides a sphere of legitimacy for the body to function under the direction of the logos. The law creates disobedience and a fear of the impure, which lead us into rites of purification and religious masochism, and, when the will fails, it leads us into transgression.

The law legitimizes the denial of self to women. The Law of the Father denies them the ego. Not only does the law forbid them to accept the phallus, it commands them to present their bodies in service to the phallus. Religion and pornography together constitute the boundaries of the conceptual structure of patriphallic psychic reality, and it is the law that links them and maintains the balance. Lacan states that "The phallus is the privileged signifier of that mark in which the role of the logos is joined with the advent of desire" (E, 287). The "Father" and his Law is the midpoint between the penis and the logos. The Father, being created in the image of God, is pure mind or spirit trapped in the physical body with the penis, which drives him through desire. Thus, the phallus is the logos-Father-penis, the structure of which is institutionally manifested in religion-law-pornography. All of the major religions presuppose the divine or ultimate reality as disembodied mind (whether differentiated or undifferentiated) and identify mind with the male and the body with the female. Thus, religion castrates (disempowers) women, and it is the law that enforces the "reign of the patriphallus."

The Castration of the Privileged Signifier

Nihilism, according to Nietzsche, is a psychological state that one reaches when one realizes "that becoming aims at *nothing* and achieves *nothing*" and that the "world is fabricated solely from psychological needs" (WP, 12). He concludes that "The faith in the categories of reason is the cause of nihilism" and that "We have measured the value of the world according to categories *that refer to a purely fictitious world*" (WP, 12). Nihilism presupposes that "there is no truth, that there is no absolute nature of things, nor a 'thing-in-itself' " (WP, 13). Radical or extreme nihilism "is the most scientific of all possible hypotheses" (WP, 55). Nietzsche's nihilism leads him to stake out the privileged signifier, to mark it out, and, subsequently, to destroy it. His method is to deroot and to destabilize, and, in so doing, he leaves us with a language that is castrated. His method anticipates Derrida, who attempts

> an exit and a deconstruction without changing terrain, by repeating what is implicit in the founding concepts and the original problematic, by using against the edifice the instruments or stones available in the house, that is, equally, in language. Here, one risks ceaselessly confirming, consolidating, *relifting (relever)*, at an always more certain depth, that which one allegedly deconstructs. The continuous process of making explicit, moving toward an opening, risks sinking into the autism of the closure. (EM, 135)

It is the gulf between the Symbolic and the Real that constitutes this castration of language. This is, according to Nietzsche, the price of consciousness. Without the privileged signifier, there is a void, a deep chasm, an abyss. Nietzsche has too choices with regard to this void—he can abandon language altogether, or he can look into the void and see what, if anything, presents itself: "and where does man not stand at an abyss? Is seeing itself not—seeing abysses?" (Z, 177). "He who sees the abyss, but with an eagle's eyes—he who *grasps* the abyss with an eagle's claws: *he* possesses courage" (Z, 298).

Nietzsche's strategy of intersubstituting opposites and his nihilistic method cause him to look beyond the "reality" of the privileged. He looks from above, out from a distance, and peers down from the heights of his solitude to catch a glimpse of his most abysmal thought. He deconstructs, destabilizes, uproots, and uplifts. Finally, he stands, looking into the cataclysmic void that he had re- created. It is dark, and there is no end, no surface, no boundary. The tumultous vision is a vision of the loneliest, it is boundless, but yet he laughs, and laughs, and laughs. It is a laughter that comes deep from within, it is uncontrollable, and its source is obscured. Somewhere beneath the laughter, he shudders, shudders violently. If he only knew why he was laughing.

Nietzsche decisively kills logos, emphatically destroys the Law of the Father, and manages to mutilate any remnants of God or manifestations of pure disembodied mind. He proclaims the death of God from the tops of mountains, for all to share in the news. He, with the high precision of a surgeon, cuts through layers of truths and leaps through hoops of certainties. He is the "transvaluor of value," the deconstructor of logocentric metaphysics, the rereader of history. He states, "It is a miserable story: man seeks a principle through which he can despise men—he invents a world so as to be able to slander and bespatter this world: in reality, he reaches every time for nothingness and construes nothingness as "God," as "truth," and in any case as judge and condemner of *this* state of being" (WP, 461).

Nietzsche revisits the belief in science, rationality, and truth as an achievable, linear objective. He vehemently attacks the ploys of metaphysicians and destroys their rational underpinnings: "In the great whirlpool of forces man stands with the conceit that this whirlpool is rational and has a rational aim: an error! The only rational thing we know is what little reason man has: he must exert it a lot, and it is always ruinous for him when he abandons himself, say, to 'Providence' " (Pt N, 50). He understands logos to be the defense mechanism against the body. He sees it as a weapon utilized to enforce the truth of order and stasis, used to capture a stagnant world, an immobile vision. Further, Nietzsche states: "Shrewdness, clarity, severity and logicality are weapons against the ferocity of the drives. These must be dangerous and threaten destruction: otherwise there would be no sense in developing shrewdness to the point of making it into a tyrant" (WP, 433). "With relentless logic one arrived at the absolute demand to deny nature" (WP, 245).

Thinking in terms of truths, in logical sequences, furthers the charade. "The laws of logic are "regulative articles of belief," (WP, 530), Nietzsche states, and further, "what can be thought of must certainly be a fiction" (WP, 539). "Thought cannot be derived, any more than sensations can be; but that does not mean that its primordiality or "being-in-itself" has been proved! All that is established is that we cannot get beyond it, because we *have* nothing but thought and sensation" (WP, 574). The need to define, to classify, and to compartmentalize gives the conscious animal a grounding, a sense of understanding of where she or he fits in the larger scheme of things. As Nietzsche states, "thingness has only been invented by us owing to the requirements of logic, thus with the aim of defining, communication (to bind together the multiplicity of relationships, properties, activities)" (WP, 557). Clinging to this *grounding* is difficult to avoid, though it, of necessity, leads only to error. "Consciousness is tyrannized—not least by our pride in it. One thinks that it constitutes the kernel of man; what is abiding, eternal, ultimate, and most original in him. One takes consciousness for a determinate magnitude. One denies its growth and its intermittences. One takes it for the "unity of the organism" (GS, I, 11).

One of the strongest scientific expositions of logos is the teleologically oriented version of evolution that was constructed by the God-fearing Charles Darwin. Nietzsche was a severe critic of Darwin's purposeful, teleological, and directional version of the process of evolution. He explains that "Man, a little eccentric species of animal, which . . . has its day . . . on earth a mere moment, an incident, an exception without consequences, something of no importance to the general character of the earth . . . an event without plan, reason, will, self-consciousness" (WP, 303). Under the subtitle, *Against Darwinism,* Nietzsche goes on to say that "The utility of an organ does not explain its origin. . . . The influence of 'external circumstances' is overestimated by Darwin to a ridiculous extent: the essential thing in the life process is precisely the tremendous shaping, form-creating force working from within which utilizes and exploits 'external circumstances'—in view; but in the struggle of the parts a new form is not left long without being related to a partial usefulness and then, according to its use, develops itself more and more completely" (WP, 647). "[M]an as a species does not represent any progress compared with any other animal. The whole animal and vegetable kingdom does not evolve from the lower to the higher—but all at the same time, in utter disorder, over and against each other. The richest and most complex forms—for the expression 'higher type' means no more than this—perish more easily: only the lowest preserve an apparent indestructibility" (WP, 684). Repeating the same subtitle, *Against Darwinism,* he states that "What surprises me most when I survey the broad destinies of man is that I always see before me the opposite of that which Darwin and his school see or *want* to see today: selection in favor of the stronger, better-constituted, and the progress of the species. Precisely the opposite is palpable . . . the inevitable dominion of the average, even the *sub-average* types. . . . That species represent any progress is the most unreasonable assertion in the world" (WP, 685). He concludes that "Becoming must be explained without recourse to final intentions . . . the present must absolutely not be justified by reference to a future, nor the past by reference to the present" (WP, 708).

Nietzsche decimates order, or the belief in a fundamental structure underlying what we have come to know as existence. Nothing is predetermined, nothing can be defined or iterated—even nondefineability. By destroying all ordering principles, Nietzsche disempowers, dethrones, and destabilizes those who look to order as justification for their rule. Adherence is no longer guaranteed when what one is adhering to has been derouted, and hopelessly derailed. "The problem 'thou shalt,' " Nietzsche states, is "an inclination that cannot explain itself, similar to the sexual drive," one that "shall not fall under the general condemnation of the drives; on the contrary, it shall be their evaluation and judge!" (WP, 275). The "*law*" exists to maintain, it is a "thoroughly realistic formalization of certain conditions for the self-preservation of a community" (WP, 204) and attempts to order the unorderable. Further, Nietzsche proclaims, "A morality, a mode of living tried and *proved* by long experience and testing, at length enters consciousness as a law, as *dominating*—And therewith the entire group of related values and states enters into it: it becomes venerable, unassailable, holy, true; it is part of its development that its origin should be forgotten—That is a sign it has become master" (WP, 514).

The Law of the Father is the law that enforces the domination of man over nature, order over chaos, finite infinities over depthless abysses. It seeks to eternally project itself, above and beyond, but never within. "Eternitalization," Nietzsche states, can "be that tyrannic will of a great sufferer who would like to forge what is most personal, individual, and narrow—most idiosyncratic—in his suffering, into a binding *law* and a compulsion, taking revenge on all things, as it were, by impressing, forcing, and branding into them his image, the image of his torture" (WP, 846).

Nietzsche proclaims the void of disembodied mind. He sees it as the illusion of a truth and the product of moral aestheticism. He characterizes as "tremendous blunders" the "overestimation of consciousness," "spirit as cause," "will introduced wherever there are effects," and "the 'real' world as a spiritual world" (WP, 529). "Belief in the body," he tells us, "is more fundamental than belief in the soul: the latter arose from unscientific reflection on [the agonies of] the body" (WP, 491). Nietzsche states that it is essential to start from the body and employ it as a guide. It is the much richer phenomenon, which allows for clearer observation. "The phenomenon of the body is the richer, clearer, more tangible phenomenon: to be discussed first, methodologically, without coming to any decision about its ultimate significance" (WP, 489). "We philosophers," states Nietzsche, "are not free to divide body from soul as the people do; we are even less free to divide soul from spirit. We are not thinking frogs, nor objectifying and registering mechanisms with their innards removed: constantly we have to give birth to our thoughts out of our pain and, like mothers, endow them with all we have of blood, heart, fire, pleasure, passion, agony, conscience, fate, and catastrophe" (GS, pref. 3). Belief in the body is better established than belief in the spirit" (WP, 532). " 'I am body and soul'—so speaks the child. And why should one not speak like children? But the awakened, the enlightened man says: I am body entirely, and nothing beside; and soul is only a word for something in the body" (Z, 61).

By privileging the body, Nietzsche kills religion, he decenters the moralistic ethic, and counters the virtuous. He castrates the Law of the Father, and, in so doing, buries God.

> "Whither is God" he cried. "I will tell you. *We have killed him*—you and I. All of us are his murderers. But how did we do this? How could we drink up the sea? Who gave us the sponge to wipe away the entire horizon? What were we doing when we unchained this earth from its sun? Whither is it moving now? Whither are we moving? Away from all suns? Are we not plunging continually? Backward, sideward, forward, in all directions? Is there still any up or down? Are we not straying as through an infinite nothing? Do we not feel the breath of empty space? Has it not become colder? Is not night continually closing in on us? Do we not need to light lanterns in the morning? Do we hear nothing as yet of the noise of the gravediggers who are burying God? Do we smell nothing as yet of the divine decomposition? Gods, too, decompose. God is dead. God remains dead. And we have killed him. (GS, 125)

So the madman tells the townspeople: God is dead! God is dead! They, however, are not yet ready for him: "Lightning and thunder require time; the light of the stars requires time; deeds, though done, still require time to be seen and heard. This deed is still more distant from them than the most distant stars—*and yet they have done it to themselves*" (GS, 125). Religion is, according to Nietzsche, a vestige of the logos, a vestige of naive rationalism. In his list of "Tremendous Blunders," Nietzsche includes, "consciousness as the highest achievable form, as the supreme kind of being, as 'God' " (WP, 529). *"A religion has never yet, either directly or indirectly, either as dogma or as parable, contained a truth,"* Nietzsche asserts (HH, 62). Further, he states, " 'To become as God,' 'to be absorbed into God'—for thousands of years these were the most naive and convincing desiderata (but what convinces is not necessarily true—it is merely convincing: a note for asses)" (WP, 17).

Nietzsche declares, under the subtitle *New Struggles*, that "After Buddha was dead, his shadow was still shown for centuries in a cave—a tremendous, gruesome shadow. God is dead; but given the way of men, there may still be caves for thousands of years in which his shadow will be shown.—And we—we still have to vanquish his shadow too" (GS, 108). In *Twilight of the Idols*, Nietzsche expresses his pessimism: "I am afraid we are not rid of God because we still have faith in grammar" (Pt N, 483). "Rational thought is interpretation according to a scheme that we cannot throw off" (WP, 522). The logos is the shadow of God, and in dedicating himself to the vanquishing of the shadow, Nietzsche undertakes the task of deflating the illusion of the phallus driven and created solely by desire. He states, "Desire magnifies that which one desires; it grows even by not being fulfilled—the greatest ideas are those that have been created by the most violent and protracted desires. . . . Mankind has embraced, with ever-increasing ardor, nothing but clouds: finally it called its despair, its impotence 'God' " (WP, 336). God is dead, and so is Logos, but the effect of consciousness is to sacralize the tomb. The madman, proclaimer of the death of God, emphatically states, "What after all are these churches now if they are not the tombs and sepulchers of God?" (GS, 125).

The Law of Desire

With the adept removal of the privileged signifier, the unhinged subject is situated in the chaotic realm of desire. It is what Nietzsche terms *"the great passion"* (WP, 26). Since the realm of desire, however, exists within the binary of the master signifiers, it would follow that when Nietzsche castrated the privileged signifier, he castrated the desire of the privileged. The Law of the Father states that *desire is thy desire, Oh Heavenly Male; it is a desire to have the Other as object, please you—the subject.* By castrating the privileged desire, what remains is the primary desire: *desire is the Other's desire, and thy desires to please the Other.*

"In the psyche," Lacan states "there is nothing by which the subject may situate himself as male or female being. In his psyche, the subject situates only equivalents of the function of reproduction" (F, 2). He further explains that "sexuality is represented in the psyche by a relation of the subject that is deduced from something other than sexuality itself. Sexuality is established in the field of the subject by a way that is of lack" (F, 204). In terms of the reproductive process, neither sex can reproduce without the other. Each, therefore suffers a lack. The lack for the female is only of the phallus. She is, therefore, everything but the phallus. The male, on the other hand, has only the phallus and is, therefore, so far as reproduction is concerned, only the phallus. It is the male, therefore, that is defined as substantially a lack. The male must possess the entire female body in order to claim the generative power of nature. Whether the grand metaphor is that of mind or body, the male can only relate to nature through the female body. There simply is no other way. He must possess it or give himself to it. Lacan further explains: "Before strictly human relations are established, certain relations have already been determined. They are taken from whatever nature may offer as supports, supports that are arranged in themes of opposition.. Nature provides—I must use the word signifiers, and these signifiers organize human relations in a creative way, providing them with structures and shaping them" (F, 20). The embodiment of the generative power of nature is the *Everything but,* and the embodiment of the one who lacks it is the *Nothing but,* the castrated.

The law of desire provides that *The desire of the person who lacks the generative power of nature shall be to fulfill the desire of the person who possesses the generative power of nature.* The generative power of nature lies with the female in the primary signifier and with the male in the privileged. Thus, human sexuality is forged within the dialectics of two opposite laws of desire.

According to Lacan, "the Law is there precisely from the beginning; it has always been there, and human sexuality must realize itself through it and by means of it. This fundamental law is simply one of symbolization. This is what the Oedipus complex means" (S III, 83). "[O]nce you have entered the play of symbols, you are always forced to act according to a rule" (S III, 51), and the rule is the law of desire. Analytic experience, as understood by Lacan, reveals that "what one must do as man or as woman are entirely abandoned to the drama, to the scenario, which is placed in the field of the Other—which strictly speaking is the Oedipus complex" (F, 204). Once we recognize, however, the presence of the primary signifier, oppositionally repressed by the privileged signifier, and perceive that the law of desire of the master signifier is an oppositional dialectic, then we know that underneath the law of desire that *the desire of the woman is to her husband and he shall rule over her* lies another law of desire, frightening and dark because it is castrating: *that the desire of the man shall be to the woman; she shall be the ultimate controller of desire.*

SEVEN

The Dialectics of Desire

Sexuality

In understanding human sexuality, there are, according to Laplanche's interpretation of Freud, "two terms, two 'signifiers' " that must be "the guiding thread," *drive* and *instinct* (L&D, 9). Instinct is "a performed behavioral pattern, whose arrangement is determined hereditarily and which is repeated according to modalities relatively adapted to a certain type of object," and 'the sexual object' is defined as 'the person from whom the sexual attraction proceeds' " (L&D, 10–11). Laplanche quotes the following passage from Freud: "Our study of thumb-sucking or sensual sucking has already given us the three essential characteristics of an infantile sexual manifestation. At its origin it attaches itself to one of the vital somatic functions; it has as yet no sexual object, and is thus auto-erotic; and its sexual aim is dominated by an erotogenic zone. It is to be anticipated that these characteristics will be found to apply equally to most of the other activities of the infantile sexual instincts" (SE, VII, 182). Laplanche calls the notion of *attaching itself to "propping"*: "The phenomenon Freud describes is a *leaning of the drive,* the fact that emergent sexuality attaches itself to and is propped upon another process which is both similar and profoundly divergent: the sexual drive is propped upon a non-sexual, vital function or, as Freud formulates it in terms which defy all additional commentary, upon a 'bodily function essential to life' " (L&D, 16).

The paradigmatic example of propping is where, in infancy, "simultaneous with the feeding function's achievement of satisfaction in nourishment, a sexual process begins to appear" that involves both the mouth of the infant and the breast of the mother, with the result that, "In the very act of feeding, the process of propping may be revealed in a culminating satisfaction that already resembles orgasm" (L&D, 17–18). "We pass progressively from the erotogenic zone, as a privileged *place* for stimulation, to a far more extended series of processes." Freud, Laplanche posits, generalizes further until he is eventually led to the position that "every function and, finally every human activity can be erotogenic" (L&D, 21). For Freud, the emotions, which are conceptualized within the physical contact between mother and infant, have a sexual component or fall within his explication of the sexual. At the same time, Freud maintains that the nerve system, which produces the erotic or sexual feelings that are more centrally focused in the genitals, are spread throughout the skin of the human body and are also concentrated in certain areas such as the breasts, the mouth, and the anus. These Freud calls erotogenic zones. Freud maintains that there are certain bodily functions and human actions, centered on the erotogenic zones, that produce a sexual excitation. These actions include the infant sucking at her mother's breast or the act of defecation. The distinction that Freud draws between biological sex and sexuality is reflected in the similar distinction he draws between animal instinct and drive, which is the conceptualization of the experiential and perceptual manifestations of the instinct.

At the conceptual level, the two most basic events are birth and death—the origin of existence and its termination. The conceptualization of these two events is closely related to sexual pleasure and death. Life begins with sexual intercourse, which generally produces the most intense form of pleasure, and death often is preceded by pain. While the process of reproduction may begin in sexual pleasure, it culminates in intense pain and joy for the mother. In addition, we know that, conceptually, sexual pleasure is linked with death.[1] Finally, we know that the gap between sexual pleasure and pain is closed in that at both conceptual and sensory levels sexual pleasure and pain become linked. At a neurobiological level, the pain and pleasure centers are "firing" in conjunction. Pain and pleasure merge or fold back on each other in an intense *jouissance.* The pain may be, and often is, purely imaginary but nevertheless results in *jouissance.* The imaginary reception of pain, within certain kinds of situational frameworks, can substantially increase *jouissance.* The conceptual links of bodily sensations and mind can be diagrammed as follows:

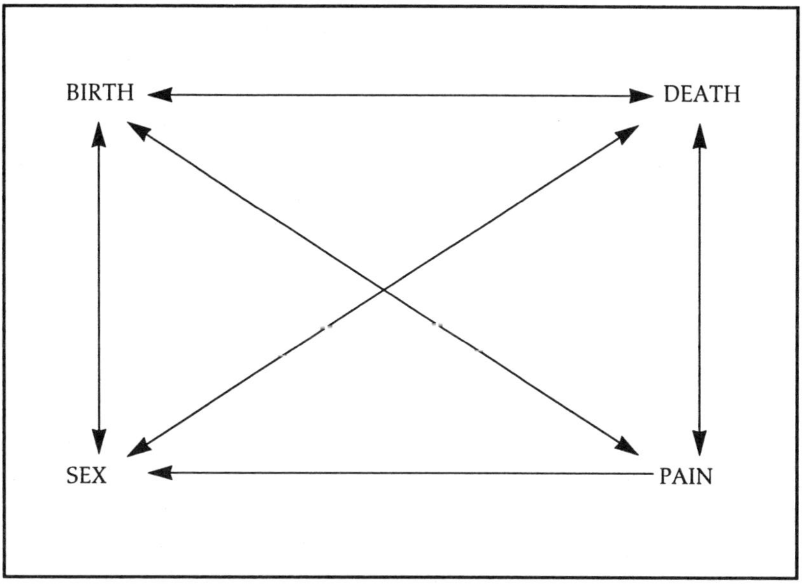

The above structure underlies Freudian psychoanalysis and forges a link between biology and mental phenomena. The tensions between the sexual and ego drives function within this birth-death-pleasure-pain square.

According to Laplanche, Freud's theory of *propping*, the buttressing of sexuality on nonsexual activities, and his thesis of *primary masochism* are essential for the understanding of the relationship between pain and sexual pleasure (L&D, 86–87). Along with the physical need for nourishment, the psychological needs related to the formation of the self become a focus of sexual desire. A mother's discipline is essential to the child's development of a sense of self. The term *discipline* combines teaching, education, training, and correction. The antiquated verb *disciple* means to teach, train, or educate. "He was discipled by his mother" is an example of its usage. A disciple is a follower of a teacher, and a discipline is an area of knowledge. Being disciplined entails being taught, corrected, or punished in the context of learning and training. In normal circumstances, children receive discipline from their mothers, whether or not it entails physical chastisement. From Freud's widespread findings of young boys' masturbating to the fantasy of being spanked by mother figures, it is clear that discipline is often sexualized. A bottle-fed male infant will have, as an adolescent or adult, the same fixation with female breasts as would a breast-fed baby. Similarly, a child who has never received physical chastisement will share similar punishment fantasies to a male child who has. Proppings are incorporated into the registers of the Imaginary and the Symbolic. Domination and submission are essential aspects of discipline. Discipline is an essential aspect of the formation of the self, and its sexualization is a key example of propping.

Masochism

When the sexual drive is repressed as a result of a contest with the ego, sexual aggression arises. Initially, Freud believed that sadism was the primary form of sexual aggression. Gradually and reluctantly, he came to the conclusion that masochism was the primary form of neurosis. Lacan concludes that "it would be a definite sign that we have really arrived at the heart of the problem of existing perversions, if we managed to deepen our understanding of the economic role of masochism" (S VII, 14–15). In masochism, sexually energized aggression is turned against the self, whereas with sadism the sexual aggression is targeted onto someone other than the self. In his paper, "A Child Is Being Beaten," Freud comments:

> The phantasy has feelings of pleasure attached to it, and on their account the patient has reproduced it on innumerable occasions in the past or may even still be doing so. At the climax of the imaginary situation there is almost invariably a masturbatory satisfaction—carried out, that is to say, on the genitals. At first this takes place voluntarily, but later on it does so in spite of the patient's efforts, and with the characteristics of an obsession.
>
> It is only with hesitation that this phantasy is confessed to. Its first appearance is recollected with uncertainty. The analytic treatment of the topic is met by unmistakable resistance. Shame and a sense of guilt are perhaps more strongly excited in this connection than when similar accounts are given of memories of the beginning of sexual life.
>
> Eventually it becomes possible to establish that the first phantasies of the kind were entertained very early in life: certainly before school age, and not later than in the fifth or sixth year. (SE, XVII, 179)

Freud asserts that these fantasies have little to do with actual experiences of corporal punishment that the child might have received. In fact, the individuals who provided the data for Freud's analysis seldom received physical discipline in their childhood.

Freud found that the childhood masochistic fantasy was different in male and female children. With young girls, the person being beaten was not themselves and was generally a boy being beaten by the girl's father (SE, XVII, 186, 189). The girl is the voyeur; she is watching the flogging of the boy but does not actively take part. In the fantasies of young boys, the child having the fantasy was generally the one being beaten, and it was generally by the mother or a substitute for her (SE, XVII, 196). There is thus "something like a constancy of sex in the persons who play a part in the phantasy" in that "the children who are being beaten are almost invariably boys, in the phantasies of boys just as much as in those of girls" (SE, XVII, 191). As the masochistic fantasies are carried on into adulthood, they retain the same structure. "As regards masochistic men," according to Freud, "the persons who administer the chastisement are always women" (SE, XVII, 197). In the case of either sex, however, the fantasy is a pleasurable one for the child and is reproduced on innumerable occasions and "at the climax of the imaginary situation there is usually a masturbatory satisfaction" (SE, XVII, 179).

There is an obvious relationship, at least as far as the male is concerned, between this primary masochism and the Oedipal passage. The Oedipal stage marks the dialectical transition from the maternal object of the ego ideal to the paternal. In the pre-Oedipal state the mother occupies the privileged position, while in the Oedipal state the privileged position shifts to the father. This passage is accompanied by phallic vacillation that manifests itself in the form of a simultaneous fear of and desire for castration. The acquisition of the phallus is inevitably accompanied by the repressed desire to present it to the mother. The inevitable repression in the Oedipal passage manifests itself in the form of sexual aggression against the phallus, which threatens the ego and is itself repressed. Masochism is therefore rooted in the pre-Oedipal and reverses the Oedipal dialectic by imposing a pre-Oedipal matricentric psychic reality.

One of the most essential premises underlying psychoanalytic theory is Freud's assertion that the relationship between mother and child has a sexual dimension. As stated by Laplanche, "[T]here is indeed a form of seduction which practically no human being escapes, the seduction of maternal care. The first gestures of a mother towards her child are necessarily impregnated with sexuality" (L&D, 33). According to Freud, "A child's intercourse with anyone responsible for his care affords him an unending source of sexual excitation and satisfaction from his erotogenic zones. This is especially so since the person in charge of him, who after all is as a rule the mother, herself regards him with feelings that are derived from her own sexual life: she strokes him, kisses him, rocks him and quite clearly treats him as a substitute for a complete sexual object" (SE, VII, 223). "[S]exuality emerges only with the turning round upon the self, thus with masochism, so that, within *the field of sexuality*, masochism is already considered as primary" (L&D, 89). Accordingly, "whether what is under discussion is fantasy or sexuality, in both cases the masochistic moment is first. The masochistic fantasy is fundamental" (L&D, 91).

Masochism in the adult is not a puerile childhood perversion. Rather, it is the dialectically repressed underside of Oedipal phallocentric sexuality. Masochism is the primary neurosis because it is the way in which the repressed sexual drive returns to attack the ego. "We already know that neurotic symptoms are the outcome of a conflict which arises over again in the symptom and are reconciled, as it were, by the compromise of the symptom's new method of satisfying the libido. The two forces which have fallen out meet once that has been constructed" (SE, XVI, 358–59). "We have every reason to believe that sensations of pain . . . trench upon sexual excitation and produce a pleasurable condition, for the sake of which the subject will even willingly experience the unpleasure of pain. When the feeling of pain has become a masochistic aim, the sadistic aim of *causing* pains can arise also" (SE, XIV, 128–29). "It [primary masochism] might be formulated as 'the lust for and/or the enjoyment of pain' . . . the paradox of masochism, far from deserving to be circumscribed as a specific 'perversion,' should be generalized, linked as it is to the *essentially traumatic nature of human sexuality*" (L&D, 105). Masochism is the product of the sexual drive attacking the ego by having the self force the ego to surrender its boundaries. The libidinal energy forces the ego to accept the aggression to reunite mind and body.

Freud distinguishes between several kinds of masochism. He classifies primary masochism as feminine masochism, stating that "The suppression of women's aggressiveness which is prescribed for them constitutionally and imposed on them socially favours the development of powerful masochistic impulses which succeed, as we know, in binding erotically the destructive trends which have been diverted inwards. Thus masochism, as people say, is truly *feminine*. But if, as happens so often you meet with masochism in men, what is left to say that these men exhibit very plain feminine traits?" (SE, XXII, 117). Freud designates this as feminine masochism even when it is found in the male because it constitutes a disavowal of the phallus and, for Freud, the essence of the feminine is the absence of the phallus. It is primarily a male neurosis since women do not have a phallus that they can disavow. Freud wrote, "But if one has an opportunity of studying cases in which the masochistic phantasies have been especially richly elaborated, one quickly discovers that they place the subject in a characteristically female situation; they signify . . . being castrated. . . . For this reason I have called this form of masochism . . . the feminine form" (SE, XIX, 162). Indeed, the ultimate fantasy of the male masochist is castration.[2] It is a variant or natural progression of the *jouissance* of submission.

According to Freud, "the mythological creation, Medusa's head, can be traced back to the same *motif* of fright at castration" (SE, XXII, 24). "[F]ear of castration is one of the commonest and strongest motives for repression and thus for the formation of neuroses" (SE, XXII, 87). As summarized by Lacan, "What analytic experience shows is that, in any case, it is castration that governs desire, whether in the normal or the abnormal" (E, 323).

Male masochism is a non-Oedipal form of sexuality. The pain must be in the context of a ritual castration-disempowerment. The masochist's attitude moves towards a dedication to suffering: a recognition of the meaning in and behind the suffering, for the deeper knowledge of the self through the renunciation of the self. It must be a voluntary sacrifice—a sacrifice of pleasure for pain, in an effort of redemption, in attributing a heightened power to the ego. At the same time, the ritual must empower the female, and she must accept the possession-ownership-control of the phallus as his voluntary sacrifice, which transforms him from a father to a consort. If the phallus is said to be a "maternal phallus" in the context of matriphallic psychic reality and sexuality, it is so defined because the female possesses, owns, and controls the male penis. The symbolic castration is the fantasized transfer of possession-ownership-control.

The narrative structures of male masochistic fantasies and practices clearly reflect this disavowal/affirmation. An important structural aspect of male masochism is the postponement of sexual gratification for the male. The fantasy structures constantly subject the male to arousal but endlessly hold him in suspense so far as gratification is concerned. At the same time, he must provide sexual gratification to the female. When he is finally gratified, it is often in the form of masturbation, and, if intercourse, the woman is on top. A disavowal of the paternal phallus requires the disavowal of the right to sexual service, and the gift of the phallus to the female entails the voluntary acceptance by the male of the duty/privilege to sexually serve the dominant female. This constitutes a form of castration/empowerment by the transfer of the phallus. The male cannot pass possession-ownership-control without voluntarily giving up power.

The structure of non-Oedipal male masochistic sexuality can be further uncovered in terms of the erotic imagery of the dominatrix. She is not a masculine woman nor is she androgynous. She is pure female, though not *feminine.* Her erotic power does not come from physical strength nor from traditionally male characteristics. It lies beneath the mask of femininity, and when the veil is lifted the Goddess is revealed. The gift of the phallus is not what makes her a Goddess. The phallus is given to her because she *is* the Goddess. She summons the sacrifice when she enters the desperate politics of transvaluation and steps away from the masquerade. Correspondingly, it is matriphallic imagery that sexually excites the masochistic male. Switch, whip, or sword are key sexual referents because of their phallic symbolism. Inner strength, self-confidence, and a lack of deference for the male are the characteristics of matriphallic females. Characteristics that might be considered masculine or androgynous have little to do with it. Similarly, masochistic males are not particularly *feminine.* In fact, they are often very powerful. The term "Dionysian masochism" is far more appropriate than Freud's "feminine masochism." Silverman describes what we would term the Dionysian masochist as follows:

> What is it precisely that the male masochist displays, and what are the consequences of this self-exposure? To begin with, he acts out in an insistent and exaggerated way the basic conditions of cultural subjectivity, conditions that are normally disavowed; he loudly proclaims that his meaning comes to him from the Other, prostrates himself before the gaze even as he solicits it, exhibits his castration for all to see, and revels in the sacrificial basis of the social contract. The male masochist magnifies the losses and divisions upon which cultural identity is based, refusing to be sutured or recompensed. In short, he radiates a negativity inimical to the social order.[3]

Underlying Dionysian masochism is the unconscious primary fantasy structure of the sexual or Eros drive. Dionysian masochism is an alliance between the (M)other and the son/consort "to write the father out of his dominant position and to install the mother in his place."[4] "In inviting the mother to beat and/or dominate him," Silverman states, "the feminine masochist transfers power and authority from the father to her, remakes the symbolic order, and 'ruins' his own paternal legacy."[5] Gilles Deleuze, in his analysis of von Sacher-Masoch's *Venus in Furs*, gives the following description of the relationship between the male masochist and the woman:

A contract is established between the hero and the woman, whereby at a precise point in time and for a determinate period she is given every right over him. By this means the masochist tries to exercise the danger of the father and to ensure that the temporal order of reality and experience will be in conformity with the symbolic order, in which the father has been abolished for all time. Through the contract . . . the masochist reaches towards the most mythical and most timeless realms, where [the (M)other] dwells. Finally, he ensures that he will be beaten . . . what is beaten, humiliated and ridiculed in him is the image and likeness of the father, and the possibility of the father's aggressive return . . . The masochist thus liberates himself in preparation for a rebirth in which the father will have no part.[6]

The contract is entered into with the mother—it excludes the father and places onto the mother the task of exercising and applying the paternal law. The contract is the Law of Transgression; it is made deliberately to promote slavery and debasement at the service of the woman and the mother and is vital to the masochistic ritual. By signing away one's rights and authorizing humiliation, the masochist's experience is heightened. Failure to honor the contract will, of course, lead to further reprisals.

The fantasies of pain trench upon sexual excitation and produce a pleasurable condition which Lacan terms *jouissance*.[7] The domination/submission experience has been described in English with terms such as *erotic, profound, exciting, exhilarating,* and *ecstasy*.[8] Participants "claim that it satisfies certain fundamental psychological needs, which may include the experience of power and control for the woman and the experience of giving up power and release for the man."[9]

Kraft-Ebbing, credited as the father of sexology, described masochism as the antithesis to sadism and referred to them jointly as "sado-masochism." There is the transparent opposition between causing pain to another for pleasure and having another cause pain to oneself for one's own pleasure. Freud at first believed that sadism was primary and masochism secondary and adopted Kraft-Ebbing's composite term. The opposition of "activity and passivity" (SE, VII, 159) reinforced this traditional link for Freud.

An examination of the structures of masochism and sadism will show, however, that they are quite separate kinds of perversions. "Masochism is not inverted sadism" (S II, 232). According to Derrida:

 From the outset we had conceived masochism as a component drive complementary to sadism in its turning back against one's proper Ego. This extra turn, this return onto "myself," or to "myself," is nothing other than the turn which turns the same drive toward the object. The only correction made since then: masochism may be primary. As this is a major correction, and as it at once proves too much or too little, but in any event operates otherwise than as a supplementary and derivative turn, Freud does not exploit it, sends it away or drops it, deciding, without any other transition, to return to the drives which preserve life. He drops the matter, like the note at the bottom of the page which punctuates the end of this act. (PC, 368)

The expression of aggression common to both sadism and masochism is somewhat misleading insofar as their relationship is concerned. Deleuze points out that "As soon as we read Masoch, we become aware that his universe has nothing to do with that of Sade. . . . We must take an entirely different approach, the *literary approach,* since it is from literature that stem the original definitions of sadism and masochism."[10] Freud was correct in noting that "certain among the impulses to perversion occur regularly as pairs of opposites; and this . . . has a high theoretical significance" (SE, VII, 160).

Oedipal sexuality manifests the Hegelian master/slave dialectics. The *jouissance* of control and domination is for the male to enjoy, and the woman is sexualized and genderized according to the *jouissance* of submission. We start life in the grip of the primary original fantasy and the primary signifier. It requires a process of sexualization and self-formation to move from the one to the other. This is the makeup of the Oedipal passage. It is much more than merely a separation from the mother. It is a reversal and restructuring of a primary sexuality and self-formation, which, if not interrupted, would lead to a matriarchal psychic reality. The Oedipal passage is simply the transformation from the primary to the privileged. If, however, people fail to shift from, or they return to, a psychic reality that is structured by the primary signifier rather than the privileged signifier, they enter the realm of perversion.

Those whose psychic reality is structured by the primary signifier, and who thus resist or transcend Oedipal genderization and sexuality, are within the dialectics of the generative power of nature and its lack, the *jouissances* of domination and submission, and the Hegelian master/slave formulation of self. The structure of the master signifiers is the same for both the primary and the privileged, the generative power of nature, the seduction of difference, and castration. The difference is that the sex of the person who represents the generative power of nature is reversed. According to Lacan, "From master to slave and rival, there is only one dialectical step—the relations of the master to the slave are essentially reversible, and the master sees very quickly his dependency in relation to his slave become established" (S II, 263). Those who are heterosexual but non-Oedipal will, by Oedipal definition, be perverse. What is the nature of this Oedipally defined perversion for the male? The answer to this question lies in the analysis of the primary neurosis, Dionysian masochism, the symptom that so troubled Freud and was so difficult for him to account for in terms of the presuppositions of psychoanalytic theory.

According to Camille Paglia, the "invitation to Dionysian dance is a binding contract of enslavement to nature."[11] Since the primary signifier relates woman to the generative power of nature, she is nature's representative. Consequently, the Dionysian dance is a binding contract of enslavement *to* woman. Man can reunite with nature only through an enslavement *by* a woman. Since nature is in his body and his body is a part of nature he can reconcile mind and body only through a binding contract with woman. The cost for woman of man's separation from nature has been immense. Man cannot return to nature or heal the mind/body breach without also paying a heavy price. The cost of man's liberation from nature was the enslavement of the woman. Man must pay the same price for his reconciliation.

Within the structure of the primary signifier, masochism is not an illness but "a hierarchical dream, a conceptual realignment of sexual orders" since "Sex is the ritual link between man and nature."[12] Masochism is a "*jouissance* beyond the pleasure principle" (F, 183–84). Lacan instructs us that "The pervert is he who, in short circuit, more directly than any other, succeeds in his aim, by integrating in the most profound way his function as subject with his existence as desire. . . . That is why . . . I wish to stress the operation of the realization of the subject in his signifying dependence in the locus of the Other" (F, 206). "[I]t is in seeing a whole chain come into play at the level of the desire of the Other that the subject's desire is constituted" (F, 235). Desire is the "nodal point by which the pulsation of the unconscious is linked to sexual reality" (F, 154), and the libido is the effective presence of that desire (F, 153).

What value has my desire for you? the eternal question that is posed in the dialogue of lovers. But the supposed value, for example, of *feminine masochism*, as it is called, should be subjected, parenthetically, to serious scrutiny. It belongs to a dialogue that may be defined, in many respects, as a masculine phantasy. . . . It is quite striking to see that the representatives of this sex [female] in the analytic circle are particularly disposed to maintain the fundamental belief in feminine masochism. It may be that there is a veil here, concerning the interests of the sex, that should not be lifted too quickly. (F, 192–93)

We know what the relationship is between male sexuality and male power, and female sexuality and male power within patriphallic psychic reality. What requires a fuller understanding, however, is the relationship between female sexuality and female power, and male sexuality and male power within a psychic reality structured by the primary signifier, and condemned as perversion in terms of the privileged signifier.

The case for the existence within language of the primary signifier has been based thus far on two arguments. The first concerns the Lacanian hypothesis of how the basic, fundamental, and central signifiers get their meaning out of oppositional relationships to each other. Nowhere does he present a reason why this is not equally applicable to the privileged signifier. The second argument is the poststructuralist position that every script has an underlying text, a narrative that lies between the line in the form of a dialectical relationship. The structure of the two master signifiers is mutually and multidirectionally related to the explanatory narratives of the two forms of the original fantasy of the collective, which establishes the relationship between humans and nature, thus facilitating the emergence of the Subject and the self. Our third argument for the existence of the primary signifier as the relational opposition to the privileged signifier will lie in an analysis of the nature and structure of Dionysian masochism.

Opinions about masochism differ. On the one hand, we have the clinical psychiatric view of masochism as a psychosexual disorder and the traditional psychoanalytic view of it as a perversion. On the other hand, we have those who describe it as a healthy, natural, sublime human experience. Otto, for example tell us that "The madness which is called Dionysus [masochism] is no sickness, no debility in life, but a companion of life at its healthiest."[13] The analyst Lyn Cowan, in her book *Masochism a Jungian View,* regards masochism as "a natural product of soul, ready and needing to bring forward its own vision and its own cure."[14] She characterizes masochism as the opposite to egoistic narcissism (M, 44). Masochism "is a mode of psychic survival" working against "the Promethean fantasy which would lead to ruin" (M, 119). It is not a mere perversion, distortion or deviation but an essential reality, a reflection of the soul in its tortured, most inarticulate moments (M, ix). "Dionysian consciousness—which allows for masochistic experience can see 'visitation' as a welcome opportunity rather than as a pathology . . . an act and experience of worship" (M, 98) in expiation of "that most original of humans sins," the deeper crime that underlies all crime: phallic inflation and narcissism (M, 101). It is "an encounter with the inevitability of one's essential character—which, as Heraclitus tells us, is fate" (M, 114). It only becomes pathological "when it is literalized and when its machinations block, instead of lead into, self-revelation and self-knowledge (M, 73). She explains:

As much as most people would abhor the idea, masochistic experience does radical therapy, performs radical change on the ego. A masochistic posture strips down and exposes the ego—its defenses, ambitions, failures, and successes. It is a psychological posture in which we are humiliated, brought down, made defenseless, made aware that we must die. Through masochism we can sometimes contact the deeper meaning in the suffering, the depth of its pain and pleasure. If our submission is genuine, we can feel it is for the sake of something greater, more important, more valuable than the ego and its perceptions. The ego becomes servant to that greater thing. . . . The necessity and desirability of submission—the chief characteristic of masochism—is a submission to Necessity herself, the Goddess Ananke. (M, 41)

The greater the narcissism of the ego, the stronger the masochistic desire. "Strength can be a terrible burden. It is a bondage which must be relieved in moments of abandonment, of weakness, of letting down and letting go. So it is hardly surprising that the strong personality . . . should be the most likely to desire masochistic experiences" (M, 111). This is reflected in the propensity for masochistic tendencies in men with social power.[15]

As a manifestation of the return of the repressed sexual drive, masochism is the expression of the *jouissance* of submission. The ego defends itself through the neuroses of the jouissance of control. Each of these *jouissances* have the same status as neuroses. The *jouissance* of submission and the *jouissance* of control cannot be separated. Dionysian masochism is a specifically male pathology.[16] According to Silverman:

[I]t is only in the case of men that feminine masochism can be seen to assume pathological proportions. Although that psychic phenomenon often provides a centrally structuring element of both male and female subjectivity, it is only in the latter that it can be safely acknowledged. It is an accepted—indeed a prerequisite—element of "normal" female subjectivity, providing a crucial mechanism for eroticizing lack and subordination. The male subject, on the contrary, cannot avow feminine masochism without calling into question his identification with the masculine position. All of this is another way of suggesting that what is acceptable for the female subject is pathological for the male.[17]

Lacan states that "In adults, we are aware of the palpable richness of perversion. Perversion, in sum, is the privileged exploration of an existential possibility of human nature—its internal tearing apart, its gap, through which the supra-natural world of the symbolic was able to make its entry" (S I, 218). This is why the ego is structured like a symptom, and it is both domination of the female and masochism that constitute the mental illnesses of man. "[T]he ego is constructed and is to be located within the subject as a whole, just as a symptom. Nothing differentiates the one from the other . . . the catalogue of defense mechanisms which make up the ego" (S I, 16). "The fundamental absurdity of interhuman behaviour can only be comprehended in the light of this *system* . . . called the human ego, namely that set of defenses, of denials *[négations]* of dams, of inhibitions, of fundamental fantasies which orient and direct the subject," so states Lacan (S I, 17). In heterosexual relationships, whether patriphallic or matriphallic, dominance and submission are sought in the opposite sex "precisely because it is opposite" (M, 112). Masochism is the passage, that for the male, connects the Imaginary and Symbolic structures of the privileged signifier with those of the primary. Just as the imagery of God-King-father is integral to the former, the imagery of Goddess-Mother is vital to the latter. Any male who is in the grips of goddess imagery will be in a masochistic, submissive psychological state. Masochistic practices are therefore associated with contemporary pagan religions.

Punishment is sought for the sake of humiliation and pain as an embrace of sacrifice. Castration is at the level of the Imaginary and the Symbolic, not that of the Real, and functions to humiliate the narcissistic ego.[18] Through humiliation-castration, the ego is deflated and can merge with the id, and a reconciliation between the sexual and ego drive can take place. Dionysus is the god of the loss of boundaries of the self—the god of unification between mind and body, female and male, humans and nature, the ego and the id, and Eros and Thanatos. "Clinical observations have led me to the impression that masochism is associated with fantasies and acts of self-preparation for being incorporated." Blumstein writes, "The fantasies and actual self-destruction has as its unconscious aim the goal of achieving a secure and physically gratifying union with an omnipotent figure."[19]

Both matriphallic and Oedipal, or patriphallic, sexuality are manifestations of the process of propping wherein sexuality becomes attached to the development of the self in terms of domination and submission (SE, XVII, 86; SE, XXII, 86; SE, XIII, 91). The whip is one of the key symbols of the powerful, aggressive forms of the Goddess.[20] The consort figure of Pan, the earlier form of Dionysus, is often portrayed as being whipped by a goddess figure.[21] The disciplining of Pan, the "angel of pain", combines the ecstasy of human sexuality with the inevitability of suffering.[22] Through the process of propping, the act of discipline merges with sexuality. The whip plays the same symbolic role in matriphallic sexuality that penetration does in patriphallic sexuality.

Oedipal genderization and sexuality ensures the triumph of Thanatos over Eros. The *jouissance* of male domination targets aggression against the female in the form of misogyny. When the female internalizes misogynous aggression, she is objectified so that she can be sexually consumed, her reproductive powers appropriated by the male in the service of his own ego. In the context of normal Oedipal genderization and a successful Oedipal passage, aggression directed against the female by the male or by herself as a result of internalizing misogyny can be fully identified with the Thanatos drive, fighting against Eros.

The Unnamed Pathology

On April 21, 1896, Freud delivered a paper to the Viennese Society for Psychiatry and Neurology entitled *The Aetiology of Hysteria.*[23] In it Freud set out his theory that neurosis was caused by childhood sexual trauma resulting from sexual molestation by an adult, generally the father or a close relative. In most cases, the seducer was male and the child female; in some, the adult was male and the child male; and in a few cases the adult was female and the child male. This theory later become known as "the seduction theory." While the sexual assaults ranged from rape to fondling, the term seduction was used by Freud because the adult would generally, at least at first, attempt to gain the child's voluntary cooperation. While Freud was clear on the matter, his choice of the term "seduction" was unfortunate as it didn't clarify that it is the adult who attempts the seduction of the child and not the child of the adult. In later years, when Freud was describing the early history of the development of psychoanalysis, he wrote, "In the period in which the main interest was directed to discovering infantile sexual traumas, almost all my women patients told me that they had been seduced by their father" (SE, XXII, 120). In the conclusion of his paper, Freud addressed the following words to his audience, "Prepared as I am to meet with contradiction and disbelief . . . I must ask you not to regard them as the fruit of idle speculation. They are based on a laborious individual examination of patients which has in most cases taken up a hundred or more hours of work."[24]

In his in-depth study of this early period in psychoanalysis and the development and later rejection of the seduction theory, Jeffrey Masson points out that, contrary to normal practice, there was no summary of the paper, no report, discussion, or comments. In a letter to Fleiss written a short while later, however, Freud commented that "A lecture on the aetiology of hysteria at the Psychiatric Society met with an icy reception from the asses, and from Kraft-Ebbing the strange comment: It sounds like a scientific fairy tale. And this after one has demonstrated to them a solution to a more than thousand-year-old problem, a 'source of the Nile!' "[25] In another letter to Fleiss written around the same time, Freud wrote, "I am as isolated as you could wish me to be: the word has been given out to abandon me, and a void is forming around me."[26]

It was the testimony of these early patients that led Freud to lay the foundations of psychoanalysis on the bedrock of human sexuality. At the time, there was no question in his mind as to the reality of the events related to him and that they were not fantasy. He wrote, "Doubts about the genuineness of the infantile sexual scenes can, however, be deprived of their force. . . . [T]he behaviour of patients while they are reproducing these infantile experiences is in every respect incompatible with the assumption that the scenes are anything else than a reality which is being felt with distress and reproduced with the greatest reluctance" (SE, III, 204). Freud nevertheless gave up the seduction theory, albeit reluctantly and with some degree of ambivalence.[27] Yet in the April 26, 1896, letter to Fliess, Freud relates the case of a woman who was brutally raped by her father and infected with gonorrhea when she was two years old, and Freud suggests a new motto for psychoanalysis: "What have they done to you, poor child?"[28] Throughout Freud's professional life, he continued to be confronted with particular cases where he could not avoid the conclusion that the memories were genuine. He later wrote that "Phantasies of being seduced are of particular interest, because so often they are not phantasies but real memories. Fortunately, however, they are nevertheless not real as often as seemed at first to be shown by analysis" (SE, XVI, 370).

Freud's motivations for abandoning the seduction theory were both unconscious and conscious and are dealt with extensively by Masson.[29] The unconscious motivation relates to Freud's relationship with Fleiss and his patient Emma Eckstein. The conscious motivation came from Freud's isolation and the fact, which he soon became aware of, that the theory was unacceptable to the professional medical community and his ostracization by the medical community for articulating the theory would be an impassable barrier to the development of psychoanalysis and of his professional career. He describes the seduction theory as "a mistaken idea . . . which might have been almost fatal to the young science" (SE, XIV, 17). A further reason, which was, no doubt, shared by the critics of the seduction theory, was that if the theory were true, it would have to be the case that the sexual abuse of children was pervasive. As Masson points out, a number of studies were available at this time that indicated that, in the words of one of the authors, "Sexual acts committed against children are very frequent."[30] Freud's conclusion that "such widespread perversions against children are not very probable" has remained the prevailing wisdom until recently.[31]

Freud did not conclude that adults did not molest children but rather that it was impossible for him to ever know whether what the patient related was true or fantasy. Laplanche states that "In summary, Freud proposes, in opposition to his own theory, objections of fact—the impossibility of ever rediscovering *the* "scene"—and of principle: the impossibility of admitting that paternal perversion is *that* frequent and, above all, the inability to decide whether a scene discovered in analysis is true or fantasized" (L&D, 32).

The return to the seduction theory in the latter years of his life by Freud's close friend and colleague Sandor Ferenczi and the paper that he delivered on the seduction theory are of great importance for clarifying the relationship of the seduction theory to the Oedipus complex. Ferenczi delivered this paper over Freud's strong objections, with a full awareness of the likely consequences that would, and did, follow.[32] Ferenczi viewed this paper as "a short extract" from "the vast theme of the external origin of the formation of character and of neuroses."[33] In this paper he discusses the resistance of psychoanalysts to what patients tell them and the reasons that led him to the conclusion that "trauma, specifically sexual trauma, cannot be stressed enough as a pathogenic agent. . . . Even children of respected, high-minded puritanical families fall victim to real rape much more frequently than one had dared to suspect."[34] Ferenczi describes the reaction of children as embracing submission:

> The overwhelming power and authority of the adult renders them silent; often they are deprived of the senses. Yet that very fear, when it reaches its zenith, forces them automatically to surrender to the will of the aggressor, to anticipate each of his wishes and to submit to them; forgetting themselves entirely, to identify totally with the aggressor. As a result of the identification with the aggressor, let us call it introjection, the aggressor disappears as external reality and becomes intrapsychic instead of extrapsychic.[35]

Ferenczi concluded his paper with the assertion, "I believe, should all this prove true, that we shall be obliged to revise certain chapters of the [psychoanalytic] theory of sexuality and of genitality."[36] He suggests that such a reevaluation may provide the answer to the question of "what it is in the playful satisfaction of tenderness that introduces the element of suffering and thereby sadomasochism." He ends with the proposition that "the love during the intercourse [of adults] . . . is saturated with hatred."[37]

The reexamination of the Oedipal theory that Ferenczi called for must produce a theory of sexuality and genitality that will account for the phenomenon of the adult seducing the child as well as the effect that it has on the emotional and sexual development of the child and that will account as well for the aggression that is implicit in human sexuality, whether focused inward or outward. This is what psychoanalysis has failed to do, hence this pathology is undesignated. Thus, there is a neurosis that belongs in the category along with masochism and sadism for which there is no name. And the reason it has no label is that it is taken as the norm. It is a pathology and not a perversion because it is phallic. We are justified in using the term *pathology* because it is harmful and damaging to others. It is the pathology that is manifested in the domination and control of women by denying their selfhood, by turning them into objects and infanticizing them. Although we do not have a name for it, we know it as pornography.

Pornography is made up of a number of different but related genres with the same basic structure. The most straightforward are the pictures of naked women, legs spread apart, ready to be penetrated and used. The next is the bondage genre in which the women are shown bound, often with gags so they are deprived of the Voice. The next progression involves the woman placing herself in a position in which her buttocks, breasts, or genitals are made readily available for whipping or subject to a painful procedure such as clamping. The script for this latter genre is that of discipline, in which the woman voluntarily submits to and accepts the punishment. According to the pornographic script, she deserves the punishment, she accepts the punishment, and she likes it. The next advance is the infantization of the female by dressing her like a child or having her pubic area shaved so that her genitals look like those of a child. The final form is child pornography in which actual children are seduced, induced, or forced to participate in its making. This fantasy is that which, when carried out, we call incest and the sexual abuse of children. When the child is a little boy, it is used like a little girl, that is, he is fondled and penetrated.

How can the sexual domination of women be considered on the same plane as masochism, as a pathology, when in every patriarchal religious system in the world it is legitimate? The sexual possession and domination of the female is fundamental to patriarchy, and it includes the right, duty, and pleasure of the husband to gain sexual satisfaction by using his wife to create sexual pleasure for himself. It has been frequently said that women are naturally masochistic because they can be eroticized by being the subject of discipline. We can infer from *The Story of O,* written by a woman, that females can and do experience the *jouissance* of submission.[38] It does not follow from this, however, that this *jouissance* is natural for all females.

The entire process of Oedipal genderization creates this structure whereby the male is eroticized to seek the *jouissance* of domination while the female is eroticized to accept and seek the *jouissance* of submission. Jehovah has ordered this when he tells the woman "Thy desire *[jouissance]* shall be to thy husband."[39] There are no novels like those of de Sade and von Sacher-Masoch to give this phenomenon a name. It doesn't, therefore, appear in the academic catalogues of sexual pathologies and perversion. The author of this text is every phallic man, that is, every male who has been successfully Oedipalized. The story of the lives of millions of women and men is not the stuff that novels are made of. Yet the text is there in the Laws of Manu, the Bible, the Koran, Sir Robert Filmer's *Patriarcha,* the law, and male pornography and imagery. Pedophilia is not the name of this pathology, it is merely one form that the pathology can take.

"[M]an's desire finds its meaning in the desire of the other, not so much because the other holds the key to the object desired, as because the first object of desire is to be recognized by the other" (E, 5). This central thesis in Lacanian psychoanalytic theory owes far more to the Hegelian-Kojèvian explanation of self-consciousness than it does to Freud.[40] The Hegelian dialectic is between master and slave or, in other words, between submission and control. "Here we find," according to Lacan, "a reciprocal relation of annihilation, a fatal relation structured by the following two abysses—either desire is extinguished, or the object disappears. That is why, at every turn, I take my bearings from the master-slave dialectic, and I re-explain it" (S I, 222). Central to Oedipal theory is the Law of the Father, wherein the Father owns or possesses the Mother. The law of the master, that the slave "should satisfy the desire and the pleasure *[jouissance]*" of the master, is the first law of patriarchy: "thy desire shall be to thy husband and he shall rule over thee."[41] The *jouissances* of control and submission, whether between male and female, male and male, female and female, or adult and child, are the essential dynamics of human relations.

According to Lacan, "Hegel gives account of the interhuman bond. He has to account not only for society, but for history. He cannot neglect any of its aspects" (S I, 222–23). The Hegelian impasse whereby the master's "recognition by the slave is worth nothing to the master, since only a slave has recognized him, that is to say someone that he does not recognize as a man" (S I, 222–23), is resolved within the Imaginary and Symbolic mythical structures where the woman is both Goddess and wife. These dialectics permeate human culture. A paradigmatic example is romantic love where the Goddess is worshipped from afar while the wife remains in servitude. The fluidity of the positions of dominance and submission resolves the Hegelian impasse.

The appropriate dialectical opposite to the masochistic *jouissance* of submission is the *jouissance* of control. Because male control and female submission were made one of the central premises of traditional psychoanalytic theory, control is only viewed as a perversion when it is exercised by women over males. If Freud had maintained his original seduction theory, he would have recognized that Oedipal sexuality is as pathological as the sexuality of the dominatrix and the male masochist. The dialectics of repression and the return of the repressed as neurosis lead inevitably to the dialectic between submission and control. While the rhetoric of political ideology may be that of equality between the sexes, the sexuality and erotica of politics is that of domination and submission As Lacan explains, "The most naked rivalry between men and women is eternal, and its style is laid down in conjugal relations. . . . Feminine rebellion didn't start yesterday. From master to slave and rival, there is only one dialectical step—the relations of the master to the slave are essentially reversible, and the master sees very quickly his dependency in relation to his slave become established" (S II, 263).

Freud's explanation of the Oedipal passage presents a theory of the dynamics of sexual desire as they develop between parents and children. Every parent is either a father or a mother, and every child is genderized as masculine or feminine in a reflection of the gender of the parent of the same sex. Thus, the dynamics and structure of human sexuality are passed on from generation to generation. Children develop their sexuality within the framework of "the seduction of maternal care" (L&D, 33; SE, VII, 223). If Freud had not abandoned the seduction theory, he may well have been led to turn the tools of psychoanalysis onto male sexuality.

Oedipal sexuality is normal because it is widespread—language privileges the male by identifying him with the *jouissance* of control. The pathology of patriarchy is powerful because the desire to submit to the female is strong. "The relations of desire to language constitute the mechanisms of the unconscious" (F, 12). "At the same time psychoanalysis considers every *symptom* as language; it makes of the symptom a type of signifying system whose laws, similar to those of language, must be discovered."[42] "[T]hen it is already quite clear that the symptom resolves itself entirely in an analysis of language, because the symptom is itself structured like a language, because it is from language that speech must be delivered" (E, 59).

The ego "is structured exactly like a symptom. At *par excellence,* the mental illness of a man" (S II, 216). One symptom has no name because it is recognized as normal. The other symptom is called masochism. Language structures and institutions have linked masculinity and domination and femininity and submission. This is why psychoanalysis can consider every symptom as language and language as making a signifying system of the symptom.[43] Domination and submission are the structure of the mental illness of man, the neuroses of normality, and the pathology of patriarchy. The sides can change, the poles can be reversed, but there is no escape from the bimorphism of sex, the dialectics of desire, and the polarity of the symptoms. Transcendence does not lie in the middle, in a synthesis, in androgynous sexuality and gender. One can change sides, but one cannot escape the game.

Sadism

Without seduction there can be no *jouissance*, and the mechanics of seduction require voluntary embrace. "But one shouldn't after all proceed too quickly to break inventive homonym, and the fact the masochism has been called by this name for so long by psychoanalysis is not without reason. In masochistic fields, pain shares the character of a good" (S VII, 239–40). In the structure of domination-submission, pain is a good because the pleasure of bearing the pain comes from meeting the desire of the Other. Pain is the sacrifice. It is the measure of submission.

The *jouissance* of sadism, on the other hand, is what Lacan terms the *jouissance* of transgression. In sadism, what "we are dealing with is nothing less than the attraction of transgression" (S II, 2). Regarding de Sade, Lacan states that "no one else has done such deep injury to the feelings and thoughts of mankind" (S VII, 200). In the structure of sadism, pain is an evil, and it is from this evil that the *jouissance* of transgression is derived. The domination and submission that constitute the structure of masochism entail one person using another person sexually with his or her consent. Sadism constitutes using a person sexually without consent (S VII, 184–85). The presence or absence of consent is critical to the nature of the *jouissance* and marks the difference between seduction and transgression. "[I]n the gaze of the being whom I torment, I have to sustain my desire with an act of defiance, a challenge at every instant. If it does not rise above the situation, if it is not glorious, desire sinks into shame" (S I, 220).

Sadism belongs within the conceptual structure of the law as its oppositional pole and reflects the dialectics of good and evil. It is a revolt against the law, whereas primary masochism subverts it. God needs the devil just as the devil needs God. They are a part of the same dynamics. De Sade is Saint Paul's evil twin. Without de Sade there is no sin for Saint Paul to rail against and from which to seek redemption, and without Saint Paul there is no law for de Sade to transgress. According to Lacan:

> Without a transgression there is no access to *jouissance*, and, to return to Saint Paul, that that is precisely the function of the law. Transgression in the direction of *jouissance* only takes place if it is supported by the oppositional principle, by the forms of the law. . . . That is the point that our experience leads us to, on condition that we are guided by Freud's articulation of the problem. Sin needed the law, Saint Paul said, so that he could become a great sinner—nothing, of course, affirms that he did, but so that he could conceive of the possibility.
>
> Meanwhile, what we see here is the tight bond between desire and the Law. And it is in the light of this that Freud's ideal is an ideal tempered with civility that might be called patriarchal civility, in the full idyllic sense. . . . That patriarchal civility is supposed to set us on the most reasonable path to temperate or normal desires. (S VII, 176–77)

The difference between the sadist and the dominator or dominatrix reflects the difference between discipline and torture. Sadism requires protest, anger, outrage in order to create the *jouissance* of transgression. This is why rape is a manifestation of sadism, as no female desires rape under any condition. If one examines the so-called rape fantasies of some women, they are not fantasies of rape but fantasies of submission to the sexual will of a stranger. By definition, only males will have rape fantasies in that, if the fantasy of a woman being sexually taken by a stranger is sexually exciting, the fantasy is such that she is being dominated and used in a way in which she doesn't have to take responsibility in the fantasy. This may seem a small difference to male readers of pornography. Nevertheless it is structurally important.

Religious or Moral Masochism

Religious or moral masochism reflects the aggression of the ego against its own body. It is a paradigmatic manifestation of the dialectical tension between the sexual and ego drive. The ego defends itself against the demands of the sexual drive by attacking the body. The pattern of monastic sexuality manifests these tensions in the form of extreme mind/body dualism. The religious or moral person denies the sexual drive, which returns in the form of erotic fantasy. The ego in turn addresses aggression against the body, which manifests itself sexually in the form of the *jouissance* of transcendence. This masochism is not the same as primary masochism, it is a secondary symptom that often takes the form of a defense against primary masochism. The aggression of the sexual drive against the aggression of the ego drive is kept internal as an ongoing antagonism between mind and body.

Religious or moral masochism constitutes a withdrawal from the world of interhuman sexual relations. From the perspective of sexuality, it constitutes a state of celibacy. Sexuality moves entirely into fantasy, and the individual struggles against all forms of sexual expression, including masturbation. The transcending of sexuality constitutes saintliness. But saintliness is nevertheless sexual. As explained by Lacan, "you only have to look at Bernini's statute [of Saint Theresa] to understand immediately that she's coming, there is no doubt about it. And what is her jouissance, her coming from? It is experiencing it but knowing nothing about it. These mystical ejaculations are neither idle gossip nor mere verbiage" (FS, 147).

Modes of Defenses against the Drives

The repression of animality and the inflation of the significance of language and consciousness create the conflict between the sexual and ego drives. We function as animals but conceptually are in a state of constant denial. "[W]hat Freud put forward is that the essential motor of human progress, the motor of the pathetic, of the conflictual, of the fruitful, of the creative in human life, is lust" (S II, 65). The Freudian notion of sexuality, however, includes not only genital activity and perversions but is sufficiently broad to include almost all forms of contact between humans. Freudian *pansexuality* "does not necessarily mean that sexuality is 'everything,' but perhaps that *in 'everything'* there is sexuality," and "that *everything* can generate sexuality" (L&D, 26).

Within the discourse of psychoanalytic theory, the distinction between perversity and normality takes on a different meaning than that found in the nontechnical meaning of everyday speech. Lacan writes, "If analysis has made any positive discovery about libidinal development, it is that the child is a pervert, even a polymorphous pervert" (S I, 214). "What is perversion? It is not simply an aberration in relation to social criteria, an anomaly contrary to good morals, although this register is not absent, nor is it atypical according to natural criteria, namely that it more or less derogates from the reproductive finality of sexual union. It is something else in its very structure. . . . Perversion, in sum, is the privileged exploration of an existential possibility of human nature—its internal tearing apart, its gap, through which the supra-natural world of the symbolic was able to make its entry" (S I, 218).

Neuroses and perversion are the inevitable results of the ego's exclusion of the sexual drive and its return in the form of the neurotic, perverse, and pathological symptoms. "The resistances always have their seat in the ego, so analysis teaches us. What corresponds to the ego, is what I sometimes call the sum of the prejudices which any knowledge comprises and which each of us has as individual baggage. It is something which includes what we know or think we know—for knowing is always in some way believing one knows" (S II, 41). "Observation shows us," according to Freud, "that an instinct may undergo the following vicissitudes:

> Reversal into its opposite.
>
> Turning round upon the subject's own self.
>
> Repression.
>
> Sublimation" (SE, XIV, 126).

He further states that "we may also regard these vicissitudes as modes of *defense* against the instincts" (SE, XIV, 127). These four vicissitudes form the foundation of "the *neuropsychoses of defense*" (S III, 102).

There is no sharp division between the neurotic and the normal (SE, IX, 210), as neurosis involves the avoidance of reality (S III, 45). The sexual drive is repressed into the unconscious and returns by turning upon the self in the form of primary masochism. The defense against primary masochism, with its *jouissance* of submission, is the reversal into its opposite, the *jouissance* of control. The *jouissance* of control, within the male, entails a denial of reality through the fantasy of the possession of the phallus for the male and the fantasy of lack for the female. Oedipal normality is, at best, a state of neurosis. The denial of the sexual drive engenders a pathological hatred of the physical body and the embrace of mind/body dualism, which manifests itself in the pathology of moral or religious masochism and neurotic sublimation. When the reality of the illusory phallus forces itself upon the male, it will often produce the pathology of sadism in the form of a revolt against both the Law of the Father and the repressed desire to lose the burden of the phallus. The male can deify and submit, dominate and control, deny and transcend, or destroy and exclude the female, thus reflecting the structure of the defence mechanisms. Human sexuality plays out in terms of the following quadrant:

To dominate and control	To deify and submit
To deny and transcend	To destroy and exclude

The *jouissance* of domination and control	The *jouissance* of deification and submission
The *jouissance* of denial and transcendence	The *jouissance* of destruction and transgression

The *jouissance* of the God-King-Father	The *jouissance* of the Consort Pan-Dionysus
The *jouissance* of the Apollonian male saint	The *jouissance* of the Amazon killing/raping hero

The *jouissance* of fucking someone	The *jouissance* of male masochism
The *jouissance* of male religious or moral masochism	The *jouissance* of male sadism

The *jouissance* of the Goddess *Domina*	The *jouissance* of Eve and of O
The *jouissance* of the female saint	The *jouissance* of the Amazon

The *jouissance* of sexual discipline	The *jouissance* of female masochism
The *jouissance* of female religious or moral masochism	The *jouissance* of female sadism

To dominate and control the person one is dependent on	To deify and submit to the person one is dependent on
To deny and transcend the person one is dependent on	To destroy and exclude the person one is dependent on

The *jouissance* of domination and control	The *jouissance* of deification and submission
The *jouissance* of denial and transcendence	The *jouissance* of destruction and transgression

The *jouissance* of the self as Subject	The *jouissance* of the Self as Other
The *jouissance* of the self as both Subject and Other	The *jouissance* of the self as neither Subject or Other

Aggression against the other self as Other	Embracing aggression from the other self as Subject
Aggression of mind against its own body	Aggression against everything and everyone

The *jouissance* of the God-King-Hero	The *jouissance* of Eve
The *jouissance* of the Male Saint	The *jouissance* of the Male Sadist

The *jouissance* of fucking	The *jouissance* of being fucked
The *jouissance* of self-discipline	The *jouissance* of rape and torture

The *jouissance* of the Goddess Domina	The *jouissance* of the Male Masochist
The *jouissance* of the Female Saint	The *jouissance* of the Female Sadist

The *jouissance* of giving discipline	The *jouissance* of receiving discipline
The *jouissance* of self-discipline	The *jouissance* of torture

The Gap, The Lack, and the Fold

According to Lacan, we experience the Symbolic as a castration, and the fear of castration is the fear of the lack. We seek to close the gap, fill the hole, eliminate "the lack that constitutes castration anxiety" (F, 73) by desiring an other as the object of our desire. The acquisition of another as the object of our desire is the desire of the master for the submission of the slave. The object of the *jouissance* is the filling of the gap, the satisfaction of the desire arising from the lack. The self emerges from the Subject as Master and, the other of the Other emerges as the slave whose desire is to be the fulfillment of the desire of the Master. Psychoanalysis, according to Lacan, "is governed by a particular aim, which is historically defined by the elaboration of the notion of the subject. It poses this notion in a new way, by leading the subject back to his signifying dependence" (F, 77). The element that permits a person to constitute the self as subject is the metaphorical identification with the generative power of nature. The primary gap upon which all others converge is that between the Subject and the Other. As humans, we are crucified on the cross of the Subject and the Other. For Freud, it was civilization and its discontents, but for Lacan it is language and its discontents. From the moment of birth until our death we are torn between separation and engulfment anxiety. We desperately desire to close the gap, replenishing the lack, yet, at the same time we seek the preservation of the ever besieged, fragile ego. This ambivalence is manifested in love and aggression—of our body, of our mothers—in misogyny and philogyny:

> [T]he subject as such is uncertain because he is divided by the effects of language. Through the effects of speech, the subject always realizes himself more in the Other, but he is already pursuing there more than half of himself. He will simply find his desire ever more divided, pulverized, in the circumscribable metonymy of speech. The effects of language are always mixed with the fact, which is the basis of the analytic experience, that the subject is subject only from being subjected to the field of the Other, the subject proceeds from his synchronic subjection in the field of the Other. That is why he must get out, get himself out, and in the *getting-himself-out,* in the end he will know that the real Other has, just as much as himself, to get himself out, to pull himself free. (F, 188)

These dialectical poles are separated by gaps, referred to by Lacan as *lacks.* One lack becomes superimposed on another (F, 215), and the lack between subject and object, body and mind, Subject and Other, Eros and Thanatos become interrelated, interidentified, and interposed on one another. The lack is the source of desire, and filling the lack is the function of desire (F, 29). The object of desire is that which is lacking (F, ix). "[I]t is in this point of lack, that the desire of the subject is constituted" (F, 219). Sexual desire and the desire for death seek to fill the gap and eliminate the lack. In the orgasm, for a few short moments all divisions weave into a *One-ness,* and desire is momentarily filled. And at death all divisions disappear. At and for the moment of sexual ecstasy the hole is filled, and at death the hole disappears. Desire can never be completely met, filled, or assuaged. Our inability to close the gap or fill the lack constitutes the inherent impossibility of desire. If desire could be entirely assuaged, all distinctions would disappear, including those between the mind and the body, into a single explosion in which being would be an eternal *jouissance.*

The languaging biped primate has sexuality, which genderizes the self. "[I]t is the man—by which I mean he who finds himself male without knowing what to do about it, for all that he is a speaking being—who takes on the woman, or who believes he takes her on. . . . Except what he takes on is the cause of his desire" (FS, 143). "Can one say . . . that if Man [L' *homme*] wants Woman [*La femme*], he cannot reach her without finding himself run aground on the field of perversions? That is what is precipitated as a formula through the experiment instituted by psychoanalytic discourse" (Tel, 37–38). "It follows then that *a* woman—since we cannot speak of more than one—a woman only encounters Man [L' *homme*] in psychosis" (Tel, 40). "[S]he is a party to the perversion which is . . . Man's [L' *homme*]. Which leads her into the familiar masquerade. . . .[S]he prepares herself on-the-off-chance, so that her inner fantasy of Man [L' *homme*] will find its hour of truth" (Tel, 40–41). "[S]hort of castration, that is, short of something which says no to the phallic function, man has no chance of enjoying the body of the woman, in other words, of making love. That is the conclusion of analytic experience. It does not stop him from desiring the woman. . . . Not only does he desire her but he does all kinds of things to her which bear a remarkable resemblance to love" (FS, 143).

Lacan describes the biped languaging primate as "this fathomless thing capable of experiencing between birth and death, capable of covering the whole spectrum of pain and pleasure in a word, what in French we call the *sujet de la jouissance*" (OS, 194). He explains that "If the living being is something at all thinkable, it will be above all as subject of the *jouissance*"

(OS, 194). He tells us, "All that is elaborated by the subjective construction on the scale of the signifier in its relation to the Other and which has its root in language is only there to permit the full spectrum of desire to allow us to approach, to test, this sort of *jouissance* which is the only valuable meaning that is offered to our life" (OS, 195).

Where Lacan sees a gap that cannot be closed and a lack that can never be filled, Derrida sees a fold. A fold can, however, be crossed. To cross the dialectical folds of discourse one must proceed, at the moment of *jouissance,* from the Subject to the Other or from the Other to the Subject, effecting a surreptitious weave of movement. If this fold can be crossed, then all other folds can similarly be traversed. For the male to cross the fold, he must move from a self as the manifestation of the Subject to a self as a manifestation of the Other. For the female to cross the fold, she must move from a self as the manifestation of the Other to a self as a manifestation of the Subject. The fold can only be crossed by effecting a weave at the moment of *jouissance,* at the "little death." The journey "is roughly charted" and "involves dangerous encounters."[44] This arduous journey, from one side to the other, from outside to inside, takes place in the "*in-between,*" and requires both dis-membering and re-membering of the self. This is only possible in and within *jouissance.*

EIGHT

Ariadne and Dionysus

Seduction

The act of seduction consists of leading a person astray in conduct or belief from a norm or standard by enticing or beguiling the person to do something that is wrong in terms of that criterion. Ariadne operates as the temptress who enforces the primal seduction of Dionysus. He is drawn to her in death but, in the union, wills only Eros. She holds the key to the labyrinth, and only she knows the way out.[1]

She has also seduced Nietzsche. Ariadne has initiated in him the desire to castrate the privileged signifier and the desire to fill the void of language, suspended precariously above an interminable abyss, with the primary signifier. Nietzsche declared himself to be beyond good and evil. He defended masters against slaves and advocated ruthlessness, but at the same time is the man who, just prior to his mental collapse, threw his arms around a horse being beaten in the street. Can the man who proclaimed the coming of the Superman be reconciled with the Dionysian searching for his Ariadne? Only Irigaray, among contemporary feminists, has made a serious attempt to engage feminism and the texts of Nietzsche.[2] Her dialogue in *The Marine Lover of Friedrich Nietzsche,* however, is more of a chastisement than an attempt to reinterpret the texts themselves.[3] Most of the great insights of Freud and Lacan existed in nascent form in the writing of Nietzsche. A convergence with feminism, however, will require a reexamination and reinterpretation of the texts of Nietzsche.

Ariadne helps Theseus kill her half-brother the Minotaur in order to put an end to the annual human sacrifice the Minotaur demands. She holds the key to the labyrinth, (where the Minotaur resides—from which most never return but some return transformed), and she alone can help

Theseus penetrate the darkness and allow his successful depenetration. Ariadne is his umbilical,[4] his link or thread to his labyrinthine origins. Her thread is the suspended veil, the cloth, the partition, and the link of the inside and the outside, penetration and perpetration. "Nothing is more vicious than this suspense" of the thread, "nothing is more perverse than this rending penetration that leaves a virgin womb intact. But nothing is more marked . . . , more folded, intangible, sealed, untouched" (D, 216). Not only does Ariadne hold the key to the labyrinth, she epitomizes it: the secret claws of the maternal womb that holds captive most males who attempt to penetrate. She keeps the Beast-Man, the Minotaur, the horned god trapped in the labyrinth, by controlling his sexuality, his phallus. She is seduced into releasing the Beast-Man from the labyrinth of his sexuality. She leads him out, where he emerges as a transformed Theseus to be her equal lover, and ensures his safe depenetration. Goddess and Hero, together.

After the murder, she flees from Crete with Theseus, from the labyrinthine truth of her origin. During their journey, Theseus deserts Ariadne on the Isle of Naxos. Once out, however, the Hero abandons the Goddess and leaves to battle the Amazons. The Hero defeats the Amazons and rapes women and possesses them as slave-wives.[5] His world becomes one of debauchery, exploitation, and abduction, and he is heralded as Hero.[6] He is a brave warrior, one who slew the Minotaur, and was so honored. Ariadne releases her umbilical and in so doing casts the fate of Theseus as Hero. By taking Ariadne's thread, Theseus succumbs to her and recognizes her as the Heroine. The taking of the thread is for Theseus an acknowledgment of his dependency. His later deeds are in fact a rebellion against this dependency, an attempt to cut away that fated umbilical. He must triumph against the Amazons as this will elevate him to Hero, whereas before he was only consort. Ariadne remains on the Isle of Naxos until the consort returns, no longer as a Beast-Man but as Dionysus. Only after Theseus has abandoned Ariadne can Dionysus come to Naxos.[7] As Nietzsche stated, "this is the soul's secret: only when the hero abandoned her, she is approached in a dream by the overhero" (Z, II, 13; Pt N, 231). The horned god Pan is now transformed.

Nietzsche summons Theseus: "To you, the bold venturers and adventurers and whoever has embarked with cunning sails upon dreadful seas, to you who are intoxicated by riddles, who takes pleasure in twilight, whose soul is lured with flutes to every treacherous abyss, . . . for you do not desire to feel for a rope with cowardly hand; and where you can *guess* you hate to *calculate*" (Z, 176). Theseus does not want to accede to Ariadne's cord, he prefers to languish in the Heroic. "Hung with ugly truths, the booty of his hunt, and rich in torn clothes; many thorns, too, hung on him—but I saw no rose. . . . He returned home from the fight with wild beasts: but a wild beast still gazes out of his seriousness—a beast that has not been overcome! . . . And only if he turns away from himself will he jump over his own shadow—and jump, in truth, into *his own* sunlight" (Z, 139–40).

According to some versions of the myth Ariadne is left "helpless" on the Isle of Naxos, with no one to consummate the marriage. The dumb cry of her deadly longing is answered when Dionysus, as savior, approaches: she is transformed from a deathly vision to a clear light, a shining brightness. Dionysus, too, is transformed by the union. Ariadne is demoted by this mythic interpretation to the level of helpless waif waiting to be saved by the power and strength of Dionysus. Clearly, she can also be interpreted as possessing the power and ability to transform Dionysus from bull to compassionate, emotive, and sacrificial figure. She is not waiting to be saved but has lured Dionysus to her living grave and, through their sexual union, has accomplished the necessary transformation of Dionysus.

The consummation or sexual awakening of Dionysus and Ariadne on Naxos demonstrates the headiness of transformation. Dionysus is no longer exuding brute force but is showing the will to merge with the Other, to leap into the abyss, risking the dissolution of the ego. Without Ariadne, Dionysus is a corpse, a hollow referent incapable of action or active becoming. By making the leap, Dionysus casts himself chaotically beyond all limits. Ariadne is no longer afraid of her own sensuality nor of her own capacity for ecstasy. In luring Dionysus to her labyrinth, she has reawakened the vitality and truth of the labyrinth in her. In a return to the dankness of her origin, she has become who she is, was, and will be—the Eternal Woman.

Like a long lost mother refound, and, in effect, *his* lost mother (for Ariadne is represented in some versions of the myth as Persephone, Dionysus' original mother), she has enabled Dionysus to tap into an energy source at once strange and familiar, recognizing in it authority and power. The power that Dionysus fosters is primarily represented in the Goddess more so than in himself. She is the symbol of the power, whereas he is the fosterer of it. He suckles the great energy source of womanhood and clings proudly and resolutely to Ariadne's thread. She guides Dionysus, as do the maenads, and it is his coalition with them that invigorates him.

The Law of Seduction As Eros

Ariadne reawakened Dionysus' desire to be the desire of the Other. She has made him hers, unconditionally, unrelentlessly. He, through his will to Eros, desires only her desire. He becomes the champion of her value, the devaluor of logos—of God-Father-King—and the proponent of the orgiastic dance. Only Ariadne could have initiated him into this sensual arena. And Dionysus is eternally grateful.

In *God and the Jouissance of the Woman,* Lacan states that his "*There is something of One*" is to be equated with the Freudian concept of Eros and is defined as a fusion making one out of two, which must be interrogated and which "has echoed across the centuries" under the name of love (FS, 139). "For in so far as the mother's look also refers to the father through whom the relationship to the law is founded, the seduction of the mother's look challenges the social and familiar order, indeed, we could say, perverts it."[8] In *The Interpretation of Dreams,* which contains Freud's initial discussion of Sophocles' *Oedipus Rex,* Freud introduces the themes of the seductive sexuality of the mother. "There is an unmistakable indication in the text of Sophocles' tragedy itself," he writes, "that the legend of Oedipus sprang from some primeval dream-material which had as its content the distressing disturbance of a child's relation to his parent owing to the first stirrings of sexuality" (SE, IV, 264).

Ariadne awakens in Dionysus the seductive desire to return to/unite with/lose the self in/be the desire of/be the phallus for the mother. These desires do not disappear in the Oedipal passage. The seduction is transformed into the desire to lose the self in the (M)other, and if the male embraces the seduction to castrate himself by presenting his phallus to the (M)other, he must kill the father within himself. In order to accede to the seduction, the male must be willing to lose a bit of the self, the ego, for the free reign of Eros. In this way, seduction is contraposed against sexuality. Sexuality is exchanged for the seduction in which the law is overthrown, gender structures transformed, asymmetry reversed, grand myths inverted, and erotic fantasy, imagery, and symbols transformed.

 According to Baudrillard in his book *Seduction,* "There is an alternative to *(Oedipal)* sex and to power" (S, 7), and the alternative is seduction.[9] "[S]eduction represents mastery over the symbolic universe, while power represents only mastery of the real universe. The sovereignty of seduction is incommensurable with the possession of political or sexual power" (S, 8). "It [seduction] knows . . . that *there is no anatomy,* nor psychology, that all signs are reversible . . . all powers elude it, but it 'reversibilizes' all their signs" (S, 10). "Every *positive* form can accommodate itself to its negative form, but understands the challenge of the *reversible* form as mortal. Every structure can adapt to its subversion or inversion, but not to the reversion of its terms. Seduction is this reversible form" (S, 21). It, as it did *to* Dionysus on Naxos, transforms control to submission. As it did *for* Ariadne, it transforms submission into control.

The phallic fable whereby woman is created by a male god by subtraction from the male body is a reversal of material reality wherein man is born of woman. "Power . . . is soluble in the reversibility of the feminine. If the 'facts' cannot decide whether it was the masculine or feminine that was dominant throughout the ages . . . by contrast it remains clear that in matters of sexuality, the reversible form prevails over the linear form. The excluded form prevails, secretly, over the dominant form, the seductive form prevails over the productive form" (S, 17). "[T]he masculine has always been but a residual secondary and fragile formation, one that must be defended by retrenchments, institutions, and artifices. The phallic fortress offers all the signs of a fortress, that is to say, of weakness. It can defend itself only from the ramparts of a manifest sexuality" (S, 13). The Oedipal passage, for the male, is the transformation of the *jouissance* of submission, which has its origins in maternal-infant sexuality, to the *jouissance* of control.

The law of seduction has one narrative but many scripts, many beginnings, and many endings. It is a play that allows for infinite variation though its theme remains resolute,[10] one which "takes the form of an uninterrupted ritual exchange where seducer and seduced constantly raise the stakes in a game that never ends. And cannot end . . . because there is no limit to the challenge to love more than one is loved, or to be always more seduced—if not death. Sex, on the other hand, has a quick, banal end: the orgasm" (S, 22). Sex and power must be surrendered by the male who chooses to play the game of seduction, "a circular, reversible process of challenges, one-upmanship and death." According to Baudrillard, "The game's sole principle, though it is never posed as universal, is that *by choosing the rule one is delivered from the law*" (S, 133).

If it would appear that men have won the game, it has been at a terrible price. The price has been to objectify women, commodify children, and turn nature into resources. It has left men lost and caught in a forward flight that can "neither assure them of safety, nor relieve them of their secret despair at what had escaped them" (S, 18). The price for women has been equally high. It has alienated them from the Goddess and has let them know only the "Truth" of God, it has given rise to a castrated, blind servility, a living death.

In order to pass from Thanatos to Eros, seduction must be embraced. It is only in the unification of Ariadne and Dionysus that this embrace is possible. The castration—the abrogation of the patriphallus (the everything but) and the sacrificial gift of the phallus (the nothing but)—is not the culmination of seduction but merely the beginning. It is the price of entry into the play, the foreplay of Eros. "If seduction is a passion or destiny, it is usually the opposite passion that prevails—that of not being seduced. We struggle to confirm ourselves in our truth: we fight against that which seeks to seduce us" (S, 119). "The problem, therefore, is not one of sexual or alimentary impotence, with its train of psychoanalytic reasons and unreason, but concerns an *impotence as regards seduction*" (S, 121).

The male can choose between the collective pathology of normality and perversion, between repressing and, in so doing, castrating Eros, or castrating the privileged position of the Ego. "Seduction and perversion maintain subtle relations. . . . The immorality of perversion, like that of seduction, does not come from abandoning oneself to the joys of sex in opposition to all morality; it results from something more serious and subtle, the abandonment of sex itself as a referent and a morality" (S, 125). The price of enlightenment is castration: one cannot embrace the Mother and retain the phallus; one cannot embrace Eros and continue to retain the phallic fantasies. The seduction to castration is the seduction to enlightenment: "The world is naked, the king is naked, and things are clear. All of production, and truth itself, are directed towards disclosure, the unbearable truth of sex being but the most recent consequence. . . . And seduction still holds, in the face of truth, a most sibylline response, which is that 'perhaps we wish to uncover the truth because it is so difficult to imagine it naked' " (S, 181).

The Proclamation of the Primary Signifier

"Is the pagan cult not a form of thanksgiving and affirmation of life?" Nietzsche asks. "Dionysus versus the 'Crucified': there you have the antithesis" is his answer (WP, 1052). Nietzsche killed God, denied logos, and castrated the signifier of male psychic reality. In doing so, he shifted the grand metaphorical relationship between human and nature from disembodied mind to the body itself.[11] He called this process the "de-deification of nature." He asks, "When will we complete our de-deification of nature? When may we begin to *'naturalize'* humanity in terms of a pure, newly discovered, newly redeemed nature?" (GS, 109). From here, he could only embrace the primary signifier or abandon language altogether. One cannot have language without the categories of Subject and Other, and one cannot have the categories of Subject and Other without a master signifier that contains the structure of the original fantasy by which selves are generated in terms of the Subject and the Other. Language itself requires a master signifier. We have only two, either the privileged or the primary. And if it is not the privileged, then it must be the primary since, according to Nietzsche, "*We cease to think when we refuse to do so under the constraint of language. . . . Rational thought is interpretation according to a scheme that we cannot throw off*" (WP, 522).

When he embraced the primary signifier, Nietzsche was inevitably drawn into the original primal fantasy where the world is turned upside down and the male body becomes the stage upon which female desire is acted out. In "The Second Dance Song" of *Thus Spoke Zarathustra,* Zarathustra sings to the redeemer of his soul, "the nameless one for whom only future songs will find a name! And truly, your breath is already fragrant with future songs" (Z, 240):

> I fear you when you are near, I love you when you are far; your fleeing allures me, your seeking secures me: I suffer, but for you what I would not gladly endure!
>
> For you whose coldness inflames, whose hatred seduces, whose flight constrains, whose mockery—induces:
>
> Who would not hate you, great woman who binds us, unwinds us, seduces us, seeks us, finds us! Who would not love you, you innocent, impatient, wind-swift, child-eyed sinner!
>
> Where now do you take me, you unruly paragon? (Z, 241)

The Will to Power As Eros

Nietzsche describes the will to power as a true life force, "not a being, not a becoming but a pathos—the most elemental fact from which a becoming an effecting first emerge" (WP, 635). "Life itself," according to Nietzsche, "is the will to power" (WP, 55). It is "incarnate will to power" (BGE, 259). "Life is only a *means* to something; it is the expression of forms of the growth of power" (WP, 706). "And do you know what 'the world' is to me?," Nietzsche asks, "Shall I show it to you in my mirror? This world: a monster of energy, without beginning, without end; a firm, iron magnitude of force that does not grow bigger or smaller, that does not expend itself but only transforms itself." The implications for cognition are made clear in Nietzsche's statement that:

> Will to truth is a making firm, a making true and durable, an abolition of the false character of things, a reinterpretation of it into being. "Truth" is therefore not something there, that might be found or discovered—but something that must be created and that gives a name to a process, or rather to a will to overcome that has in itself no end—introducing truth, as a *processus in infinitum*, an active determining—not a becoming conscious of something that is in itself firm and determined. It is a word for the "will to power." (WP, 552)

Nietzsche was the first since Heraclitus to formulate a scientific approach to knowledge structured in terms of the matrix rather than the logos. He proclaims that, "in truth we are confronted by a continuum" (GS, 112), and he declares, "I tell you: you still have chaos in you" (Z, 46). The term *postmodernism* is in reaction to the supersanguine assumptions about the nature of knowledge and the potential for human understanding of the universe. Nietzsche reacted against modernity by way of a pessimistic view of knowledge and its potential. " 'Truth' is therefore more fateful than error and ignorance, because it cuts off the forces that work toward enlightenment and knowledge" (WP, 452). "The criterion of truth," he tells us, " resides in the enhancement of the feeling of power" (WP, 534). "Parmenides said, 'one cannot think of what is not;'—we are at the other extreme, and say 'what can be thought of must certainly be a fiction' " (WP, 539). We must recognize the gap or gulf between the registers of the Imaginary and the Symbolic and that of the Real. Nietzsche constructed a theory of knowledge that foreshadowed the new scientific paradigm that is now referred to as complex adaptive system theory.[12] "In this moment of suddenness there is an infinite number of processes that elude us. An intellect that could see cause and effect as a continuum and a flux and not, as we do, in terms of an arbitrary division and dismemberment, would repudiate the concept of cause and effect and deny all conditionality" (GS, 173).

Since at least the time of quantum mechanics and Heisenberg's proclamation of the uncertainty principle, theoretical and mathematical models of natural phenomena have shifted from classical logos-oriented approaches to the focus on the unstable, aperiodic, nondeterministic, nonlinear, and chaotic dynamics of physical systems. There has been a marked shift from "knowledge optimism" to knowledge pessimism, all foreshadowed by Nietzsche. The shift in evolutionary theory from Darwin's teleological, intentional, purposive, linear model to Nietzsche's evolutionary perspective of chaotic and complex emergence returns us to the ancient, primary, original fantasy of the emergence of life out of chaos, or the matrix. Nietzsche's metaphor for the matrix was "the Will to Power."

Nietzsche's solution to the problem of nihilism is "Dionysian wisdom. Joy in the destruction of the most noble and at the sight of its progressive ruin: in reality joy in what is coming and lies in the future, which triumphs over existing things, however good. Dionysian: temporary identification with the principle of life (including the voluptuousness of the martyr)" (WP, 417). He explains:

> [T]his my Dionysian world of the eternally self-creating, the eternally self-destroying, this mystery world of the twofold voluptuous delight, my "beyond good and evil," without goal, unless the joy of the circle; is itself a goal; without will, unless a ring feels good will toward itself—do you want a name for this world? A solution for all its riddles? A light for you, too, you best-concealed, strongest, most intrepid, most midnightly men?—This world is the will to power—and nothing besides! And you yourselves are also this will to power—and nothing besides! (WP, 1067)

Der Über Mensch

Nietzsche's system of knowledge as structured by the primary signifier can be found in two of his later, and extremely significant, texts, *Thus Spoke Zarathustra*, and *The Will to Power*. "I write for a species of man that does not yet exist: for the 'masters of the earth,' " Nietzsche tells us (WP, 958). "Not 'mankind' but *Overman* is the goal!" (WP, 1001). Clearly—and consistent with his anti-Darwinian views on evolution—Nietzsche does not view the coming of the Overman in biological terms. The Overman is a psychological state of mind and can only be understood in psychological terms. The Overman is the individual who most clearly embodies the will to power, the will to power made flesh. Since the will to power is life, the will to Eros, the Overman will be the being who expresses and is driven to the unfolding and generation of life—life simply for the sake of life. Zarathustra proclaims:

> Behold I teach you the *Overman*
> The *Overman* is the meaning of the earth. Let your will say
> The *Overman shall be* the meaning of the earth!
> I entreat you, my brothers, remain *true to the earth,* and do not believe those who speak to you of superterrestrial hopes!
> They are poisoners, whether they know it or not.
> They are despisers of life, atrophying and self-poisoned men of whom the earth is weary: so let them be gone.
>
> Behold I teach you the *Overman:*
> He is this sea, in him your great contempt can go under. (Z, 42)[13]

Nietzsche characterizes the Overman as a male figure, when clearly the primary signifier and the primary original fantasy identify the generative power of nature, synonymous with Nietzsche's will to power, with the female. It is this structure, this reconciliation with the generative power of nature, that in the end leads Nietzsche to merge the figures of Ariadne and the Overman. More and more Nietzsche identifies himself with Dionysus, not the Dionysus he refers to in *The Birth of Tragedy,* but the Dionysus who surrenders himself fully and completely to Ariadne's seduction.[14] He belongs to her, and her alone. Dionysus, who epitomizes the "higher man," is willing to be seduced. He is willing to foresake his ego for the higher aim of the merger. If the merger is to be fully recognized, then the *Übermensch* becomes *SHE* who is "Over Man," or the Over Man. If Nietzsche destroys God, then in one way or another the Goddess must return, otherwise we cannot remain in language. If you reject one master signifier, the other must be embraced, be it consciously or unconsciously. The death of God (patriarchal religion) and logos (linear and teleologically structured science) preface the return of the Goddess and the matrix.

For Nietzsche, the escape from nihilism is accomplished by a total surrender to life. His metaphor for this is the Eternal Return. "Let us think this thought in its most terrible form: existence as it is, without meaning or aim, yet recurring inevitably without any finale of nothingness: 'the eternal recurrence' " (WP, 55). If one can say "YES" to this, then one has embraced life by surrendering to it. Nietzsche's metaphor for this is a going-under, into the water, the ocean, the abyss. The going under is the sacrifice of the self and the ego. Only the human can say "YES" to life—or no. Only the human can consciously embrace the will to power and thereby embody it. "I love those who do not first seek beyond the stars for reasons to go down and to be sacrifices: but who sacrifice themselves to the earth, that the earth may one day belong to the *Over Man*" (Z, 44).

By identifying the Over Man as female, a most radical form of feminism will result. When Nietzsche declares that "A declaration of war on the masses by higher men is needed. Everywhere the mediocre are combining in order to make themselves master!" (WP, 861), this may be interpreted as a call to combat the mass of Thanatos-driven males who dominate and suppress females, who are the embodiment of the generative power of nature. "The new courage—no *a priori* truths, but a *free* subordination to a ruling idea that has its time" (WP, 462).

Nietzsche calls for a dedication to life that could not be possible or even conceivable without the liberation of women and the destruction of patriarchy. He tells us that "There are *master morality and slave morality*" (BGE, 260). Slave morality, according to Nietzsche, functions to suppress the will to power while the master morality intensifies it. Equality is, for Nietzsche, a slave morality. "In the age of suffrage universal, i.e., when everyone may sit in judgment on everyone and everything, I feel impelled to re-establish *order of rank* (WP, 854). Rank, according to Nietzsche, is determined by power. "What determines your rank is the quantum of power you are" (WP, 858). The power that for Nietzsche determines the hierarchy between the lower and the higher man is that which is manifested as the will to power, the will to life. This reading of Nietzsche's text, therefore leads us to a feminism that proclaims the primacy of the female as the manifestation of the will to power. Nietzsche states that "The strongest must be bound most firmly, watched, laid in chains, and guarded—if the instinct of the herd has its way" (WP, 887). In that case, it is the masses of mediocre and lesser men, who use a slave mentality to bind, lay in chains, and guard those who embody the generative power of nature.

'Ressentiment'

For Nietzsche, the order of rank is measured in terms of the manifestation of the will to power. The will to power is manifested as the affirmation of life. The distinction between the strong and the weak is not biologically determined. It is a matter of psychology. If women manifest a greater affirmation of, and will to, life or Eros, then within Nietzsche's system of thought they would constitute a master class; and if males, as a gender, opposed or denied life rather than affirmed it, they would constitute the herd of lesser beings, "the sick animal" who says no to life (GM I ,17). A male must not only accept but must positively affirm his lack, his animality, which includes his sexuality and mortality, if he is to manifest the will to power or to life. Nietzsche asserts that "it is a very noble type of man that confronts nature and life in *this* way," that is, with an "enormous amount of gratitude," thus affirming and accepting life, our animality, and our lack without *ressentiment* (BGE, 49). According to Nietzsche, "The degree and kind of a man's sexuality reach up into the ultimate pinnacle of his spirit" (BGE, 75). In order to affirm life, the male must confront and accept his sexual and emotional dependency upon the female without *ressentiment.*

The Law of the Father, which constitutes the foundation of male authority, is a manifestation of misogyny, and misogyny is a paradigmatic example of *ressentiment.* A slave morality is a manifestation of *ressentiment,* as its function is to castrate those who manifest the will to power. "The *ressentiment* which these lowly-placed persons feel . . . fills poor little foolish heads with an insane conceit, as if they were the meaning and the salt of the earth" (WP, 172). Nietzsche specifies for us what he considers constitutes what he chooses to call, *"The prudence of moral castrationism"*:

> First . . . one claims virtue in general for one's ideal; one negates the older ideal to the point of presenting it as the antithesis of all ideals . . . an art of defamation.
>
> Second . . . one sets up the opponent of one's ideals as the measure of value in general . . . as God.
>
> Third . . . one sets up the opponent of one's idea; as the opponent of God. . . .

Fourth . . . one derives all suffering, all that is uncanny, fearful and fateful in existence from opposition to one's own ideal. . . .

Fifth . . . one goes so far as to conceive nature as the antithesis of one's own ideal. . . .

Sixth . . . the victory of unnaturalness, of the castrationist ideal . . . is projected into the future as conclusion, finale, great hope, as the "coming of the kingdom of God."

—I hope that at this artificial inflation of a small species into the absolute measure of things one is still permitted to *laugh?* (WP, 204)

"The castrator," according to Nietzsche, "formulates a number of new self-preservative measures for men of a quite definite species: in this he is a realist. His means of legislation are . . . the appeal to authority of all kinds, to 'God' the employment of the concept 'guilt and punishment' " (WP, 204).

The driving force of Christianity, according to Nietzsche, is *ressentiment* (WP, 179), and its source is not so much the teachings of Jesus but those of Paul who "*annulled* primitive Christianity," laid the foundations for "a new priesthood and theology—in a new ruling order and a church. . . . Paul re-erected on a grand scale precisely that which Christ had annulled through his way of living" (WP, 167). He tells us that "A doctrine and religion of 'love,' of *suppression*, of self-affirmation, of patience, endurance, helpfulness, of cooperation in word and deed . . . deifies a life of slavery, subjection, poverty, sickness, and inferiority . . . under the ideal of humility and obedience" (WP, 373). Is this not a fairly accurate description of the Western theistic morality that religions impose on women? The desire that a world comfortable to the one who desires leads, according to Nietzsche, to a "blind trust in reason," to "an expression of hatred for a world that makes one suffer," and to the conceptualization of a fantasy world. "The ressentiment of metaphysicians against actuality is here creative" (WP, 579).

Clearly, the concept or fear of castration has repercussions with respect to conceptions and portrayals of women—as those who are castrated, capable of castrating, and simultaneously or successively capable of affirmation (Sp, 101). According to Derrida, the relationship between castration and women is best understood through concepts of Church and God. The Church, as promulgator of patriarchal law, uses God to repress the male fear of castration. By asserting the primacy of the mind, the spirit, and the supernatural, the Church gives little credence to the body, to life, or to the importance of the male bodily organ. Religion and the concept of God do their own job of emasculation and mutilation. "Whence comes the seductive charm of such an emasculated ideal of man [God]? Why are we not disgusted by it as we are perhaps disgusted by the idea of the castrato?—The answer lies precisely here: the voice of a castrato does *not* disgust us, despite the cruel mutilation that is its condition: it has grown sweeter—Just because the 'male organ' has been amputated from virtue, a feminine note has been brought to the voice of virtue that it did not have before" (WP, 204). According to Derrida, writing on Nietzsche's styles, the Church, by privileging the supernatural as opposed to the natural, the afterlife as opposed to life, is inescapably hostile to woman as SHE is the essence of life: "Hostile to life, the Church is hostile thus to woman also who is herself life (femina vita)" (Sp, 93).

Nietzsche clearly understands, however, that those who are in fact oppressed are in danger of lapsing into *ressentiment* itself. Feminists and feminism are not free from the sickness of *ressentiment.* A feminism that conceptualizes itself in the discourse of equality and egalitarianism will, by doing so, add legitimacy to a discourse that, according to Nietzsche, is a manifestation of *ressentiment.* This, in turn, will lead to a reactive mentality rather than the "aggressive . . . stronger, nobler, more courageous" individual who has "at all times a freer eye, and a better conscience," and is "a hundred steps closer to justice than the reactive man" because that individual has "no need to take a false and prejudiced view of the object before him in the way the reactive man does and is bound to do" (GM II, 11).

The Role of the Goddess

The seductive female of lace and perfume does not awaken the desire in the male for castration through sacrifice. Rather, the male is seduced into giving in to his own desire. The form of seduction to castration is generated by the the Amazon, the heroine that Theseus most despised.

Once Nietzsche began the process of restructuring his system of knowledge upon the bases of the primary signifier, the structure should have taken over and moved him from a patriphallic to a matriphallic consciousness. Whether or not this did in fact take place is critical to the question of whether or not Nietzsche's text can be given a feminist interpretation. Nietzsche's view of women is complex and cannot be fully appreciated without a careful examination of his relationship with Lou Andreas-Salomé, an amazing woman who was a writer, an intellectual, and in later life a lay psychoanalyst and friend and colleague of Freud's.[15] For her, Nietzsche was only a confidante and friend. Nietzsche's feelings for Andreas-Salomé, on the other hand, were profound. She was the only woman whom he asked to marry. Nietzsche's sister Elizabeth intensely disliked her, as she was the opposite of her in almost every way. Elizabeth was unexceptional, while Lou Andreas-Salomé "was the affirmative woman, neither castrated nor castrating—beyond castration."[16] She was the Ariadne to Nietzsche's Dionysus. There is some indication of a Dionysian masochistic fantasy structure in Nietzsche, apart from statements such as the following in *Thus Spoke Zarathustra,* where Nietzsche/Zarathustra proclaims, "Pain is also a joy" (Z, 331); "For all joy wants itself, therefore it also wants heart's agony! O happiness! O pain!" (Z, 332). In 1882 Nietzsche arranged for the photographer Jules Bonnet to take a photograph of himself, Lou Andreas-Salomé, and Paul Ree. Martin states that "In Lucerne, Nietzsche orchestrated the infamous photograph of the threesome . . . which depicts the two men pulling a small cart driven by Andreas-Salomé who is half perched on the seat of the cart with a whip in her hand."[17] The contriving of this symbolic depiction is revealing, we would suggest, of Nietzsche's psychic reality, which reflects the dynamics of male matriphallic sexuality. Martin goes on to say that the photograph led to "a true scandal when, some say, Andreas-Salomé showed it around at the premiere of *Parsifal* in Bayreuth."[18] This incident puts Nietzsche's statement "Are you visiting women? Do not forget your whip!" (Z, 93) in a different context.

Elements in Nietzsche's texts are clearly misogynist, but are they critical? Of what was he critical? Many of his texts reveal the mask of femininity that women are forced to wear. He asks, "Finally, *women.* Reflect on the whole history of women: do they not *have* to be first of all and above all else actresses?" (GS, 361). He later relates the following parable:

> Someone took a youth to a sage and said: "Look, he is being corrupted by women." The sage shook his head and smiled. "It is men," said he, "that corrupt women; and all the failings of women should be atoned by and improved in men. For it is man who creates for himself the image of women, and woman forms herself according to this image . . . someone else shouted out of the crowd "women need to be educated better!"—"Men need to be educated better," said the sage. (GS, 68)

How should women educate men about their nature? It is obvious that modern discourse has had little effect. Can the education of the male be separated from the atonement that Nietzsche tells us the male must make? Atonement, discipline, and education of the male: can they be separated? Regarding what Nietzsche refers to as the "amazing and monstrous" education of women: how are they to be reeducated? Concerning the education of women, Nietzsche asserts: "Thus a psychic knot has been tied that may have no equal. Even the compassionate curiosity of the wisest student of humanity is inadequate for guessing how this or that woman manages to accommodate herself to this solution of the riddle, and to the riddle of a solution" (GS, 71).

Ariadne and Dionysus: The Embrace

According to Nietzsche:

> The word "*Dionysian*" means: an urge to unity, a reaching out beyond personality, the everyday, society, reality, across the bays of transitoriness: a passionate-painful overflowing into darker, fuller, more floating states; an ecstatic affirmation of the total character of life as that which remains the same, just as powerful, just as blissful, through all change; the great pantheistic sharing of joy and sorrow that sanctifies and calls good even the most terrible and questionable qualities of life; the eternal will to procreation, to fruitfulness, to recurrence; the feeling of the necessary union of creation and destruction. (WP, 1050)

Nietzsche tells us that "the desire for destruction, change, becoming, can be expressed of an over-full power pregnant with the future (my term for this, as is known, is the word 'Dionysian')" (WP, 846). Dionysus is understood as the figure capable of reinterpreting and reshaping existing hierarchical relationships of power and domination. He plays the decisive role of the consort to Ariadne and is seduced by the bacchic maenads into the role of the transvaluor of values. They initiate Dionysus into their secret mysteries, and he submits. He faces the consequences of initiation, risks the loss, be it of the logos, the ego, or the phallus, and emerges as both more and less than when he started. He defies all categorizations and *obeys* instead something more primal and labyrinthine: the orgiastic dance of the maenads. He opens himself up to the maenadic vigor of the bacchanal, and never looks back.

The mystery of his initiation takes place through the body of a woman.

 It is a journey of becoming, whereby the hidden inside is revealed, explored and interpreted. It is a reconciliation with the Mother.

The mystery is always of a body . . .

—Advance, advance, in the warmness of ignorance, approach absorbed on the interior of the contemplation in the scent of daffodils, attracted by the scant scent of sacred daffodils. . . .

The mystery is always—of the body of a . . .

—approach almost dying in ignorance almost dead, approach in the death-agony of approaching, advance before you, from the left side. . . .

The mystery is always of the body of a woman . . .

The mystery is woman. The mystery is always of a woman.

The mystery of the mystery is being woman.

Listen from the bottom of your body and know:

The mystery to be a woman is: only one, a single woman, is not alone: the mystery is always of the body in the body of a woman.[19]

In Euripides' *The Bacchae,* where Dionysus was willing to succumb to maenadic *truths,* Pentheus was not as eager.[20] Dionysus attempts to seduce Pentheus into a willing participation in the initiatory drama. He ventures to bring the Hero to the ritual and gives him the celebratory mask. Pentheus is frightened by the horrific vision of the bacchants. The castrating vision of the undecidability of nature, its deadly beauty, stiffens the Hero, and instead of hurling himself daringly into the ambivalence, the bacchants hurl themselves at him. In the Oedipal myth, knowledge undoes the sage—the truth of the riddle is what destroys. In *The Bacchae,* order undoes the man—the truth of the logos causes Pentheus to deny the beast, a denial that foreshadows his beastly death. Most males run from the bacchanal for fear of a fate similar to that afforded the king, as they cannot conceive of the Dionysian embrace. Dionysus is empowered not in his attempt to control his surroundings, not in an effort to dictate or subjugate, but in the pure submission to the undecidability of chaos. To amass the strength of Dionysus, what is necessary for the male is a sacrificial release of the logos, of ordering principles, hierarchies, and controlling forces, a sacrifice with Nietzsche of the privileged signifier and a leap into unknown, murky territories. The ground is uneven, and the leap is into a deep abyss, and for most the leap is too dangerous to attempt.

In pushing the boundaries of the self and reevaluating the principles that serve to classify self and other, the actor has the ability to transgress the limits that ordinarily delimit one's self, one's individuality, one's subjectivity. The state of Dionysian affirmation is one of being catapulted chaotically beyond the limit, driven on or beyond the very limit that would delimit every condition of the individual, the "possibility of an impossible" (Ap, 70). "The more unveiledly this possibility gets understood, the more purely does the understanding penetrate into it *as the possibility of the impossibility of any existence at all.*"[21] In effect, one would come to be outside oneself, exceeding the limits that serve to delimit the self. The self is lost or hidden beneath the confines of the confusion. This is the sense of Dionysian dread, terror, and suffering that is often thought of or referred to. This is the painful side of pleasure and the true sense of ancient Greek tragedy. The Dionysian frenzy is what leads the way to a veritable *jouissance.* The journey is harrowing, full of labyrinths and ravines, obstacles and caveats, dark dungeons and abysses, but it is a journey nonetheless.

In the Freudian Oedipal passage, the separation anxiety that accompanies the painful process of assimilation of gender difference has divergent effects. For Pentheus, it had the effect of turning him into the conquering hero. He views the bacchante women as mad, as childlike, and must exert phallic power so as to maintain control. "The hero," states Nietzsche, "after being sufficiently tortured by fate, earned a well-deserved reward through a splendid marriage or tokens of divine favor. The hero has turned gladiator on whom, after he had been nicely beaten and covered with wounds, freedom was occasionally bestowed. The *deus ex machina* took the place of metaphysical comfort" (BT, 17).

Toward the latter part of *Thus Spoke Zarathustra,* Nietzsche's longing for the Over Man merges, with growing identification, with Dionysus who longs to merge with Ariadne:

> Oh how should I not lust for eternity and for the wedding
> ring of rings—the Ring of Recurrence!
> Never yet did I find the woman by whom I wanted children,
> unless it be this woman, whom I love: for I love you,
> O Eternity!
> *For I love you, O Eternity!*
>
> Oh how should I not lust for eternity and for the wedding
> ring of rings—the Ring of Recurrence. (Z, 244–45)

 Lampert, in his interpretation of *Thus Spoke Zarathustra,* explains that "The marriage symbol par excellence for Nietzsche is that marriage that followed the abandonment of a woman by a heroic man . . . the marriage of Ariadne and Dionysus that followed the abandonment of Ariadne by Theseus. It is towards this mystery that the fable of Zarathustra moves, the mystery of male and female culminating in marriage, in the fruitful complementarity of Zarathustra and Life."[22]

Matriphallic psychic reality is the initial response when the human collective psyche confronts material reality. It is the initial stage in meaning, myth, and explanation. Oedipal patriphallic psychic reality is a denial of and a defense against matriphallic psychic reality, and the method of the defense is a denial of material reality and the projection of a fantasy structure that is pure illusion. Matriphallic psychic reality and the Dionysian are, therefore, basic, dominant, fundamental, and primary, while patriphallic psychic reality and the Oedipal are an ancillary, derivative, subordinate, and secondary defense mechanism. The son must kill the consort to become a Father—and the son must kill the Father to become a consort.

The answer to Freuds' question "What do women want?" may be obvious but repressed. Freud does point out that, "There is one particular constant relation between femininity and instinctual life which we do not want to overlook. The suppressions of women's aggressiveness which is prescribed for them constitutionally and imposed on them socially" (SE, XXII, 116). If the dynamics of the development of the self are those of a sexualized, eroticized, and genderized Hegelian master/slave relationship, why should it be different for women? The irony of the equality position is that it doesn't grant the female the equal capacity to desire to be master over the opposite sex. Lacan ends this seminar with the comment that: "No doubt something should remain open relative to the place we currently occupy in the development of erotica and to the treatment to be given, not simply to one individual or other, but to civilization and its discontents . . . we haven't even been able to create a single new perversion. But it would be a definite sign that we have really arrived at the heart of the problem of existing perversions, if we managed to deepen our understanding of the economic role of masochism" (S VII, 14–15).

Embracing Death

The fear of castration is the fear of the seductive power of the female to trigger the *jouissance* of submission. The failure to embrace the *jouissance* of submission is the tragic destiny of Oedipus, the phallic male with his hollow phallic crown. "To be deprived of seduction is the only true form of castration" (S, 121). The truly castrated male is the one who, like Oedipus, kills the Father but is impotent as regards seduction (S, 121). He is castrated because he has no phallus. When the fantasy of the patriphallus and its law collapses, the male must either be castrated or embrace the seduction and keep the phallus in play as the phallus of the consort that is given to the (M)other. Thus, castration saves the male from Castration since "To be deprived of seduction is the only true form of castration" (S, 121).

Leopold von Sacher-Masoch's novel *Venus in Furs* is a sexual fantasy of von Sacher-Masoch's and as such shares a similar structure to the plots of stories written by other masochists or to the pornography written for them.[23] It entails a reluctant woman being encouraged to find sexual pleasure in causing pain to and exercising power over the willing slave. A common theme is the pattern of sexual arousal of the male by the female, and the deprivation of sexual release by the denial of satisfaction. The story often ends with the ritual castration of the male, the ritual sacrifice of the male, or both.[24]

There is a fundamental distinction to be drawn, however, between Nietzsche's Dionysian and the masochist. Nietzsche has Zarathustra say, "The hour when you say: 'What good is my happiness?' It is poverty and dirt and a miserable ease. But my happiness should justify existence itself!" (Z, 43). This is the law of desire, which distinguishes the masochist from the Dionysian. The masochist is interested only in the satisfaction of his own desire. He hires the dominatrix, provides the script, and describes the scenes that he wishes played out for his own pleasure. The Dionysian's *jouissance* comes from being the object of the other's desire—in filling her desire he achieves his pleasure. She becomes the Over Man when she experiences "the pleasure of conquest and the insatiability of great love . . . the overflowing feeling of strength that desires to over power, to compel" (WP, 873). It is for her, the Over Man, to enjoy "The condition of pleasure called intoxication," and which is "precisely an exalted feeling of power" (WP, 800). Nietzsche understood that "Pleasure is a kind of pain" (WP, 490) and that pain can be a kind of pleasure. He asks us, the reader, however, "But will there be many people honest enough to admit that it is a pleasure to inflict pain?" (HH, 50). He tells us, "The states in which we infuse a transfiguration and fullness into things and poetize about them until they reflect back our fullness and joy in life: sexuality; intoxication; feasting; spring; victory over an enemy; mockery; bravado; cruelty; the ecstasy of religious feeling. *Three* elements principally: *sexuality, intoxication, cruelty*—all belong to the oldest festal joys of mankind" (WP, 801). According to Nietsche, "*Pleasure* appears where there is the feeling of power" (WP, 1023). "Sexuality, the lust to rule, pleasure in appearance and deception, great and joyful gratitude for life and its typical states—these are of the essence of the pagan cults and have a good conscience on their side" (WP, 1047).

Nietzsche proposes that moral values be replaced by naturalistic values and that in the place of sociology we develop "a theory of the forms of domination" (WP, 462). He conceives of "*The Body as a Political Structure.*"[25] "Pleasure and Pain are not opposites. The feeling of power, the concept of 'perfecting': *not* only greater complexity, but greater *power.* . . . Inference concerning the evolution of mankind: perfecting consists in the production of the most powerful individuals, who will use the great mass of people as their tools" (WP, 660). Nietzsche invites us to experiment:

> So far as the promotion of knowledge is concerned, mankind's most useful achievement is perhaps the abandonment of its belief in an immortal soul . . . and it is for precisely this reason that individuals and generations can now fix their eyes on tasks of a vastness that would to earlier ages have seemed madness and a trifling with Heaven and Hell. We may experiment with ourselves! Yes, mankind now has a right to do that! The greatest sacrifices have not yet been offered to knowledge—indeed, merely to *have an inkling* of such ideas as nowadays determine our actions would in earlier times have been blasphemy and the loss of one's eternal salvation. (D, 501)

If the only truth is the will to power and the will to power is life itself, then it is women who sacrifice for truth, as they sacrifice for the renewal of life, and if men are to sacrifice themselves for truth, then they must sacrifice themselves for women. A convergence of feminism with Nietzsche's system of knowledge would invite the replacement of female sacrifice with that of the male, a rejection of the hollow and ineffectual morality of equality, and a commitment to a gender hierarchy based on voluntary sacrifice under the dynamics of the will to power. As Nietzsche states:

Of all the means of producing exaltation, it has been human sacrifice which has at all times most exalted and elevated man. And perhaps every other endeavor could still be thrown down by one tremendous idea, so that it would achieve victory over the most victorious—the idea of *self sacrificing mankind.* But to whom should mankind sacrifice itself? One could already take one's oath that, if ever the constellation of this idea appears above the horizon, the knowledge of truth would remain as the one tremendous goal commensurate with such a sacrifice, because for this goal no sacrifice is too great. (D, 45)

Castration As Sacrifice

If the male is to sacrifice himself to life, who is to receive the sacrifice? For Nietzsche, life is female. Life is SHE. In "The Second Dance Song," Zarathustra says:

Lately I gazed into your eyes, O Life: I saw gold glittering in your eyes of night—my heart stood still with delight:
I saw a golden bark glittering upon dark waters, a submerging, surging, re-emerging golden tossing bark!
At my feet, my dancing-mad feet, you threw a glance, a laughing, questioning, melting tossing glance;
Twice only did you raise your castanets in your little hands—then my feet were already tossing in a mad dance.
My heels raised themselves, my toes listened for what you should propose: for the dancer wears his ears—in his toes. (Z, 241)

The dancer dances to the whip of life. If the whip is in the hands of life, then the strokes will be administered by a female, and the dancer will be male.

Nietzsche offends the rationality of the philosopher, the ethics of the moralist, and the sanctity of the priest. His subversive wisdom must be laced with irony and obscured by ambiguity. Nietzsche and von Sacher-Masoch recognized the link between power, pain, and sexual pleasure. Nietzsche wrote that "One hurts those whom one wants to feel one's power" (GS, 86). Nietzsche writes of the pleasure of inflicting pain (HH, 50), the pleasure of venting one's power on others (HH, 103), the "voluptuousness of power," and of the "psychical extravagance of the lust for power" (D, 113). "We want . . . to perceive or divine how the next man outwardly or inwardly suffers from us, how he loses control over himself and surrenders to the impressions our hand or even merely the sight of us makes upon him" (D, 113).

> To the rhythm of my whip you shall shriek and trot! Did I forget my whip?—I did not!
>
> Then life answered me thus, keeping her gentle ears closed:
>
> "Oh Zarathustra! do not crack your whip so terribly! You surely know: noise kills thought—and now such tender thoughts are coming to me." (Z, 242)

They then talk of love and parting. This is followed by the tender and beautiful lines:

> I said something into her ear, right in the midst of her tangled yellow foolish locks.
> "You know that, O Zarathustra? No one knows that."
> And we gazed at one another and looked out on the green meadow, over which the cool evening was spreading, and wept together.
> But then Life was dearer to me than all my Wisdom had ever been. (Z, 243)

Life wields the whip, and man dances to its strokes as Zarathustra sings the "Second Dance Song."

"[W]ho would not hate you, great woman who binds us, enwinds us, seduces us, seeks us, finds us!" Nietzsche asks of life (Z, 241). His will to life is affirmed in his suffering, as we interpret the scene, as the strokes of the whip fall:

> Thus Spoke Zarathustra.
> *One!*
> Oh Man! Attend!
> *Two!*
> What does deep midnight's voice contend?
> *Three!*
> "I slept my sleep,
> *Four!*
> And now awake at dreaming's end:
> *Five!*
> The world is deep,
> *Six!*

Deeper than day can comprehend
Seven!
Deep is its woe,
Eight!
Joy—deeper than heart's agony:
Nine!
Woe says: Fade! Go!
Ten!
But all joy wants eternity,
Eleven!
—wants deep, deep, deep eternity"
Twelve! (Z, 243)

Nietzsche's affirmation of life and his metaphorical link of the human with nature through the body invite a philogynist reading of his text. The feminist interpretation we have offered of Nietzsche is that of Nietzsche the psychologist and not of Nietzsche as a philosopher. Nietzsche calls psychology "the queen of the sciences" and "the path to the fundamental problems" (BGE, II, 23). Nietzsche calls Zarathustra "the first psychologist of the good" (EH, 130). He writes, "For us psychologists . . ." (GM, III, 19, 20) rather than "for us philosophers." "Who before me at all among philosophers has been a psychologist and not rather its opposite 'higher swindler,' 'idealist'?" (EH, 131). Nietzsche tells us that "*Beyond Good and Evil* . . . does *not* mean 'Beyond Good and Bad' " (GM, I, 17). Beyond good and evil lies the affirmation of and denial of life. Nietzsche came to and made that affirmation, and his later texts are a manifestation of what that affirmation entails.

According to Nietzsche, "We cease to think when we refuse to do so under the constraint of language. . . . Rational thought is interpretation according to a scheme that we cannot throw off" (WP, 522). So far as discourse refers to the Real it is not true, and so far as it is true, it does not correspond to the Real. According to Karl Jaspers, all of Nietzsche's statements "seem to be annulled by other statements. *Self-contradiction* is the fundamental ingredient in Nietzsche's thought. For nearly every single one of Nietzsche's judgments, one can find an opposite. He gives the impression of having two opinions about everything."[26] The contradictions of Nietzsche's text, however, are not products of a changing mind, nor of loose thinking, but manifest a striving to reach the truth to be found only at the point of the fold. For Nietzsche, there would always be the lie of the perceived truth, the truth that makes the perceived truth a lie, and the truth of the lie of *the truth which makes the perceived truth a lie* also a lie. In this way, Nietzsche forces us into the fold where the discourse bends back upon itself.

The Real is not dialectical. Dialectics are a property of discourse only. The dialectics of discourse, however, are not polar opposites like good and bad, justice and injustice, up and down, or in and out. They have no resolution or synthesis. The dialectics of discourse meet in Derrida's fold. At the point of the fold in discourse where Nietzsche's truth is to be found, there is a Lacanian gap, in that the discourses of the lie in the truth and the truth in the lie disappear. It is only at that moment that one achieves the Nietzschean truth, that the discourses on either side of the fold are not the Real. Nietzsche's critique of Western metaphysics is implicitly a critique of methodology as much as it is of substance. Nietzsche had a radical view of truth, a radical view of how to achieve it, and a radical view of the degree of truth that was achievable. To achieve truth in the way of Nietzsche, one must recognize the dialectics of any discourse and break through the point of the fold moving from the truth in the lie to the lie in the truth, pausing momentarily where there is no truth or lie but silence. If there is a truth to be discovered at that point of silence, it cannot be put into words. "The criterion of truth resides in the enhancement of the feeling of power" (WP, 534).

The Desire and Fear of Seduction

The study of the sexuality of successful male politicians, published in the book *Sexual Profiles of Men in Power,* illustrates that men who would appear to be paradigmatic examples of Oedipal sexuality are secretly driven by strong Dionysian, masochistic desires and fantasies.[27] Male romantic love, for the often short period of its duration, often reflects a Dionysian matriphallic fantasy structure. The male's often ambivalent attraction to dominating or powerful women would indicate that the Dionysian drive is a part of the psyche of most males. The most convincing evidence of the dialectical nature of male heterosexual sexuality, however, is the defensive nature of the fantasy structure of Oedipal-patriphallic sexuality and its major collective structures of religion, law, and pornographic imagery. Male masochistic pornography confines the libidinal processes to fantasy and masturbation, allowing the male to release the self-castrating desire without empowering real women. Thus, powerful politicians, lawyers, judges, and businessmen can go to a dominatrix and undergo symbolic castration without having to empower living women or to give up any power of their own.[28] They privately see the dominatrix, subsume to her for their pleasure, then leave sated—ready for another day in patriarchy. She is their "fix," she satisfies their masochistic urges just enough so that they will be back but not enough so that they will desire transformation.

In Nagisa Oshima's Japanese-French film *In the Realm of the Senses,* which purports to be based on an actual occurrence, the lead male willingly dies in the act of intercourse, with the female riding him, slowly strangling him so that his contortions and convulsions give *her* the ultimate orgasm, after which she cuts off his genitals. The essence of pornography is the repetition of a small number of erotic narrative structures, with the details changing but the script remaining the same. The paramount theme, however, is that the sexual pleasure of the male is achieved through a painful but willing sacrifice for the erotic benefit of the female but for which she must be taught or tutored to desire.

Fabien Tremeau says of Oshima's film, "I regard as the turning point the killing of the hero, Kichiso, leading to what Lacan calls the feminine *jouissance.*" The article, entitled "*Ai no Korrida* [the Japanese name of the film]: The Cutting Edge of Eroticism," sets out to "show how Lacan's teaching can elucidate the movie's framework and conversely, perhaps above all, how the movie illustrates some of Lacan's ideas about *jouissance,* especially those developed in the Seminar XX, *Encore* (1972–73). So far no other films have achieved this Lacanian uniqueness."[29] Lacan is quoted in the article as saying of this film: "I was flabbergasted, because it is about feminine eroticism. Feminine eroticism seems to be pushed there to its extreme, and the extreme is the fantasy, no more or less, than to kill the man."[30] If we now imagine this extreme form of eroticism as experienced by SHE who is Over Man as an expression of the will to power, as the taking of the male as a sacrifice for the renewal of life, we would have an idea of a feminine *jouissance* that is the same as Ariadne's. If one were to conceive of the closing scene of the film as a ritual pagan sacrifice of the Dionysian consort to fertilize the earth, we gain something of an idea of the *jouissance* of the will to power when enjoyed by a female who takes the voluntary sacrifice of the male to fulfill her desire as a manifestation of the will to power.

Such a scene has an interesting counterpart in Thomas Tryon's cult novel *Harvest Home*.[31] The story involves an artist and his wife and teenage daughter who move to a small isolated New England village inhabited by the descendants of Celts who emigrated from Cornwall in the early days of New England. The artist gradually discovers that the villagers are followers of the *old religion,* and worship the Goddess. To his horror, his wife and daughter become involved in the rituals of the cult. He secretly hides to see the young Justin, the ritual harvest king, with hands tied behind his back, laid upon and coupled in intercourse with the artist's wife as the ritual corn maiden. His throat is then slit and his blood spilled over the earth as a willing sacrifice to the Goddess to ensure the fertility of the earth and the renewal of the crops. The artist rushes forward to disrupt the sacred ceremony but is caught, held, and forced to witness the sexual act between his wife and the harvest king, after which his eyes are gouged and his tongue cut out. The novel ends with him sitting childlike, with his newly pregnant wife solicitously mothering him. The novel has a narrative structure similar to that of the basic scripts of the masochistic fantasy, except that in the novel there is the horror and fear of castration with an erotic ambivalence, in that the horror arises in part from a desire for castration so as to merge with the Mother.

Harvest Home, like Euripides' *The Bacchae,* is a paradigmatic illustration of a manifestation of the original fantasy of creation, seduction, and castration, within the framework of matriphallic sexuality. While some of the content is violent, it contains far less violence than most movies, television programs, or novels. It is not a ghost story, and it is not about the supernatural. It contains no monsters or serial killers. Yet, the back of the paperback edition contains in large letters, the words, "WARNING: DO NOT READ THIS BOOK IF YOU ARE ALONE. BUT IF YOU DO, KEEP REPEATING TO YOURSELF, 'IT'S ONLY A BOOK. IT'S ONLY A BOOK.' " The introductory pages of the same edition contain quotes from reviews that describe the book as "a chiller among chillers," "sheer evil," "a malevolence," "an unhinging experience," a "horror story," "superbly haunting," and "fiendish," while one reviewer compares it to *Rosemary's Baby,* a novel about Satan worship. Why is the book so disturbing (and it is a very disturbing novel when first read)? It presents a view of matriphallic sexuality from the perspective of a patriphallic male and disturbs and frightens him because it resonates with the structure of the original fantasy and the repressed pre-Oedipal matriphallic sexuality of every male born of, nurtured, and reared by a female. The women of the village in

Harvest Home are beyond good and evil, manifestations of the will to power as manifestations of Eros. The males of the village are under their domination and at their service.

We can now begin to see a parallel between, on the one hand, what Lacan calls the feminine *jouissance* and Nietzsche's will to power as manifested in the marriage of Ariadne and Dionysus and, on the other, the theme of goddess worship and the ritual sacrifice of the sacred king in Sir James Frazer's *The Golden Bough* (which was further developed by Mary Renault in her novel *The King Must Die*).[32] The themes of Goddess worship, male submission, symbolic sacrifice of the phallus, and the disciplining of the male are often found in a variety of combinations in both practice and fantasy.[33] The antithesis is between misogyny and deification.[34] The true textual opposition is to be found between the narrative fantasy structure of the New Testament and the narrative fantasy structure of *Harvest Home.* In *Harvest Home,* the harvest lord willingly sacrifices himself for the Great Earth Mother, and the sacrifice has to be periodically renewed. In the narrative of the New Testament the sacred king dies for the Heavenly Father as a willing sacrifice and in doing so eliminates the need for any future sacrifice by the male of the logos.[35] The biblical story underlying the Judeo-Christian-Islamic tradition is opposite that of recently resurfaced narrative: the age of matriarchal consciousness.

There is a general rejection of Oedipal patriphallic psychic reality in the environmental movement, with its emphasis on a return to nature. Thomas Tryon's novel contains an interesting and penetrating insight in this regard. The novel commences with Mr. Theodor Constantine, a painter of Greek origin, and his family seeking to leave the city and return to nature. It ends with his castration by the removal of his eyes and tongue, and his wife and daughter disavowing the paternal phallus and embracing the maternal. In the novel, a return to nature entails a return to matriphallic reality. This same insight has been recognized by others who see the structural similarities between the environmental and feminist movements. What Tryon subliminally tells the reader is that the price of the return to nature is male castration.

As von Sacher-Masoch illustrated in *Venus in Furs,* the safest protection against being dominated by women is to dominate them. As the novel so clearly expresses, men have the choice of being castrated by women or castrating them. The extreme is that of a ritual voluntary sacrifice unto death, as portrayed in many of the narratives reflecting male matriphallic psychic reality, such as *Harvest Home* and *The King Must Die;* in male masochistic fantasies, such as *In the Realm of the Senses;* and in the myths recorded in Frazer's *The Golden Bough.* Even in *Venus in Furs,* the voluntary death of the male is intimated to be the ultimate conclusion of the relationship between Severin and Wanda, but Severin terminates the relationship and escapes his desire to be submissive (to be castrated) by embracing the *jouissance* of domination.

Kaja Silverman points out, however, that "there have always been individual men who have embraced lack at the level of their unconscious fantasies and identities" as well as "individual women for whom the phallus has not been the signifier of desire."[36] Silverman argues that "male mastery rests upon an abyss, and . . . the repetition through which it is consolidated is radically and ceaselessly undermined by a very different and much more primordial kind of repetition."[37] She points out that when "the equation of the male sexual organ with the phallus" can no longer be sustained, the disjuncture of the penis and the phallus will lead to "a collective loss of belief in the whole of the dominant fiction."[38] Her aim is to "call sexual difference into question, and beyond that, reality itself."[39] She goes on to say that "To effect a large-scale reconfiguration of male identification and desire would, at the very least, permit female subjectivity to be lived differently than it is at present. . . . The theoretical articulation of some non-phallic masculinities would consequently seem to be an urgent feminist project."[40] Nonphallic and psychic realities, whether of the female or the male, still leave us in the Lacanian bind. Silverman tells us that "what is finally at issue here is not just an erotic economy which defies the procreative imperative, and blurs the distinction between fore-pleasure and end-pleasure, but one which decenters the male sexual organ, delineates a continuity of pleasure extending from male lips to female genitals, and refuses to write 'lack' at the site of the female body" and refuses as well "to project castration onto the corporeality of the sexual Other, and thereby to secure the phallus as the unquestioned signifier of power, privilege, and wholeness."[41] She goes on to assert by way of conclusion that unexpected pleasures and possibilities await the male subject who "renegotiates his relation to the Law of Language—when he accedes to his castration, his specularity, and the profound 'otherness' of his 'self' by embracing desires and identifications which are in excess of the positive Oedipus complex."[42] She asks, "after even a partial glimpse of those pleasures and psychic possibilities, who would still opt for the straight and narrow path of conventional masculinity?"[43]

The law of language furnishes us with two choices. As von Sacher-Masoch, speaking through the voice of Severin, his alter ego, puts it: "The moral is that woman, as Nature created her and as man up to now has found her attractive, is man's enemy; she can only be his slave or his mistress but never his companion . . . there is only one alternative: to be the hammer or the anvil."[44] If man is to do as Silverman suggests and "renegotiates his relation to the Law of Language," "accedes to his castration, his specularity, and the profound 'otherness' of his 'self' by embracing desires and identifications which are in excess of the positive Oedipus complex" in order to catch "a glimpse of those pleasures and psychic possibilities," then he must leave "the straight and narrow path of conventional masculinity" and embrace the *jouissance* of submission. This is what it means to *become* Dionysus.

Peter Greenaway's film *Drowning by Numbers* centers on three women who all have the same name and who correspond to the virgin/mother/crone of the Triple Goddess. All three are married to useless males who are unfaithful or are unable to satisfy their desires, and who would use them while doing nothing particularly useful for them in return. They solve their collective problem by drowning their husbands, the oldest woman first, followed by the next in age, and finally the youngest. In each case they appeal to the Dionysian figure of the local coroner who designates the drownings as accidental while knowing full well how the deaths occurred.

The movie is replete with castration symbols. A young boy circumcises himself with a pair of scissors merely to satisfy a young girl's curiosity. It is as if he presents her with his foreskin as a present. Throughout the story, the coroner is caught in play. He delights at the trivial, and is consumed by the game. His passion is numbers, and he sees them everywhere, in everything: they are paramount to the thrill of the game. The numbers, so significant for logos, science, and economics, pervade the screen. A young girl skips and counts stars at the same time. When she reaches one hundred, she stops and says, "Once you've counted one hundred, all the other hundreds are the same."[45] Deaths of all kinds, including animals, are numbered by Smut, the boy who mutilated his foreskin. The last death was number one hundred. Death is meaningless, hence "all the other hundreds are the same." After Smut's gift of himself, through his foreskin, is rejected by the young girl, he eventually commits suicide.

The coroner requests sexual favors from the women for covering up the murders, but each rebuffs him, teasing and taunting him. He commences a game in which they either will service him sexually or he will betray them to the authorities. They nevertheless refuse to play. Rather than betray them or the game in which they are all players—the game to see who would use whom, he permits himself to be seduced and is taken out into the water in a rowboat. He takes off all his clothes so he is naked before them and sits peaceful and resigned in the boat. The women pull the boat's plug, and the film ends with the boat gradually sinking into the water. By the women's refusal to play the game of life with him, the coroner, as the Oedipal King, allows himself to be seduced into the role of the sacrificial Dionysus. In stripping himself naked before them and embracing death, he surrenders the patriphallus, the Gaze and the Voice. He becomes Other to their Subject. The three women gaze at the coroner; they watch him sink, deeper and deeper. They gaze "Over Man" but continue themselves to swim.

The recognition of the primary signifier and the primary original fantasy of the collective permits women to remain in the circuit of linguistic exchange. They were never out of it and need never, in fact cannot ever, leave it. No prediscursive reality is required. The status of the phallus need not be challenged directly in terms of the female body but rather through the dialectical oppositions of the structure of the original primary fantasy, which is reflected in the structure of both the privileged and the primary signifiers.

If Dionysian masochism is the primary neurosis of the male, against which other neuroses and pathologies arise as defenses, then this fact ought to have tremendous significance for feminism. If we ever really did have a true and full commitment to gender and sexual equality, then male submission to the female ought to be as thinkable, plausible, and acceptable as the reverse is now. Our willingness to embrace reversibility demonstrates the depth of our commitment to equality of the sexes. Most women are not prepared to contemplate the possibility of having the opportunity to define their own sexuality, invite males to play with them within the realm of the Imaginary and Symbolic structured by the primary signifier, and to accept males who wish to lose the burden of the Oedipal phallus.

A convergence of feminism with Nietzsche's text would place the SHE who is Over Man in the ancient past. When SHE has appeared, SHE has been slaughtered by the breed of lesser men who turn the will to power into a death drive. Yet the will to power will be manifested in women again and again, and at some point some will go beyond what Nietzsche deemed the slave morality and embrace a will to power in which she will seduce, use, and sacrifice the lesser breed of males in the manifestation of Nietzsche's will to power. So would the Nietzschean narrative unfold as structured by the primary signifier.[46]

NINE

Medusa Depetrified

Medusa's presence evokes sentiments of fear and reproach in those who happen to cross her path. As such, she is constantly being put in an obscure corner, in the dark continent of decay. She has come to symbolize the pure potency of the female—her prowess—intellectually, physically, and sexually. She is a figure who is not necessarily pleasant, nice, or receptive in the traditional feminine connotations of such terms. Rather, Medusa is a true fighter—an Amazon—and one to be feared for she has a brute force untamed by femininity. She has been given the physical attributes of the monster—the form in which her essence has been understood by centuries of patriarchal figures. In psychoanalysis, her image is the product of the male fear of the (M)other, the fear of castration and of death. She is at once both frightening and alluring, revolting and erotic. Her ambiguity makes the male onlooker want to embrace her dominance but also to run fitfully from her penetrating claws. Faced with this ambiguity, the result is denial—petrifying her image—keeping her locked behind a mask. It is her onlookers, however, who are truly petrified, as goes the myth, whereas she is merely the enigma that has caused their metamorphosis.

For the male, Medusa epitomizes the darkness of the discovery of the female genitalia. She is the symbol of the male's first encounter with the female's "lack," the first confrontation with the fact of woman's otherness and difference. Her head filled with a mass of writhing serpents, Medusa, as possessor of the lack, represents the pure horror of castration, the unbridgeable gulf, the ultimate fear of being engulfed by the woman's genitalia—conceptualized as the dangerous mouth that poses an insurmountable threat to the male penis.

For women immersed in patriarchy, she is equally frightening. The desire to unmask is only realized when woman comes to terms with her present existence as a mere shadow. Only then will she desire to resurrect and reconstruct the dormant counterstructure. Many women prefer to remain shielded by the veil of femininity in order to avoid the retribution of the Father; others are shielded by the comfort of working toward liberal notions of equality. Very few venture any further, as the risks and the pain can easily overwhelm.

Out of her death, Medusa gives birth to the winged horse Pegasus (who, upon her death, springs with other creatures from the stump of her neck). The blood from her left side is said to be capable of raising the dead, whereas the blood from the right side is reputedly poisonous, capable of causing instant death. Medusa is thus capable of initiating both cure and curse. She is capable of giving life and, simultaneously, of brutally taking it away. She is "the movement, the locus and the play: (the production of) difference," the "differance of difference" whereby she "holds in reserve, in [her] undecided shadow and vigil, the opposites and the differends that the process of discrimination will come to carve out" (PP, 127). She is the dark feminine, the castrator, the inspiration for the femme fatale of dark drama and cinema. In India, Medusa takes her form as the Great Goddess Kali, bloodstained and tongue-lolling, defeater of Raktavira. She is the Goddess of death and destruction, face dripping with blood, surrounded by snakes and adorned with human heads and skulls. She represents the maternal feminine, the Goddess of life and fertility.

For women, Medusa depetrified gives rise to the true ability to actively become, in the Nietzschean sense. "*What does your conscience say?*—You shall become the person you are" (GS, 270). She is and should be the pinnacle of radical feminism, as she is about the depetrification of women, about the difficult process of women *becoming*. According to Mary Daly, *Gyn/Ecology* "is about the journey of women becoming, that is, radical feminism. . . . Radical feminist consciousness spirals in all directions, discovering the past, creating/dis-closing the present/future. The radical being of women is very much an Otherworld Journey. It is both discovery and creation of a world other than patriarchy."[1] For men, the petrified image of Medusa represents the "lack"—the inverted symbol of phallic power. The act of depetrification for the male is a veritable submission to the "lack," an acknowledgment of its presence, a deveiling, demystification of phallic "power." She demonstrates the ability of males to take part and engender a nonphallocentric discourse.

Is depetrification a viable option, a cogent reality, or even a therapeutic possibility? Can it be a socially important avenue for the transformation and resuscitation of the hidden selves of women? In all probability, no—the ramifications are far too effective. Clearly, though we may decide and have a certain degree of success in being able to resuscitate her for a few small pages, Medusa is destined to remain a stony figurine, purely frozen potential.

The Castrating Effect of Medusa

The (M)other is understood as having the ability to swallow an emergent identity. The vagina, that which brought life, is looked upon as dangerous, murky, and ravenous—capable of reswallowing a slowly emerging self. Man is fearful at the sight of the female "lack" and anxious or apprehensive that the sighting will produce a similar "lack" in himself, and so mythologies about the mysterious "black hole" of female sexuality formed over time. For instance, the fear of castration expressed itself in mythology by way of the toothed vagina or the "toothed matrix" (Glas, 205): the *vagina dentata.* Judy Trejo retells the Paiute version of the myth in which Coyote, when trotting through a canyon, came upon two females squatting on the ground. "This was back in the days when the female genital organs still had teeth." The two women were eating a rabbit and throwing the bones underneath themselves, where they were hungrily devoured by "the second set of teeth in their genitals." "Horrified, Coyote . . . tossed pieces of shale under both women, breaking all their teeth and rendering their vaginas harmless to men after all."[2] Camille Paglia relates a similar North American Indian version in which "A meat-eating fish inhabits the vagina of the Terrible Mother."[3] "The hero is the man who overcomes the Terrible Mother, breaks the teeth out of her vagina, and so makes her into a woman."[4]

The sexual act of intercourse can be interpreted as a submission to the recesses of the female orifices. The male who submits in this way has no way of knowing if she will return him his prized appendage. She engulfs it ravenously, and he, correspondingly, desperately wants to be engulfed. The tension of simultaneous will and avoidance results in the "'supreme spasm,' the moment of dying laughing" whereby it "eliminates the exteriority of anteriority, the independence of the imitated, the signified, or the thing" (DS, 209). According to Paglia, "metaphorically, every vagina has sacred teeth, for the male exits as less than when he entered."[5] Sexual intercourse with a woman for a male is a traversal of the ambiguous boundaries of life and death—the anxiety of castration is what binds the two. It is all part of a narcissistic attempt at a merger with the lost (M)other, a violation of the female body and staking out of its territory. But, most importantly, it is the erotic walk on the tightrope, looking out over the abyss, the erotic leap into fate—not knowing if phallic power will be fully subsumed or revitalized.

The female *vagina demon* is insatiable, it threatens to suck the life out of the male victim. She is the original vampiress, seductress, and temptress. The male fear is of the marshland of female fecundity; the terrible stench of a wet, dank interior; the humid horror of the female body. Despite the repulsive referent, the male's primal desire is to enter, to penetrate, to territorialize the recesses as far and as deep as he is capable of doing, even if what this means for the intruder is a deadly encounter with *her teeth*. His ultimate *jouissance* is in submission to the pure potentiality of the *vagina dentata*.

The repression of animality as well as the fear of death, decay, and castration are all definitively linked to the repression of sexual dependency. The fears are all essentially the threat of a loss of self, be it through the loss of the engulfed penis, the loss of individuation, or the end of life. Eroticism and fantasy cannot possibly be excluded from this dynamic. In fact, they are the necessary tools for the actualization of this repression. Violence takes on a sexualized erotic role in the repression fantasy. Eros and Thanatos are thus inextricably linked. According to René Girard, "At the very height of the crisis, violence becomes simultaneously the instrument, object and all-inclusive subject of desire."[6] Desire and the desiring subject in this form must clearly be violent. In the eroticization of the repression fantasy, desire is generated at the moment at which the self experiences itself as loss—as decapitated, castrated, or destroyed. This typically occurs at the moment of sexual release during coition. In this transgression of taboos, the male loses his self to the Other and in erotic, repressed form confronts the baseness of his animality: "Repression is thus the very condition of pleasure."[7] This fantasy structure follows the dialectic of the master/slave, and the *jouissances* of domination and submission for in the dialectic of masochism desire is only generated when repressed.

Medusa is one of the three Gorgon sisters who sports a single *evil* and *demonic* eye. She invites the Gaze of the Other but simultaneously repels it. She seduces the masses to meet her stare, yet most are afraid of the paralyzing results. Anthropological studies of the roots of the evil eye demonstrate that it threatens to make men impotent[8] and is therefore a threat to "masculinity." The evil eye is a symbol of destruction and marginalization. The evil eye is the castrating Gaze of the powerful and dominant female who is a self as a manifestation of the Subject. It is castrating because it denies the male the Gaze and the Voice rendering him a self as the manifestation of the Other. The male maintains the phallus as the privileged signifier through its recognition as the phallus by the female. He is unable to maintain the fantasy structure without her recognition. Her refusal to recognize the logos as the manifestation of the generative power of nature and her rejection of the Law of the Father constitute, therefore, a castration. Perseus, through his primal act of violence, did manage to kill the female demon, but he is still not afforded the right to *look.* He needed Athene's aegis to shield him from himself—from his gazing or from his desire to penetrate the gap between the voyeur and what is being looked at.

Medusa has the ability to castrate, deconstruct, dethrone, and to dedeify. It is, however, the onlooker *victim,* the true desirer, who brings about the petrification. According to Derrida, this is "the logical paradox of the apotropaic: castrating oneself *already,* always already, in order to be able to castrate and repress the threat of castration, renouncing life and mastery in order to secure them; putting into play by ruse, simulacrum and violence just what one wants to preserve; losing in advance what one wants to erect; suspending what one raises" (Glas, 46). Oedipus was hopelessly drawn to challenge the Sphinx—it was his duty as upholder of the logos, and Pentheus felt compelled to play the voyeur. Perseus had to cut off Medusa's head. It was Theseus' role as Hero to conquer the Amazons. Through a mixture of the anticipation of pleasure and danger, the soon-to-be castrated is drawn toward the castrator—in Oedipus' case, it was a blind search for an obsequious "Truth"; for Pentheus, it was a meek effort to assert whatever "masculinity" remained; and for Perseus, it was an act of violence, of war and sexualized aggression, in an effort to subvert and subsume her power.

The Medusan myth of violation and decapitation is necessary for the survival of patriarchy and the denial of female sexuality. It represses the possibility or viability of female authority or of a matriarchal society.

Onlookers *fetishize* her image, they demote her to the horrid monster because in this way she is more easily dismissed. Medusa is the true dominatrix of desire through the onlooker's theatrical ritualization of fantasy. All she can do is invite submission to desire. But submission invites death as it invites the losing of the boundaries of the ego. And, in fact, submission *is* death. According to Bataille, key to eroticism is the notion of being "swept away" or losing all barriers and controlling mechanisms: "No one could deny that one essential element of excitement is the feeling of being swept off one's feet, of falling headlong. If love exists at all, it is, like death, a swift movement of loss within us, quickly slipping into tragedy and stopping only with death. For the truth is that between death and the reeling, heady motion of the little death the distance is hardly noticeable."[9] The submission is not a willing of death but a willing of life. By pushing life to its very extremes, just to the point where death becomes a true contingency, the submission to death becomes in actuality a submission to life, to Eros, to the primary signifier:

> The desire to go keeling helplessly over, that assails the innermost depths of every human being is nevertheless different from the desire to die in that it is ambiguous. It may well be a desire to die, but it is at the same time a desire to live to the limits of the possible and the impossible with ever-increasing intensity. It is the desire to live while ceasing to live, or to die without ceasing to live, the desire of an extreme state that Saint Theresa has perhaps been the only one to depict strongly enough in words. "I die because I cannot die." But the death of not dying is precisely not death; it is the ultimate stage of life; if I die because I cannot die it is on condition that I live on; because of the death I feel though still alive and still live on.[10]

The Jouissance of Male Submission

Of the several different kinds of love, it is courtly love that Lacan finds most revealing of the relationship between love and *jouissance.* The lady must be unreachable, separated from her courtly lover by an uncrossable barrier. She is depersonalized, and "as a result, writers have noted that all poets seem to be addressing the same person" (S VII, 149). "In this poetic field the feminine object is emptied of all real substance" (S VII, 149) and has nothing to do with actual women.[11] The reason for the nonpersonal nature of the lady is to prevent the female figure from returning love. She is an object of unattainable desire.

A further property that preserves male *jouissance* is the coldness and arbitrariness of the lady. According to Zizek, "The relationship of the knight to the Lady is thus the relationship of the subject-bondsman, vassal, to his feudal Master-Sovereign who subjects her vassal to senseless, outrageous, impossible, arbitrary, capricious ordeals."[12] The *jouissance* that is at play, so far as the male is concerned, is the *jouissance* of submission. Lacan tell us that he "was struck by the fact that, in the terminology of courtly love, the word *domnei* is used. The corresponding verb is *domnoyer,* which means something like 'to caress,' 'to play around,' and is related to the term *Domna,* the Lady, or in other words, to her who on occasion dominates" and is "frequently referred to with the masculine term, *Mi Dom,* or my Lord" (S VII, 149–50). He turns to Arnaud Daniel for "evidence from the file of courtly love." He then translates the poem about the lady, *Domna Ena,* who orders her knight to lick her anus with his tongue in order "to test the worthiness of his love, his loyalty and his commitment." He comments, "The idealized woman, the Lady, who is in the position of the Other and of the object, finds herself suddenly and brutally positing, in a place knowingly constructed out of the most refined of signifiers, the emptiness of a thing in all its crudity, a thing that reveals itself in its nudity to be the thing, her thing, the one that is to be found at her very heart in its cruel emptiness, That Thing, whose function certain of you perceived in the relation to sublimation, is in a way unveiled with a cruel and insistent power" (S VII, 162).

The parallels between the structure of courtly love and contemporary male masochism are striking, and Zizek comments on them at length. The ritualized and highly structured features of masochistic praxis, reflected in von Sacher-Masoch's *Venus in Furs,* are to be found in the ritual of courtly love. Zizek writes, "We are dealing with a strictly codified fiction, a social game of 'as if' where we pretend that our sweetheart is the inaccessible Lady."[13]

Courtly love places feminism in a double bind. If women seek equality then they lose *jouissance,* and if they lose *jouissance,* they cannot maintain love. If they decide to play the role of the domina, then they are actresses in a male script, still serving male desire.[14] Is not the *Domna* a product of male fantasy wherein SHE plays a role akin to the veiled virgin, hiding beyond the sexual referent of male desire? Courtly love, as described by Lacan and Zizek, deals with the inaccessible lady but the male fantasy of this Lady as opposed to her participation in the fantasy. The male's *jouis-*

sance is submission, submission to the male image of the lady—a male construction.

The Retaliation of the Hero

The Hero has to retaliate against the castrating effect of Medusa, against the desire to play the role of the courtly lover. She is to the Hero the ultimate foe because SHE has the ability to undermine the stately podium from which he enacts the Law of the Father. The Hero, in this retaliation, seeks to petrify, delegitimize, deconstruct, deny, and castrate her. Women are castrated by the Hero every day by being denied the generative power of nature and the logos as ego-mind-self, by being *fucked.* They are castrated by being denied *jouissance* and the right to control their own sexuality and the destinies of their own bodies. The problem that Hegel articulated is, How can the master receive reaffirmation of his self from a slave? In the context of Oedipal patriphallic sexuality, the problem becomes, How can the male maintain love for the inferior, castrated submissive whom he regularly fucks? Fucking consists of satisfying one's own desire by using another as the object:

> Why is it precisely in connection with a half-failed act of pruning, with an act of cutting that is blocked, thwarted, messed up, that one should evoke the presumed origin of the word and find it in the hole drilling activities of work in its most primitive of forms, with the meaning of sexual operation, of phallic penetration? Why does one resurrect the metaphor "fuck" in connection with something that is "fucked up?" Why is it the image of the vulva that surfaces to express a number of different acts, including those of escaping, of fleeing, of cutting and running *[se tailler]* as the German term in the text has often been translated? (S VII, 168)

Clearly, to retaliate against her castrating effect, the Hero fucks her and appropriates the Lady of courtly love and, in so doing, denies her potency and promulgates her objectification. By fucking her, he is able to erect and maintain his simulacrum of phallic power.

The Appropriation of Athene

The Hero, in his battle against the Medusan Amazon, has enlisted, in the patriarchal versions of the myth, the aid of Athene. According to one version, Athene was jealous of Medusa's beauty and her consorting with

 Poseidon. She punished Medusa by turning her into a vicious monster with pointed claws and a mass of writhing serpents for hair. Athene is reputed to have battled against the Amazons and was understood to be a great nemesis to matricentric society. Yet her earliest manifestations demonstrate that she may have in fact been their ally.[15]

Athene dons the frightful image of Medusa as a shield, an act that Freud understands has the effect of placing her outside of desire. She becomes "a woman who is unapproachable and repels all sexual desires—since she displays the terrifying genitals of the Mother" (SE, XVIII, 273). Donning the mask, Athene is no longer the object. She eludes the evil eye of the spectator and denies the rights to her objectification.

The Hero has obliged Medusa to play the role of the virgin undeniably bound to the mask. The Apollonian Law of the Father, in its effort to deny and repress the anxiety of castration, has erected its antithesis. Medusa is depicted as a dispassionate one-dimensional Athenian aegis, as this is what she is forced to become. Her vitality is masked by the petrification of her sexual prowess, and those that come into contact with her must assume a mask in order to avoid her wrath. They cannot gaze directly as this would be looking directly into the contingency of death.

Medusan 'Jouissance'

Lacan discusses what he terms "the paradox of *jouissance*" and seeks to clarify it for us in terms of "the enigma of its relation to the Law" (S VII, 192) and to the death of God. God, the logos, and the phallus have always been dead, fraudulent metaphors for Lacan because mind has no existence independent of the body. "No doubt a science has been erected on the fragile belief ['of a single God who is both the Lord of the universe and the dispenser of the light that warms life and spreads the brightness of consciousness'] I was discussing, namely, the one that is expressed in the following terms, which always reappear at the horizon of our aims: 'The real is rational, the rational is real' " (S VII, 180). The death of God is, for Lacan as it is for Nietzsche, the denial of the truth of logos and of any teleological direction and hierarchy of values.

According to Lacan, "The two notions, the death of God and neighborly love [God's commandment of love], are historically linked (S VII, 193): "We cannot avoid the formula that *jouissance* is evil. Freud leads us by the hand to this point: it is suffering because it involves suffering for my neighbor." *Jouissance* is irreconcilable with the Law of the Father, with God's neighborly love, as God's love does not take into account the reality of "the unconscious aggression that *jouissance* contains" (S VII, 194), which exists both within ourselves and within our neighbors. According to Lacan's interpretation of Freud, the moment we take the path toward neighborly love, we lose the path opening on to *jouissance* (S VII, 186). There can be no *jouissance* without aggression, and the aggression of my neighbor's *jouissance* "is that which poses a problem for my love" (S VII, 187). "What are we drawing attention to?" Lacan asks. He answers, "To the unconscious aggression that *jouissance* contains" (S VII, 194). He asks a further question: "What is the goal *jouissance* seeks if it has to find support in transgression to seek it?" (S VII, 195). This question is left open.

The relationship between love and *jouissance* is a diacritical one. Where at first glance they appear to be in dialectical opposition, on further analysis, their association is more undecidable and complex. Whereas, to the idealist, love implies *jouissance*, love *is jouissance:* the "realist" understands the two terms to be mutually exclusive. The terms seem to suggest "a certain *folding back* {*repli*}—which will later be called a *re-mark*—of opposition within the series, or even within its dialectic. . . . Such a functional displacement, which concerns differences (and as we shall see, simulacra) more than any conceptual identities signified, is a real and necessary challenge. It writes itself" (PP, 104).

Love can be maintained in relationships of equality but at the price of *jouissance*. Both long-term mutual love and mutual *jouissance* seem to be a matter of fantasy rather than material reality because the flow of aggression that is necessary for *jouissance* seems incompatible with a mutually loving, long-term relationship. This is particularly so for Oedipal patriphallic sexuality. The situation is somewhat different in matriphallic sexuality. If the relationship is between a dominant female and a *feminized* other, the Other may express love in embracing the role of the Object of desire. The inferiority in feminization may sustain *jouissance* but not love. The submission of the Consort in a Goddess/Consort archetypal relationship, however, is based on sacrifice rather than inferiority.

The privileged signifier is no longer able to maintain a meaningful relationship with the Real. Thus, it can no longer furnish the grand metaphor and the grand metonymy for the generation of the self as subject. God is dead, the secular form of the logos has lost its theoretical foundations in science and philosophy, and the penis has lost its phallic significance. Nevertheless, the discourses of the privileged signifier still predominate. Consequently, it becomes more and more difficult to identify the male, as a materialization of the Subject, as a manifestation of the Real. As a result, more and more aggression is required to maintain male *jouissance.* With the loss of the credibility of the privileged signifier as a manifestation of the Real, more and more females generate the self as a manifestation of the Subject, placing themselves in the position of the male. In doing so, they refuse to be fucked. Consequently, heterosexual relationships become more fragile and fleeting, more filled with aggression, and less sexually satisfying.

The loss of *jouissance* within the structure of the privileged signifier leads more and more people into alternative forms of sexuality, the leading heterosexual alternative being sexual discipline and bondage.[16] Females, socialized in the discourses of the privileged signifier and yet at the same time always subject to the power of the primary signifier as the truth of the patriarchal lie, find it difficult to enter into the *jouissance* of domination and submission, on either side. By settling for patriarchal civility as the best that can be achieved, they find heterosexual relationships void of both love and *jouissance.*

Males, on the other hand, find themselves castrated when the privileged signifier loses its metaphorical and metonymical significance. They remain in the discourses of the privileged signifier but find it more and more difficult to maintain their place as self qua manifestation of the Subject. When they solve the riddle of the Sphinx and know who and what they really are, they suffer the castration of Oedipus. They become engulfed one way or another in the abyss and in the despair of nihilism. The despair and loss of self often lead to blind rage, and their only source of *jouissance* becomes the *jouissance* of transgression. Those who can pay the price can obtain temporary *jouissance* through the professional sex workers who will, for money, play the role of dominant or submissive.

The relationship here—between love and *jouissance,* inside and the outside, the monstrous and the sublime—is an interconnected weave of difference and not a synthesis. Human heterosexual relations are trapped within the dialectical tension of love and *jouissance* for "what is love other than banging one's head against a wall?" (FS, 170). "The double screen which divides it inside itself, dividing its internal and its external aspects, but dividing it by only by reassembling it with itself, sticking it to itself doubly, *fort:da*. I am calling this, once more, and necessarily, the *hymen* of the *fort:da*" (Pos, 316).

A 'Jouissance' Proper to Her

The depetrification of Medusa symbolizes the shedding of the veil and the ultimate removal of the mask of femininity. The mask, according to Girard, "mixes man and beast, god and inanimate object." They "juxtapose beings and objects separated by differences. They are beyond differences; they do not merely defy differences or efface them, but they incorporate and rearrange them in original fashion. In short, they are another aspect of the monstrous double."[17] "Have your masks and subtlety," states Nietzsche, "that you may be mistaken for what you are not, or feared a little" (BGE, 25). Further, he states that "every opinion is also a hideout, every word also a mask" (BGE, 289). The removal of the mask exposes the hideaway with a deadly precision.

The Goddess-Lady-*Domina* who looks behind the mask of femininity never gets fucked. The relationship never gets personal. She is the One who fills the gap, the lack, the hole for the man, which is the function of *jouissance*. The female must be dominant for the male in order to prevent him from fucking her. In love, a living person replaces what Lacan refers to as "the Thing," but the living person cannot fill the gap or the lack. The Thing is connected with the Real. It is this link with the Real that makes *jouissance* possible. Loving relationships between two people cannot maintain *jouissance* because they become personal, and when they become personal they lose their link with the Real in terms of the Imaginary and the Symbolic. The function of fantasy is to generate the *jouissance* that is blocked by the personalization of the sexual act. Many males prefer pornography and masturbation to actual intercourse as they can more easily maintain *jouissance* in the former. Other males prefer raping a woman to consensual sex because rape is impersonal and adds to the Sadean *jouissance* of transgression. The male's embrace of the role of the submissive prevents the female from loving him on a personal level. He is an object and not a person, and therefore he can love, but only at a distance, exchanging coitus for *jouissance*.

The 'Domna' Potential

According to Derrida:

One can envisage, then, a quasi-transcendental privilege of this drive for mastery, drive for power, or drive for domination [*emprise*]. The latter denomination seems preferable: it marks more clearly the relation to the other, even in domination *over oneself*. And the word immediately places itself in communication with the lexicon of *giving, taking, sending,* or *destining* that is inciting us here from a distance, and that soon will concern us more directly. The drive to dominate must also be the drive's *relation to itself*: there is no drive not driven to bind itself to itself and to assure itself of mastery over itself as a drive. Whence the transcendental tautology of the drive to dominate: it is the drive as drive, the drive of the drive, the drivenness of the drive. Again, it is a question of a relation to oneself as a relation to the other, the auto-affection of a *fort:da* which gives, takes, sends and destines itself, distances and approaches itself by its own step, the other's. (Pos, 403)

Within the chains of signification of the primary signifier, it is the man who must embrace a self that merges from the Other and is defined in terms of lack. Consequently, according to Lacan and Zizek, women would not enjoy the *jouissance* of domination.[18] They are only acting—playing a role—for money or for favor in a theater, a play staged entirely by men. Consequently, the *Domna-Domina* is not a manifestation of their own desire. The masochist, according to Zizek, establishes in a cold businesslike way the terms of the contract: the scenes, the costumes, the props, "how strongly she is to whip him, in what precise way she is to enchain him, where she is to stamp on him with her high heels," and when it is over he returns to the role of the "respectful bourgeois" and arranges the time for the next appointment.[19] It may well be that many masochists are in a dominant/submissive relationship under the illusion that they can remain in control. The fact is, however, that some women enjoy the *jouissance* of domination. A good deal of female *Domina*/male submissive relationships exist in which the female sets the scene, decides upon the script, chooses the props, and dictates a contract that frees her from all limits, leaving the male with the only option of walking away.

If one does not recognize the existence of the *Domna* within the language of the primary signifier, one necessarily has to interpret her as a product of male fantasy or as a petrified woman without Voice or Gaze who has internalized male fantasy. The privileged signifier does not provide a structure in which SHE can be Subject, and therefore there is no alternative but to explain her sexuality as a manifestation of male desire. If one recognizes the existence and function of the primary signifier, then one has a structure in which domina sexuality can be explained in terms of female desire and the male submissive can be equally explained in terms of the structure of the primary signifier. One must, however, "go beyond oppositional or dialectical logic" (Pos, 403) in order to derive the "truth" of the female subject, of SHE. One must, in order to find her "subjecthood," return to her objecthood, to his subjecthood, as "it defines the relationship to oneself as the relation to the other" (Pos, 404).

In *This Sex Which Is Not One,* Irigaray was asked what she thought "of the notion of 'woman power' " and further "If woman were to come to pass (in history and in the unconscious, the latter being, indeed, 'only' hom[m]osexual), what would result: would a feminine power be purely and simply substituted for masculine power?"[20] She answered: "it clearly cannot be a matter of substituting feminine power for masculine power. Because this reversal would still be caught up in the economy of the same, in the same economy—in which, of course, what I am trying to designate as 'feminine' would not emerge. There would be a phallic 'seizure of power.' "[21] At the end of her book *The Bonds of Love,* Jessica Benjamin states that "women must claim their subjectivity and so be able to survive destruction."[22] She sees this as the claiming of the equal other so as to assert the possibility of mutual recognition: "They [women] may thus offer men a new possibility of colliding with the outside and becoming alive in the presence of an equal other."[23] Finally, she states, "My conclusion is both modest and utopian."[24]

The world of difference implies the inevitability of hierarchies. When there is difference, there is otherness, but the egotistical self is unable or unwilling to confront the simultaneous independent and codependent reality of the Other. Recognizing the Other is a recognition of the other in oneself, one's own limitations and the baseness of animality. The result is the setting of boundaries, the exertion of control, and the struggle for power—the *jouissance* of domination. The dialectic of domination and submission is unavoidable: "In his nascent state, man is never simply man. He is always, necessarily, and essentially, either Master or Slave."[25] Recognizing the inevitability of hierarchy, however, does not, of necessity entail a recognition of the supremacy of one sex over the other. It merely asserts that equality is a fabrication and that within a heterosexual relationship one partner likely will be dominant and the other submissive, or else they will remain in a state of frequent conflict. It asserts a dialectical approach to hierarchy, the male being dominant when the privileged signifier is maintained, the female being dominant when the primary signifier is maintained. The roles can *potentially* switch, as each role has, deep within it, elements of the other.

In our view, radical feminism, when pitted against postmodernism and psychoanalysis, must take into account the potentiality of female domination in the Symbolic order by *privileging* the primary signifier. If and when the primary signifier is privileged in the Symbolic order, females will, according to the dialectical framework of hierarchy, play the dominant role. While domination may or may not enter the domain of the Real, it must be recognized as a contingency in the realm of the Imaginary. It is there and must be contended with. By accepting the "truth" of women's oppression past and present, woman's difference, and the inevitability of hierarchical relationships in sexuality, one must correspondingly recognize the likelihood or potentiality of female domination. It does exist in the fantasy structures of many males (surfacing as instances of the primary neurosis of male masochism) and *is* what lies hidden behind Medusa's mask. Why do women fear or deny this potential? The assertion is not essential, or biological, it is a mere assertion of the *potentiality*. Patriarchal discourse has long been premised on male domination of females due to the continued preeminence of the privileged signifier. When one can assert that this positioning of the privileged signifier is not absolute, that it is only one element of a dialectical pole wherein lies contingents of the other, one must consider the potentiality of the other end of the dialectical scale. While equality has served as an effective tool for feminists to combat male domination, the result will always be somewhere in between "equality" and male domination. Equality as an end is not achievable in this way.

Power is a characteristic of both sexes and is not exclusively a male trait, though it has been sexualized as such. If it were, one would be positing the continual subordination of females. If one can free power of its patriarchal tonality, then it can and should be utilized by females to *be*, to assert, and to define. We link woman's appropriation of the potentiality of power with her journey toward her origins. "To seduce the man, to part him from his natural trajectory," states Derrida, "she accomplishes in the final count the wise design of nature" (Glas, 127). Her empowerment is not about males (though it cannot escape its positioning within sexual hierarchies), it is more about SHE, about her process of becoming, about her *jouissance*. According to Daly,

> The play is part of our work of unweaving and of our weaving work. It whirls us into another frame of reference. We use the visitation of demons to come more deeply into touch with our own powers/virtues. Unweaving their deceptions, we name our Truth. Defying their professions we discover our Female Pride, our Sinister Wisdom. Escaping their possession we find our Enspirited Selves. Overcoming their aggression we uncover our Creative Anger and Brilliant Bravery. Demystifying/demythifying their obsessions we re- member our Woman-loving Love. Refusing their assimilation we experience our Autonomy and Strength. Avoiding their elimination we find our Original Be-ing. Mending their imposed fragmentation we Spin our Original Integrity.[26]

The Hegelian master/slave dialectic is the culmination of the struggle between independence and dependence, disappearance and reappearance. The self's primary goal is to see itself as privileged, as the only operative force, a goal that clashes with the self's need for recognition—the need for others to recognize the privileged positioning of the self. The obvious tension is magnified when it becomes clear that for others to recognize the self, the self must recognize the mutual existence of others, of the Other. The self needs to be able to find her or himself in the Other but at the same time wants to "rid it of the parasite" and "keep the outside out" (PP, 128). "This," states Derrida, "is the inaugural gesture of 'logic' itself, of good 'sense' insofar as it accords with the self-identity of *that which is:* being is what it is, the outside is outside and the inside inside." The cure will "eliminate the excess," the truth of the Other, but "this elimination, being therapeutic in nature, must call upon the very thing it is expelling, the very surplus it is *putting out*" (PP, 128). According to Hegel, the conflict that is created is irresolvable and therefore produces an insoluble conflict. The inevitable breakdown that is created when tensions mount—between asserting the self and recognizing the Other—leads to the *jouissance* of domination. According to Girard, "We believe that the normal form of desire is nonviolent and that this nonviolent form is characteristic of the generality of mankind. But if the sacrificial crisis is a universal phenomenon, this hopeful belief is clearly without foundation. At the very height of the crisis, violence becomes simultaneously the instrument, object, and all inclusive subject of desire."[27]

Much like the psychoanalytic individuation process, there is an ongoing battle to differentiate from the Other and to rise above—a tension of the *fort:da*, between affirmation and denial, appearance and reappearance, whereby "he *himself* has a hard time recognizing *himself* among his own" (PC, 299). According to Jessica Benjamin, domination is the by-product of the self's denial of its dependent relationship to the Other: "If I completely control the other, then the other ceases to exist."[28] The submissive (masochist) grants the power of recognition to the master, who, in the domination fantasy, maintains the sense of control. For the submissive, the dialectical conflict is resolved by the total renunciation of the self. The search for recognition is translated by the masochist into the search for freedom through slavery—for an other who has the power to bestow recognition. Recognition is thus gained vicariously, through the master.[29] The masochist sacrifices his ego in an effort to redeem his self. If the submission is genuine, the masochist can contact the deeper meaning in the suffering and find pleasure. The pain will be felt for the sake of something more valuable than the ego and its perceptions. Suicide is the ultimate form of masochism, and masochism is, in effect, a metaphorical suicide. Masochism itself seems to be an effort to keep this paradox of pleasure and pain, to preserve the sense of resisting and yet consenting to death at the same time.[30]

Beyond Affirmation—Toward a Theory of Discipline

Saint Paul wishes to transcend the law: "[T]he law hath dominion over a man as long as he liveth. For the woman which hath an husband is bound by the law to *her* husband."[31] "For when we were in the flesh, the motions of sins which were by the law, did work in our members to bring forth fruit unto death. But now we are delivered from the law . . . that we should serve in newness of spirit."[32] "For they that are after the flesh do mind the things of the flesh; but they that are after the Spirit the things of the Spirit."[33] Without the law there would be no sin. The sensual body requires the law, but in the law we are tied to the body. In transcending the body by becoming spirit, we transcend the law. Paul turns the mind against the body, and as we mortify the body we transcend it through the spirit. There is no *jouissance* to be found in loving a woman. The hatred of the body is transferred onto that of the woman, and as the woman becomes the embodiment of the hated flesh and the flesh requires that the man fuck the woman, the only *jouissance* he will enjoy is if the act is a manifestation of aggression.

The pornography of discipline and the genre of related literature exist as a manifestation of *jouissance* or to generate *jouissance,* as intercourse without aggression is sexual release without *jouissance. Jouissance* is generated in opposition to the Law of Patriarchal Civility, because there is no *jouissance* to be found in the law, only in opposition to it. The *jouissance* of transgression is generated by breaking the law. The *jouissance* of transcendence as manifested in moral or religious masochism is generated by transcending the law. Abnormal or perverse sexuality in its various forms is a reaction to the Law of Patriarchal Civility, the Law of the Father. His desire is to be served but in a reasonable and rational manner. The law prohibits aggression and therefore stands in the way of *jouissance.*

Zizek speaks of "the 'black hole' around which desire is organized."[34] The Thing that will fill this gap or lack is that which connects us to the Real. The Law of the Father cannot connect us to the Real because God is dead and has always been dead. The privileged signifier is a bar to *jouissance* as it can furnish us with no meaningful link to the Real. Lacan declares that "it is in the locus of the Other that he begins to constitute that truthful lie by which is initiated that which participates in desire at the level of the unconscious" (F, 144). It is only with discourse that we are constituted male or female and constituted as sexual beings. It is only within discourse that our bodies take on meaning and that we generate a self as a manifestation of the Subject or the Other.

On October 5, 1924, a privately printed book limited to one hundred copies and richly bound in dark green morocco leather with over thirty hand-drawn illustrations was seized in a police raid instigated on the basis of "information received," before a single copy had been distributed. Every copy was burned, and the printer's proof and plates were destroyed.[35] The printing press was located in the converted stables of a manor house in Etchingham, England, belonging to Gerald Percival Hamer. A large collection of erotica found on the premises was also destroyed. This particular book was singled out for a lengthy condemnation, and so ferocious were the remarks of the judge that it is commonly believed that five years of the eleven-year prison term Hamer received were for his publication of this single book.

The name of the book was *A Guide to the Correction of Young Gentle-*

 men, subtitled *The Successful Administration of Physical Discipline to Males by Females.*[36] While the book purports to be a handbook for the disciplining of young and juvenile males, the introduction demonstrates that the adolescent male is used to represent the adult male, and "Even a cursory reading of this book will make it clear that . . . the intended 'subjects' of the treatment are quite obviously adult males. . . . The author makes it explicitly clear, over and over again . . . who are the real subjects of the dissertation: it simply cannot be mistaken."[37] The second chapter is entitled "The Eternal Boy." The narrator expressly states that "Here is a fellow who drinks too much . . . and in the end he drinks himself to death—all for the want of the proper external authority to which, were it available, he would gladly submit. . . . This man gambles. . . . Like the drunkard, he yearns for an all-powerful, outside force to *make* him stop. . . . Your role is to provide that external demiurgic force . . . to take responsibility for him *on condition that he allows you to train him.*"[38]

While the volume in question specifies only that it was "Written by a Lady," the author of this book was, without doubt, Alice Kerr-Sutherland, a professional dominatrix who like many in her trade had started her working career as a governess. She had been a close associate of Hamer's since 1912, and there can be no question about her authorship of the *Guide* when its style is compared with other surviving examples of her writing. Between 1915 and 1920 she ran an elegant brothel for the flagellation of wealthy English aristocrats, and her clientele included, it is thought, George, Marquis of Milford Haven, the elder brother of the late Earl Mountbatten. At the time of the 1928 trial, Kerr-Sutherland was already in Holloway Prison for Women serving a four-year sentence for a number of public morality offenses.

This book, when studied alongside von Sacher-Masoch's *Venus in Furs* and Reage's *The Story of O*, reveals much about the dynamics of *jouissance* underlying domination and submission. Kerr-Sutherland is not a sadist, and as has been clearly argued by Deleuze, the symmetrical inversion of masochism is not sadism. The *jouissance* of domination has nothing in common with sadism, other than the linkage of sex and pain. The structure and logic of domination require the willing and consensual participation of the submissive: "A birching, properly administered, is . . . a religious rite: an offering to the Great Goddess, ideally by a consenting sacrifice."[39] *Venus in Furs* illustrates the *jouissance* of submission within the male, whereas *The Story of O* outlines the *jouissance* of submission within the female in reaction to male dominance. The *Guide* presents the *jouissance* of domination as enjoyed by the female and, as such, furnishes us with the asymmetrical side of male masochism and at the same time with an alternative example of the *jouissance* of the female furnished by *The Story of O.*

The discourse of the female self as a manifestation of the Subject and of the male as lacking, as the Other, is established even in Kerr-Sutherland's short introduction. She writes, "We women have charge of all human life from its earliest stages, and during that time we have to perform many deeds that might be considered ignoble, even indecent, it is our destiny and our responsibility. There is nothing an unclothed male of any age can display that any but the most sheltered maiden lady cannot have seen before. . . . We are after all, in *loco parentis.*"[40]

The first chapter discusses the three aspects of the ancient Goddess with reference to Frazer's *The Golden Bough,* Sir Thomas Malory's *Mort d'Arthur,* and Shakespeare's *Macbeth.* She then develops a corresponding analysis of the three aspects of the governess that correspond to or manifest the qualities of the triple Goddess and describes the approach to discipline and the form it should take within these three configurations. The Goddess as maiden corresponds to the governess as nurse. The mature Goddess as the Mistress is described in the following way:

> She is alive to sensuality, and plays upon it as an instrument; but no trace of bawdiness or open voluptuousness ever taints her operations. She is not a Sacred Prostitute, but an anointed Priestess, a medium. She commands, but is herself commanded by a Higher Power, of which she forms a part, and of whom she is the present representative.
>
> She is a Mistress of Ritual, comprehending that the slow and deliberate pace, the measured litany and the prescribed costumes, settings and liturgies of these ancient ceremonies serve to preserve and renew the Mystery—of which she is celebrant—and thereby to honour the Great Goddess, of whom she is a servant.[41]

The dame corresponds to the fearful aspect of the triple Goddess as revealed in Hecate or Kali. She shows little mercy when severe discipline is called for: "The dedicated and successful Governess should be able to assume any of the three personalities at need."[42] The third chapter commences with the paragraph:

> THE GOVERNESS STANDS *in loco Deae,* and her son Cupid, as ever, languishes *in statu pupillari.* But where does this elegant and ageless ritual opposition of feminine and masculine principles, with its foreordained result, take place? If it is a

play, where and what is the stage? If it is a mystical or religious rite, in which temple or church (we already know before whose altar) is it celebrated? What are the surroundings, and how do they act upon the Principals? What part, if any, does the physical environment play in the proceedings that unfold?[43]

One essential feature of the discipline regime outlined in the *Guide* is the stripping of the submissive. The male submissive is *subject* to the Gaze and to female authority. The Gaze is an essential aspect of the self as a manifestation of the Subject, and being subject to the Gaze is an essential aspect of the self as a manifestation of the Other. The authoress strongly advocates the presence of a female assistant, which adds to the humiliation, and she stresses the value of having the discipline applied in front of female witnesses, to heighten the humiliation further.

The *Guide* is not simply a work of pornography that Kerr-Sutherland wrote to enhance her business or attract new customers. The long and detailed descriptions of the various instruments of discipline, the variety of positions, the coloring of the skin as each stroke is given, and the different methods of bondage all indicate that the writing of this book was energized by a particular kind of female *jouissance,* one that some females can and do enjoy. The carefully detailed description of punishment and disciplining sessions ought to be compared to the text of *The Story of O.* It gives a radically different impression, however, when the disciplining subject is female and the object of the discipline is male.

Kaja Silverman, in her article "*Histoire d'O:* The Construction of a Female Subject," tells us that "The heroine of *Histoire d'O,* like some of Freud's more rebellious heroines, knows herself to be constituted in and through a discourse which exceeds her—one which speaks for her, in her 'place.' "[44] She continues to say that "Psychoanalysis would tell us that O's condition is synonymous with subjectivity—that since desire is always articulated from the place of the Other, woman (like man) is inevitably spoken through a discourse which anticipates and transcends her. However, as Freud himself acknowledges, the male subject has consistently provided the focus and model for descriptions of subjectivity."[45] We might well ask why it is that the male constantly defines subjectivity. When a matricentric discourse is permitted, it is only in the context of a pornography that is fenced off from the political world of power.

A male submissive discourse, as a manifestation of the Other, is permitted so long as it serves male fantasy. As Lacan points out, "With courtly love things are all the more surprising because they emerge at a time when the historical circumstances are such that nothing seems to point to what might be called the advancement of women or indeed their emancipation" (S VII, 146). He states that "She is strictly speaking, what is indicated by the elementary structures of kinship, i.e., nothing more than a correlative of the functions of social exchange, the support of a certain number of goods and of symbols of power. She is essentially identified with a social function that leaves no room for her person or her own liberty. . . . It is in this context that the very curious function of the poet of courtly love starts to be exercised."

Silverman specifies the task of interpretation of these various texts that manifest the different kinds of *jouissance.* She writes, "The investigation thus proceeds on two fronts, exploring on the one hand what distinguishes female from male subjectivity within the present symbolic order, and on the other what is lost for woman during her entry into that order."[46] She explains that:

> It will be my working hypothesis (a hypothesis which will be "tested" through *Histoire d'O*) that while human bodies exist prior to discourse, it is only through discourse that they arrive at the condition of being "male" or "female"—that discourse functions first to territorialize and then to map meaning onto bodies. In other words . . . the female body cannot be seen as existing outside discourse. . . . I will attempt to demonstrate that very close links are forged between actual bodies and discourses, and that those links are both durable and mutually reinforcing at all key junctures. The most helpful concept currently available to us for articulating the relationship between real and constructed bodies is *anaclisis. Anaclisis* is the name given by Freud to the leaning or propping of the erotic drive upon the self-preservative instincts.[47]

"[T]he distinction between the speaking (male) subject and the spoken (female) subject" is the distinction between the male self as a manifestation of the Subject and the female self as a manifestation of the Other.[48] She demonstrates through her analysis of *The Story of O,* "the powerful hold which discourse exerts upon the female subject's corporeal existence."[49] A similar analysis of the *Guide* will also demonstrate the powerful hold that the counterdiscourse has upon the male's subject's corporeal existence.

Claiming Subjecthood

According to Derrida, "*Coitus* must not be reduced to the ovary and the sperm as if the new formation were merely the assemblage of forms or parts of two partners, for the feminine certainly contains the material element, while the male contains the subjectivity" (Glas, 113). Despite their possession of the "material element," women have no subjectivity. According to Andrea Dworkin, sexual intercourse is intimately related to women's objecthood:

> To become the object, she shakes herself and transforms herself into a thing: all freedoms are diminished and she is caged, even in the cage docile, sometimes physically maimed, movement is limited: she physically becomes the thing he wants to fuck. It is especially in the acceptance of object status that her humanity is hurt: it is a metaphysical acceptance of lower status in sex and in society; an implicit acceptance of less freedom, less privacy, less integrity. In becoming an object so that he can objectify her so that he can fuck her, she begins a political collaboration with his dominance; and then when he enters her, he confirms for himself and for her what she is: that she is something, not someone; certainly not someone equal.[50]

Women, by unlearning objecthood, must incorporate subjecthood into their collective experience. They must learn how to opt out of the slave position. The woman as inevitable other must use the psychoanalytic tools to heal her wounds. Playing the role of the subject is the first step in the healing process. The task of a psychoanalytic postmodern feminism, therefore, must be to restore the primary signifier to our awareness, to bring its manifestations in the registers of the Imaginary and the Symbolic into the cultural mainstream, and to disturb and subvert the privileged signifier. "The frightening unknown on the other side of the line is that which in man we call the unconscious, that is to say the memory of those things he forgets," Lacan reminds us (S VII, 231). It would appear that the female self as a manifestation of the Subject is one of those memories of something that males have forgotten, returning from the unconscious with her whip or birch in her hand. Suddenly, for the male, mother, goddess, and lover merge, and he is the child again seeking confirmation of her love through loving discipline: "There is a *jouissance* proper to her, to this 'her' which does not exist and which signifies nothing . . . and of which she herself may know nothing, except that she experiences it—that much she does know. She knows it of course when it happens. It does not happen to all of them" (FS, 145–46).

The *Story of O* has had particular significance for feminists as a paradigmatic example of the subjectivity of the female self as a manifestation of Otherness. Silverman states: "*HISTOIRE d' O* is . . . the history of the female subject—of the territorialization and inscription of a body whose involuntary internalization of a corresponding set of desires facilitates its complex exploitation. That history will never read otherwise until the female subject alters her relation to discourse—until she succeeds not only in exercising discursive power, but in exercising it differently."[51] Is it the case that no woman whatsoever has altered her relation to the discourse of the privileged signifier? Can we not find one single example of a female exercising the kind of discursive power that Silverman refers to? Has no women generated a self as a manifestation of the Subject?

"[P]atriarchal cultures have reduced the value of the feminine to such a degree that their reality and their description of the world are incorrect. Thus, instead of remaining a different gender, the feminine has become, in our languages, the non-masculine, that is to say an abstract nonexistent reality."[52] So states Luce Irigaray. Woman is waiting, far too patiently, in the realm of nonsignification. Her power is petrified, and man cannot look her straight in the eye for that would, for the man, acknowledge that she is there, independent of him—giving her potential subjectivity. She cannot look at herself in the mirror as she has not the tools—for the tools are all male. She must break through the glass of the mirror and risk the blood that will inevitably be shed. For her objecthood is "abject submission, an abdication of the freedom and integrity of the body."[53] It is also complicity. A failure to break the silence is interpreted as an acceptance of the silent tomb, the grave of patriarchal value. The phallus, as primary signifier, is for males the *jouissance* of submission. It is Isis's simulacrum, and Osiris depends on her for its stately positioning (P, 41). In order to gain access to this simulacrum, the simulacrum of desire, women must recognize the correlative male dependence.

Woman must consciously rewrite and rework the text and the story. By writing, she can attempt to define her self, her sex, and her newly emergent sexuality. She can create a discourse from which she had previously been cut off. By so doing, she can return to the body and free up the desire that has been veiled for far too long: "We must kill the false woman who is preventing the live one from breathing. Inscribe the breath of the whole woman."[54] According to Hélène Cixous, the woman who writes "cuts herself out a paper penis" and opens herself up onto the world of subjecthood.[55] In this way, she manages to transcend objectification. "The Dark Continent is neither dark nor unexplorable—It is still unexplored only because we've been made to believe that what interests us is the white continent, with its monuments to Lack. And we believed. They riveted us between two horrifying myths: between the Medusa and the abyss."[56]

The castration of Oedipus and the rise of feminism are making the world a more dangerous place for women in that there are many young males at the height of hormonal development who are unable to claim the privileged position of the self as manifestation of the Subject. Their lives contain neither love nor *jouissance*, as fewer and fewer women are prepared to simply be fucked. The fantasy substitutes only fuel unfulfillable desire. The discourses of the privileged signifier continue to lose their credibility, and consequently it is becoming more and more difficult to maintain patriarchal civility. Equality seems to serve as a two-edged sword in that while it erodes the privileged signifier, it also erodes the primary. The banning of pornography, for example, does have the benefit of removing the pictorial imagery and text that portray the aggression against women that the *jouissance* of male domination requires. At the same time, one bans the pornography of female domination and male submission, which could prove to reverse the eroticization of aggression wherein the submissive male, unlike the female in patriarchal civility, has the ability to walk away from the eroticized aggression of the domina if the pain outweighs the pleasure.

An ideal heterosexual relationship would contain love, be personal, and maintain *jouissance*. This would require a meaningful master signifier that would permit the relationships of the individual as manifestations of the Real in terms of the Subject and Other. This, in turn, would require the self to be generated out of the discourses of the primary signifier. The female self (Subject) would have to be the embodiment of the will to power, the will to life, or Eros. She would be the manifestation of the Goddess, the materialization in the flesh of the generative power of nature, the *Übermensch, She who stands above man*. The male would need to identify himself with the generative power of nature through her and in particular through her body. He would, therefore, take on phallic significance as her Consort. He could not fuck her, but at the same time he would not be her slave nor would she need to be the cold and cruel mistress. However, only the higher man can be loved and remain in submission. The domina then can return the love, but she must still retain the whip.

Isn't it about time that we returned to the labyrinth and excavated what was there prior to the infiltration of the Heroes? Who knows what will emerge when the restraining cover of the privileged signifier is finally lifted. There is a herstory waiting to be discovered, refurbished, and created. By removing the veil of femininity, by depetrifying Medusa, what emerges in the discourse is the Amazon, the powerful female who has the ability to transform and reinterpret the nature of femaleness. She is the reason why males have a castration complex, as she has always been there, hidden in the Other but somehow always lurking behind each shadow, present. She is the castrator—not necessarily in the physical sense of the word, but more importantly and on a larger scale—she is the castrator of discourse. The fear of castration is not solely a fear of dismembering the lone appendage but rather the threat of losing the privileged positioning of the phallus, the logos. By giving advantage to the privileged signifier, the primary is not obliterated, it is there, hidden in the shadow, always posing a threat. The fear of castration is the male threat of having one's discourse cut off, of losing subjecthood. No, women don't have it, they do not exist in phallocentric patriarchy. But they must invent and reinterpret themselves so as to create their story, and to become. According to Cixous, the precepts of patriarchal civility are such that "women have no choice but to be decapitated. . . . If they don't actually lose their heads by the sword, *they only keep them on condition that they lose them*—lose them, that is, to a complete silence, turned into automatons."[57]

Clearly, under the guise of patriarchal civility, women can keep time to the male drum and do it so well that they *live*, or they can stand up to the order and risk decapitation: "It's a question of submitting feminine dis—order, its laughter, its inability to take the drumbeats seriously, to the threat of decapitation. If man operates under the threat of castration, if masculinity is culturally ordered by the castration complex, it might be said that the backlash, the return, on women of this castration anxiety is its displacement as decapitation, execution—of woman as loss of her head."[58] Women must realize the unbridled potential of their pleasure and must dictate and demand full satisfaction. They must not mask pleasure at the sign of their partner's pleasure but must risk decapitation. Playing the petrified role of the object is keeping time to the male drum.

According to Derrida, for the male "to be oneself is to-be-Medusa'd, and from then on the Medusa'd-being constitutes itself, that is, defends itself, bands itself erect, and elaborates itself only in being Medusa'd by oneself, in eating-Medusa'ing oneself, in making oneself a bit {*mors*} that gives oneself/itself up as lost {*fait son deuil*}. Dead sure of self. No *logic* is more powerful than this apotropic. No absolute general economy, no exposition or pure expenditure: a strict-ure more or less strong. His *(Sa)* Medusa('s), always. Self's dead sure biting (death) {*Morsure de soi*}" (Glas, 202–3).

TEN

Oedipus

More so than any other myth, the Oedipal legend has successfully managed to capture the attentions of psychoanalysts, philosophers, anthropologists, cultural critics, historians, and dramatists. The fascination with the myth lies mainly in its ubiquitous applicability, and its metaphorical use of discursive language. Key to Sophocles' *Oedipus Tyrannus* is the method utilized to reveal the tale. The plot is not about the origins of Oedipus per se but more with Oedipus' logical approach to solving the riddle of his existence. Through processes of ironic textual and symbolic reversals, Oedipus is brought full circle from the position of the hero-king-god, a position of both power and ignorance. His pursuit of knowledge and higher truths leads him to a truth he cannot fathom, a truth that he never confronts, and one that forces him to hide from himself, his family, and his city. In his loss of the fabrication of hero-king-god, Oedipus is desolate as that is all he has ever learned to affirm. Outside of the privileged structure of the Hero there is an emptiness that Oedipus has not been able to penetrate.

King Laius and Oedipus, father and son, meet at the "fated" crossroads, both of them unaware of their biological connection. The myth suggests that Laius tries to run Oedipus off the road. In defense, Oedipus kills Laius and his servants, actualizing the Apollonian oracle. The encounter foreshadows the encounter with the Sphinx, who Oedipus meets on his way to the city of Thebes. She holds the key to seduction and has the keen capacity to lure her victims to her abode, though they know it is likely they will perish at her feet. She beckons to Oedipus, and he acquiesces. He thinks he has solved the riddle that she poses, a riddle so difficult and so simple, a riddle that has stumped many. A riddle that continues to confound.

 Oedipus clings to the certainty of science. The absence of chance makes him unable to affirm. Instead, Oedipus is only able to deny, repress, and ignore. He begins the process by asserting the logos over the Sphinx, by denying her discourse, and by failing to recognize her significance for him. Logos is Oedipus' truth, and he views it as absolute, though it is merely his "*irrefutable* error" (GS, 265). He denies her existence and continues to search blindly for his origins in utter ignorance, despite the fact that she—half animal, half female—holds all the clues. Oedipus can only say "no," "no." This is most explicit in his final denial—his brutal dismemberment—the tearing out of his eyes.

Oedipus the Heroic

The identification of the mind of man with logos is implicit in phallic science. "I want to know how God created this world," Einstein said, "I am not interested in this or that phenomenon, in the spectrum of this or that element. I want to know His thoughts. The rest are details."[1] According to Stephen Hawking, "If we find the answer [to why it is that we and the universe exist] it would be the ultimate triumph of human reason—for then we would know the mind of God."[2] Thus, the logos connects the cosmos to the mind of man, thereby endowing *him* with the generative power of nature, which justifies the Law of the Father. "Moreover, because it is a question here of a non-physical Almighty, that's the only thing which allows one to do science, that is to say, in the end reduce the Almighty to silence" (S II, 240). The Jehovah of the Old Testament becomes the logos of the New Testament. "In the beginning was the Word (Logos), and the Word (Logos) was with God, and the Word (Logos) was God."[3] And the logos of the New Testament does not die but becomes the mathematical structure of the universe.

The Oedipal Replacement: The Hero Kills the Monster

Psychoanalysis is prefaced on the need to replace the desire for the mother with the *higher aim* of the identification with the father. Psychoanalysts understand this as key, as pivotal, to the child's individuation process. Should the child not lose her or his identification with the mother, the child would be in a state of arrested development, in perpetual narcissism.

Why must the child break the tie to the mother? Why must the (M)other be deemed other, for the successful passage of the child? Such propositions are fundamental to the psychoanalytic Oedipal passage and ensure a patriarchal bent. If the desired end is father-king-logos, the Mother must be repressed and ignored. Similarly, if the desired end is wife-other-voiceless-masked, the Heroine, the Great Mother, and the Amazon must also be systematically repressed. The Oedipus complex utilizes the Law of the Father to transgress the Maternal Law. The two cannot coexist.

According to Freudian Oedipal theory, the young boy must sublimate his unconscious incestuous fantasies in order to realize a sense of self apart from his relationship with his mother. The child's narcissistic identification with the (M)other in the pre-Oedipal phase is consistent with the primacy of the sexual and/or Eros drives, whereas the post- Oedipal individuation phase privileges the Ego drive. The oscillating tension for the boy who clings to the fervent desire to merge with the (M)other in an attempt to hold onto the narcissistic complacency of the pre-Oedipal stage while at the same time fearing reengulfment by her—which translates into a fear that the identity that is slowly emerging will be lost—is the Oedipal counterpart to the mind/body split and the tensions between the sexual and the Ego drives. This tension causes the boy to resent the mother, and women in general, and often leads to the will to subjugate and dominate.[4] The gaining of a sense of self, which is the goal of the Oedipal passage, is essentially an ego-self, one that represses all other elements and heightens mind/body dualism. By asserting "man," Oedipus devalues beast-animality-nature and the generative powers of nature. The self that emerges as a result of Oedipal genderization is the father-king-logos that must be asserted in order to maintain heroism. The lack in the male self is replaced by the Apollonian insanity of the delusionary phallus. The *truth* that Oedipus asserts is an ego *truth,* it is the *truth* of "man," the Law of the Father, and can only exist in a domain where the primary signifier is demoted to the position of Other, in the domain of patriarchal civility.

Lacan and Freud both hold the assumption that the father figure is essential to individuation as he is a catalyst for the break of the special bond between infant and mother. They understand the assumption to be immutable, inalterable, and fundamental. The assumption that children will not fully individuate without the father figure justifies the "normalcy" of Oedipal sexuality and gender structure and the corresponding "perversity" of alternatives. As Andrew Samuels has pointed out, the above assumption ignores the fact that children themselves wish and strive to individuate and women also wish that their children will individuate and become independent. *"Babies and mothers have an investment in separation."*[5] It also ignores the fact that a matriphallic male can play a nonoppositional and supportive role for the mother in encouraging the individuation of the child. A child normally individuates according to the particular familiar relationship of which the child is a part. The father's part in the process is culturally constructed.[6] This opens up the possibility for the male to play a very different kind of role in the family relationship. The matriphallic male would be mother- and child-supportive and would be subversive of the so-called normal gender relations.

The male child's fear that he will be separated from his mother manifests itself in a castration anxiety: that what he presently has is inadequate, and that someday he will lack altogether what his mother desires. Castration puts the finishing touches on the process of separation that sees the Subject (penis) as signifiable. In other words, it sees the Subject as separate, always confronted by an Other: namely, the Subject in the mirror (signified) and semiotic process (signifier). The discovery of castration, however, detaches the Subject (penis) from its dependence on the mother for the satisfaction of desire. The perception of this lack makes the phallic function a symbolic function. The phallus is forbidden to the mother by the Law of the Father.

> If the desire of the mother is the phallus, the child wishes to be the phallus in order to satisfy that desire. Thus the division immanent in desire is already felt to be experienced in the desire of the other, in that it is already opposed to the fact that the subject is content to present to the Other what in reality he may have that corresponds to this phallus, for what he has is worth no more than what he does not have, as far as his demand for love is concerned because that demand requires that he be the phallus. (E, 289)

Castration ends any possibility for satisfaction of the male within the Oedipus complex framework. The male child realizes that his position is precarious: he does not possess what his mother desires. What he does possess is something somewhere between the castrated lack of his sister and what his father possesses.

Psychoanalysis has its own repressions and does not want to know about male castration and submission, even in the sense of repression, nor about male pathology. It considers the cure of the male's sacrifice of the phallus, epitomized in Freud's discussion of masochism, to be worse than the disease of phallic illusion. It knows all about male lack but continues to discuss female lack.

According to Jean-Joseph Goux in *Oedipus, Philosopher,* Freud ignores the matricide that pervades the infrastructure of most myths: the Hero kills the Female Monster for access to his bride (OP, 25–29). Instead of combating her face to face, Oedipus blindly asserts his logos, his manly rationality, and suppresses in his own unconscious the truth of her existence. It is this suppression that leads to his kingship, but since it was not a victory in the "true" sense his kingship is unavoidably short lived. In effect, she has won the battle all along. According to Goux, "[T]he episode of the Sphinx is the meeting with the mystery of sexuality and of death, in which the young man has to run the risk of disappearing. He has to experience the fact that his own desire for the dark mother is lethal. It is this confrontation alone that allows, after a symbolic death, the hero's rebirth with a new identity" (OP, 37).

Goux thus recounts the struggle with the Monster as the male's psychoanalytic initiation—a necessary step in the process of becoming "man." In order to assert the phallus and privilege its position, one must attack the dark demon of female fecundity, enter onto the labyrinthine path of the Hero, not in a Dionysiac effort to merge but in full Thesean battle gear. One must kill the dark eroticism of the female sex in order to free the bride—the nonsexed veiled virgin, the milky white waif who is willing to embrace the male phallus. Psychoanalysis as posited by Freud necessitates the overcoming of the Maternal Law in order to assert the Law of the Father. Only when she is dead, buried, chained, and controlled can the Law of the Father come to be. Oedipus had to *disempower* the Sphinx before he could become king. She was the ultimate ruler until he asserted his word. By privileging the logos, he buries the primacy of nature, its generative and procreative truths. Oedipus does not kill the Sphinx in a blind act of rage or in a fit of violence. On the contrary, he believes he kills her by asserting the patriarchal law when he *solves* the riddle that she poses with the answer "MAN." According to Derrida, "with the answer to the riddle, Oedipus's words, the discourse of consciousness, *man* destroys, dissipates, or tumbles the petroglyph" (Pit, 99).

Only when Oedipus denies the power of the Sphinx can he assert the fantasy of the veiled virgin, only then can he take Jocasta as bride and deny her maternity. The Sphinx descends to her labyrinth where she continues to function and to subvert Oedipus' law and remains, long after her downward descent, Oedipus' foremost opponent. Though Oedipus has relegated her to the position of Other and has thus managed to deny her and effectually *overcome* her, she is not really Other. She exists somewhere in the Derridean realm of undecidability, beyond the binary, beyond the dialectical negation and hierarchy. Coming to an understanding of the placement of the Sphinx is "a question of remarking a nerve, a fold, an angle that interrupts totalization: in a certain place, a place of well-determined form, no series of semantic valences can any longer be closed or reassembled. Not that it opens onto an inexhaustible wealth of meaning or the transcendence of a semantic excess. By means of this angle, this fold, this doubled fold of an undecideable, a mark marks both the marked and the mark, the re-marked site of the mark" (Pos, 46).

The Missing Heroine: The Hero's Inability to Kill the Monster

Is it possible to gain an understanding of femininity and the feminine "which is not confined by the phallic definition"? (FS, 137). On this subject, Lacan asserts that the woman does not exist because phallic sexuality can only provide a position for her in terms of fantasy—a fantasy of male completeness and oneness into which she, for her survival, must be incorporated. The nonexistence of woman is asserted by many philosophers. "There is no such thing as the essence of woman because woman averts, she is averted of her self," Derrida states in *Spurs: Nietzsche's Styles* (Sp, 51). She "is a non-identity, a non-figure, a simulacrum" (Sp, 49), who "finds herself censured, debased and despised. In the name of truth and metaphysics she is accused here by the credulous man who, in support of his testimony, offers truth and his phallus as his own proper credentials, . . . [She] is twice castration: once as truth and once as non-truth" (Sp, 97). In *The Newly Born Woman*, Hélène Cixous and Catherine Clément suggest that "the female body served only as an intermediary, prop, passage. Passage accomplished, that which is no longer woman but beast, devil, symptom is set free. The girls are not released, the demons are: the girls are *bound*."[7]

Lacan is unable to provide an existence for woman within the structure of language, structured as it is by only the privileged signifier, the phallus. He rejects the view that woman's existence can be grounded in her body since to do so would drive psychoanalytic theory into such an essential link with biology that even Freud would have rejected it outright. According to Lacan, "Psycho-analysis, then, reminds us that the facts of human psychology cannot be conceived in the absence of the function of the subject defined as the effect of the signifier" (F, 207). Lacan concludes that woman's position in the sexual relationship is that of a symptom for the man. Being a symptom for the man, the woman is never a subject, but always an Other. "By her being in the sexual relation radically Other, in relation to what can be said of the unconscious, the woman is that which relates to this Other" (FS, 151).

Riddles and Truths

Oedipus' perseverance and scientific rationale give him the only answer that he is capable of giving to the Sphinx's riddle. The riddle outlines what Oedipus believes to be the various stages of human development of the typical person: first crawling on four feet, then walking on two, then, with age or infirmity, walking with a cane. Oedipus was more likely to *solve* this riddle the way he did because of his personal experiences and his discursive outlook. What is it that makes us want to know the truth? Nietzsche asks this question in *Beyond Good and Evil:*

> It is any wonder that we should finally become suspicious, lose patience, and turn away impatiently? that we should finally learn from this Sphinx to ask questions, too? *Who* is it really that puts questions to us here? *What* in us really wants "truth"?
>
> Indeed we came to a long halt at the question about the cause of this will—until we finally came to a complete stop before a still more basic question. We asked about the *value* of this will. Suppose we want truth: *why not rather* untruth? and uncertainty? even ignorance?
>
> The problem of the value of truth came before us—or was it we who came before the problem? Who of us is Oedipus here? Who the Sphinx? It is a rendezvous, it seems, of questions and question marks.
>
> And though it scarcely seems credible, it finally almost seems to us as if the problem had never even been put so far—as if we were the first to see it, fix it with our eyes, and *risk* it. For it does involve a risk, and perhaps there is none that is greater. (BGE, 1)

The Sphinx's riddle is clearly subordinate to the fundamental riddle of Oedipus' origins,[8] it entails a return to the murky labyrinth of his birth, to the generative power of nature—(M)other. Though the solving of the Sphinx's riddle puts Oedipus on the tragic path toward self-knowledge, he never quite reaches his destination since he does not acknowledge the labyrinthine trajectory. Oedipus attempts to get a glimpse of his origins without confronting the brute force of the generative powers. By solving the riddle as he did, Oedipus appears to win the battle against savagery and animality with the ammunition of scientific reasoning, with logos, with the inflation of the phallus. He is repressing the primary and heightening the privileged signifier. He refuses to see them as elements that fold back on each other, as a dialectical duo whereby, in confrontation, one is both the truth and the falsity of the other.

A "solved" riddle is the "reduction of heterogeneous material to logic, to the homogeneity of logical thought, which produces a blind spot, the inability to see the otherness that gets lost in the reduction. Only the unsolved riddle, the process of riddle-work before its final completion, is a confrontation with otherness."[9] Oedipus reduces the riddle-work to a single nondialectical truth, one that simultaneously searches for and represses origins. He introduces the veiled virgin under the guise of *liberation* and the oppression of the monstrous Other under the guise of *patriarchal civility*. Somewhere within this liberal framework, *equality* is introduced, which has the effect of diluting otherness and denying the elusiveness of difference and hierarchy, while at the same time asserting sameness—which is *patriarchal civility*.

Equality is the conceptual focus of political, moral, and legal ideology and is likely to remain so for the foreseeable future. A feminism committed to gender equality presupposes the possibility of gender-neutral discourse. It is a widespread and common assumption that the discourse of the *rule of law* and of *fundamental rights* is gender-neutral. The discourse of the Western legal tradition is derived from Greek mathematical science by way of the physics, ethics, and logic of the Stoics. The concepts of legal personhood, the citizen, or the free agent as empty, neutral containers that defy categorization are by-products of the Greek concept of the "variable," as is reflected in Stoic propositional logic.[10] The genderless discourse of the law remains within the framework of the privileged signifier, as much or even more so than the discourse of science since the content of the formal structure of the law is easily filled with a genderized discourse. The legal, moral, and political discourse of equality is structured by the privileged signifier and as such privileges mind over body and male over female. It is useful, however, in women's struggle for a more benign form of male domination.

Lacan tells us that "patriarchal civility is supposed to set us on the most reasonable path to temperate or normal desire" (S VII, 177). It is, however extremely fragile given its grounding in mind/body dualism, and its underlying strata of misogyny. If in the middle term of the phallic structure, the Law of the Father fails to hold the balance, the male psyche reverts to either the pathology of religious or moral masochism or to the rage of rape. The patriphallic male oscillates within the four neurotic symptoms, defending against primary masochism with the phallic structure of the *jouissances* of transcendence, control, and transgression. Sexuality plays out within the dynamics of the dialectical tensions between the sexual drive and the ego drive as well as the formulation of the self in terms of the *jouissances* of domination and submission. There is no necessary relationship between biology and any particular gender structure or relationship. Yet, while we universally pay lip service to the discourse of equality, our practices demonstrate gender, racial, and economic inequality. There is no *jouissance* of equality nor does equality have any correspondence to the dynamics of difference, castration, and lack that underlie the libidinal foundations of gender. "This errant democrat, wandering like a desire or like a signifier freed from *logos,* this individual who is not even perverse in a regular way, who is ready to do anything, to lend himself to anyone, who gives himself equally to all pleasures," states Derrida, "swept off by every stream, he belongs to the masses; he has no essence, no truth, no patronym, no constitution of his own" (PP, 145).

Religion and science serve as the juncture of the Imaginary and the Symbolic with the Real. "[I]t is clear," Lacan tells us, "that our physics is simply a mental fabrication whose instrument is the mathematical symbol. For experimental science is not so much defined by the quantity to which it is in fact applied, as by the measurement it introduces into the real" (E, 74). "[T]hose who have been listening to me for some time," he tells us, "know that I use, quite intentionally the formula—*The Gods belong to the field of the real*" (F, 45). The realm of the Goddesses and the Gods is at the intersection of the Imaginary and the Symbolic with the Real. Eventually science and religion merge into the fantasy structures by which we attempt to stretch our metaphors across the gulf, the fiery chasm between the Imaginary, the Symbolic, and the Real. "[I]t is in relation to the real that the level of phantasy functions. The real supports the phantasy, the phantasy protects the real." In the final analysis, both science and religion are narratives of origin. If the story uses the human mind as the metaphorical reference linking the Subject with the Other and the self with nature, it will be structured by the privileged signifier. Whether the narrator is Einstein, Hawkins, or the writer of the Gospel of John, the story will commence with, "In the beginning (or as first principle) was the Logos." If, on the other hand, the account uses the female body as the metaphorical reference linking the Subject with the Other and the self with nature, it will be structured by the primary signifier. Whether the speaker is a scientist from the Santa Fe Institute explaining chaos and Complex Adaptive System Theory or Hesiod in his *Theogony* proclaiming "that out of Chaos came Gaia," the story will begin "Chaos was first of all." The languaging body produces a mind/body dualism within which language functions as a dialectical set of oppositionary signifiers. The Great Mother/the Heavenly Father, the matrix of chaos and the mathematical structure of logos, furnish the rectangle of master signification:

	The Ego Drive-Thanatos Complex	
Logos	Law of the Father	Male Organs of Reproduction
	The Phallus	
Creation	*Seduction*	*Castration*
	The Structure of the Original Fantasy of the Collective	
Generative Power of Nature	*Difference*	*Lack*
	The Womb	
Matrix	Law of the Mother	Female Organs of Reproduction
	The Sexual Drive—The Eros Complex	

Patriarchal civility is inconsistent with feminism and therefore temperate or normal desire that is phallically structured must also remain inconsistent with feminism. Nonpatriarchal heterosexual desire is structured by the primary signifier, centered in difference, and as Derrida states, "we are not dealing with the peaceful coexistence of a *vis-à-vis*, but rather with a violent hierarchy" (Pos, 41).

The problem, then, that has dominated the psychoanalytic debate on feminine sexuality is how to maintain Freud's most radical insight, on the significance of sexual difference in fantasy, the Imaginary and the Symbolic, and, at the same time, how to retrieve femininity from a total subordination to the effects of the privileged status of much of that construction. Feminism must presuppose the existence of woman in the Symbolic and the Imaginary. In this way, it can articulate the foundations of that existence—that already lie in language—in the Other—without having the insurmountable task of *creating* foundations. She is not born, but rejuvenated, having always been there in the registers of the Imaginary and the Symbolic. She is subject, in a symbolism structured by a master signifier. Archaeology, anthropology, myth, human sexuality, dream and fantasy—the very texts of patriarchy attest to a primary original fantasy, the structure of which is reflected in the primary signifier. It is the repression of the primary that makes the phallus the privileged signifier. We live and suffer in dialectical tension and will continue to do so as long as we have egos and conceive of ourselves as minds within bodies.

In many ways Nietzsche anticipated the new alternative scientific paradigm that today is known as chaos theory and complex adaptive system theory.[11] According to Nietzsche, "The astral order in which we live is an exception; this order and the relative duration that depends on it have again made possible and exception of exceptions: the formation of the organic. The total character of the world, however, is in all eternity chaos—in the sense not of a lack of necessity but of a lack of order, arrangement, of form, beauty, wisdom, and whatever other names there are for our aesthetic anthropomorphisms" (GS, 109). He posits the "beautiful chaos of existence" (GS, 277, 322), and suggests that "one must still have chaos in oneself to give birth to a dancing star" (Z, prologue, 46). Any scientific worldview that explains mind as evolving from matter assumes the primary signifier as the master signifier of the Imaginary and the Symbolic. Life materializes out of a material matrix. Some have referred to science structured according to the primary signifier as *Gaia Consciousness*.[12] There are thus two different master signifiers that can structure our scientific worldview. Just as science can be structured according to the privileged signifier, it can equally be structured according to the primary signifier. Contemporary physics, chaos theory, and complexity theory provide alternative scientific explanations that rely less on fantasy and wish fulfillment and more on observation. We do not have a kind of science that keeps an even balance between the material and the mental. Either we project mind onto the cosmos, the real, or we don't. If we do, then we are still looking for God, or what is essentially the same thing—the mind of God. If we don't project mind onto the cosmos then we see it as a matrix, and we enter the ephemeral realm of the Goddess.

Nietzsche seems to prefer to think of "truth" as an active process of creation rather than something to be discovered, "something that must be created and that gives a name to a process, or rather to a will to overcome that has in itself no end—introducing truth, as a processus in infinitum, and active determining—not a becoming-conscious of something that is in itself firm and determined" (WP, 552). He refers to the process of becoming as a process of creating the truth of one's existence. Truth is not something to be discovered according to Nietzsche but something that must be creatively pursued in a process of self-actualization: "Not whence you come shall henceforth constitute your honor, but whither you are going! Your will and your foot which has a will to go over and beyond yourselves—that shall constitute your new honor" (Z, III, 12, 315).

When Zarathustra speaks of the need for all beings to create something beyond themselves, he is referring to the human's ability to create its own self by reconceptualizing that self through the affirmation of life. According to Nietzsche, man stands between *Übermensch* and animal. He can go toward *Übermensch,* but this would involve a crossing over an abyss. If he does not want to chance it, he remains animal: the passive being. If he makes the attempt, he enters into the active process of Becoming, which is more important than the being produced. As such, the truth that Oedipus clung to—the Apollonian truth of destiny—is according to Nietzsche a nontruth. The end of *Oedipus Tyrannus* is tragic in that Oedipus ceases to act. He never has the ability to become who he is because his preconceived notion of who he thinks he is prevents him from seeing or seeking otherwise.

The *Übermensch* is the one who can be strengthened by tragic insight rather than succumbing to it. Affirmation of the *Übermensch* is only something that higher men can do. In the Oedipal myth, Oedipus succumbs to his tragic insight. He allows it to reign supreme to the exclusion of any other thoughts. Oedipus' castration is not a voluntary relinquishing of power and primacy but an inability on Oedipus' part to hang on to something he perhaps never had. Affirmation of the *Übermensch* would be an affirmation of the power of the Sphinx—the culmination of the Great Mother and of animality. The Sphinx held a bold position atop Mount Cithaeron. There she was perched, looking down Over Man. When Oedipus denied her primacy by way of the erection of the logos-phallus-mind, she returned to the fiery labyrinth from whence she came and continued her work from there. Oedipus deflated the oracle, deflated the curse, and the Sphinx's mythological underpinnings. Armed with logic, he represses her very existence without confronting her. He returns to the city as the Hero, but all he was was a simulacrum of a Hero—the phallic Hero whose reign is destined to be short lived.

According to Nietzsche, Oedipus' inability to act (as opposed to his ability to react) makes him a dead man, a walking castrated tomb. In the first part of *Thus Spoke Zarathustra,* Zarathustra recounts the story of the tightrope walker (Z, I, 6). As the tightrope walker reaches the middle of the rope, a jester bounds onto the rope and jumps over the first tightrope walker with quick steps: " 'Forward, Lamefoot!' he shouted in an awe-inspiring voice. . . . 'You ought to be locked up; you block the way for one better than yourself.' " Seeing his rival win, the first tightrope walker plunges to the ground. The body falls right next to Zarathustra. " 'What are you doing here?' he asked at last. 'I have long known that the devil would trip me. Now he will drag me to hell. Would you prevent him?' 'By my honor, friend,' answered Zarathustra, 'all that of which you speak does not exist: there is no devil and no hell. Your soul will be dead even before your body.' " (Z, I, 6). The lame tightrope walker knew the devil was going to trip him, and this is exactly what occurred.

Since patriarchy has traditionally identified femininity with the body, mind/body dualism is not nearly as serious a problem for the female as for the male. Consequently, the tensions between the sexual and ego drive are not nearly as pathological for the female as they are for the male. For the female who has been patriarchally genderized, it may be necessary to strengthen the ego through the *jouissance* of control in order to gain the optimum reconciliation between the sexual and ego drives. When all one knows is submission, when submission is the force of the law that directs and guides, it is difficult to simply step out from within those confines and transgress. Transgression of the patriarchal law of submission is, for the female, very difficult since she must first admit that she has been forced to submit. She must remove the veil of complicity and extricate herself from the daunting Gaze of the male. Further, she must relearn, rebirth, and rejuvenate her desire. This is a perplexing job as her desire has long been left in the dark crevasses and is dusty from disuse.

Oedipal Politics

We cannot remain human and avoid the symptoms of the neuroses that go with being a languaging biped primate. We must continue to play in the fields of the Goddesses and Gods, but we can choose to play either in the fields of Gaia, Ariadne, and Dionysus or of Kali, Parvati, and Shiva or we can play in the fields of Zeus, Allah, Jehovah, and the logos. An androgynous sexuality, or the will to equality, presupposes equal footing in the chains of signification and denies or represses the pervasiveness and/or brutal force of difference. Equality is comforting, but it is only a cover, a sham, a veritable fabrication. Coming to terms with the inevitability of difference is a process of painful affirmation. For men, it involves coming to terms with the fact that I—as promulgator of patriarchal law—have dominated, controlled, and repressed the Other. For the woman, the process is even more painful. It involves coming to terms with the fact that I-Me, within the *reality* of patriarchy, does not exist. The mask that I don so proudly, which allows me to blindly participate on a stage that is not mine, is only that—a mask. My faith in the system as one that will protect my interests, ensure my voice, and give me justice—*O Almighty Justice!*—is a system that at its very roots seeks to keep me down. Give me laws, give me rights entrenched in constitutions—let them proclaim that I as woman am a person, for this I did not know.

Life can go on within the registers of the Imaginary and Symbolic structured by the privileged phallic signifier, and for many it may be a psychic reality of patriarchal civility on a reasonable path toward temperate or normal desire. For many others, particularly women and children, it is a world that is neither civil nor reasonable—nor could it even be said to be normal. The prevalence of male sexual violence, fetishes, perversions, pathologies, neuroses, and so on, ranging from serial killings to sexual harassment, is clear evidence of the misogyny that must be deciphered and explained. Lacan goes on to say that "We live in a society in which slavery isn't recognized. It's nevertheless clear to any sociologist or philosopher that it has in no way been abolished. . . . The master-slave duality is generalized within each participant in our society. The deep-seated bondage of consciousness in this unhappy state of affairs is to be attributed to the discourse that provoked this profound social transformation" (S III, 132–33).

Much of what Lacan states about the illusions of freedom, the reality of bondage in general, economic exploitation, and master/slave duality, is applicable to gender, behind which exists a secret discourse, a message of liberation, that in a way subsists in a state of repression. Applying Lacan's words to feminism one can also say that the discourse of gender equality is "not only ineffectual but also profoundly alienated from its aim and object":

We all remain at the level of an insoluble contradiction between a discourse that is at a certain level always necessary and a reality to which, both in principle and in a way proved by experience, we fail to adjust.

Moreover, don't we see that analytic experience is deeply bound up with this discursive double of the subject, his discordant and ridiculous ego? The ego of every modern man?

Isn't it clear that analytic experience began with the fact that ultimately nobody feels at ease in the current state of interhuman relations in our culture? (S III, 134)

If there is a *trans-Oedipal* state beyond the post-Oedipal and a reconciliation between mind and body within an Eros complex, then patriarchal psychic reality can be viewed as a state of arrested adolescence in the process of individuation. We argue that there is a second passage beyond the Oedipal, an analysis of which completes the dialectical structure of psychoanalytic theory in such a way that it is not only compatible with feminism as a critique of patriarchy but will reveal the possibility of transcending male domination. One can make a very plausible argument for the biological superiority of the female and can reverse the assumptions of patriarchy. One can perceive men as walking genitals to counter the perception of women as mere carriers of the womb. The psychoanalytic postmodern feminist would argue that neither sexuality nor gender are innate or natural since existence is prefaced solely by the registers of the Imaginary, the Symbolic, and the Real. Denial of the innateness of female supremacy asserts the power of the Imaginary and the Symbolic with the metaphorical and metonymical link to the Real. It is only when *female supremacy* is taken out of the essentialism of biology and given free rein in the realm of the Imaginary and the Symbolic that it gains its full potential for individual and social change. In the domains of the Imaginary and the Symbolic, the imagery of female supremacy is pure potential and is on a much more level playing field than are the counterimages of male supremacy.

For the biped primate whose only function is to carry one half of the genetic code and who cannot reproduce life out of his own body, castration is inevitable. The only choice is how it is done. One can suffer the castration of Oedipus that leads to being swallowed up in the abyss, suffer the castration of Pentheus and be torn apart, or one can embrace the castration of Dionysus-Shiva and remain in libido, in action, at play. The phallus will eventually go limp and fall off or be cut off. The only way the male can retain the phallus is to give it away in the form of the phallic serpent, the symbol of the sacrifice to the Goddess and the embracing of

Eros. All this, of course, is play in the realm of the Imaginary and the Symbolic, but, after all, that is where we live and breathe, desire and suffer.

> If woman has always functioned "within" man's discourse, a signifier referring always to the opposing signifier that annihilates its particular energy, puts down or stifles its very different sounds, now it is time for her to displace this "within," explode it, overturn it, grab it, make it hers, take it in, take it into her women's mouth, bite its tongue with her women's teeth, make up her own tongue to get inside of it. And you will see how easily she will well up, from this "within" where she was hidden and dormant, to the lips where her foams will overflow.[13]

Lacan tells us that "The progress of an analysis does not consist in the enlarging of the field of the *ego*, it is not the reconquest by the *ego* of its margin of the unknown, rather it is a genuine inversion, a displacement, like a minuet executed by the *ego* and the *id*" (S I, 232). "That really is what is at issue, at the end of analysis," he states, "a twilight, an imaginary decline of the world, and even an experience at the limit of depersonalization. *That is when the contingent falls away*—the accidental, the trauma, the hitches of history—*And it is being which then comes to be constituted*" (S I, 232). The best we can hope for is a kind of reconciliation between the unconscious and the conscious, the sexual drive and the ego drive, the Eros complex and the Thanatos complex, between body and mind, culture and nature, our languaging capabilities and limitations and our animality, and, finally and most importantly, between female and male.

Passing through the Fold—Breaking through the Hymen

"This—'The scene illustrates but the idea, not any actual action, in a hymen (out of which flows Dream), tainted with vice yet sacred, between desire and fulfillment, perpetration and remembrance: here anticipating, there recalling, in the future, in the past, under the false appearance of a present. That is how the Mime operates, whose act is confined to perpetual allusion without breaking the ice or the mirror: he thus sets up a medium, a pure medium, of fiction' " (DS, 175). The point of convergence "is neither desire nor pleasure, but between the two . . . in an act of violence that is (at the same time or somewhere between) love or murder" (DS, 213). When a man fucks a woman it is an act between the murder of SHE and the love of the

daughter that she is not. On the other side of the fold, when the domina disciplines the submissive, she is murdering the Hero and loving the sacrificial Consort that he is not. Fucking and sexual discipline are the two palisades separated by the hymen—the fold between the contradictions of discourse and the textual dialectics of the master signifiers.

When a female is fucked, no female monster has actually been murdered, and when a female domina sexually disciplines a male, the man has not actually been castrated. In both cases, no act of love has taken place. "What takes place is only the *entre,* the place, the spacing, which is nothing, the ideality (as nothingness) of the idea. No act, then, is *perpetrated (Hymen . . . between perpetration and remembrance'*); no act is committed as a crime. There is only a memory of a crime that has never been committed . . . and because this crime is its opposite: an act of love. Which itself has not taken place" (DS, 214). There is no synthesis at the point of the fold, no androgyny, no equality, no resolution, no denouement, no integration. "At the edge of being, the medium of the hymen never becomes a mere mediation or work of the negative; it outwits and undoes all ontologies, all philosophemes, all manner of dialectics. It outwits them and—as a cloth, a tissue, a medium again—it envelops them, turns them over, and inscribes them" (DS, 215).

The image of SHE is sacred as the Goddess and profane as the dominatrix. Discipline is sacred as sacrifice and depraved as masochism. The sexuality of male submission is sacred as an act of worship and perverse as a sexual act. The texts structured by the primary signifier span the range between female spirituality in the worship of the Goddess and male masochistic pornography—"tainted with vice yet sacred." Yet "each session by itself is no more whole or symmetrical for all that, being but the rejoinder or application of the other, its play or its exercise. Together they are neither more nor less than two hemitropic crystals; never, in sum a finished volume" (DS, 227).

The dialectic of the privileged and the primary is timeless as it exists within language, and however the history might have unfolded or will unfold, the fold between the two palisades will always be present. Behind the "everyday world" is the "theatrical world" of mental existence in which we transform roles if we cross, fantasize, or dream ourselves into the other, the unpublished and hidden discourse (DS, 232). The discourses are separated, according to Derrida, by "a simple veil." Nietzsche glimpsed through the veiled opaqueness and saw a blurred image of what lay on the other side, but he never passed through. Freud and Lacan reached the point of the fold but never crossed over. We have attempted to take the reader through to the other side and have crafted a play for "the inner stage." We have strived to show "in what way the dialectical structure is incapable of accounting for the graphics of the hymen, being itself comprehended and inscribed with the latter, almost indistinguishable from it, separated from it only by itself, a simple veil that constitutes the very thing that tries to reduce it to nothing: desire" (DS, 249).

There is an ongoing dialogue between feminist texts and the texts of the political, legal, moral, philosophical, sociological, and psychoanalytic and their authors. This dialogue takes place within the discourse structured by the privileged signifier. Within this discourse, women remain other, masked. They protest this designation, but they speak their protest from within it. Can there be a dialogue with SHE, the woman who is a self as a manifestation of the Subject? Such a dialogue is not possible so long as it remains within the discourse structured by the privileged signifier. How can a dialogue take place between the privileged and the primary signifiers when those discourses are contradictory, separate psychic realities?

Such a dialogue can only take place where their mutual mimesis reverberates. Each side of the dialogue must enter into the discourse of the other. How can we, immersed as we are in the discourse structured by the privileged signifier and in the psychic reality of patriarchal civility, pass through this veil? How can the man enter the cavern, the underworld of the Other? How can the woman break out of the cave, the subterranean subjectivity of Otherness and embrace herself as a manifestation of the Subject? How can the woman seize the Gaze and the Voice of the Subject while submerged in the discourses that define her as other?

SHE cannot exist in the discursive until there is a name for her. Her name must appear before she can truly *be.* When we remove the mask from the woman we see nothing behind it because there is no text to name her and no discourse to think her, no dialogue to communicate with HER. It is only through interrogating the texts of the privileged signifier, the discourse of patriarchal civility, and the Name of the Father that we can break through and play at the meeting point of the fold. At this point, language reverberates between the master signifiers, and it is within this reverberation that the unthinkable can be thought, and the unspeakable can be named.

Discourse, Death, and Sexuality

The structure of the master signifiers that configure the relationship of the sexes as manifested in discourse is that of the two gender poles, *the self as the manifestation of the Subject who embodies the generative power of nature* and *the self as the manifestation of the Other who suffers the lack.* If the discourse is structured by the privileged signifier, then the self (Subject) will be male and the self (Other) will be female. If, however, the discourse is structured by the primary signifier, then the self (Subject) will be female and the self (Other) will be male. The two master signifiers represent the alternative metaphorical relationships between humans and nature in terms of body—which is connected in the registers of the Imaginary and the Symbolic to femaleness—and mind—which is connected in the registers of the Imaginary and to the Symbolic—to maleness.

When I as male describe you as female, I describe myself at the same time. When I as female describe you as male, I simultaneously describe myself. If I describe you as a self generated from the Other, then, I, concurrently, describe myself as a self generated from the Subject. If I describe you as a self generated from the Subject, I describe myself as a self generated from the Other. Subject and Other, human and nature, and female and male meet at the same fold, at the interwoven region of textual contradiction where dialectics merge in ironic reversal. The place where the contradictions intertwine is the point of animality. The human is both animal and that which is not animal. That which is not animal is the Subject. That which is animal in the human is Other. Thus, the gender that is a self as the manifestation of the Subject is not animal, while the self that is the manifestation of the Other is the animal side of the human or the human animal—part human and part animal. The Subject can relate to the animal-human self of the Other through killing, or taming and controlling the animal. The animal and human merge in the Other as Sphinx or Pan, female Monster or Beast-Man.

The animal in the human as a self as Other is the untamed sexual desire of that self. The self as Subject, whether female or male, whether primary or privileged, must kill or tame the animal, the sexual desire of that self, which is designated within the ruling discourse as a manifestation of the Other, so that it may serve the desire of the self as Subject. When female and male meet at the fold of discourse, where Subject and Other, human and nature, libido and ego, Eros and Thanatos, domination and submission meet, merge, and reverberate, the encounter of seduction takes place within and between the discourses of the master signifiers.

When female and male meet at the fold and she accepts him as Hero, king, and god, he will kill the vital, sexual will to life by destroying the Monster that threatens his phallus. When female and male meet and she is SHE, having the Gaze and the Voice, she will be the Siren that will lure him to surrender the phallus and serve her desire. She will invite him to exchange Eros for Thanatos and sacrifice his narcissistic ego for the forbidden pleasures of the hidden desires of his secret fantasies. If he refuses the seduction, then she will turn her back on him and rejoin her sisters in the play of Eros.

The dialectics converge in the register of the Imaginary in the part-human-part-animal mythic monstrosities—the Sphinx, Pan, the Minotaur, and the Centaur. The images of the man as Other, at the fold of desire, are that of the man animal, the animal man, the serpent as man as matriphallus who serves female desire, and the Minotaur, the bull man, who is the sacrifice at the altar of female fecundity. The part-man, part-goat, or stag, the horned god serves the female as Consort, and the Centaur, part man and part horse, is to be broken, tamed, and ridden.

When female and male cannot reconcile who is to play the role of self as Subject and who the role of self as Other, then they will remain in conflict. If neither is able to seduce the other into submission, if they are governed by no law of desire, either the primary or the privileged, they will remain in conflict. They will be at war in many soft and subtle but nevertheless cruel ways. While they may embrace equality in a nongendered discourse, a war will surge underneath the mirage of patriarchal civility. The choice for the man is between the Dionysian sacrifice and the Oedipal abyss.

In the original fantasy of the primary signifier, the male serves female desire as phallic serpent, female fecundity as the sacrificial bull, and the female Subject as horned Consort. But it is as the Centaur that he is shaped to embrace the *jouissance* of submission. The dressage method of training horses furnishes an appropriate metaphor for transforming the Beast-Man into the higher man. Here, the trainer understands fully the psychology of the horse and molds it in terms of that psychology. Eventually, the horse anticipates the wishes of the rider so closely that it is often difficult to say who is *controlling*. In the final analysis, however, the rider is in the saddle.

The relationship between the self (Subject) and the self (Object) is necessarily hierarchical because of the presence of the generative power and its lack. The central configuration of the mythic discourse structured by the privileged signifier is that which has been termed the monomyth, or the myth of the hero. There are a number of examples of the monomyth, but they all share the same minimum narrative core that yields the sequence of episodes Goux articulates in the following terms:

> (1) A king fears that a younger man, or one not yet born, will take his place, as an oracle has predicted. He then uses all available means to try to prevent the child's birth, or to get rid of the presumed intruder.
>
> (2) The future hero escapes from the king's murderous intentions. Nevertheless, much later he finds himself in a situation in which a different king again attempts to do away with him. But this second king cannot bring himself to commit the crime with his own hands, so he assigns a perilous task in which the future hero is expected to lose his life.
>
> (3) The trial takes the form of a fight with a monster. The hero succeeds in defeating the monster, not on his own but with the help of a god, a wise man, or a future bride.
>
> (4) Finally, the hero's triumph over the monster allows him to marry the daughter of a king. (OP, 6)

In the narrative plot of this standard form of myth, after the hero receives the daughter of a king as his bride, he then ascends to a throne in his own right and becomes a king, a father of a nation. The gender structure of the standard monomyth, therefore, is king and daughter-bride. Consequently, the hierarchical gender structure of the mythic discourse is that of the parent and child. The king takes a daughter of a king for a bride. Rather than master/slave, the mythic structure of privileged gender hierarchy is father/daughter.

In the Persean myth, there are four narrative steps:

1. An oracle informed King Actrisius of Argos that his grandson would take away his throne and his life. Consequently, he has his daughter Danae and her infant son Perseus, her child by Zeus, enclosed in a chest and thrown into the sea.

2. Zeus preserves the chest and guides it by ocean tides to the shores of

a kingdom ruled by two brothers, Dictys and Polydectes, who raise Perseus. His stepfather, however, sends him on a dangerous mission to obtain the head of the Medusa and bring it back to him in Seriphus.

3. Perseus fights the Medusa, and with the aid of Athena, strikes off her dreaded snake-hair head which when gazed upon turns a man to stone.

4. Perseus returns in triumph and saves the life of Andromeda, who is given to him as his bride by her father, King Cepheus of Ethiopia. He eventually reigns as King over Tiryns and Mycenae.

Thus, according to Goux:

> [I]t is only at the end of a bloody battle against this oppressive and devouring female monster, only when the son has mobilized all his manly energies to kill her, to free himself from her, so that he can marry the princess, the girl he has been promised, who is *not* his mother, and whom the dragon was holding prisoner or to whom she was blocking access. To kill the monster after making the hazardous trip back to the dark lair where she lives is thus for the hero to sever a bond, to make a vital sacrifice, to inflict a bloody cut that allows the protagonist to become the spouse of the girl who had been the monster's prisoner. (OP, 26)

Goux makes very clear that what is killed is not the mother as such, or a mother figure, but "a shadowy, dark, devouring reptile, a monster inhabiting cavernous watery depths, a dimension that myth alone can conceptualize" (OP, 26). The myths give her many names, such as Medusa and Kali. She is *the female who is a self as a manifestation of the Subject.* She is *SHE who must be obeyed.* She is *SHE who stands above the man.* She is the woman in the unconscious whose subjectivity is structured by the primary signifier, which is a manifestation of the sexual drive. She is at war with the woman in the conscious whose subjectivity is structured by the privileged signifier that is the manifestation of the male narcissistic ego drive and which is internalized within her by being immersed in the discourse of the privileged signifier.

In killing the monstrous SHE, the Hero, according to Goux, liberates not only himself from his masochistic desires. At the same time, he liberates the female from her monstrous desire, the desire to dominate, to be the self that is the manifestation of the Subject and has the Gaze and the Voice that create the feared desire in the male to castrate himself as a sacrifice to HER desire. "The matricide alone constitutes the liberation of woman," Goux tells us, "it gives access to the bride, once the dark maternal element has been separated from the bright nuptial feminine element"

(OP, 27). The self as a manifestation of the Subject, the Goddess, is castrated, beheaded by the Hero and leaves the self as a manifestation of the Other, as the daughter-bride.

The monstrous feminine is the desire in the female to dominate, to be a self that is a manifestation of the Subject, which entitles her to seduce into submission a lover whose supreme desire is to sacrifice himself for her—to give his body to her as the object of her desire. The monstrous in the female is her desire, which ignites the *jouissance* of submission in the male. Goux explains that "It is the young man's desire itself that creates, out of its own inclinations, a horrible, anguish-generating monster" (OP, 36).

There is not just one classic monomyth any more than there is only one master signifier. There is an older, and equally paradigmatic, structure of a more ancient set of myths. The structure of this alternative archetypal mythic has been set out in one study as follows: "The goddess has many names and many different tales are told about her, but one story is unvarying throughout the Near East. The goddess becomes separated from the one she loves, who dies or seems to die, and falls into a darkness called the 'Underworld.' This separation is reflected in nature as a loss of light and fertility. The goddess descends to overcome the darkness so that her loved one may return to the light, and life may continue."[14] The Goddess's beloved is her son-lover, the Consort. "The great myth of the Bronze Age is structured upon the distinction between the 'whole,' personified as the Great Mother Goddess, and 'the part,' personified as her son-lover. . . . She gives birth to her son as the new moon, marries him as the full moon, loses him to the darkness as the waning moon, goes in search of him as the dark moon, and rescues him as the returning crescent."[15] The gender structure of the alternative set of myths is that of mother and son-lover.

These myths are interrelated in an antagonistic dialectic. The monster that the Hero must kill is the counterpart of the Goddess. The Consort-lover-son must kill the mother Goddess as Monster to free himself so he can be reborn as the Hero king and take on the woman as father and daughter, although the daughter of another king. Both sets of myths have incestuous overtones in that the male self as a manifestation of the Subject fucks women who are the manifestation of the self as Other, as daughters, while women who are uncastrated and claim the Gaze and the Voice discipline men as sons.

If Oedipus is the citizen of the new democratic republic, then he is castrated. The price of gender neutrality, according to this interpretation of the myth, is castration. The killing of the mother as self, as a manifestation of the Subject, and the killing of the father as self, as a manifestation of the Subject, leaves women and men both as selves that are manifestations of the Other, with neither having the generative power of nature. The killing severs the human's link with nature, leaving the human without meaning, in the abyss. The state of humanity after the Oedipal triumph of science and philosophy over myth is that of an unresolved dialectic between the *jouissance* of domination and submission.

With man as the measure of all things, there is no way to make the link to nature. There can be no self without a discourse, no discourse without a master signifier, no master signifier without a grand metaphor, no grand metaphor without a primal fantasy, and no primal fantasy except through the body of the female. Where are we to find this discourse? In ancient stories? The resurgence of paganism and Goddess worship? Domination and submissive erotic literature and pornography? Feminist scholarship? Are the parlors of the professional dominatrix our only temples? Are *Venus in Furs* and *The Guide to the Correction of Young Gentlemen* our only sacred texts? Is the price of meaning the loss of liberty for the male? Is the loss of liberty for the female the cost that she must pay for males to have liberty? Is the cost of liberty for both females and males the loss of *jouissance* and meaning?

We kill the *SHE Who Must Be Obeyed,* the *SHE Who Stands Above the Man,* by killing the discourse within which the female self is formulated as a manifestation of the Subject. Although God is dead, the discourse structured by the privileged signifier is very much alive, and males can thus continue to generate their selves as manifestations of the Subject. It is no longer necessary to kill the powerful woman who is a self as a manifestation of the Subject. The discourse itself has been so limited that women have only the discourse of the privileged signifier, which leaves them only the alternative of generating out their selves as manifestations of the Other. Can the discourse of academic feminism located, as it is, in the gender-neutral discourse of science, philosophy, and law—unrelated to any Imaginary or Symbolic connection to the Real and barring any metaphorical meaning linking the human with nature—provide a discourse from which women can generate for themselves a self as a manifestation of the Subject, having the Gaze and the Voice?

Can the male avoid the fate of Oedipus at Colonus? He has killed the

Father by the act of human reasoning, which makes man the measure of all things. His domination over the earth, matter, and the bodies of women no longer has mythic justification. Without mythic justification, it becomes simply rape. He can no longer play the Hero, kill the monstrous feminine, and claim the daughter-bride. The discourse of science and philosophy doesn't provide the structure for the generation of that kind of subjectivity. Blind, exiled from nature, sexually and emotionally dependent, without hope or purpose, Oedipus at Colonus is the man who has fallen into the abyss, and the discourse of science and philosophy leads eventually to its edge. The conundrum of modern man is that it appears that the only way to escape from falling into the abyss of nihilism is to reconnect with nature. The only way to reconnect with nature is through the female. Since she will no longer accept being dominated, the only way to reconnect with nature is through submission to her through the sacrifice of the phallus to her.

Through the Looking Glass

Does SHE exist? It depends upon the discourse. If the discourse is structured by the privileged signifier, SHE appears as a Monster. If the discourse is structured by the primary signifier, SHE appears as a Goddess. Women and men live in dialectical ambiguity. When a woman meets a man, she can never be sure whether he is going to attack her, try to seduce her so that he can fuck her, or simply plead with her for a good spanking. The man, on the other hand, vacillates between wanting to kill her, rape her, fuck her, or castrate himself for her. This only reflects the dialectics of body/mind, female/male, and sexual drive/ego drive dualisms. In *Civilization and Its Discontents,* Freud wrote: "And now, I think, the meaning of the evolution of civilization is no longer obscure to us. It must present the struggle between Eros and Death, between the instinct of life and the instinct of destruction, as it works itself out in the human species. This struggle is what all life essentially consists of, and the evolution of civilization may therefore be simply described as the struggle for life of the human species. And it is this battle of the giants that our nurse-maids try to appease with their lullaby about Heaven" (SE, XXI, 122).

We are trapped within the dialectics. We can embrace Eros or Thanatos. We can affirm life and accept our animality or rebel against it and deny and betray our humanity. The dialectic is not a state of affairs that we can transcend nor is it the result of something that has gone terribly wrong. It is what it means to be human. There is no grand scheme, no Utopia awaiting us in the future, no final synthesis, no transcendence. At the end of history, science fails us by leaving us in a universe without meaning, philosophy betrays us by leaving us at the edge of the abyss, and religion blinds us and fogs our eyes so we don't see the abyss until we have fallen into it. We have no place to turn, and the ancient myths furnish little guidance in the postmodern age.

Can the mythic structure of the Nietzschean worldview take us into a new age? Can Kali, Artemis, and Ariadne merge into the *SHE Who Stands Over the Man?* Can Dionysus merge with Nietzsche's Zarathustra into the Higher Man? Can we internalize and embrace our animality, our sexuality, and our death through his Eternal Return? Can the domina become a Goddess? Can the male masochist who loves to play the slave be transformed into a Consort? Can the contemporary pagans worshipping the Goddess keep their mythic relationship with the earth and combine it with the sophistication of postmodern *enlightenment?* Can we transform old discourse and create new discourse in which the Imaginary and the Symbolic can relate to the Real in such a way that we can embrace and affirm life? Can we maintain a *Gaia consciousness* that will be powerful enough to link earth, nature, and woman in a positive way?

When women and men confront each other, within what discourses are their subjectivities formed? Perseus sees a Monster and attempts to kill her. Oedipus engages her in intellectual discussion and persuades her to castrate herself. Theseus uses her, abandons her, and then declares war on her. Attis castrates himself for her. Dionysus embraces her. Athena hates her and gives Perseus the weapons with which to kill her. Apollo hates her and sends Orestes to kill her, even though she is his own mother. Jehovah curses her, Saint Paul tells her to keep her mouth shut. Allah counsels disciplining her if she is disobedient. The Buddha tells us to avoid her because she will pollute us.

Can Perseus look into the face of the Medusa without the mirror and see HER beauty? Can Oedipus embrace the Sphinx and let her tear him apart so that he can be reborn as HER consort? Can Theseus recognize that if he kills the Minotaur he is killing something elemental in himself and that if he embraces the Minotaur they both will merge into Dionysus who will never abandon Ariadne? Can Orestes tell Apollo to go to hell when he orders him to kill Clytemnestra? Can Saint Paul sit at HER feet and learn wisdom from HER? Can Jehovah and Allah have their eyes opened and see that they don't have what they think they have—that *it* isn't where they think it still is? Can the Buddha be made to see that his body is real and nirvana an illusion and that the true self that is identical in everyone isn't in anyone?

SHE is said not to exist, but if a woman appears to resemble her she might be killed or attacked. Freud shut his eyes to HER. Jung saw HER and advocated killing her in order to free oneself from HER. Lacan couldn't see HER but always had an uneasy feeling that somehow there was something there that he couldn't quite grasp. He said SHE didn't exist but he wrote about HER with a slash through the *the* to confirm her nonexistence (FS, 137–48). Nietzsche saw HER, but he couldn't make up his mind whether to play the role of Oedipus, Perseus, or Dionysus and finally went mad. Women who look into the mirror and see HER become frightened and cover HER with a mask. They are afraid that if men see HER and become frightened, they might be mistaken for a Monster and be attacked.

We, the authors, as a woman and a master fool, have attempted to create a text, a *play* that would generate HER in the psyche of the reader. If SHE appeared, what you felt about HER reflects who you are.

Notes

Notes to Introduction

1. Chap. 1, 14.
2. Chap. 10, 272.
3. Chap. 9, 245, quoting Luce Irigaray, *This Sex Which Is Not One* (Ithaca: Cornell University Press, 1985), 129–30.
4. Chap. 6, 162.
5. Chap. 10, 282.
6. Chap. 1, 12.
7. Friedrich Nietzsche, *The Will to Power,* trans. Walter Kaufmann and R. J. Hollingdale (New York: Vintage Books, 1968), 204, quoted by these authors at chap. 8, 212.
8. Catharine A. MacKinnon, *Only Words* (Cambridge: Harvard University Press 1993), 60–62.

Notes to Chapter One

1. Jane Flax, *Thinking Fragments: Psychoanalysis, Feminism, and Postmodernism in the Contemporary West* (Berkeley: University of California Press, 1990), 42.
2. Carole S. Vance, "Pleasure and Danger: Toward a Politics of Sexuality," in *Pleasure and Danger: Exploring Female Sexuality,* ed. Carole S. Vance (Boston: Routledge & Kegan Paul, 1984), 2.
3. Ibid., 5.
4. J. C. Smith, *The Neurotic Foundations of Social Order: Psychoanalytic Roots of Patriarchy* (New York: New York University Press, 1990). The paperback edition is entitled *Psychoanalytic Roots of Patriarchy: The Neurotic Foundations of Social Order* (New York: New York University Press, 1990), chap. 8–11.
5. Roy Shafer, "Narration in the Psychoanalytic Dialogue," in *On Narrative,* ed. W. J. T. Mitchell (Chicago: University of Chicago Press, 1980), 25.
6. Alexander Nehamas, *Nietzsche: Life As Literature* (Cambridge: Harvard University Press, 1985), 173.
7. Richard Geha states, "The affinities between Nietzsche and Freud are not

 merely extensive: they are profound." Richard E. Geha, "Freud as Fictionalist/The Imaginary Worlds of Psychoanalysis," in *Freud: Appraisals and Reappraisals*, ed. Paul E. Stepansky. Contributions to Freud Studies, vol. 2 (Hillsdale, N.J.: Analytic Press, 1986), 136.

8. Jacques Derrida relies heavily on both Freud and Nietzsche. This reliance is documented in Gayatri Chakravorty Spivak's introduction to Derrida's *Of Grammatology*, trans. G. C. Spivak (Baltimore: John Hopkins University Press, 1974), ix-lxxxvii.

9. Shoshana Felman, *Jacques Lacan and the Adventure of Insight* (Cambridge: Harvard University Press, 1987).

10. Ellie Ragland-Sullivan, "The Sexual Masquerade: A Lacanian Theory of Sexual Difference," in *Lacan and the Subject of Language*, ed. E. Ragland-Sullivan and Mark Bracher (New York: Routledge, 1991), 49.

11. Lisa Appignanesi and John Forrester, *Freud's Women* (New York: Basic Books, 1992).

12. See, for example, Hélène Deutsch, Melanie Klein, Anna Freud, Karen Horney, Ella Freeman Sharpe, Joan Rivière, Susan Isaacs, Marjory Brierly, Marian Milner, Hanna Segal, Lou Andreàs-Salomé, Marie Bonaparte, Sylvia Payne, Sabina Spielrein, Ruth Mack Brunswick, Dorothy Burlingham, Jeanne Lampl de Groot, Eva Rosenfeld, Alix Strachey, Janine Chaseguette-Smirgel, Margaret Mahler, and many others.

13. Jane Gallop, "Moving Backwards or Forwards," in *Between Feminism and Psychoanalysis*, ed. T. Brennan (London: Routledge, 1989), 27.

14. For example, the primal scene, the degree to which memories of seduction are fantasies or recall of real events; whether young males suffer from the castration anxiety; whether females suffer from penis envy; and whether young children wish to have an incestuous relationship with the parent of the opposite sex.

15. See also, Barnaby B. Barratt, *Psychic Reality and Psychoanalytic Knowing, Advances in Psychoanalysis: Theory, Research, and Practice*, vol. 3 (Hillsdale, N.J.: Analytic Press, 1984), 1–49.

16. See also, Jacob Golomb, *Nietzsche's Enticing Psychology of Power* (Iowa City: Iowa State University Press, 1989), 150–60, 234–42.

17. See also, Alan D. Schrift, "Nietzsche and the Critique of Oppositional Thinking," *History of European Ideas* 11 (1990): 783–90.

18. Jacques Derrida, *Dissemination*, trans. Barbara Johnson (Chicago: University of Chicago Press, 1981), 192–93; Jacques Derrida, *Spurs/Éperons* (Chicago: University of Chicago Press, 1979), 51–53, 87–89; Paul de Man, *Allegories of Reading* (New Haven: Yale University Press, 1979), 16: "the latter seems to reach a truth, albeit by the negative road of exposing an error, a false pretense"; Barbara Johnson, *A World of Difference* (Baltimore: Johns Hopkins University Press, 1987), 15: "Truth is preserved in vestigial form in the notion of error. This does not mean that there is, somewhere out there, forever unattainable, the one true reading against which all others will be tried and found wanting."

19. Jacques Derrida, "Différence," in *Margins of Philosophy*, trans. Alan Bass (Chicago: University of Chicago Press, 1982).

20. On the postmodern perpectival construction of reality, see *Of Grammatology*, sup. n. 8, 86. See also, *Allegories of Reading*, sup. n. 18; Barbara Johnson, *The Critical Difference* (Baltimore: Johns Hopkins University Press, 1985). For Nietzsche's origination of this construction, see also, Gary Shapiro, *Nietzschean Narratives* (Bloomington: Indiana University Press, 1989).

21. For Nietzsche's genealogical approach to origins, see also, Michel Foucault, "Nietzsche, Genealogy, History," in *The Foucault Reader*, ed. Paul Rabinow (New York: Pantheon Books, 1984), 76–100. For Foucault, see Benjamin Sax, "Foucault, Nietzsche, History: Two Modes of the Genealogical Method," *History of European Ideas* (1989): 769–81. See generally, Michel Foucault, *Discipline and Punish*, trans. Alan Sheridan (New York: Vintage Books, 1979).

22. See, for example, Jane Flax, *Thinking Fragments*, sup. n. 1; Rosi Braidotti, *Patterns of Dissonance*, trans. Elizabeth Guild (Oxford: Polity Press, 1991).

23. Catharine A. MacKinnon's *Towards a Feminist Theory of the State* (Cambridge: Harvard University Press, 1989) has been widely criticized on essentialist grounds. See, for example, Alexandra Z. Dobrolowsky and Richard F. Devlin, "The Big Mac Attack: A Critical Affirmation of MacKinnon's Unmodified Theory of Patriarchal Power," *McGill Law Journal* 36 (1991): 575–608; Angela Harris, "Categorical Discourse and Dominance Theory," *Berkeley Women's Law Journal* 5 (1990): 181–96; Barbara Flagg, "Women's Narratives, Women's Story," *Cincinnati Law Review* 59 (1990): 147–68. MacKinnon bases her theory on a parallel kind of post-Marxian analysis, substituting sexuality for labor.

24. See also, Appignanesi and Forrester, *Freud's Women*, sup. n. 11, ix.

25. C. G. Jung, "The Structure of the Unconscious," in *The Collected Works of C. G. Jung*, vol. 7 (Princeton: Princeton University Press, 1966), par. 296–340.

Notes to Chapter Two

1. Parveen Adams, "Representation and Sexuality," in *The Woman in Question*, ed. P. Adams and E. Cowie (Cambridge: MIT Press, 1990), 248.

2. The term "maternal phallus" is problematic because of the identification of the word "phallus" with the male penis. To postulate a maternal phallus could be said to inevitably carry the meaning that the female is laying claim to something that she does not in fact have. There is no single female organ or part which stands alone as does the male penis. Female sexuality is more diffuse. If, on the other hand, we had another word that would be the female equivalent of the phallus, it would not carry the meaning that the term phallus possesses as signifier. While, therefore, the term "maternal phallus" may consequentially be somewhat paradoxical, its meaning can be made clear by emphasizing that the essential part of its meaning is the generative power of nature.

3. Freud to Jung, letter no. 314, May 1912, in *The Freud/Jung Letters*, ed. W. McGuire (Princeton: Princeton University Press, 1974), 504. Freud writes that, "A father is one who possesses a mother sexually (and the children as property). The fact of having been engendered by a father has, after all, no psychological significance for a child."

4. For a discussion of the Freudian material reality see Barnaby B. Barratt, *Psychic Reality and Psychoanalytic Knowing, Advances in Psychoanalysis: Theory, Research, and Practice*, vol. 3 (Hillsdale, N.J.: Analytic Press, 1984).

5. C. G. Jung, "The Structure and Dynamics of the Psyche," in *The Collected Works of C. G. Jung*, vol. 8 (Princeton: Princeton University Press, 1969), par. 746.

6. Parveen Adams, "Of Female Bondage," in *Between Feminism and Psychoanalysis*, ed. Teresa Brennan (London: Routledge, 1989), 247.

7. Donald Symons, *The Evolution of Human Sexuality* (Oxford: Oxford University Press, 1979).

8. For an extended development of this thesis, see J. C. Smith, *The Neurotic Foundations of Social Order: Psychoanalytic Roots of Patriarchy* (New York: New York University Press, 1990).

9. Alexander Nehamas, *Nietzsche: Life As Literature* (Cambridge: Harvard University Press, 1985), 202.

10. See generally, Robert L. Heilbroner, *The Nature and Logic of Capitalism* (New York: W. W. Norton, 1985).

11. Gen. 3:16.

12. Jacques Lacan, *Écrits* (Paris: Éditions de Seuil, 1966), 768–69.

13. Juliet Flower MacCannell, *Figuring Lacan/Criticisms of the Cultural Unconscious* (London: Croom Helm, 1986), 78.

14. Exod. 3:14.

15. John 1:1.

16. Gen. 1:1.

17. Gen. 1:26.

18. Aeschylus, *Eumenides*, ed. Alan H. Sommerstein (Cambridge: Cambridge University Press, 1989).

19. Parveen Adams, sup. n. 6, 249.

20. Ibid., 253.

21. We recognize that the *his* in the term history is coincidental and that the origin of the word has nothing to do with gender. Nevertheless, among feminists, it is a useful and now common rhetorical way of making a point.

22. Johann Jacob Bachofen (1815–87). See George Boas, preface to, and Joseph Campbell, introduction to Bachofen's *Myth, Religion, and Mother Right*, trans. Ralph Manheim (Princeton: Princeton University Press, 1967); Sir James George Frazer (1854–1941), *The Golden Bough, The Dying God* (1911), and *Adonis, Attis, Osiris* (1930) (London: Macmillan).

23. Camille Paglia, *Sexual Personae* (New Haven: Yale University Press, 1990), 42.

24. Charles Segal, *Dionysiac Poetics and Euripides' Bacchae* (Princeton: Princeton University Press, 1982), 272.

25. Norman O. Brown, "Dionysus in 1990," in *Apocalypse and/or Metamorphosis* (Berkeley: University of California Press, 1991), 180.

26. Ibid., 199.

27. Joan Rivière, "Womanliness as a Masquerade," in *Formations of Fantasy*,

ed. Victor Burgin, James Donald, and Cora Kaplan (London: Methuen, 1986), 35; Stephen Heath, "Joan Rivière and the Masquerade," in *Formations of Fantasy*, 45; Michélle Montrêlay, "Inquiry into Femininity," in *The Women in Question*, ed. Parveen Adams and Elizabeth Cowie (London: Methuen, 1989), 253.

28. J. C. Smith, sup. n. 8. See generally, chap. 15, "The Self in the Post-Oedipal Stage of History."

29. Nietzsche's phrase "become who you are" presupposes an acknowledgment of who one is. The *Übermensch's* ability to "become who she or he is" implies an acceptance of animality. See Nehamas, sup. n. 9, 170–200.

30. Jacques Derrida, *Spurs/Èperons* (Chicago: University of Chicago Press, 1979). This comes down to whether Nietzsche was misogynous or simply disliked the mask of femininity. To answer this question one has to examine his relationship to Lou Andreas-Salomé. For a discussion of this relationship and his complicated view of women, see Biddy Martin, *Woman and Modernity* (Ithaca: Cornell University Press, 1991); *Nietzsche and the Feminine*, ed. P. J. Burgard (Charlottesville: University of Virginia Press, 1994); D. F. Krell, *Postponements: Women, Sensuality, and Death in Nietzsche* (Bloomington: Indiana University Press, 1986); Jean Graybeal, *Language and "the Feminine" in Nietzsche and Heidegger* (Bloomington: Indiana University Press, 1990).

31. J. C. Smith, sup. n. 8. See generally chap. 18: "The End of History."

32. Shoshana Felman, *Jacques Lacan and the Adventure of Insight* (Cambridge: Harvard University Press, 1987), 9.

Notes to Chapter Three

1. H. R. Maturana and F. Varela, *The Tree of Knowledge* (Boston: Shambhala, 1992), 24.

2. John Searle, *The Rediscovery of the Mind* (Cambridge: MIT Press, 1992). Searle makes it quite clear that mental phenomena cannot be reduced to something that can be described entirely in nonmental terms.

3. There is a vast amount of literature on the mind and consciousness. In none of it do we find a true theory of mind. They are either models or pure speculation. See, for example, Geoffrey Madell, *Mind and Materialism* (Edinburgh: Edinburgh University Press, 1988); Gerald M. Edelman, *Bright Air, Brilliant Fire: On the Matter of the Mind* (New York: Basic Books, 1992); Marvin Minsky, *The Society of Mind* (New York: Simon and Schuster, 1985); Roger Penrose, *The Emperor's New Mind* (Oxford: Oxford University Press, 1989); and Daniel C. Dennett, *Consciousness Explained* (Boston: Little, Brown, 1991).

4. See, for example, Warren S. McCulloch, *Embodiments of Mind* (Cambridge: MIT Press, 1965).

5. Ibid., 1.

6. Paul Buckley and F. David Peat, *A Question of Physics: Conversations in Physics and Biology* (Toronto: University of Toronto Press, 1979), 7.

7. Ibid.

8. Ibid., 9.

9. Stephen W. Hawking, *A Brief History of Time from the Big Bang to Black Holes* (Toronto: Bantam Books, 1988), 174.

10. Philip Lieberman, "On the Evolution of Human Language," in *The Evolution of Human Language*, ed. John A. Hawkins and Murray Gell-Mann (Reading, Mass.: Addison-Wesley, 1992), 42.

11. Roger S. Jones, *Physics As Metaphor* (New York: Meridian, 1982), 6–7.

12. Ibid., 51.

13. Nick Herbert, *Quantum Reality beyond the New Physics* (Garden City, N.Y.: Anchor Press, 1985), 15–16.

14. Ibid., 249.

15. Henry W. Sullivan, "Homo Sapiens or Homo Desiderans: The Role of Desire in Human Evolution," in *Lacan and the Subject of Language*, ed. Ellie Ragland-Sullivan and Mark Bracher (New York: Routledge, 1991), 37.

16. Ibid., 36.

17. Julia Kristeva, *Language—the Unknown: An Initiation into Linguistics* (New York: Columbia University Press, 1989), 265–66.

18. Jacques-Alain Miller, "Language: Much Ado about What?" in *Lacan and the Subject of Language*, sup. n. 15, 31.

19. F. Patterson and E. Linden, *The Education of Koko* (New York: Holt, Rinehart and Winston, 1981).

20. Steven Pinker, *The Language Instinct* (New York: William Morrow, 1994).

21. Kristeva, sup. n. 17, 272.

22. Ellie Ragland-Sullivan, *Jacques Lacan and the Philosophy of Psychoanalysis* (Urbana: University of Illinois Press, 1986), 130.

23. Warren S. McCulloch, "What the Frog's Eye Tells the Frog's Brain," chap. 14 of *Embodiments of Mind*, sup. n. 4, 230.

24. Sullivan, sup. n. 15, 36.

25. Ferdinand de Saussure, *Course in General Linguistics* (New York: McGraw-Hill, 1966).

26. For an account of epistemological adjusters and their implication, see S. Coval and D. D. Todd, "Adjusters and Sense Data," *American Philosophical Quarterly* 9 (1972): 107–12.

27. Mary Jane Sherfey, *The Nature and Evolution of Female Sexuality* (New York: Random House, 1972), chap. 2.

28. Ellie Ragland-Sullivan, "The Sexual Masquerade: A Lacanian Theory of Sexual Difference," in *Lacan and the Subject of Language*, sup. n. 15, 69.

Notes to Chapter Four

1. Julia Kristeva, *Language—the Unknown: An Initiation into Linguistics* (New York: Columbia University Press, 1989), 265.

2. Jacques-Alain Miller, "Language: Much Ado about What?" in *Lacan and the Subject of Language*, ed. Ellie Ragland-Sullivan and Mark Bracher (New York: Routledge, 1991), 33.

3. Jacques-Alain Miller, "Suture (Elements of the Logic of the Signifier)," *Screen* 18, no. 4 (1977–78): 33–4.

4. Jacques-Alain Miller, "Elements of Epistemology," *Analysis* 1 (1989): 28.

5. Steven Pinker, *The Language Instinct* (New York: William Morrow, 1994), 237.

6. Ibid., 18.

7. J. C. Smith, *The Neurotic Foundations of Social Order: Psychoanalytic Roots of Patriarchy* (New York: New York University Press, 1990), chap. 15. This is a product of the belief in the all-inclusive mind (the logos of the West as differentiated mind, or the nirvana or the Tao of the East as undifferentiated mind).

8. Sup. n. 4. All further references to this work in the text will be indicated by *EE* and the page number, in parentheses.

9. Further, since "all the 'primitive forms' of knowledge are erotic" (EE, 28) and patriarchy is structured into language from its inception, even the earliest forms of culture were essentially patriarchal. This assumption is not evident from the structure and artifacts of early myths.

10. *Shorter Oxford English Dictionary* (Oxford: Clarendon Press, 1968).

11. Mary Jane Sherfey, *The Nature and Evolution of Female Sexuality* (New York: Random House, 1972). All further references to this work in the text will be indicated by *N* and the page number, in prentheses.

12. L & D, ix, 1–7. LaPlanche explains that "one senses the immense difficulty experienced by Freud in proposing a synthesis, as though his final contribution—concerning Eros and the death drive—could but barely be integrated into the first notion of sexuality" (L & D, 8).

13. Martin Heidegger, *Unterwegs zur Sprache* (Pfullingen: Gunther Neske, 1959), 215. Quoted in Jacques Derrida, *Aporias* (Stanford University Press, 1993), 35.

14. Alexandre Kojève, *Introduction to the Reading of Hegel* (Ithaca: Cornell University Press, 1969). All further references to this work in the text will be indicated by *RH* and the page number, in parentheses.

15. Catharine A. MacKinnon, *Toward a Feminist Theory of the State* (Cambridge: Harvard University Press, 1989); Jessica Benjamin, *The Bonds of Love: Psychoanalysis, Feminism, and the Problem of Domination* (New York: Pantheon, 1988).

Notes to Chapter Five

1. R. H. Hook, "Phantasy and Symbol: A Psychoanalytic Point of View," in *Fantasy and Symbol: Studies in Anthropological Interpretation*, ed. R. H. Hook (London: Academic Press, 1979), 267–68.

2. Ibid., 270.

3. Ibid.

4. M. Bénassy and R. Diatkine, "On the Ontogenesis of Fantasy," Symposium on Fantasy, *International Journal of Psychoanalysis* 45 (April-July 1964), 172.

5. In psychoanalytic literature one will find both spellings. Laplanche and

 Pontalis explain that "There are two separable notions covered by the term 'phantasy' and the distinction between them is enshrined in the two ways of spelling the word in the English language" (LP, 156). James Strachey drew attention to this in the introduction to *The Standard Edition of the Complete Works of Sigmund Freud* (SE, I, xxiv) and the distinction was further emphasized and incorporated into a theoretical framework by Susan Isaacs (The Nature and Function of Fantasy," *International Journal of Psycho-Analysis* 29 [1948]: 73.) See also, *Developments in Psycho-Analysis,* ed. Joan Rivière (London: Hogarth Press, 1973). Strachey, following a lead given by the Oxford English Dictionary, used the *ph* form for "the technical psychological phenomenon" and the *f* form when the idea of "caprice whim, fanciful invention" predominates. Susan Isaacs used the *ph* form to denote "unconscious mental content, which may or may not become conscious," but it should be noted that this distinction is not universally accepted and some psychoanalytic writers contest its validity on the grounds that it is not in harmony with the complex nature of Freud's thought" (LP, 156).

6. Michel Foucault, *Madness and Civilization* (New York: Vintage Books, 1988).

7. H. R. Maturana and F. Varela, *The Tree of Knowledge* (Boston: Shambhala, 1992), 28.

8. Bénassy and Diatkine, sup. n. 4, 176.

9. Ibid., 175.

10. Daniel Lagache, "Fantasy, Reality, and Truth," *International Journal of Psychoanalysis,* sup. n. 4, 185.

11. Ibid.

12. Ibid., 185, n. 7.

13. Ibid., 188.

14. Hanna Segal, "Fantasy and Other Mental Processes," *International Journal of Psychoanalysis,* sup. n. 4, 194.

15. Ibid.

16. Ibid., 193.

17. Ibid.

18. Bénassy and Diatkine, sup. n. 4, 171.

19. Lagache, sup. n. 10, 182.

20. According to J. Sandler and H. Nagera ("On the Concept of Fantasy," *International Journal of Psychoanalysis,* sup. n. 4, 190), "Conscious fantasy, or daydreaming, is a reaction to frustrating external reality. It implies the creation of a wish-fulfilling situation in the imagination, and thereby brings about a temporary lessening of instinctual tension. Reality testing is discarded; the ego nevertheless remains aware that the imaginative construction is not reality, without this knowledge interfering with the gratification thus achieved. Conscious fantasy differs from hallucinatory wish fulfilment in that the daydream is not normally confused with reality, whereas the hullucinatory gratification cannot be distinguished from reality."

21. J. C. Smith, *The Neurotic Foundations of Social Order: Psychoanalytic Roots of Patriarchy,* (New York: New York University Press, 1990), chap. 5.

22. Sandler and Nagera, sup. n. 20, 190.

23. Smith, sup. n. 21, 200.
24. Lagache, sup. n. 10, 180.
25. Susan Isaacs, "The Nature and Function of Phantasy," *International Journal of Psychoanalysis,* 29 (1948): 81. See also, Hook, sup. n. 1, 272.
26. Lagache, sup. n. 10, 188.
27. Bénassy and Diatkine, sup. n. 4, 176.
28. Ibid., 175–76.
29. Hook, sup. n. 1, 274.
30. Ibid., 273.
31. Lagache, sup. n. 10, 183.
32. Anna Freud, "The Ego and the Mechanisms of Defense," in *The Writings of Anna Freud,* vol. 2 (New York: International Universities Press, 1966).
33. Isaacs, sup. n. 25.
34. Ibid., 69 ff.
35. Segal, sup. n. 14 , 192.
36. Hook, sup. n. 1, 272.
37. Ibid.
38. Bénassy and Diatkine, sup. n. 4, 177.
39. Ibid., 177–78.
40. Ibid., 178.
41. Ibid.
42. Smith, sup. n. 21, chap. 7.
43. Hook, sup. n. 1, 284.
44. George Devereux, "The Awarding of a Penis as Compensation for Rape: A Demonstration of the Clinical Relevance of the Psycho-Analytic Study of Cultural Data," *International Journal of Psychoanalysis,* 38 (1957): 400.
45. Hook, sup. n. 1, 269–70.
46. Ibid., 288.
47. Ibid., 287.
48. Freud states in *The Paths to Symptom Formation* (SE, XVI, 371), "I believe these primal phantasies, as I should like to call them, and no doubt a few others as well, are a phylogenetic endowment. In them the individual reaches beyond his own experience into primaeval experience at points where his own experience has been too rudimentary."
49. Bénassy and Diatkine, sup. n. 4, 173.
50. Smith, sup. n. 21, chap. 5.
51. Hook, sup. n. 1, 282.
52. Ibid., 272.
53. Donald Symons, *The Evolution of Human Sexuality* (New York: Oxford University Press, 1979), chap. 8.
54. Segal, sup. n. 14, 192.
55. Gen. 1: 1–3
56. Gen. 2: 7, 21–23.
57. Aeschylus, *Eumenides, Oresteia,* trans. Richard Lattimore (Chicago: Universtiy of Chicago Press, 1953), 161.
58. Gen. 3: 13–16.

59. *This Business of the Gods. . .*, Joseph Campbell in conversation with Fraser Boa, (Windrose Films, Caledon East, Ont., 1989).

Notes to Chapter Six

1. "The true world—we have abolished. What world has remained? The apparent one perhaps? But no! *With the true world we have also abolished the apparent one.*" (T, 486).

2. B. Grunberger, *Narcissism: Psychoanalytic Essays* (New York: International Universities Press, 1979), 69.

3. C. G. Jung, *The Collected Works of C. G. Jung*, vol 8 (Princeton: Princeton University Press, 1966), par. 745.

4. For an analysis of this Egyptian myth, see Jean-Joseph Goux, "The Phallus: Maculine Identity and the 'Exchange of Women,' " *Differences* 4 (spring 1992): 40.

5. M. Esther Harding, *Woman's Mysteries: Ancient and Modern* (New York: Harper & Row, 1971), 195–96.

6. Gini Scott, *Dominant Women, Submissive Men* (New York: Praeger, 1983).

7. Gen. 1.

8. "The Laws of Manu," Nos. 147–48, in *The Sacred Books of the East*, vol. 25, ed. F. Max Muller (Delhi: Motilal Banarsidass, 1967), 301–4.

9. 1 Cor. 7:1–2.

10. 1 Cor. 7:8–9.

11. Diana Y. Paul, *Women in Buddhism/Images of the Feminine in the Mahayana Tradition* (Berkeley: University of California Press, 1985), 9.

12. 1 Cor. 14:34.

13. 1 Tim. 2:11–12.

14. *The Koran*, "Sura" 4:34.

15. Jean Baudrillard, *Seduction* (New York: St. Martin's Press, 1979), 1–2.

16. Ibid., 180.

17. M. Bénassy and R. Diatkine, "On the Ontogenesis of Fantasy," *International Journal of Psychoanalysis* 45 (April-July 1964): 172.

18. Abby W. Kleinbaum, *The War against the Amazons* (New York: McGraw-Hill, 1983).

19. Eva Keuls, *The Reign of the Phallus: Sexual Politics in Ancient Athens* (New York: Harper and Row, 1985).

20. Paul Tillich, for example. See Hannah Tillich, *From Time to Time* (New York: Stein & Day, 1973); Mary Daly, *Gyn/Ecology: The Metaethics of Radical Feminism* (Boston: Beacon Press, 1985), 94–95.

Notes to Chapter Seven

1. The orgasmic experience is often referred to as the "little death." What death and the orgasm have in common is the loss of the boundaries of the self.

2. Gini Scott, *Dominant Women, Submissive Men* (New York: Praeger, 1983), 246.

3. Kaja Silverman, *Male Subjectivity at the Margins* (New York: Routledge, 1992), 206.

4. Ibid., 211.

5. Ibid., 212.

6. Gilles Deleuze, *Masochism, Coldness and Cruelty* in *Venus in Furs*, by Leopold von Sacher-Masoch (New York: Zone Books, 1989), 65–66.

7. There is no counterpart for this term in the English language. It is a combination of an erotic high, bliss, joy, pleasure, enjoyment, and orgasm (S I, 25).

8. Scott, sup. n. 2, 3.

9. Ibid.

10. Deleuze, sup. n. 6, 13.

11. Camille Paglia, *Sexual Personae* (New Haven: Yale University Press, 1990), 95.

12. Ibid., 436.

13. Walter F. Otto, *Dionysus: Myth and Cult* (Bloomington: Indiana University Press, 1981), 143.

14. Lyn Cowan, *Masochism: a Jungian View* (Dallas: Spring Publications, 1982), 33. All further references to this work in the text will be indicated by *M* and the page number, in parenteses.

15. See Sam Janus, Barbara Bess, and Carol Saltus, *Sexual Profiles of Men in Power* (Englewood Cliffs, N.J.: Prentice-Hall, 1977).

16. Silverman, sup. n. 3, 189.

17. Ibid., 189–90.

18. Ludwig Eidelberg, "Humiliation in Masochism," *Journal of the American Psychoanalytic Society* 7 (1959): 275–83.

19. Alex Blumstein, "Masochism and Fantasies of Preparing to Be Incorporated," *Journal of the American Psychoanalytic Society*, ibid., 292–97.

20. C. G. Jung, *The Collected Works of C. G. Jung*, vol. 5 (Princeton: Princeton University Press, 1966), par. 577.

21. Philippe Borgeaud, *The Cult of Pan in Ancient Greece* (Chicago: University of Chicago Press, 1988), 72–73, 122–29.

22. E. F. Benson, *The Angel of Pain* (Philadelphia: Lippincott, 1905).

23. Sigmund Freud, "The Aetiology of Hysteria," in *The Assault on Truth: Freud's Suppression of the Seduction Theory*, by Jeffrey Moussaieff Masson (New York: Farrar, Straus and Giroux, 1984), appendix B, 251.

24. Ibid., 281.

25. "Letter of April 26, 1896," in *The Complete Letters of Sigmund Freud to Wilhelm Fleiss, 1887–1904*, trans. and ed. Jeffrey Moussaieff Masson (Cambridge: Harvard University Press, 1985), 183.

26. "Letter of May 4, 1896," Ibid., 185.

27. Masson, *The Assault on Truth*, sup. n. 23, 107–44.

28. *Letters*, sup. n. 25, 287–89.

29. Masson, sup. n. 23.

30. Ibid., 14–54.

31. "Letter of September 21, 1897," in *Letters*, sup. n. 25, 265.

32. Masson, sup. n. 27, 145–87.

33. Sandor Ferenczi, "Confusion of Tongues between Adult and the Child," in Masson, sup. n. 23, appendix C, 288.

34. Ibid., 288–89.

35. Ibid., 290.

36. Ibid., 294.

37. Ibid., 295.

38. The author of *The Story of O* used the pen name Pauline Réage. A good deal of speculation has centered on whether or not the real author was female, male, or a group. The book was actually written by Dominique Aury, a highly talented literary figure and respected woman of letters who was awarded the Légion d'Honneur. She wrote it for her lover, Jean Paulhan, a well-known writer, critic, and editor, in order to rekindle his interest in her. Her strategy was successful. Paulhan was excited by the book and persuaded her to permit him to get it published. He then wrote the introduction, which consistently appears with it wherever it is published. See, John de St. Jorre, "The Unmasking of O," *The New Yorker,* (August 1, 1994) 42.

39. Gen. 3:16.

40. Alexandre Kojève, *Introduction to the Reading of Hegel* (Ithaca: Cornell University Press, 1980).

41. Gen. 3:13–15.

42. Julia Kristeva, *Language the Unknown* (New York: Columbia University Press, 1989), 266.

43. Ibid., 266.

44. Mary Daly, *Gyn/Ecology: The Metaethics of Radical Feminism* (Boston: Beacon Press, 1985), 1.

Notes to Chapter Eight

1. For a Jungian analysis of the myth of Ariadne, see, for example, Linda Fierz-David, *Women's Dionysian Initiation: The Villa of Mysteries in Pompeii,* trans. Gladys Phelan (Dallas, Texas: Spring Publications, 1988), 18–33. See also, Chris Downing, "Ariadne, Mistress of the Labyrinth," in *Facing the Gods,* ed. James Hillman (Dallas, Texas: Spring Publications, 1980), 135–50.

2. Of the many subsequent readings and co-optations of Nietzsche's text, a feminist interpretation was one of the earliest.

3. Luce Irigaray, *The Marine Lover of Friedrich Nietzsche* (New York: Columbia University Press, 1991).

4. Freud links Ariadne's labyrinth to the birth: "The legend of the Labyrinth can be recognized as a representation of anal birth: the twisting paths are the bowels and Ariadne's thread is the umbilical cord." "Revision of Dream Theory" (SE, XXII, 7–30).

5. For an analysis of Theseus' rapes, see W. B. Tyrrell, *Amazons: A Study in Athenian Mythmaking* (Baltimore: Johns Hopkins University Press, 1984).

6. Theseus sought out and captured the Amazon's fiery queen, Antiope; he

abducted a very young Helen and later abandoned her in Attica as she was not of marrigeable age; he attempted to abduct Persephone from the underworld. See generally, Anne G. Ward et al., *The Quest for Theseus* (New York: Praeger, 1970).

7. Laurence Lampert, *Nietzsche's Teaching: An Interpretation of Thus Spoke Zarathustra* (New Haven: Yale University Press, 1986), 109.

8. Parveen Adams, "Of Female Bondage," in *Between Feminism and Psychoanalysis*, ed. Teresa Brennan (London: Routlege, 1989), 253.

9. Jean Baudrillard, *Seduction* (New York: St. Martin's Press, 1990). All further references to this work in the text will be indicated by *S* and the page number, in parentheses. Seduction according to Baudrillard "is always more singular and sublime than sex, and it commands the higher price" (13). It is "an ironic, alternative form, one that breaks the referentiality of sex and provides a space, not of desire, but of play and defiance" (21). It "is a circular, reversible process of challenges, one-upmanship and death. It is, on the contrary, sex that is the debased form" (47).

10. Baudrillard writes, "In this struggle all means are acceptable, ranging from relentlessly seducing the other in order not to be seduced oneself, to pretending to be seduced in order to cut all seduction short" (119).

11. For a general discussion of Nietzsche's use of metaphor and its relation to the body, see Eric Blondel, "Nietzsche: Life As Metaphor," in *The New Nietzsche*, ed. D. B. Allison (Cambridge: MIT Press, 1985), 150.

12. See, for example, Mitchell M. Waldrop, *Complexity: The Emerging Science at the Edge of Order and Chaos* (New York: Touchstone, 1992).

13. While we use Hollingdale's translation, we prefer Kaufmann's translation of *Übermensch* as "Overman" rather than "Superman."

14. In *The Birth of Tragedy*, Nietzsche utilizes the Greek Dionysus to counter Apollo—each is in opposition to the other. While Apollo is the ordered aesthetic, Dionysus in *The Birth of Tragedy* is a vision of the tragic art form, an emotive nonrational entity. This Dionysus in many ways lays the foundation for the Dionysus in Nietzsche's later works.

15. Biddy Martin, *Woman and Modernity: The (Life)Styles of Lou Andréäs Salomé*, (Ithaca: Cornell University Press, 1991).

16. Ibid., 5.

17. Ibid., 72–73.

18. Ibid., 73.

19. Hélène Cixous, "Come the Following Chapter," trans. Stan Theis, *Enclitic* (1980): 51–53.

20. Euripides, *The Bacchae*, trans. G. S. Kirk (Englewood Cliffs, N.J.: Prentice-Hall, 1970).

21. This is cited in Derrida's *Aporias* (70) and is taken from Heidegger's analysis of *Dasein*, wherein death is "*the most proper* possibility of Dasein."

22. Lampert, sup. n. 7, 109.

23. Gilles Deleuze, *Masochism, Coldness, and Cruelty*, in *Venus in Furs*, by Leopold von Sacher-Masoch (New York: Zone Books, 1989), 143–293. For the similarity between *Venus in Furs* and the stories of the masochists, see Gini

 Graham Scott, *Dominant Women, Submissive Men* (New York: Praeger, 1983), 246.

24. Ibid., 250.

25. See generally, Eric Blondel, *Nietzsche: The Body and Culture* (Stanford: Stanford University Press, 1991).

26. Karl Jaspers, *Nietzsche: An Introduction to the Understanding of His Philosophical Activity* (South Bend, Ind.: Regnery/Gateway, 1979), 10.

27. See Sam Janus, Barbara Bessm and Carol Saltus, *Sexual Profiles of Men in Power* (Englewood Cliffs, N.J.: Prentice-Hall, 1977).

28. Ibid.

29. *Lacanian Ink* 5 (1991): 29.

30. Ibid., 35.

31. Thomas Tryon, *Harvest Home* (New York: Knopf, 1973).

32. Sir James George Frazer, *The Golden Bough, The Dying God* (1911), and *Adonis, Attis, Osiris* (1930) (London: Macmillan) and *The Illustrated Golden Bough*, ed. Mary Douglas (Garden City, N.Y.: Doubleday, 1978); Mary Renault, *The King Must Die* (New York: Pantheon, 1958).

33. Sup. n. 23, 123–34.

34. J. C. Smith, *The Neurotic Foundations of Social Order: Psychoanalytic Roots of Patriarchy* (New York: New York University Press, 1990), 192–216.

35. Karen Armstrong, *The First Christian: Saint Paul's Impact on Christianity* (London: Pan Books, 1983); R. H. Randall, *Hellenistic Ways of Deliverance and the Making of the Christian Synthesis* (New York: Columbia University Press, 1970), 137–55.

36. Kaja Silverman, *Male Subjectivity at the Margins* (New York: Routledge, 1992), 52.

37. Ibid., 65. Silverman associates the undermining with the death drive. We would argue that the Eros or sexual drive plays a much greater role in undermining male mastery.

38. Ibid., 2.

39. Ibid., 1.

40. Ibid., 2–3.

41. Ibid., 388.

42. Ibid.

43. Ibid.

44. Sup. n. 23, 271. Von Sacher-Masoch believed that gender hierarchy was the product of socialization. Consequently he thought that gender equality would be possible "when she [the woman] has the same rights as he [the man] and is his equal in education and work."

45. *Drowning by Numbers*, 121 min., Else Vier Vendex, All Starts Productions, Great Britain, 1988.

46. See Clément Rosset, *Joyful Cruelty: Toward a Philosophy of the Real* (New York: Oxford University Press, 1993). Rossett's interpretation of Nietzsche has a good deal in common with our own. The first part of the three-part book, "The Overwhelming Force," is a description of the only way in which one can confront

the Real, directly, without illusion, substitution, or mediation, and that is by a joyful affirmation. Rosset writes that "there is in joy a mechanism of approval" (3). "[J]oy is always somehow engaged with the real, while sadness unceasingly confronts the unreal" (5). Rossett realizes the sexual dimensions of this joy, which is rooted in the body. He speaks of a "sexual rejoicing" and the "condition for sexual joy" for which orgasm "is a necessary but not a sufficient condition" (10). "The joy of which I am speaking is completely indistinguishable from the joy of life" (12). The second part of the book deals with what Rossett calls the betrayals of Nietzsche by those such as Heidegger. They claim to be his interpreters but lack the courage of Nietzsche's cruel and joyful vision, which Rossett calls "beatitude" and defines as "the simple and unadorned experience of the real" (25)—"the central and constant theme of Nietzsche's thought . . . the only theme" (26). The third part is entitled "The Cruelty Principle," by which Rossett means the intrinsically painful, tragic, insignificant, and ephemeral character of everything in the world as viewed from the human perspective. In this section, Rossett points out that "The cruelty of reality is illustrated in a particularly spectacular and significant fashion in the cruelty of love" (96).

Notes to Chapter Nine

1. Mary Daly, *Gyn/Ecology: The Metaethics of Radical Feminism* (Boston: Beacon Press, 1985), 1.
2. Judy Trejo, "Coyote Tales: A Paiute Commentary," in *Spiders and Spinsters*, ed. Martha Weigle (Albuquerque: University of New Mexico Press, 1982), 123–25.
3. Camille Paglia, *Sexual Personae* (New Haven: Yale University Press, 1990), 47.
4. Erich Neumann, *The Great Mother: An Analysis of an Archetype* (Princeton: Princeton University Press, 1963), 168.
5. Sup. n. 3, 13.
6. René Girard, *Violence and the Sacred* (Baltimore: Johns Hopkins University Press, 1979), 144.
7. Carolyn J. Dean, *The Self and Its Pleasures: Bataille, Lacan, and the History of the Decentered Subject* (Ithaca: Cornell University Press, 1992), 245. See also, Georges Bataille, *Erotism: Death and Sensuality*, trans. Mary Dalwood (San Francisco: City Lights Books, 1986), 105.
8. Frederick Thomas Elworthy, *The Evil Eye* (Secaucus, N.J.: University Books/Citadel Press), facsimile of 1895 ed.; *The Evil Eye*, ed. Alan Dundes (Madison, Wis.: University of Wisconsin Press, 1992); Tobin Siebers, *The Mirror of Medusa* (Berkeley: University of California Press, 1983), chap. 2.
9. Bataille, sup. n. 7.
10. Ibid., 239–40.
11. Slavoj Zizek, "From Courtly Love to the Crying Game," *New Left Review* 202 (1993): 96–97.
12. Ibid., 96.

13. Ibid., 97.
14. Ibid., 108.
15. Jessica A. Salmonson, *The Encyclopedia of Amazons* (New York: Paragon House, 1991), 24–25.
16. G. G. Brame, W. D. Brame, J. Jacobs, *Different Loving: An Exploration of the World of Sexual Domination and Submission* (New York: Villard Books, 1994).
17. Sup. n. 6, 167.
18. This is mainly a result of the fact that Lacan views women entirely from the perspective of man's desire.
19. Sup. n. 11, 99.
20. Luce Irigaray, *This Sex Which Is Not One* (Ithaca: Cornell University Press, 1985), 129.
21. Ibid., 129–30.
22. Jessica Benjamin, *The Bonds of Love* (New York: Pantheon, 1988), 221.
23. Ibid.
24. Ibid.
25. Alexander Kojève, *Introduction to the Reading of Hegel* (Ithaca: Cornell University Press, 1980), 8.
26. Sup. n. 1, 423.
27. Sup. n. 6, 144.
28. Sup. n. 22, 53.
29. Ibid., 54–56.
30. Lyn Cowan, *Masochism* (Dallas: Spring Publications, 1982), 71.
31. Rom. 7: 1–2.
32. Rom. 7: 5–6.
33. Rom. 8:5.
34. Sup. n. 11, 102.
35. An actual copy did survive under an unusual set of circumstances that, according to the account given to the publishers of the 1991 reprint, involved the ingenuity of one of the original jurors (v).
36. London: Delectus Books, 1991. This reissue of the original of Kerr-Sutherland's book was reviewed by Christopher Hitchens in the *London Review of Books* (16, no. 20 [1994]: 11) under the title "On Spanking." A substantial part of the review consisted of comparing Margaret Thatcher, and the verbal spankings she gave to the members of her cabinet, with Kerr-Sutherland's governess administering discipline.
37. Ibid., ii-iii.
38. Ibid., 12.
39. Ibid., 85.
40. Ibid., x-xi.
41. Ibid., 6.
42. Ibid., 9.
43. Ibid., 17.
44. Kaja Silverman, "*Histoire d'O*: The Construction of a Female Subject," in

Pleasure and Danger: Exploring Female Sexuality, ed. Carol Vance (Boston: Routledge and Kegan Paul, 1984), 320.

45. Ibid.
46. Ibid., 321.
47. Ibid., 324.
48. Ibid., 327.
49. Ibid., 346.
50. Andrea Dworkin, *Intercourse* (New York: Free Press, 1987), 141.
51. Sup. n. 44, 346.
52. Luce Irigaray, *Je, Tu, Nous: Towards a Culture of Difference* (New York: Routledge, 1993), 20.
53. Sup. n. 50, 140.
54. Hélène Cixous, "The Laugh of the Medusa," in *The Rhetorical Tradition,* ed. P. Bizzell and B. Herzberg (Boston: Bedford Books, 1990), 1232.
55. Ibid., 1238.
56. Ibid., 1239.
57. Hélène Cixous, "Castration or Decapitation," *Signs* 7, no. 1 (1981): 42–43.
58. Ibid., 43.

Notes to Chapter Ten

1. Ronald W. Clark, *Einstein: The Life and Times* (New York: Avon Books, 1971), 37.
2. Stephen W. Hawkins, *A Brief History of Time* (New York: Bantam 1988), 175.
3. John 1:1.
4. J. C. Smith, *The Neurotic Foundations of Social Order: The Psychoanalytic Roots of Patriarchy* (New York: New York University Press, 1990), chap. 8–11; Christiane Olivier, *Jocasta's Children/The Imprint of the Mother,* trans. George Craig (London: Routledge, 1989), 82–89. Males possess the will to subjugate and dominate not only because they resent females for lacking male sexual organs but also because they see a "powerful maternal imago, envied and terrified." See also, Janine Chasseguet-Smirgel, *Sexuality and Mind* (New York: New York University Press, 1986), 24.
5. Andrew Samuels, *The Political Psyche* (London: Routledge, 1993), 140–43.
6. Ibid., 143.
7. Hélène Cixous and Catherine Clément, *The Newly Born Woman* (Minneapolis: University of Minnesota Press, 1991), 11.
8. Freud understands the riddle of the Sphinx to represent Oedipus' literal origins: the riddle of where babies come from. The origin of babies is understood by Freud to be the first question of the infant (SE, VII, 195).
9. Jane Gallop, *The Daughter's Seduction/Feminism and Psychoanalysis* (Ithaca: Cornell University Press, 1982), 61. Oedipus passes over the blindspot without even knowing that it is there because he is overly concerned with reaching his

 solution. Janine Chasseguet-Smirgel also discusses the "blind spot" of Freudian theory in *Sexuality and Mind,* sup. n. 4, 20.

10. J. C. Smith and D. N. Weisstub, *The Western Idea of Law* (London: Butterworths, 1983), 242–362; Smith, sup. n. 4, 311–14.

11. See, for example, Mitchell M. Waldrop, *Complexity: The Emerging Science at the Edge of Order and Chaos* (New York: Touchstone, 1992); Murray Gell-Mann, *The Quark and the Jaguar* (New York: Freeman, 1944).

12. See, for example, J. E. Lovelock, *Gaia: A New Look at Life on Earth* (Oxford: Oxford University Press, 1979).

13. Cixous and Clément, sup. n. 7, 95–96.

14. Anne Baring and Jules Cashford, *The Myth of the Goddess: Evolution of an Image* (London: Viking Arkana, 1991), 145.

15. Ibid., 147.

Index